THE CAMBRIDGE COMPANION TO
ST PAUL

The apostle Paul has been justifiably described as the first and greatest Christian theologian. His letters were among the earliest documents to be included in the New Testament and, as such, they shaped Christian thinking from the beginning. As a missionary, theologian, and pastor Paul wrestles with theological and ethical questions of his day in a way paradigmatic for Christian theology, not least for Christianity's own identity and continuing relationship with Judaism. *The Cambridge Companion to St Paul* provides an important assessment of this apostle and a fresh appreciation of his continuing significance today. With eighteen chapters written by a team of leading international specialists on Paul, the *Companion* provides a sympathetic and critical overview of the apostle, covering his life and work, his letters and his theology. The volume will provide an invaluable starting point and helpful resource for subsequent studies.

JAMES D. G. DUNN is Lightfoot Professor of Divinity at the University of Durham, where his research interests cover the evolution of the historical critical method, the third quest for the historical Jesus, the relation between Christianity and Judaism in the first century, and the theology of the New Testament. Professor Dunn's recent publications have included *The Partings of the Ways between Christianity and Judaism*, commentaries on several New Testament books, and *The Theology of Paul the Apostle*. He is General Editor of Cambridge's New Testament Theology series, in which he authored *The Theology of Paul's Letter to the Galatians* (1993).

CAMBRIDGE COMPANIONS TO RELIGION

A series of companions to major topics and key figures in theology and religious studies. Each volume contains specially commissioned chapters by international scholars which provide an accessible and stimulating introduction to the subject for new readers and non-specialists.

Other titles in the series

THE CAMBRIDGE COMPANION TO CHRISTIAN DOCTRINE,
edited by Colin Gunton (1997)
ISBN 0 521 47118 4 hardback   ISBN 0 521 47695 8 paperback

THE CAMBRIDGE COMPANION TO BIBLICAL INTERPRETATION
edited by John Barton (1998)
ISBN 0 521 48144 9 hardback   ISBN 0 521 48593 2 paperback

THE CAMBRIDGE COMPANION TO DIETRICH BONHOEFFER
edited by John de Gruchy (1999)
ISBN 0 521 58258 x hardback   ISBN 0 521 58751 6 paperback

THE CAMBRIDGE COMPANION TO LIBERATION THEOLOGY
edited by Chris Rowland (1999)
ISBN 0 521 46144 8 hardback   ISBN 0 521 46707 1 paperback

THE CAMBRIDGE COMPANION TO KARL BARTH
edited by John Webster (2000)
ISBN 0 521 58476 0 hardback   ISBN 0 521 58560 0 paperback

THE CAMBRIDGE COMPANION TO CHRISTIAN ETHICS
edited by Robin Gill (2001)
ISBN 0 521 77070 x hardback   ISBN 0 521 77918 9 paperback

THE CAMBRIDGE COMPANION TO JESUS
edited by Markus Bockmuehl (2001)
ISBN 0 521 79261 4 hardback   ISBN 0 521 79678 4 paperback

THE CAMBRIDGE COMPANION TO FEMINIST THEOLOGY
edited by Susan Frank Parsons (2002)
ISBN 0 521 66327 x hardback   ISBN 0 521 66380 6 paperback

THE CAMBRIDGE COMPANION TO MARTIN LUTHER
edited by Donald K. McKim (2003)
ISBN 0 521 81648 3 hardback   ISBN 0 521 01673 8 paperback

THE CAMBRIDGE COMPANION TO ST PAUL
edited by James D. G. Dunn (2003)
ISBN 0 521 78155 8 hardback   ISBN 0 521 78694 0 paperback

Forthcoming

THE CAMBRIDGE COMPANION TO THE GOSPEL
edited by Stephen C. Barton

THE CAMBRIDGE COMPANION TO MEDIEVAL JEWISH THOUGHT
edited by Daniel H. Frank and Oliver Leaman

THE CAMBRIDGE COMPANION TO ISLAMIC THEOLOGY
edited by Tim Winter

THE CAMBRIDGE COMPANION TO

ST PAUL

Edited by James D. G. Dunn
University of Durham

CAMBRIDGE
UNIVERSITY PRESS

CAMBRIDGE UNIVERSITY PRESS
Cambridge, New York, Melbourne, Madrid, Cape Town, Singapore, São Paulo, Delhi

Cambridge University Press
The Edinburgh Building, Cambridge CB2 8RU, UK

Published in the United States of America by Cambridge University Press, New York

www.cambridge.org
Information on this title: www.cambridge.org/9780521781558

First published 2003
Sixth printing 2008

Printed in the United Kingdom at the University Press, Cambridge

A catalogue record for this publication is available from the British Library.

ISBN 978-0-521-78155-8 hardback
ISBN 978-0-521-78694-2 paperback

Contents

Notes on contributors

James D. G. Dunn is Emeritus Lightfoot Professor of Divinity at the University of Durham. His research interests cover the quest of the historical Jesus, the emergence of Christianity in its distinctive character, the ongoing relations between Christianity and Judaism, the theology of the New Testament and the interpretation of the New Testament. Professor Dunn's recent publications have included *The Partings of the Ways between Christianity and Judaism* (1991), commentaries on several New Testament books, *The Theology of Paul the Apostle* (1998), and *Christianity in the Making, Vol. 1: Jesus Remembered* (2003). He is General Editor of Cambridge's New Testament Theology series, in which he authored *The Theology of Paul's Letter to the Galatians* (1993).

Stephen C. Barton is Reader in New Testament in the Department of Theology, University of Durham, and a non-stipendiary minister at St John's Church, Neville's Cross. His books include *Discipleship and Family Ties in Mark and Matthew* (1994), *Invitation to the Bible* (1997), and *Life Together: Family, Sexuality and Community in the New Testament and Today* (2001).

Klaus Haacker is Professor of New Testament at the Kirchliche Hochschule Wuppertal, Germany. His books include *Die Stiftung des Heils: Untersuchungen zur Struktur der johanneischen Theologie* (1972), *Biblische Theologie als engagierte Exegese theologische Grundfragen und thematische Studie* (1993), *Paulus: Der Werdegang eines Apostels* (1997), *Der Brief des Paulus an die Römer* (1999), and *Versöhnung mit Israel: Exegetische Beiträge* (2002). Since 1977 he has been editor of the bi-monthly periodical *Theologische Beiträge*.

Morna Hooker is Lady Margaret's Professor Emerita at the University of Cambridge and Emerita Fellow of Robinson College. Her many publications include *Pauline Pieces* (1979), *The Message of Mark* (1983), *From Adam to Christ: Essays on Paul* (1990), *A Commentary on the Gospel according to St. Mark* (1991), *Not Ashamed of the Gospel* (1994), and *The Signs of a Prophet* (1997). She is Joint Editor of the *Journal of Theological Studies* and Editor of Black's New Testament Commentaries.

Arland J. Hultgren is Asher and Carrie Nasby Professor of New Testament at Luther Seminary, St Paul, Minnesota. His books include *Jesus and His Adversaries: The Form and Function of the Conflict Stories in the Synoptic Tradition* (1979), *1, 2*

Timothy, Titus (1984), *Paul's Gospel and Mission: The Outlook from his Letter to the Romans* (1985), *Christ and His Benefits: Christology and Redemption in the New Testament* (1987), *The Rise of Normative Christianity* (1994), and *The Parables of Jesus: A Commentary* (2000).

L. W. Hurtado is Professor of New Testament Language, Literature and Theology, University of Edinburgh. His books are *Text-Critical Methodology and the Pre-Caesarean Text: Codex W in the Gospel of Mark* (1981), *Mark: New International Commentary* (1989), *One God, One Lord: Early Christian Devotion and Ancient Jewish Monotheism* (1998; 2nd edn, 1998), *At the Origins of Christian Worship: The Context and Character of Early Christian Devotion* (1999), and *Lord Jesus Christ: Devotion to Jesus in Earliest Christianity* (2003).

Robert Jewett directs a bibliography project related to Paul's letter to the Romans at the University of Heidelberg, Germany, where he is a guest professor. He went to Heidelberg after twenty years at Garrett Evangelical Theological Seminary, Illinois. Among his eighteen books are *Paul's Anthropological Terms* (1971), *A Chronology of Paul's Life* (1979), *Letter to Pilgrims: A Commentary on the Epistle to the Hebrews* (1981), *The Thessalonian Correspondence* (1986), *Paul the Apostle to America* (1994), *The Myth of the American Superhero* (2002), and *Captain America in a Time of Jihad* (2003).

Luke Timothy Johnson is Robert W. Woodruff Professor of New Testament and Christian Origins in the Candler School of Theology at Emory University. He is the author of *The Writings of the New Testament: An Interpretation* (1998) and of commentaries on James, Luke–Acts, the Pastorals, and Romans. His most recent book is *The Future of Catholic Biblical Scholarship: A Constructive Conversation* (with William S. Kurz).

Andrew T. Lincoln is Portland Professor of New Testament at the University of Gloucestershire and Chair of its International Centre for Biblical Interpretation. His publications include *Paradise Now and Not Yet: Studies in the Role of the Heavenly Dimension in Paul's Thought* (1981), *Ephesians* (1990), *The Theology of the Later Pauline Letters* (with A. J. M. Wedderburn, 1993), and *Truth on Trial: The Lawsuit Motif in the Fourth Gospel* (2000).

Bruce Longenecker is Lecturer in New Testament Studies at the University of St Andrews. His publications include *The Triumph of Abraham's God* (1998), *Eschatology and the Covenant: A Comparison of 4 Ezra and Romans 1–11* (1991), *Narrative Dynamics in Paul: A Critical Assessment* (2002), and *The Lost Letters of Pergamum: A Story from the New Testament World* (with Ben Witherington, 2003).

Margaret M. Mitchell is Associate Professor of New Testament in the Divinity School and Chair of the Department of New Testament and Early Christian Literature in the Humanities Division at the University of Chicago. She is the author of *Paul and the Rhetoric of Reconciliation: An Exegetical Investigation of the Language and Composition of 1 Corinthians* (1991) and *The Heavenly Trumpet: John Chrysostom and the Art of Pauline Interpretation* (2000), and co-editor, with

Adela Yarbro Collins, of *Antiquity and Humanity: Essays on Ancient Religion and Philosophy Presented to Hans Dieter Betz on his 70th Birthday* (2001).

Robert Morgan has taught New Testament and Christian theology at Lancaster (1967–76) and Oxford, where he is now Reader in New Testament Theology and Vice-Principal of Linacre College. His publications include *The Nature of New Testament Theology* (1973), *Ernst Troeltsch: Writings on Theology and Religion* (with Michael Pye, 1977), *Biblical Interpretation* (with John Barton, 1988), and *Romans* (1995).

Jerome Murphy-O'Connor, OP has been Professor of New Testament at the Ecole Biblique et Archéologique Française, Jerusalem, since 1972. His most recent books are *Paul: A Critical Life* (1996) and *St Paul's Corinth: Texts and Archaeology* (3rd edn, 2002).

Calvin J. Roetzel is Arnold Lowe Professor of Religious Studies at Macalester College in St Paul, Minnesota. He is author of *The Letters of Paul: Conversations in Context* (4th edn) and *Paul: The Man and the Myth* (1998), winner of the BAR award for the 1998 New Testament Book of the Year. His *The World that Shaped the New Testament* will appear in a revised edition. Roetzel was active for ten years as a co-chair of the Pauline Theology Group of the Society of Biblical Literature, and is under contract to write a commentary on 2 Corinthians and books entitled *Paul: The Marginal Jew* and *Pauline Interpretation in the First Three Centuries.*

Brian S. Rosner, formerly lecturer at the University of Aberdeen, is Senior Lecturer in New Testament and Ethics at Moore Theological College and Honorary Senior Research Fellow in the Department of Ancient History at Macquarie University in Sydney. His publications include *Paul, Scripture and Ethics: A Study of 1 Corinthians 5–7* (1994, 1999), *Understanding Paul's Ethics: Twentieth-Century Approaches* (editor, 1995), and the *New Dictionary of Biblical Theology* (co-editor, 2000).

Alan F. Segal is Professor of Religion and Ingeborg Rennert Professor of Jewish Studies at Barnard College, Columbia University. He is the author of *Two Powers in Heaven: Early Rabbinic Reports about Christianity and Gnosticism, Rebecca's Children: Judaism and Christianity in the Roman World, The Other Judaisms of Late Antiquity*, and *Paul the Convert: The Apostolate and Apostasy of Saul of Tarsus*. He is currently finishing a book on life after death, tentatively called *Charting the Undiscover'd Country: The Afterlife in the West.*

Graham N. Stanton is Lady Margaret's Professor of Divinity at the University of Cambridge. Recent publications include *A Gospel for a New People: Studies in Matthew* (1992), *Gospel Truth? New Light on Jesus and the Gospels* (1995), *The Gospels and Jesus* (2nd edn, 2002), *Tolerance and Intolerance in Early Judaism and Christianity* (edited with G. G. Stroumsa, 1998), and *Jesus and Gospel* (2003). He is a General Editor of the International Critical Commentaries.

Loren T. Stuckenbruck is Westcott Professor of Biblical Studies at the University of Durham. His publications include monographs on *Angel Veneration and*

Christology (1995) and *The Book of Giants from Qumran* (1997). He is a specialist in early Jewish apocalyptic literature, the Dead Sea Scrolls, Pauline theology, and the Apocalypse of John. On the editorial boards of several journals, he is Editor in Chief of the forthcoming Commentaries on Early Jewish Literature.

Ben Witherington, III is Professor of New Testament at Asbury Theological Seminary, Wilmore, Kentucky. He has recently authored *New Testament History: A Narrative Account* and *The Gospel of Mark: A Socio-Rhetorical Commentary*. He is also the General Editor of the New Cambridge Bible Commentary Series. Among his twenty other books are *The Jesus Quest, The Paul Quest, The Acts of the Apostles: A Socio-Rhetorical Commentary, Conflict and Community in Corinth: A Socio-Rhetorical Commentary on 1 and 2 Corinthians, Grace in Galatia: A Socio-Rhetorical Commentary on Galatians, Women in the Ministry of Jesus,* and most recently *The Poetry of Piety* (with Christopher Armitage).

Glossary

agape a feast held by the early Christians in connection with the Lord's Supper; also Christian love

antinomianism the doctrine that the law is not binding on Christians

binitarianism belief in a Godhead of two persons

bishop an officer of the early church, who supervised the ministry of the community. The Greek term is *episkopos*, 'overseer'.

Christ a title from the Greek *Christos*, translation of Messiah, 'the anointed one'; Christians regard Jesus as the Messiah; *see also* Messiah

christology the doctrine of the person of Jesus

christophany an appearance or manifestation of Christ, usually from heaven

codex an ancient manuscript in book form

cruciform in the shape of a cross

deacon an officer of the early church. The Greek term is *diakonos*, also translated as 'servant' or 'minister'.

Decalogue the Ten Commandments

diaspora the dispersal of the Jews among the Gentiles; also the Jews so dispersed

docetism the belief that Jesus' body was merely a semblance or else of ethereal substance

doxology an ascription of glory to God

Ebionites an early Christian sect believing that Jesus was merely human and that the Jewish law was binding on Christians

ecclesiology doctrine of the church

eschatology the doctrine concerning the last things

Frühkatholizismus early Catholicism

glossolalia the gift of tongues (strange or unknown languages)

Gnosticism a religious system or teaching emphasizing knowledge (*gnosis*), often knowledge available only to the initiated

grace the undeserved favour of God

halakhah rulings or interpretation of points of Jewish law

Hauptbriefe 'the principal letters', i.e. 1 and 2 Corinthians, Romans, and Galatians, sometimes regarded as a canon within the Pauline canon

Hellenists Greek-speaking Jews from the Western diaspora

kerygma proclamation, especially of the Christian gospel

Kirchenrecht canon law

Kyrios 'Lord': Greek translation of the Hebrew word for God, used also of Jesus in the New Testament

Manichaeism a religious system founded by Manes or Mani and followed in the third to the fifth century. It taught that there are two basic principles, light and darkness, or good and evil.

Marcionites adherents of the ascetic sect founded by Marcion of Sinope in the second century

Messiah a Hebrew title, 'the anointed one', given to Jesus; *see also* Christ

midrash the Hebrew exposition of the Old Testament

millenarian believing in the millennium, the 1,000 years Jesus was prophesied to reign in person on the earth

Mishnah the Jewish oral law

Montanism a second-century ascetic movement founded by Montanus of Phrygia

nomistic based on law or scripture

parousia 'coming', usually Jesus' second coming

Pastoral Letters the letters to Timothy and Titus

Pharisees a Jewish sect characterized by strict observance of the law

presbyter an officer of the early church. The Greek term is *presbyteros*, 'elder'. The presbyters formed a council with a 'ruling' function, and some of them were engaged in preaching and teaching.

pseudepigrapha spurious writings

Religionsgeschichtliche Schule the 'History of Religions School' of the late nineteenth century. It saw Christianity not just as a list of doctrines but as a religion which was practised, and viewed it in the context of the many religions of its time.

sacraments religious ceremonies or acts regarded as a means of grace

Sadducees a Jewish sect consisting mainly of high-priestly families who controlled the temple in Jerusalem

Shema the traditional Jewish confession of the uniqueness of the God of Israel; it is found in Deut. 6:4

soteriology the doctrine of salvation

Synoptic Gospels the gospels of Matthew, Mark, and Luke, regarded as giving a synopsis of the story of Jesus, which can be read side by side (syn-optically)

Talmud the body of Jewish civil and canon law

Torah the Jewish law; the Pentateuch

Valentinians followers of the Egyptian theologian Valentinus; also members of the Gnostic sect founded by him

Yahweh the Hebrew name for God in the Old Testament

polemical – involving strong arguments for or against 'sth', often in opposition to the opinions of others.

Abbreviations

General

AB	Anchor Bible
ABD	*Anchor Bible Dictionary* (6 vols., New York: Doubleday, 1992)
AD	Anno Domini (in the year of the Lord) = CE
ANRW	*Aufstieg und Niedergang der römischen Welt*, ed. H. Temporini and W. Haase (Berlin, 1972–)
ANTC	Abingdon New Testament Commentaries
AV	(translation of the Bible)
BC	Before Christ
BCE	Before Christian Era
BNTC	Black's New Testament Commentary
ca	circa = about
CBQ	*Catholic Biblical Quarterly*
CE	Christian (or Common) Era
cf.	compare
ch(s).	chapter(s)
DPL	*Dictionary of Paul and his Letters*, ed. G. F. Hawthorne and R. P. Martin (Downers Grove, IL: IVP, 1993)
ed(s).	editor(s), edited by
e.g.	exempli gratia = for example
ET	English Translation
et al.	et alii = and others
FRLANT	Forschungen zur Religion und Literatur des Alten und Neuen Testaments
GNB	Good News Bible (translation of the Bible)
HTKNT	Herders theologischer Kommentar zum Neuen Testament
HTR	*Harvard Theological Review*
HUT	Hermeneutische Untersuchungen zur Theologie
ICC	International Critical Commentary
IGRom	*Inscriptiones graecae* (Rome)

JB	Jerusalem Bible (translation of the Bible)
JBL	*Journal of Biblical Literature*
JETS	*Journal of Evangelical Theological Society*
JSJS	Supplement to *Journal for the Study of Judaism*
JSNT	*Journal for the Study of the New Testament*
JSNTS	Supplement to *JSNT*
JTC	*Journal for Theology and Church*
JTS	*Journal of Theological Studies*
KEK	Kritisch-exegetischer Kommentar
KJV	King James Version (translation of the Bible)
LCC	Library of Christian Classics
LXX	Septuagint (= Greek translation of the OT)
NCB	New Century Bible
NCBC	New Century Bible Commentary
NCBCS	New Cambridge Bible Commentary Series
NEB	New English Bible (translation of the Bible)
NIB	*New International Bible*
NICNT	New International Commentary on the New Testament
NIGTC	New International Greek Testament Commentary
NIV	New International Version (translation of the Bible)
NJBC	*New Jerome Bible Commentary*
NovT	*Novum Testamentum*
NovTSup	Supplements to *NovT*
NRSV	New Revised Standard Version (translation of the Bible)
NT	New Testament
NTG	New Testament Guides
NTS	*New Testament Studies*
OT	Old Testament
ÖTK	Ökumenischer Taschenbuch-Kommentar
PL	*Patrologia Latina*
RB	*Revue Biblique*
RSV	Revised Standard Version (translation of the Bible)
SBL	Society of Biblical Literature
SBS	Stuttgarter Bibelstudien
SNTSMS	Studiorum Novi Testamenti Societas (= Society of New Testament Studies) Monograph Series
THNT	Theologischer Handkommentar zum Neuen Testament
TübZeit	*Tübinger Zeitschrift*
WBC	Word Biblical Commentary

WUNT	Wissenschaftliche Untersuchungen zum Neuen Testament
ZKG	*Zeitschrift für Kirchengeschichte*
ZNW	*Zeitschrift für die neutestamentliche Wissenschaft*
ZTK	*Zeitschrift für Theologie und Kirche*

Books of the Bible

Old Testament

Gen.	Genesis			Jer.	Jeremiah
Exod.	Exodus				
Lev.	Leviticus			Ezek.	Ezekiel
Num.	Numbers			Dan.	Daniel
Deut.	Deuteronomy	Job			
Josh.	Joshua	Pss.	Psalms	Joel	
		Prov.	Proverbs		
1–2 Sam.	1–2 Samuel				
1–2 Kgs.	1–2 Kings	Isa.	Isaiah		
				Hab.	Habakkuk
				Mal.	Malachi

LXX/Deuterocanonical books

1–4 Macc.	1–4 Maccabees	Wis.	Wisdom of Solomon
Sir.	Sirach		
Tobit			

Old Testament pseudepigrapha

Apoc. Abr.	Apocalypse of Abraham	Pseudo	Phocylides
Ascension of Isaiah		T. Isaac	Testament of Isaac
2 Bar.	2 Baruch		
1 Enoch			
4 Ezra			

New Testament

Matt.	Matthew	1–2 Thess.	1–2 Thessalonians
Mark		1–2 Tim.	1–2 Timothy
Luke		Titus	
John		Phlm.	Philemon
Acts		Heb.	Hebrews
Rom.	Romans	Jas.	James
1–2 Cor.	1–2 Corinthians	1–2 Pet.	1–2 Peter
Gal.	Galatians	1–3 John	
Eph.	Ephesians		
Phil.	Philippians		
Col.	Colossians		

Chronology

(This is intended as illustrative rather than definitive; most Pauline scholars would agree the broad outline, with divergence on key dates limited to two or three years.)

Birth in Tarsus	around the turn of the century
Education primarily in Jerusalem (Acts 22:3)	
Crucifixion of Jesus	30
Conversion of Saul (Acts 9 etc.)	32/33
First Jerusalem visit (Gal. 1:18)	35/36
Antioch – teacher and missionary	early and mid 40s
(Jerusalem visit? Acts 11:30)	
– 'the first missionary journey' (Acts 13–14)	
Jerusalem council (Gal. 2:1–10/Acts 15)	48/49
Aegean mission – Corinth (Acts 18:11)	50–2
1 and 2 Thessalonians	
Galatians	
Jerusalem visit (Acts 18:22)	52
Aegean mission – Ephesus (Acts 19:10)	53–5
1 and 2 Corinthians (Philippians,	
Colossians and Philemon?)	
Aegean mission – final phase (Acts 20:3)	56
Romans	
Arrest in Jerusalem (Acts 21:33)	57
Imprisonment in Caesarea (Acts 24:27)	57–9
Journey to Rome (Acts 27:1–28:16)	59–60
Imprisonment in Rome (Acts 28:30)	60–2
Philippians, Colossians, and Philemon	
Probable date of execution	62/63
(Possible release and further mission	62–4?)
(Ephesians, Pastoral Epistles)	

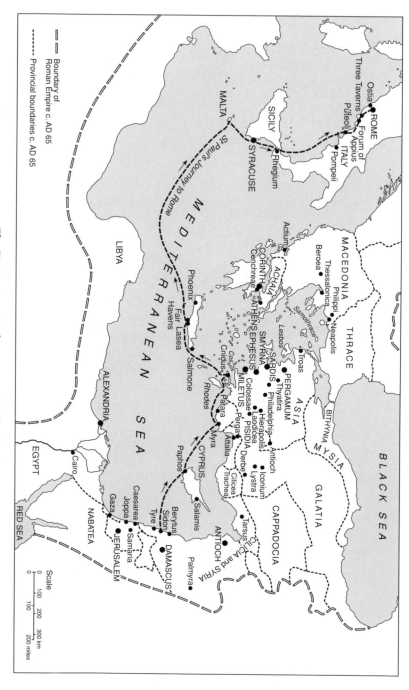

The First-century Mediterranean World of Paul

ROME
Three Taverns
Forum of Appius
Ostia
Puteoli
ITALY
Pompeii

SICILY
Rhegium
SYRACUSE

MALTA

St Paul's Journey to Rome

LIBYA

M E D I T E R R A N E A N   S E A

Phoenix
Fair
Lasea
Havens
Salmone

Actium
Beroea
Thessalonica
MACEDONIA
Philippi
Neapolis
THRACE
CORINTH
ACHAIA
Cenchreae
ATHENS
EPHESUS
Samothrace
Lesbos
Troas
MYSIA
BITHYNIA
BLACK SEA
SMYRNA
SARDIS
PERGAMUM
Thyatira
Chidus
Cos
Colossae
Philadelphia
Hierapolis
Laodicea
Rhodes
MILETUS
Perga
Patara
Myra
Attalia
PISIDIA
Derbe
Antioch
Lystra
Iconium
GALATIA
Cilicea
Trachea
Tarsus
CILICIA and SYRIA
CAPPADOCIA
Palmyra

ALEXANDRIA

EGYPT
Cairo

RED SEA

NABATEA

CYPRUS
Paphos
Salamis

Caesarea
Joppa
Gaza
Samaria
JERUSALEM
Tyre
Sidon
Berytus
DAMASCUS
ANTIOCH

Scale
0   100   200   300 km
0   100   200 miles

Introduction

JAMES D. G. DUNN

A 'TROUBLER OF ISRAEL'

Paul has always been an uncomfortable and controversial figure in the history of Christianity. The accusation against the prophet Elijah by Israel's King Ahab, 'you troubler of Israel' (1 Ks. 18:17), could be levelled against Paul more fittingly than any other of the first Christians. He first appears on the public stage of first-century history as a Jewish 'zealot' (Acts 22:3), one who measured his 'zeal' by his attempt to violently 'destroy' (Gal. 1:13; Phil. 3:6) the embryonic movement within Second Temple Judaism, then best characterized as 'the sect of the Nazarenes' (Acts 24:5, 14; 28:22), two generations later as 'Christianity'.[1] Following his conversion, when he turned round and joined those whom he had persecuted (Acts 9; Gal. 1:13–16), and when he then embarked on a highly personal mission to win Gentiles to the gospel of Christ (Rom. 11:13; 15:18–20), he displayed the same sort of passionate commitment, even 'zeal' (2 Cor. 11:2) on behalf of his converts and churches.

Such out-and-out commitment to his cause created tremendous resentment among his fellow Jews, including, not least, those Jews who, like him, had also come to believe in Jesus as Israel's Messiah.[2] One of the chief reasons why we still have so many of his letters is that his teaching was quickly challenged by varying opponents from both within and without the churches he established; it was characteristic of Paul that he did not hesitate to respond vigorously to such challenges.[3] Similarly when his churches proved restive under his tutelage he saw it as part of his continuing apostolic vocation to write to further instruct, encourage and exhort them.[4] The fact that most, though not all of his letters were preserved for posterity testifies to their effectiveness; they must have been treasured by those who received them, circulated round other churches and within a generation or so have been gathered into a single collection for wider use.

Paul remained a controversial figure in the generations immediately following him. One of the main reasons why most scholars regard the Pastoral

Epistles (1 and 2 Timothy and Titus) as post-Pauline, though written from within the tradition he inaugurated, is that they seem to present a softer, somewhat idealized Paul, more amenable to the faith forms and structures of mainstream Christianity as it emerged from the first century. Similarly the Paul of Acts seems to have been stripped of much of the controversy known to us from his letters, even of some of his more distinctive teaching, and to have been shorn of most of his prickles. It should also be recalled that there were some strands diverging from mainstream Christianity in the second century which claimed that Paul was their principal inspiration (Marcion, Valentinian Gnosticism); Tertullian could even call Paul 'the apostle of the heretics' (*adv. Marc.* 3.5). Equally significant is the fact that the most direct heirs of the Jewish-Christian groupings within earliest Christianity regarded Paul as the great apostate, an arch enemy (*Epistula Petri* 2:3; *Clem. Hom.* 17:18–19). And so it becomes still more apparent that the Paul retained for Christianity was a domesticated Paul, Paul rendered more comfortable, an ecclesiasticized Paul.[5]

At the same time, the influence of Paul on subsequent Christianity has been incalculable. Not for nothing was he hailed a century ago as 'the second founder of Christianity'.[6] And for the most part his influence has been positive and creative, challenging new generations as he did his own to a renewed appreciation of 'the truth of the gospel', provoking leading exponents of Christianity to fresh insights into what it means to be 'christian' and 'church', and stimulating again and again fresh theological syntheses at the fulcrum point of epochs in transition. It was under the influence of Paul that Irenaeus and Tertullian were able to steady the boat of Christianity, rocked as it was in the second half of the second century by 'heresy' and competing religious systems. The great paradigm formulated by Augustine which enabled western Christianity to survive the fall of the Roman Empire and to endure through 'the dark ages' owed much to Paul. The Reformation, built on the foundation of Paul's teaching on 'justification by faith (alone)', resulted in a Protestantism which can be justly characterized as a kind of Paulinism. Methodists delight to recall that it was when he had been listening to a reading of Luther's preface to Paul's epistle to the Romans that John Wesley felt his 'heart strangely warmed'. It was the commentary of Karl Barth on the same Pauline letter which fell like a bomb in the playground of Europe's theologians after the First World War, inaugurating a new phase in twentieth-century theology and churchmanship. And in the last two decades of the twentieth century the so-called 'new perspective on Paul' has been a major factor in reinvigorating interest in what had become a stereotyped appreciation of earliest Christianity and a rather moribund treatment of Pauline theology.

The following pages reflect something of the fascination that Paul exerts, as well as something of the irritation he causes. Many of the issues are relatively humdrum – particularly the 'who wrote what where and when and why' questions which Introductions to ancient writings have to ask. Were all thirteen letters attributed to Paul actually written by him? There has rarely been much doubt about the principal letters (*Hauptbriefe*) – Romans, 1 and 2 Corinthians and Galatians; 1 Thessalonians and Philippians usually slip easily under the rope too. And not many have the heart to deny Paul the intriguing personal note to Philemon. But for nearly two hundred years there have been weighty voices raised against the Pauline authorship of 2 Thessalonians and Colossians, and still more against the Pauline authorship of Ephesians, even though it can be justly described as a classic exposition of 'Paulinism'. And it is probably a minority of modern scholars who would regard the Pastoral Epistles as penned or dictated by Paul himself. Over that period the debate on Pauline authorship has ebbed to and fro, without much final resolution being achieved, beyond the universal agreement that the letter to the Hebrews was not by Paul, despite old church tradition reflected in the heading of the King James Version (KJV). The chief factors to be considered in such introductory questions regarding the thirteen letters of the Pauline corpus, together with an analysis of each letter, can be followed through in Part two below.

Of more intrinsic interest are the larger questions regarding Paul's life and role as 'apostle to the Gentiles', the distinctive character of each of the letters, the themes of Christian teaching and practice which he addressed, and the heritage which he left behind him through these letters. Since these questions provide the principal subject matter for this *Companion*, and since most of the current thinking on these questions reflects in greater or less degree the influence of earlier phases of thinking on them, it is important that readers of the *Companion* have some idea of that earlier thinking.

F. C. BAUR

There is one overarching question which more than any other has dominated the study of the historical Paul during the last two centuries. That is the issue of Paul's role in transforming a Jewish messianic renewal movement into a religion which captured the allegiance of most of the Graeco-Roman world within three centuries and so became the dominant religious and intellectual influence on European thought and culture.

The question was first posed in the modern period by F. C. Baur. As he expressed it at the beginning of his treatment of Paul, the principal challenge is to understand 'how Christianity, instead of remaining a mere form of

Judaism . . . asserted itself as a separate, independent principle, broke loose from it' and became a new religion.[7] Baur had already found the clue to Paul's role in the references to conflict between different parties in 1 Cor. 1:12. Hence the second part of the title of his most famous article: 'The Opposition between Petrine and Pauline Christianity in the Earliest Church'.[8] Baur's thesis was that this conflict between two factions, one with distinctive Jewish tendencies, and the other, Pauline Christianity, shaped the history of Christianity for the first two centuries of its development. And who made the ultimately decisive contribution to free Christian universalism from Jewish particularism? Paul, of course. So too it was Baur who insisted that the opponents of Paul in all his letters were 'judaizers', proponents of a stultifying Jewish Christianity who insisted that Paul's Gentile converts conform to the restrictions of the Jewish law.[9] Not altogether surprisingly, Baur saw in this conflict a foreshadowing of the Reformation conflict between Catholicism (characterized as like Judaism in its attachment to the formal and external) and Protestantism (regarded as like Pauline Christianity in its attachment to the inner and spiritual). Well into the twentieth century, indeed, the key question was when 'old Catholicism' or 'early Catholicism' (*Frühkatholizismus*) first emerged – only after Paul (the Pauline epistles) or already within Paul's own church organization.[10]

THE HISTORY OF RELIGIONS SCHOOL

The terms of the debate only began to change in the late nineteenth century when the developments in embryonic Christianity began to be looked at from the opposite direction; that is, when the focus began to shift from asking how Christianity emerged *from Judaism* to asking how Christianity became influenced *by Hellenism* (the Greek culture which had increasingly pervaded the eastern Mediterranean since the conquest of Alexander the Great nearly four centuries earlier). This was the phase in the study of Christianity's origins identified with the 'History of Religions School'. The *Religionsgeschichtliche Schule* was a movement which insisted that Christianity should be seen not simply as a list of *doctrines* believed but as a *religion* practised. To understand earliest Christianity it was necessary to look at it in relation to other religions and religious currents of the time, that is, to see Christianity not as separate from but as part of the history of its times, not as something unique but as one religion among many. Here again, in the 'hellenization' of Christianity, Paul was the one to be credited with making the decisive breakthrough.

The impact of the History of Religions movement changed the face of New Testament study, particularly in regard to Paul, to whose writings most attention was given. For example, by reading Paul's account of the effects of the Spirit within his churches Hermann Gunkel shifted the perception of 'spirit' from the idealized world spirit of Hegel to something much more primitive – the experience of empowering.[11] In effect Gunkel's changed focus anticipated the emergence of Pentecostalism in the early twentieth century, characterized by a similar emphasis on the experience of the Spirit. The emphases cut little ice for the mainstream theological and ecclesiastical developments of the first half of the twentieth century, but the growth of the 'charismatic movement' in the second half aroused an equivalent interest in the charismatic and experiential dimension of Paul's writings in Pauline scholarship.[12]

Not unrelated was a famous debate between Rudolph Sohm and Adolf Harnack which spanned the turn of the nineteenth to the twentieth century – in effect complementary to the *Frühkatholizismus* debate. Sohm sharpened an already recognized contrast between 'function' and 'office' in early church organization into a sharp antithesis between 'charisma' and 'canon law' (*Kirchenrecht*). His argument, based principally on Paul, was that 'the organization of Christendom is not a legal one, but a charismatic organization'; 'Christendom is organized through the distribution of spiritual gifts'.[13] For Sohm the displacement of charismatic structure by human *Kirchenrecht*, first visible in 1 Clement (late first century AD), marked a 'fall' from the apostolic to subapostolic age. In contrast, Harnack recognized the tension between Spirit and office, but saw it not as sequential but rather as simultaneous, charismatic functions and administrative offices operating in tension more or less from the first.[14] This too is a debate which revived in the second half of the twentieth century.[15] On the one hand, the tension in Paul has been mirrored in the equivalent tensions within and between the ecumenical and charismatic movements – always with the challenge, implicit or explicit: does the character of Christian community as envisioned in 1 Corinthians 12 provide a continuing model for the church as 'the body of Christ'?[16] And on the other, the *Frühkatholizismus* issue has been restated in terms provided from the sociology of Max Weber, as to whether the 'routinization' or 'institutionalization' of charisma is best conceived as a second-generation development or as a feature within Paul's own churches.[17]

Too much of that debate was a throwback to the earlier period marked by introverted navel-gazing, as though early Christianity's history were something quite separate from the history of its time. More typical of History of Religions' concerns was interest in early church organization as influenced by and reflective of contemporary social structures. The path was pioneered by Edwin Hatch before the emergence of the History of

Religions School,[18] but was surprisingly even more neglected until the later decades of the twentieth century.[19] However, since the pioneering studies of the Corinthian church by Gerd Theissen,[20] the sociological path has become a major highway for scholarly monographs.[21] The concern has been to understand better the social dynamics of small groups meeting in private houses, sometimes small tenement apartments. What was the proportion of well-to-do and low born, of slaves and slave-owners, of Jews and non-Jews? What did it mean for Paul to work with his own hands to support himself? How did the patron/client and honour/shame conventions of the Mediterranean world impact on the conduct and relationships within the Pauline churches? What about the status of women within the house churches and their role in ministry within these churches? How did the first Christian groups survive or thrive within often hostile environments: what boundaries did they draw round themselves and what movement did they permit through these boundaries? Such questions continue to fascinate students and scholars, not least for the lessons which might be gleaned from a pre-Christendom church of possible relevance to a post-Christendom church.

An older interest which was reinforced by History of Religions' motivation was in the influence of ancient rhetoric on Paul. This was another way of approach to Paul's letters, other than viewing them as primarily statements of theology, which came to the fore in the great commentary on 1 Corinthians by Johannes Weiss.[22] But here once again it was an interest which sputtered only fitfully during the middle decades of the twentieth century when the programmes of Barthian theology largely dominated university faculties of theology. However, it too has revived in the closing decades of that century, kick-(re)started by Hans Dieter Betz,[23] and much stimulated by interaction with the lively postmodern debates within the field of literary criticism. That highly illuminating readings of Paul's letters can be achieved by familiarity with ancient epistolary and rhetorical conventions, by noting carefully the terms, idioms, and strategies employed by Paul, and by listening attentively to the effect he sought to evoke in his readers has become increasingly apparent.[24] In at least some occasions, after all, Paul's letters were but one side of an often contentious and passionate dialogue. It does *not* follow – especially for those who want to hear afresh the controversial Paul for themselves – that their content (*die Sache*) is best grasped by a dispassionate exposition.

THE ORIGIN OF THE SACRAMENTS

The thesis which most characterized the History of Religions contribution to study of Christianity's origins was the claim that Christianity's two (chief) sacraments (baptism and sacred meal) were deeply influenced in derivation by the equivalent rites of contemporary mystery cults. Where did Paul get the idea that Christians had been 'baptized into Christ Jesus (and) into his death' (Rom. 6:3)? A parallel with initiation into the cults of dying and rising gods, typically celebrating the renewal of spring (Easter!), immediately suggested itself. The Attis cult with its ghastly taurobolium, where the initiate was 'reborn' by being drenched in the blood of a bull, drew particular attention. And does not talk of eating the body and drinking the blood of Christ in the Lord's Supper suggest the idea of devouring the god which characterized the frenzied ritual of the cult of Dionysus?[25]

As so often when parallels catch the eye, however, the initial excitement pushed the thesis too far. We know too little of the mysteries of the cults; for the most part they succeeded in keeping their 'mysteries' secret. But on some of the key issues, at least, we can be fairly confident. For example, where ablutions were involved they were likely to be preparatory for initiation rather than part of the initiation itself. The suggestion of a mystical identification with the cult god is more read into than out of the texts in question. And the function of any symbolic eating and drinking within any mystery, and therefore the extent and significance of any parallel, is quite unclear.[26]

At the same time, it is true that Paul seems to acknowledge a parallel between the Lord's Supper and meals eaten in temples dedicated to gods like Sarapis (1 Cor. 10:20–1). The suggestion that the bread and wine, consumed in a wrong spirit, could have a destructive effect (1 Cor. 11:29–30) has an unnerving ring. And Paul evidently saw a dangerous parallel between the chaotic enthusiasm of the Corinthian worship (14:23) and the abandoned ecstasy of the Dionysiac cult (12:2). Yet, some such phenomenological parallels are hardly unexpected. And if the issue is the originating impulse for the Christian sacraments, the background of Jewish washings (Heb. 6:2) and Passover meal (1 Cor. 5:7) is a much more obvious source of influence. Consequently, few now find any cause to look further than Christianity's own foundational tradition of John's baptism as the beginning of the gospel (cf. Mark 1:8; 10:38; Rom. 6:3) and the last supper of Jesus with his disciples before his death (1 Cor. 11:23–6).

THE ORIGINS OF CHRISTOLOGY

Where the History of Religions approach made its greatest impact, however, was in the area of christology. The debate following Baur had brought to increasing recognition that the development of earliest Christianity could not be conceived satisfactorily simply in terms of two great blocks (Petrine and Pauline Christianity) grinding against each other. There were more layers involved: James and the primitive Jerusalem church for a start, and Gentile factions more radical than Paul; but then also the overlap of Judaism and Hellenism which was already a feature of 'the Hellenists' (Acts 6:1) and of diaspora Judaism prior to Paul. The effect was to distance Paul even more from Jesus. The more Jesus was seen simply as a Jewish teacher of love-moralism, as in late-nineteenth-century Liberalism,[27] the more difficult it was to explain where Paul was coming from in developing his conception of Christianity as a religion of redemption focused on Jesus' death and res-urrection. Paul's seeming disregard for Jesus during his earthly ministry, 'Christ according to the flesh' (2 Cor. 5:16), simply reinforced the problem. A great gulf was fixed and many were the attempts made to bridge the gap between 'Jesus and Paul'.[28]

Initially, and still with the mysteries in mind, the decisive development in the Christian way of thinking about Christ was attributed to the mystical experience of Christ as a supra-terrestrial power which was thought to have characterized the worship of the early Christian cult. Paul's own distinctive conception of being 'in Christ' was seen as a direct reflection of this cultic mysticism.[29] This line of exposition reflected a wider interest in mysticism before the Second World War, an interest which has diminished greatly since, being either diverted into a reinvigorated theology of church and sacrament, or largely overtaken by the renewed interest in the charismatic experience of the Spirit.[30]

Of weightier and more enduring influence was the growing History of Religions conviction that Gnosticism, previously regarded as simply a Christian heresy, had much deeper roots, represented a quite independent religious philosophy, and, putting the theory of influence into reverse, had been the *source* of Christianity's own theology of salvation. The high water mark of this particular tide of speculation was Rudolf Bultmann's famous claim that behind Paul's christology lay the Gnostic Redeemer myth.[31] This was the belief that the human condition was one of imprisonment and ignorance, the spirit within ('sparks of light') needing to be enlightened, given knowledge (*gnosis*) as to its true nature and origin. In the myth, salvation is brought by the 'light-person' who enters this lower world to bring the saving, life-giving *gnosis*. Bultmann was sure that passages like 2 Cor. 8:9, Phil. 2:6–11 and Eph. 4:8–10 reflected the Gnostic myth of the descent and re-ascent of the Gnostic Redeemer.

The problem is that no extant version of the Gnostic Redeemer myth predates Christianity. The Jewish talk of divine Wisdom's descent to earth (as in Sir. 24:8–12 and 1 Enoch 42) is best seen not as the broken fragment of some complete, earlier myth, but as the sort of building block out of which the later myth was constructed. The fact that redeemer figures (like Simon Magus) only appear subsequent to Jesus probably indicates that early Christian, not least Pauline christology, was itself another of the building blocks which second-century Gnosticism built into its syncretistic myth. The Nag Hammadi codices (discovered in 1945) have provided a life-support system for Bultmann's thesis (particularly *The Gospel of Philip* 58:17–22; 71:9–17 and *The Sophia of Jesus Christ* 100–1), but the thesis still depends on the false premise that 'independent means prior'. It is hardly to be denied, of course, that Paul shared with his environment language and concepts like 'knowledge' (*gnosis*) and 'spiritual' (*pneumatikos*). But it is now widely agreed that the quest for a pre-Christian Gnosticism, properly so called, has proved to be a wild goose chase. As with the sacraments, there are far more obvious roots for Paul's christology, particularly the already well-developed Jewish reflection on Adam and Wisdom.[32]

THE NEW PERSPECTIVE ON PAUL

On the issue of the decisive influences on Paul's theology, the tide began to turn with the work of W. D. Davies, who protested against the undue History of Religions concentration on Paul's Hellenist background and insisted that the key to understanding Paul was his Jewish origins.[33] However, there was a major stumbling block in any attempt to shed light on Paul from that source – namely, the deeply rooted, albeit unconscious, prejudice in so much Christian scholarship against Judaism. Judaism was what Paul had turned away from, was it not? His conversion had surely liberated Paul from the slavery of the law and from a legalistic Pharisaism. Was not his central doctrine, justification by faith, formulated precisely in opposition to a Judaism which taught that justification depended on one's own efforts ('works')? Thus it could be said that the History of Religions School had in effect continued to be motivated by Baur's conception of Christianity as a universal religion which could become itself only by freeing itself from the narrow particularistic bonds of Judaism. So far as the History of Religions School and its heirs were concerned, it was the influence of the universal spirit of Hellenism which had saved infant Christianity from a Jewish childhood of stunted growth and enabled it to achieve maturity.

Every so often voices were raised against such a parody both of second temple Judaism and of Paul's debt to his Jewish heritage.[34] But it was not until E. P. Sanders attacked the parody in a bare-knuckled way that the wrongheadedness of much of the earlier disregard of Paul's Jewish background became widely recognized, although the bluntness of his polemic provoked considerable resentment, particularly within German scholarship.[35]

Sanders observed that the starting point for Judaism's self-understanding as the people of God (both second Temple Judaism and rabbinic Judaism) was the covenant made by God with Israel; the covenant was nowhere regarded in Jewish writings as an achievement of human merit. And although Jews had the responsibility to maintain their covenant standing by obedience to the law, the repeated emphasis on repentance, and the centrality of a sacrificial system which provided atonement for the repentant within Israel's pattern of religion, meant that the characterization of that religion as legalistic and merit-based was misconceived, unjustified, and prejudicial. Sanders coined the phrase 'covenantal nomism' to embrace both aspects – the divine initiative of God's choice of a 'not people' (covenant), and the response of obedience required from that people (law/nomism).

This was 'the new perspective on Paul'. In reality it was a new perspective on Paul's 'Judaism'. But it called for a new perspective on Paul himself. If Paul was not reacting to a legalistic Judaism which understood salvation to be dependent ultimately on human achievement, then what was he reacting to? Sanders himself saw Paul's reaction to be essentially confused.[36] But James Dunn argued that the new perspective shed light on Paul's theology by allowing us to see that its polemical thrust was directed not against the idea of achieving God's acceptance by the merit of personal achievement (good works), but against the Jewish intention to safeguard the privilege of covenant status from being dissipated or contaminated by non-Jews. Paul was reacting primarily against the exclusivism which he himself had previously fought to maintain. In particular, he was reacting against the conviction (shared by most other Christian Jews) that 'works of the law', such as (or particularly) circumcision and laws of clean and unclean, continued to prescribe the terms of covenant relationship for Gentiles as well as Jews. It was in and from this conflict that Paul's doctrine of justification by faith alone achieved its classic expression (Gal. 2:1–21).[37]

THE ONGOING DEBATE

The contours of the ongoing debate remain unclear. An overdue response to Sanders from German scholarship, from Friedrich Avemarie, observes that the rabbinic evidence is more mixed and argues that Sanders has pushed the covenant side of his 'covenantal nomism' too hard.[38] It has been more fully recognized that the language of 'justification' should be used in reference not only to the initial acceptance through faith but also to the final judgment. Also that the central Jewish idea of salvation, as a balance between divine initiative and human response, a status both received as a gift (election) and to be maintained (by doing God's will), is not so very different from Paul's. If Jewish hope of salvation is founded upon God's choice of Israel to be his people, so Paul's is founded upon the grace of God in Christ received through faith. If Jewish hope of life in the world to come depends on human obedience (nomism), no less does Paul speak in terms of judgment according to works for believers too (Rom. 2:6–11; 2 Cor. 5:10). In fact, it is evident that a fresh assessment of the balance between divine initiative/grace and human response/responsibility is required both in regard to Paul's theology and in early Judaism.

Within this overarching scheme, any continuing role for the Torah (Jewish law) in Paul's ethics is a matter of continuing controversy. How to do justice to the positive as well as the negative thrust of what Paul says about the law? Are his ethics simply charismatic ('walk by the Spirit')? Can the old distinction between moral law (still applicable) and ceremonial law (discarded) be revived in a more credible form than previously? How could Paul pick and choose between individual commands as he does – some no longer applicable (circumcision, food laws) but others still in force (against idolatry and sexual licence) – when they all have the same divine sanction in scripture? Is it possible to discern clear and consistent principles, not least scriptural (OT) principles, governing Paul's advice and his own conduct, or is this one of the areas where criticisms of inconsistency and manipulation have some force?[39]

Some attempts have been made to open up new ways of interpreting Paul's letters. A decade-long seminar at the annual Society of Biblical Literature attempted to refocus the old questions about a centre or core of Paul's theology and about a discernible development through his letters; but found itself becoming bogged down in the problem of deciding whether 'the theology of Paul' is the theology of each letter as such, or is better conceived as the theology upon which Paul drew to write the letters and which he shaped by writing them.[40] Feminist interpreters have attempted to tackle head-on the passages which have given Paul over the years at least the impression of being hostile to women having authority in church;[41] typical of a deeply rooted patriarchalism had been the refusal to allow that Phoebe in Rom. 16:1–2 could have been a deacon and a benefactor, and that Paul could have greeted a female apostle called Junia a few verses later (Rom. 16:7), despite the clarity of the terms he used.

Other old controversies have been reinvigorated and given fresh life. For example, is it so clear that Paul entertained no interest in the popularly miscalled 'historical Jesus', when so many of his exhortations seem to echo teachings explicitly attributed to Jesus in the Synoptic Gospels?[42] The fresh appreciation of the vitality of Jewish mysticism at the time of Paul has reinvigorated the idea of Pauline mysticism, now in terms of Paul's conversion experience and other claims to visions and revelations (2 Cor. 4:4–6; 12:1–7);[43] should Paul's soteriology be seen in terms more of spiritual participation ('in Christ') than of legal 'justification'? And one of the most fascinating discussions on Paul's reconfiguration of his Jewish heritage focuses on Paul's christology – now not simply on the extent to which he was influenced by Jewish Wisdom speculation, but on whether he had in effect so redefined Jewish monotheism as 'christological monotheism' (1 Cor. 8:5–6) as effectively to have turned his back on his Jewish faith in God as one (Deut. 6:4).[44]

A more radical approach has been signalled by J. L. Martyn in his insistence that predominant weight must be given to the apocalyptic dimension of Paul's theology.[45] In terms reminiscent of Barth's dismissal of the relevance of History of Religions parallels for an adequate grasp of Paul's gospel, Martyn maintains that Paul's talk of 'new creation' (Gal. 6:15) relegates to irrelevance all issues of continuity with Israel's past. Like Barth he wants to hear afresh the gospel of Paul in all its raw power and offensiveness. In common with many other (particularly American) scholars, Martyn reinforces the christocentric character of Paul's gospel by advocating that Paul's talk of 'faith' in his key polemical discussions on the theme is a reference not to human trust (*pistis Christou* = 'faith in Christ') but to the faithfulness of Christ (*pistis Christou* = 'faith of Christ').[46]

From a different perspective, the debate is whether Paul's turning his back on his 'Judaism' (Gal. 1:13–14) was only(!) his conversion from one Jewish sect to another,[47] or the first stirring of Christianity's subsequent and long-running anti-Judaism with its horrific outworkings in twentieth-century Europe.[48] It is whether in insisting on reading the scriptures through christological spectacles, that is, as 'Old Testament', Paul was not opening the door to a Marcionite disowning of or at least disregard for the scriptures of his ancestral religion. It is whether Paul in seeking for the movement he represented an identity which was not (only) Jewish made it impossible for Jewish believers in Jesus Messiah to retain their cultural identity as Jews.[49] Or whether Paul can still be heard as an authentically Jewish voice seeking to understand the scriptures from within and to live out what he saw to be Israel's God-given mission to be 'a light to the nations'.[50]

Thus we can see that the wheel has come full circle, from Baur in the early nineteenth century to the present debate. How are the theology and historical contribution of Paul, the Jew become believer in Jesus Messiah, the Pharisaic zealot become apostle to the Gentiles, to be adequately grasped and assessed? If not as the founder of Christianity, then certainly as the one who more than any other of his generation ensured that the Jewish Nazarene renewal movement would break out of the matrix of his native

Judaism and become Christianity of the Gentiles. And yet as one who sought to bring non-Jews to faith in the one God proclaimed by Israel through Israel's Messiah Jesus, who saw the churches (*ekklesiai*) he established as of a piece with the assembly (*ekklesia*) of Israel, and who was convinced that his gospel was in accord with Israel's scriptures. It is that paradox, apostle of Israel or apostate from Israel, with which Paul confronts his twenty-first-century readers, both students of Christianity's beginnings and Christians eager to hear afresh 'the truth of the gospel' preached by Paul. Unless the paradox is taken fully into account, the heart of Paul's theology and historical contribution, not to mention Paul himself, will remain an unresolved enigma.

Notes

1 Ignatius, *Magnesians* 10:1–3; *Romans* 3:3; *Philadelphians* 6:1.
2 E.g. Acts 21:20–1; Rom. 3:8; 15:31; 2 Cor. 11:22, 24.
3 Gal. 1:6–9; 2 Cor. 10–13; Phil. 3:2–6.
4 E.g. 1 Corinthians; Phil. 2:1–18; 1 Thess. 4–5.
5 See further J. D. G. Dunn, *Unity and Diversity in the New Testament* (London: SCM, 1977; 2nd edn, 1990) 288–96.
6 W. Wrede, *Paul* (London: Philip Green, 1907) 180.
7 F. C. Baur, *Paul: The Apostle of Jesus Christ* (1845; ET 2 vols., London: Williams & Norgate, vol. 1, 1873) 3.
8 F. C. Baur, 'Die Christuspartei in der Korinthischen Gemeinde, der Gegensatz des petrinischen und paulinischen Christentums in der ältesten Kirche, der Apostle Petrus in Rom', *TübZeit* 5/4 (1831) 61–206.
9 At the time of Paul 'Judaize' was a term used for Gentiles who sympathized with Judaism and adopted some Jewish customs; the usage introduced in the nineteenth century and dominant since was unknown in the first century.
10 See further Dunn, *Unity and Diversity* 341–66.
11 H. Gunkel, *Die Wirkungen des Heiligen Geistes nach der populären Anschauung der apostolischen Zeit und der Lehre des Apostels* (Göttingen: Vandenhoeck & Ruprecht, 1888).
12 See particularly J. D. G. Dunn, *Jesus and the Spirit: A Study of the Religious and Charismatic Experience of Jesus and the First Christians* (London: SCM, 1975); G. D. Fee, *God's Empowering Presence: The Holy Spirit in the Letters of Paul* (Peabody, MA: Hendrickson, 1994).
13 R. Sohm, *Kirchenrecht* (1892; Munich: Duncker & Humblot, 1923) 1.1, 26.
14 A. Harnack, *The Constitution and Law of the Church in the First Two Centuries* (London: Williams & Norgate, 1910).
15 E.g. H. von Campenhausen, *Ecclesiastical Authority and Spiritual Power in the Church of the First Three Centuries* (1953; ET London: A. & C. Black, 1969); E. Schweizer, *Church Order in the New Testament* (ET London: SCM, 1961).
16 Cf., e.g., H. Küng, *The Church* (London: Burns & Oates, 1967).
17 See particularly M. Y. MacDonald, *The Pauline Churches: A Socio-Historical Study of Institutionalization in the Pauline and Deutero-Pauline Writings*, SNTSMS 60 (Cambridge: Cambridge University Press, 1988).

18 E. Hatch, *The Organization of the Early Christian Churches* (London: Longmans, 1888).

19 Indicative was the long neglect suffered by E. A. Judge, *The Social Patterns of Christian Groups in the First Century* (London: Tyndale, 1960).

20 G. Theissen, *The Social Setting of Pauline Christianity* (Philadelphia: Fortress/Edinburgh: T. & T. Clark, 1982).

21 See particularly J. K. Chow, *Patronage and Power: A Study of Social Networks in Corinth*, JSNTS 75 (Sheffield: JSOT, 1992); R. F. Hock, *The Social Context of Paul's Ministry: Tentmaking and Apostleship* (Philadelphia: Fortress, 1980); D. G. Horrell, *The Social Ethos of the Corinthian Correspondence: Interests and Ideology from 1 Corinthians to 1 Clement* (Edinburgh: T. & T. Clark, 1996); B. J. Malina, *The New Testament World: Insights from Cultural Anthropology* (London: SCM, 1983); W. A. Meeks, *The First Urban Christians: The Social World of the Apostle Paul* (New Haven: Yale University Press, 1983).

22 J. Weiss, *Der erste Korintherbrief*, KEK (Göttingen: Vandenhoeck & Ruprecht, 1910).

23 H. D. Betz, *Galatians*, Hermeneia (Philadelphia: Fortress, 1979).

24 See, e.g., R. N. Longenecker, *Galatians*, WBC 41 (Dallas: Word, 1990); M. M. Mitchell, *Paul and the Rhetoric of Reconciliation: An Exegetical Investigation of the Language and Composition of 1 Corinthians* (Louisville: Westminster/John Knox, 1991).

25 The classic study was by W. Heitmüller, *Taufe und Abendmahl* (Göttingen: Vandenhoeck & Ruprecht, 1903); for an up-to-date survey see H.-J. Klauck, *The Religious Context of Early Christianity* (Edinburgh: T. & T. Clark, 2000) ch. 2.

26 A. D. Nock, 'Early Gentile Christianity and its Hellenistic Background', *Essays on Religion and the Ancient World* (Oxford: Clarendon Press, 1972) 1.49–133; A. J. M. Wedderburn, *Baptism and Resurrection: Studies in Pauline Theology against its Graeco-Roman Background*, WUNT 44 (Tübingen: Mohr Siebeck, 1987).

27 Classically in A. Harnack, *What is Christianity?* (1900; ET London: Williams & Norgate, 1901).

28 J. W. Fraser, *Jesus and Paul* (Abingdon: Marcham Manor, 1974); A. J. M. Wedderburn, ed., *Paul and Jesus: Collected Essays*, JSNTS 37 (Sheffield: Sheffield Academic Press, 1989).

29 Most famously W. Bousset, *Kyrios Christos* (1921; ET Nashville: Abingdon, 1970).

30 See further my *The Theology of Paul the Apostle* (Grand Rapids: Eerdmans/ Edinburgh: T. & T. Clark, 1998) 390–6.

31 Especially R. Bultmann, *Theology of the New Testament* (ET London: SCM, vol. 1, 1952) 164–83. Particularly significant examples were the teachings of Hermes Trismegistus, above all the treatise on Poimandres (see now B. P. Copenhaver, *Hermetica* (Cambridge: Cambridge University Press, 1992)), and 'the Song of the Pearl' in the third-century *Acts of Thomas* 108–13.

32 See, e.g., M. Hengel, *The Son of God: The Origin of Christology and the History of Jewish-Hellenistic Religion* (London: SCM, 1976); J. D. G. Dunn, *Christology in the Making* (London: SCM, 1980; 2nd edn, 1989) chs. 4 and 6.

33 W. D. Davies, *Paul and Rabbinic Judaism* (London: SPCK, 1948; 4th edn, 1981).

34 Particularly G. F. Moore, 'Christian Writers on Judaism', *HTR* 14 (1922) 197–254.

35 E. P. Sanders, *Paul and Palestinian Judaism* (London: SCM, 1977).

36 E. P. Sanders, *Paul, the Law and the Jewish People* (Philadelphia: Fortress, 1983); H. Räisänen, *Paul and the Law*, WUNT (Tübingen: Mohr Siebeck, 1983).

37 J. D. G. Dunn, 'The New Perspective on Paul' (1983), *Jesus, Paul and the Law: Studies in Mark and Galatians* (London: SPCK, 1990) 183–214; more recently *Theology of Paul* ch. 14; insufficiently appreciated has been the earlier K. Stendahl, *Paul among Jews and Gentiles* (Philadelphia: Fortress, 1976/London: SCM, 1977).

38 F. Avemarie, *Tora und Leben: Untersuchungen zur Heilsbedeutung der Tora in der frühen rabbinischen Literatur*, WUNT (Tübingen: Mohr Siebeck, 1996).

39 See, e.g., S. Westerholm, *Israel's Law and the Church's Faith: Paul and his Recent Interpreters* (Grand Rapids: Eerdmans, 1988); J. D. G. Dunn, ed., *Paul and the Mosaic Law*, WUNT 89 (Tübingen: Mohr Siebeck, 1996).

40 *Pauline Theology* (4 vols.), ed. J. M. Bassler (vol. 1, 1991), D. M. Hay (vol. 2, 1993), D. M. Hay and E. E. Johnson (vol. 3, 1995; vol. 4, 1997); vols. 1–3 (Minneapolis: Fortress), vol. 4 (Atlanta: Scholars).

41 E. Schüssler Fiorenza, *In Memory of Her* (New York: Crossroad, 1994).

42 Dunn, *Theology of Paul* 183–95.

43 See particularly A. F. Segal, *Paul the Convert: the Apostolate and Apostasy of Saul the Pharisee* (New Haven: Yale University Press, 1990).

44 C. C. Newman, J. R. Davila, and G. S. Lewis, eds., *The Jewish Roots of Christological Monotheism*, JSJS 63 (Leiden: Brill, 1999).

45 J. L. Martyn, *Galatians*, AB 33A (New York: Doubleday, 1997).

46 Particularly R. B. Hays, *The Faith of Jesus Christ: An Investigation of the Narrative Substructure of Galatians 3:1–4:11* (Chico: Scholars, 1983; 2nd edn, Grand Rapids: Eerdmans, 2002).

47 Segal, *Paul the Convert.*

48 The issue was given unavoidable impetus by R. R. Ruether, *Faith and Fratricide: The Theological Roots of Anti-Semitism* (New York: Seabury, 1974).

49 J. M. G. Barclay, *Jews in the Mediterranean Diaspora from Alexander the Great to Trajan (323 BCE–117 CE)* (Edinburgh: T. & T. Clark, 1996).

50 J. D. G. Dunn, 'Paul: Apostate or Apostle of Israel?', *ZNW* 89 (1998) 256–71; also 'Who did Paul Think he was? A Study of Jewish Christian Identity', *NTS* 45 (1999) 174–93.

Part one

Paul's life and work

1   Paul's life

KLAUS HAACKER

Opinions of Paul have always been divided. He had been a man of conflict before his sudden conversion on the road to Damascus, bitterly opposed to the Jesus movement. He remained a subject of controversy after that event not only among his conservative Jewish countrymen but also within the early church. In modern times generations of scholars have hailed or blamed him as the true founder of Christianity, granting that Jesus himself had not crossed the borders of ancient Judaism. Obviously the apostle of the Gentiles was and is a challenge that leaves little room for indifference. Nevertheless sound scholarship must aim at balanced views that have a chance of convincing a majority of those who are ready and able to dig deeper and listen to the sources rather than to the praise or disdain of modern friends or foes. Positive or negative judgments on Paul are usually based upon some well-known doctrinal statements of his, isolated from the argument of their context and quoted without regard to the circumstances of his life and times. Instead of such more or less arbitrary opinions, to do justice to the person and work of the apostle demands a careful consideration of the character of our sources and an interpretation of his teaching as conditioned by his social and religious background and as part of his ministry of founding and fostering young churches in the Mediterranean world outside Judaea.

THE SOURCES

Historical knowledge of the life of Paul comes almost entirely from the New Testament, mostly from the Acts of the Apostles as the only narrative source, supplemented by a number of autobiographical passages or remarks in the letters of Paul (including some letters whose authorship is disputed). Both types of source concentrate on the years when Paul was a leading figure of the missionary outreach of the early church, i.e. the 50s of the first century CE, leaving large parts of his life open to speculation. In what evidence they offer, both sources are historically valuable but not free of tendencies to stress certain aspects and to leave out others, paying tribute to the perspective of their authors at the time of their writing. While Paul certainly knows his life better than the author of Luke–Acts, the occasions of his autobiographical statements are always marked by conflict, so that what he says has to serve very special concerns of his. Only some aspects of the controversies surrounding Paul (mostly those with people outside the early church) are also reflected in Acts and have influenced Luke's portrait of Paul.

CHRONOLOGY

The only sure basis for the chronology of Paul's missionary career is his encounter with the proconsul L. A. Gallio in Corinth according to Acts 18:12–17. Gallio's period in office can be dated from an inscription from Delphi to AD 51–2, and Paul's eighteen months at Corinth (Acts 18:11) must *somehow* have overlapped with this period. (Contrary to a widespread mis-understanding, the narrative does not say that the event occurred at the *end* of Paul's stay and at the *beginning* of Gallio's term of office.) Prior to this event, we hear of two 'missionary journeys' of Paul (Acts 13–14 and Acts 16–18) leading him from Antioch in Syria first to Asia Minor and then to Macedonia and Greece. The Jerusalem conference described in Acts 15 seems to be identical with a visit of Paul to Jerusalem mentioned in Gal. 2:1–10 which he dates to three and fourteen years after his calling (Gal. 1:18 and 2:1). This is in accord with the information given in 2 Cor. 11:32 (cf. Acts 9:23–5) that Paul had to flee from Damascus some time after his conversion at the time of (the Nabataean) King Aretas – who ruled from 9/8 BC to AD 40/1.[1] The death of Paul cannot be dated with any certainty because it is not related in the New Testament and only vaguely hinted at in 1 Clem. 5:7 and because we do not know the exact date when Porcius Festus (who died in AD 62) became governor of Judaea;[2] it was he who sent Paul to Rome for his trial at the court of Caesar (Acts 25–6). According to Acts 27–8, Paul arrived there only after shipwreck and a winter on the island of Malta. Acts 28:30 speaks of two more years of waiting for his trial under house arrest, and 1 Clem. 5:7 seems to imply that Paul was not sentenced to death at the end of this trial but did visit Spain, as had been his plan when writing the letter to the Romans (cf. Rom. 15:24). Possibly he died during the Neronian persecution in AD 64 after the fire of Rome. What age Paul was when he died can only be guessed at from the fact that he is mentioned as a 'young man' at the time of the martyrdom of Stephen (Acts 7:58) prior to his conversion.

BIRTH AND EDUCATION

There can be no doubt that Paul was Jewish by birth (Rom. 11:1; 2 Cor. 11:22; Phil. 3:5). More precisely he claimed to be a member of the tribe of Benjamin (Rom. 11:1; Phil. 3:5), and therefore it makes good sense that his parents gave him the name of Israel's first and only king from this tribe, *Saul* (used by the risen Lord in Paul's Damascus vision, Acts 9:4; 22:7; 26:14 and with the Greek ending (*Saulos*) by Luke for Paul from Acts 7:58 to 13:9). Since Benjamin was the youngest of the sons of Jacob/Israel, Paul may be alluding to his Benjaminite origin in 1 Cor. 15:8, where he calls himself the last and smallest of the apostles and in some sense the product of an abnormal birth (cf. Gen. 35:16–20). The name Paul (of Latin origin – meaning 'small'!), under which he became famous, was not a result of his conversion but a second name to be used in communications with a Graeco-Roman public (like Silvanus along with Silas).

According to Acts 9:11; 21:39; 22:3 Paul was born and at home in Tarsus in Cilicia, and was therefore a member of the Jewish diaspora. As such he visited the synagogues of Hellenistic Jews at Jerusalem (Acts 9:29). On the other hand he called himself a 'Hebrew' (2 Cor. 11:22) or even 'a Hebrew of Hebrews' (Phil. 3:5) – a term which in the light of Acts 6:1 marks the opposite of Hellenistic Jews, i.e. Jews of the motherland who spoke 'Hebrew' (or rather Aramaic, in our terms). Even according to Luke, Paul could and did speak 'Hebrew' when addressing a crowd in Jerusalem (Acts 21:40; 22:2). The apparent contradiction is bridged by the information given in Acts 22:3 (in Paul's own words): 'I am a Jew, born in Tarsus of Cilicia, but brought up in this city here [Jerusalem] . . . ' As W. C. van Unnik has shown, the term 'brought up' (*anatethrammenos*) refers to early childhood and not to later education or formal training for a profession.[3] So Paul seems to have come to Jerusalem as a child. His family must have had close ties to Jerusalem: Acts 23:16 mentions a son of his sister who lived there and helped to rescue Paul from a plot against his life.

Acts 22:3 mentions Gamaliel (i.e. Rabban Gamliel the Elder), a famous Pharisaic teacher of Torah (Acts 5:34), as the one who was responsible for young Paul's initial or later education (the name is placed between the participles *anatethrammenos* and *pepaideumenos*). This has caused many interpreters to conclude that Paul had been trained to become a teacher of Torah himself. But *paideuo* is not the usual term for any sort of professional training, and in the following clause the result of the influence of Gamaliel on Paul is not spelled out in terms of wisdom but in terms of religious zeal leading to action. Paul must have been brought up in the house of Gamaliel or in a school under the supervision of Gamaliel. There is no evidence that Paul was or was preparing to become a teacher of the Torah.

Some scholars have doubted the historical value of Acts 22:3 because in Acts 5:34–9 Gamaliel is depicted as rather tolerant towards the Jesus movement. However, if one of these two Gamaliel traditions in Acts is wrong, the reasons for doubt are stronger in the case of Acts 5, where the chronology of Theudas and Judas cannot be reconciled with the information given by Josephus. Apart from this, Gamaliel's plea for tolerance must be seen in the context of the rivalry between Pharisees and Sadducees (cf. Acts 5:17 and 23: 6–9), and as an example of the general tendency of the Pharisees to avoid death sentences (even where demanded by the written Torah), while Sadducees were stricter in their application of criminal law. Apart from this, the situation of Acts 5 was different from the development after the conflict with Stephen when the disciples of Jesus lost the support of the populace (cf. Acts 5:26 and 6:12).

After all, in mentioning Gamaliel as the main influence on young Saul/Paul, Luke does nothing more than give a name and circumstances, while Paul himself claims to have been a Pharisee (Phil. 3:5; Acts 26:5) or 'a Pharisee, born of Pharisees' (Acts 23:6). Thus, the Jewishness of Paul is specified as an allegiance to one of the three or four major strands of ancient Judaism, according to Josephus the most influential one in his lifetime. Joachim Jeremias made a case for the heritage of Gamaliel in Paul to be identified in terms of a *Hillelite* tradition which he thought could be detected even in the later writings of the apostle.[4] But the points of contact which he described are not sufficiently distinctive of Hillelite teaching or can be traced back to the Jesus tradition which Paul must have somehow embraced after his conversion. Above all, Jacob Neusner has shown that the rabbinic tradition that Gamaliel was a (descendent and) follower of Hillel is too late and a product of later concerns, so that it cannot be trusted historically.[5] Neusner goes even further and draws attention to certain affinities of some Gamaliel traditions with teachings of the stricter school of Shammai.[6]

EARLY EXCELLENCE IN A MILITANT RELIGIOUS TRADITION

A Pharisaic background alone cannot account for the most conspicuous fact of Paul's pre-Christian career: his commitment to exterminate the Jesus movement (cf. Acts 7:58; 8:1; 9:1–2, 5, 13–14, 21; 22:4–5, 7, 19; 26:9–11, 14; 1 Cor. 15:9; Gal. 1:13, 23; Phil. 3:6; 1 Tim. 1:13). He mentions it among those things he could be proud of as a Jew (Phil. 3:6) and as the aspect of his life by which he exceeded his Jewish contemporaries (Gal. 1:13–14).

This activity was not the result of an office he held but born out of his own conviction and initiative (Acts 8:1.3; 9:1–2). It included imprisonment (Acts 8:3; 22:4; 26:10) and beating (Acts 22:19) of Christians, pressure or even torture in order to force Christians to 'blaspheme' (i.e. to curse Christ; cf. Acts 26:11 with 1 Cor. 12:3). In Acts 26:10 Paul even confesses to having voted for death sentences against Christians. (We do not know which Jewish court of his time had the *right* to capital punishment. The allusion could be to conspiracies of vigilantism such as that mentioned in Acts 23:12–15.) Not content with his successes in Jerusalem, Paul planned to extend this activity to centres of the Jewish diaspora to which members of the Jesus movement had fled in order to escape persecution (Acts 8:1; 11:19).

As for the reasons for this commitment, the relevant texts give us but one explanation: Paul was inspired by the ideal of *zeal* (for the Lord or his law); see Acts 22:3–4; Gal. 1:13–14; Phil. 3:6. As a religious motive of violence against renegades this ideal goes back to famous figures of biblical history such as Phineas (cf. Num. 25:6–13; Ps. 106:30–1; Sir. 45:23; 1 Macc. 2:26.54; 4 Macc. 18:12), Saul (cf. 1 Sam. 28:9), Elijah (1 Kgs. 18:40; 19:14), Jehu (2 Kgs. 10:16).[7] Its popularity even among diaspora Jews of Paul's day is documented by Philo of Alexandria, who speaks of 'thousands of vigilantes, full of zeal for the laws, strictest guardians of the ancestral traditions, merciless to those who try to abolish them' (*Spec. Leg.* 2. 253).

It is this ideal of Judaism which Paul strove to live by, which he left behind at the turning point of his life (Phil. 3:7–11), and which he still has in mind when commenting on the essence of Judaism (Rom. 10:2) or reacting fiercely to Jewish opposition to his missionary work (Gal. 4:29; 1 Thess. 2:14–16).

This background must be kept in mind when Paul's criticism of Judaism is compared with Jewish sources and the character of Judaism which they reveal: rabbinic Judaism did not follow this militant line, which had contributed to leading Israel into the repeated catastrophes of rebellion against the Romans. It had been the Judaism of Paul himself and of his equals (Acts 22:3) which called for action in order to free Israel from God's impending anger. It is this strategy of human effort which the apostle decries as not only unnecessary and futile but also hostile to the all-sufficient work of Christ in his sacrificial death on the cross (Gal. 2:21; 5:2–4; 6:12–14).

CONVERSION: SURPRISED BY GRACE

Paul and his experience on the road to Damascus have become proverbial for a life that is divided in two by a decisive turning point. Therefore it is justified to speak of his 'conversion' – as long as it is clear that his was not a conversion from one *religion* to another,[8] and not a decision taken upon hearing a piece of Christian proclamation. The nature of this event is attested by both types of evidence – Acts and Pauline letters – as a visionary encounter with Jesus, risen from the dead and normally hidden in the realms of heaven. In 1 Cor. 15:8 this experience is grouped with such visions of the risen Lord as are reported in the final chapters of the gospels. This is also true of the result of these God-given revelations: the witnesses of Christ being alive are commissioned to be messengers of his vindication by God; the visions regularly aim at a calling. But in the case of Paul this calling implies an act of *grace* (Rom. 1:5; 1 Cor. 15:9–10; Gal. 1:15). The threefold Lukan report of the event does not use this term, but corroborates its essence by narrative means. The most distinctive element of the dialogue between the heavenly Lord and Saul/Paul is the repeated reproach: 'Saul, Saul, why do you persecute me?' and 'I am Jesus, whom you are persecuting' (Acts 9:4–5; 22:7–8; 26:14–15).[9] In the tradition of prophetic language of the Old Testament such an indictment should lead to the announcing of a divine judgment. Instead, Paul is called to serve the one whose memory he had tried to erase (Acts 9:15–16; 22:14–15; 26:16–18). No wonder that 'grace' became a hallmark of Paul's proclamation of the gospel which he defended relentlessly whenever he met with (or suspected) efforts to earn or justify God's favour by human achievements, however deeply rooted in biblical tradition (cf. Rom. 4:4, 16; 6:14–15; 1 Cor. 1:4; Gal. 1:6; 2:21; 5:4; Phil. 3:6–9).[10] It is open to question whether this calling immediately included the specification on the lines of Gentile mission. It is only the last, less literal repetition of the Damascus story in Acts 26 which makes this an explicit content of the Damascus vision. In this case Luke seems to incorporate the content of the vision of Acts 22:17–21 into the Damascus vision, thus 'telescoping' the two events. Likewise in Gal. 1:16 Paul himself stresses that it had been God's intention to send him to the non-Jews, but not that this aim had been revealed to him right at the beginning.

THE EARLY YEARS AS A MEMBER OF THE CHURCH

In the light of Galatians 1 and Acts 9 alike there can be no doubt that Paul's conversion took place at (or near) *Damascus* and that he joined the Jesus movement in this prominent Hellenistic city on the border of Roman political influence. In Acts 9:2, 20 Luke rightly mentions the existence of more than one synagogue; according to Josephus (*War* 3.561; 7.368) 10,000 or even 18,000 Jewish inhabitants of Damascus were killed by their pagan fellow citizens at the outbreak of the Jewish rebellion in AD 66.

According to Gal. 1:17–18 Paul did not return to Jerusalem immediately after his conversion but stayed at Damascus for 'three years' (in our terms, one full year and at least parts of two years; Acts 9:23 speaks of a 'considerable' time), only interrupted by a visit to Arabia. The duration and purpose of this trip to Arabia are a matter of speculation which need not detain us here. Little more can be said about the reasons for the threat to Paul's life which caused his dramatic departure from the city, although some details (flight in a basket through an opening in the city wall) are reported in Acts 9:25 and 2 Cor. 11:33. In view of the original purpose of Paul's journey to Damascus it sounds plausible when Acts 9:23 speaks of a Jewish conspiracy against Paul's life in close connection with a summary statement about his powerful witness to Jesus Christ among the local Jews (verse 22).

Upon his return to *Jerusalem* Paul says that he stayed with Peter for a fortnight and met no other apostle except James, the brother of Jesus (Gal. 1:18–19). Acts 9:26–30 is less precise but adds the information that 'the disciples' at Jerusalem at first did not welcome Paul because they did not trust the sincerity of his conversion. Later, when he disputed with Hellenistic Jews in the capital, his opponents plotted violence against him (as against Stephen earlier: Acts 6:9–14). The Jerusalem church, however, had no wish for another martyr but escorted Paul to Caesarea on the sea, with a ticket for Tarsus (Acts 9:30).

A similar reaction is recorded in connection with Paul's last journey to Jerusalem (cf. Acts 21:10–11), when conservative Jewish Christians were displeased at Paul's visit because public opinion held him to be an apostate from the law (Acts 21:20–1). The persecutor turned preacher was felt to be a danger to the peaceful development (Acts 9:31) of a church that was eager to convince its countrymen of its full loyalty to the national heritage. Thus Luke does not conceal the tensions between Paul and Jerusalem which the apostle, too, has to concede and to discuss time and again (cf. Rom. 15:31b; Gal. 2:4.12).

We do not know how long Paul stayed in Tarsus, where he had been born, nor what he did there until he was called by Barnabas to join him in ministry in the Syrian metropolis of Antioch (Acts 11:25–6). We may guess that it was at this time that he received his training as a tent-maker (Acts 18:3) – a craft that fitted well into the economic profile of Cilicia. There was also scope during this period for further progress in secular Hellenistic education. Philosophical and religious influences which in former times (irrespective of Acts 22:3) were attributed to Paul's being *born* in Tarsus might have reached him now and contributed to his way of thought and ability to speak and write in Greek. There is not the slightest hint in our sources of the existence of Christian communities founded by the apostle during this Cilician period of his life. A conviction that he was called to become a messenger to the Gentiles (Gal. 1:16; Acts 22:21) need not have led to immediate action without proper preparation.[11] We have to keep in mind that Paul's original zealot mentality must have created a rather hostile attitude towards Gentiles (except when they decided to undergo circumcision: Gal. 5:11). The sudden revelation of the truth of the gospel in that one moment on the road to Damascus does not preclude the necessity of a longer process of remodelling and development of new concepts for Paul's future life and ministry, especially in view of the universal scope of his new commission.

The first 'parish' or 'pulpit' of Paul was located at *Antioch*, once the capital of the empire of the Seleucids, then capital of the Roman province of Syria and the centre of Rome's military presence in the East. Until his move from Tarsus to Antioch Paul had acted upon his personal sense of calling but had no accepted function within the structures of the early church. It was Barnabas who made him a leading member of the church at Antioch and shared with him his task of teaching (Acts 11:25–6; 13:1). The nucleus of this congregation had come from Judaea as refugees from persecution after the death of Stephen, and some of them had started a deliberate evangelistic outreach to the Greeks (Acts 11:19–20).

Another novelty of the development at Antioch was that (according to Acts 11:26) it was there that the Jesus movement came to be known as *Christianoi* – a Latin term, apart from the Greek ending, styled after other terms for the followers of some leader, whether still living or already dead (such as *Pompeiani* and *Caesariani*). Apparently it was this logic of the term *Christianoi* that caused Roman authorities to conclude that the quarrels among Roman Jews that led to their expulsion from the city under Claudius were the work of a ringleader named Chrestus (wrongly for *Christus* in Suetonius, *Life of Claudius* 25.4). It is open to question whether the term was coined by the Christians themselves (and only then could the new name reveal some new feature of their identity) and not by the Roman authorities, who had to register and survey any new association.[12] In any case it is quite wide of the mark to regard this designation as proof of a break with Judaism and the emergence of a new religion. The very form of the term *Christianoi* does not sound like the name of a new cult worshipping Christ: the appropriate term for such a cultic fellowship would have been *Christiastai*.[13]

In twentieth-century studies on the history of the primitive church, the congregation of Antioch has been the object of flourishing speculations. Scholars viewed the city as a melting pot of cultures and traditions comparable to places like New York or Los Angeles today. Wilhelm Bousset

(1865–1920) and his followers in the History of Religions School (such as Rudolf Bultmann, 1884–1976) regarded Antioch as the scene of a rapid process of hellenization and other pagan influences on early Christian thought. Important New Testament features such as the titles 'Son of God' and 'Lord' for Jesus were attributed to this assumed hot-bed of religious and theological innovation. From the last decades of the twentieth century, however, perceptions have changed. It has been increasingly recognized that 'Hellenists' (i.e. Greek-speaking Jews from the Western diaspora) had already played an important part in the 'mother church' at Jerusalem in her first years (Acts 6:1–7) and that by the time of the primitive church even the Jewish homeland had been hellenized (to a lesser degree, of course) for three and a half centuries.[14] Those who were open to the influences of Greek culture had sufficient opportunities to follow their inclinations in Jerusalem and in cities nearer to Jerusalem than Syrian Antioch. On the other hand, the inclusion of Gentiles in the church (and the beginning of an organized missionary outreach to other regions) is the only innovation of Antioch that is mentioned in the New Testament. And according to Gal. 2:11–14, the conviction of the Christians at Antioch that Jews and Gentiles could share their daily life and services (including table fellowship) was not firm enough to withstand the pressure of more conservative Jews coming from Jerusalem. Many scholars believe that this conflict was the beginning of a parting of the ways between Paul and this congregation (and between Paul and Barnabas, although Acts 15:36–41 gives a different reason). Luke mentions only one more stay of Paul at Antioch (Acts 18:22–3). Sometimes it is inferred from Phil. 4:10–16, 2 Cor. 11:8–9, and Acts 18:5 that the congregation at Philippi became the new major support of Paul's missionary activities in the regions around the Aegean Sea, while Ephesus seems to have been the place of his longest stay in one place as a free man (Acts 19:10).

PAUL'S PROFILE AS AN APOSTLE 'AT LARGE'

When Paul speaks of his ministry he sometimes stresses two priorities: (1) that he considered himself as called to evangelize among non-Jews (Rom. 11:13; Gal. 1:16; 2:7); (2) that he preferred as a rule to play the part of a missionary pioneer in planting churches and not to 'build on the foundations laid by somebody else' (Rom. 15:20; 1 Cor. 3:6; 4:15; Gal. 4:19).

There is evidence, however, that he did not restrict his work to activities in line with these two criteria. First, in 1 Cor. 9:20 he writes: 'To the Jews I became like a Jew, to win the Jews.' This is in principle confirmed by Rom. 11:14 (although this text does not speak explicitly of a work *among*

Jews), and by several stories in Acts where Paul at each new place of his missionary journeys first visits the synagogue and tries to win believers from the Jewish congregations (see Acts 13–14 and 17–19). The wording of Rom. 1:5–6 suggests that Paul may have understood the Gentile destination of his calling as a matter more of geography than of ethnicity: 'apostleship to provoke the reaction of faith *among* all nations (or non-Jews) . . . *among* whom you, too, are living, called by Jesus Christ'. In Acts 22:17–21 Luke even suggests that Paul would have preferred to remain a witness to Jews but was compelled by a command from heaven to leave this vision behind in order to become a missionary to the Gentiles.

We cannot be sure whether Paul considered this principle of 'non-intervention' in congregations founded by others as imperative or whether he simply preferred it when he had a choice. In Rom. 15:20 he calls it his 'ambition', and that puts the matter on a level with his decision not to receive his livelihood from the communities he served (1 Cor. 9:12–18). Of course we know from Acts of quite a number of places where Paul (together with colleagues and helpers) founded a church or – to use more modest terms – at least assembled a group of believers: in Cyprus, in the cities of southern Galatia, at Philippi, Thessalonica, Beroea, Athens, and Corinth. But Ephesus (where Paul worked for more than two years) can hardly be added to this list (cf. Acts 18:19–21, 24–7), and even at Corinth Aquila and Priscilla had already settled before Paul appeared on the scene (Acts 18:2). Can we imagine that their household had not been a house *church* prior to Paul's arrival? In both cases, Corinth and Ephesus, we get the impression that Paul 'founded' these local congregations by organizing separate meetings and structures, i.e. by initiating their independence from the synagogue (Acts 18:7–8; 19:8–10). This development is also reported from other cities and appears to have resulted from either Jewish resistance, or increasing numbers of non-Jews responding to Paul's message, or a combination of both factors. In the interpretation of Rom. 15:20 perhaps too much weight has been given to the restrictive element in what Paul says. In verse 22 his use of the principle as an excuse for his not yet having visited Rome simply means that he has had more urgent tasks, and the following verses speak of his plan to evangelize in Spain and to visit Rome on the way there. The main idea in Paul's mind seems to have been his commission to missionary work in universal dimensions, i.e. to permeate with the gospel what his contemporaries considered the 'Western world' and liked to talk of as 'the inhabited world' (*oikoumene*), that is, the Mediterranean world under Roman rule. It is this 'universal' horizon of Paul's sense of calling that made him feel responsible for 'all churches' (2 Cor. 11:28) or allowed him to send greetings to Rome from 'all churches' (Rom. 16:16).[15]

IN-HOUSE CONTROVERSIES DURING THE MINISTRY OF PAUL

If we were dependent on the Pauline letters as our only sources we could scarcely know much about how Paul worked as a missionary. Fortunately 1 Thessalonians, possibly Paul's earliest surviving letter, gives a summary of the contents of his preaching (1 Thess. 1:9–10) and a reminder of his behaviour among the new converts as a model for their own lifestyle (cf. 2:1–12 with 4:1–12). On the whole, the epistles of Paul are a mirror of Paul's concerns as a teacher and 'spiritual director' if not leader of existing churches. They offer corroboration of his central message, ethical teachings in general terms or advice on topical questions or queries, and a large amount of argument against opinions and activities which the apostle deemed dangerous for the churches and contrary to 'the truth of the gospel' (Gal. 2:5.14).

In the early decades of the twentieth century many scholars, especially in Germany, were fond of the idea that Paul had to fight a 'war on two fronts' (a term coined for the nightmare of German foreign policy under Bismarck and which came true in the First World War), that is, a war against (primarily Jewish) *legalism* and (primarily Gentile) 'enthusiasm' coinciding with libertinism – an idea modelled on Martin Luther's struggles with the papacy on one hand and the enthusiasts (*Schwärmer*) on the other. However, the efforts (especially of Wilhelm Lütgert, 1867–1938) to trace these two menaces through the letters of Paul did not prevail. The only challenge that threatened larger parts of the Pauline mission field and its relations with the 'mother church' in Judaea was the attempt of conservative Jewish Christians to combine Christian evangelism with Jewish proselytism by urging Gentile Christians to convert to Judaism (in the case of men including the rite of circumcision). This programme emerged as a criticism voiced by Jewish Christians of the missionary strategy of the congregation of Antioch and had been rejected at the Jerusalem 'council' (Acts 15 and Gal. 2:1–10). But it lived on as a 'counter-mission' backed by parts of the Jerusalem church (Gal. 2:11–14) and promised to 'complete' the work which Paul had begun by his preaching of the gospel (Gal. 3:3). The movement seems to have reached its climax in Galatia, i.e. in the congregations founded during the first missionary journey who lived in a region with a very strong Jewish presence (Acts 13–14).[16]

Paul reacted with a fierce counter-attack in his philippic to the Galatians (much too polemical to be labelled as an apology!) and in Philippians 3 (a chapter that cannot be dated with certainty). Romans 1–11 continues to discuss topics that had been prominent in this controversy, and the news which Paul received on his arrival at Jerusalem (according to Acts 21:20–1) revealed that the majority of believers in Judaea had been won over by his opponents or at least believed the charges that had been circulated against him.

Other conflicts reflected in Paul's letters seem to have been restricted to local congregations and to matters of less fundamental relevance. Especially at Corinth, opposition to Paul emerged, partly because of some members' enthusiasm for other church leaders such as the apostle Peter and Apollos, a learned teacher and impressive speaker (1 Cor. 1:10–17; 3:1–4:21; Acts 18:24–6), and partly because of different concepts of apostleship (2 Cor. 10–13). Even in this context influences from Judaea can be discerned (2 Cor. 11:22). Of course Paul could never rid himself of the handicap that he had not belonged to the inner circle of the original apostles of Jesus. He can only refer to his having seen the same Risen Lord as they had (1 Cor. 9:1; 15:8) and to the miracles which the Lord had worked through him, too, which were cherished as 'signs of an apostle' (2 Cor. 12:12; cf. Rom. 15:19). But the polemical aspect of Paul's theology has been exaggerated by scholars who tended to detect a 'front' or 'group of opponents' as the implied target of every solemn affirmation of Paul. Not every weakness or danger which Paul saw or suspected in his congregations was the result of a position or programme, and many exhortations may have been given as a precaution.

LOCAL CONFLICTS WITH JEWISH OR GENTILE OPPONENTS OF CHRISTIANITY

In Acts we read of a number of conflicts between Paul and local officials and representatives of the Roman Empire. In the light of Paul's own list of calamities in 2 Cor. 11:23–6 these reports are a mere selection from a much longer story. They seem to have been chosen in order to draw attention to typical points of conflict.

In Pisidian Antioch (Acts 13:45,50), Iconium (Acts 14:2,4), Lystra (Acts 14:19), Thessalonica (Acts 17:5), Beroea (Acts 17:13), and Corinth (Acts 18:12–13) opposition arose from local Jewish communities who did not embrace the message of Paul's preaching and who were alarmed at the great numbers of Gentile sympathizers who joined Paul. These Gentiles attracted by Judaism had been a sort of buffer zone between the synagogues and pagan society. Now the Jews may have feared that they would lose their support. For some such reason they persuaded the magistrates or the masses to take action against Paul and his team. Only at Corinth the proconsul Gallio (brother of Seneca) refused to accept Jewish charges against Paul – probably an act not of tolerance against the Christians but of contempt for the Jews (Acts 18:14–17).[17]

In Philippi (Acts 16:16–24) and Ephesus (Acts 19:23–40) it was economic interests that led to accusations against Paul which were formulated as appeals to the cultural identity of the city. Both conflicts may have been more dangerous for Paul and his mission than Luke makes them appear (cf. 2 Cor. 1:3–11). The climax of these attacks is reached when Paul is accused before Antonius Felix, governor of Judaea, in the words of a professional speaker: 'We have found this man to be a troublemaker, stirring up riots among the Jews all over the world' (Acts 24:5). To the Romans, with their memories of bloody civil wars and their gratitude to the Julian-Claudian dynasty for having established universal peace, this was the worst charge that could be voiced. Luke leaves no doubt that it was feigned in order to replace an earlier accusation which had not stood the test of closer examination (cf. Acts 21:28; 23:29).

FROM JERUSALEM TO ROME

No fewer than eight chapters of Acts (21–8) are devoted to the trial of Paul that began in Jerusalem and led him to Rome, and yet the outcome is left open to the imagination (or the memory) of the readers. They cover four or five years of Paul's life (cf. Acts 24:27; 28:11,30). If this whole story has not been invented it presupposes the Roman citizenship which Paul claims in Acts 16:37; 22:25–9 (cf. 23:17).[18] While some historical details remain doubtful, no other explanation can account for the attention paid to the case by the Roman authorities. This civic status of Paul is balanced by the resolution of Paul's Jewish enemies, who regarded him as a real danger to diaspora Judaism. His accusers (who risked punishment themselves in the case of Paul's acquittal) were official representatives of the Jewish people (Acts 21:21,28; 24:5; 25:2–3.24; 28:17–19). Luke's narrative uses the whole story as an occasion to let the apostle combine his apology with his witness to the Lord who had called him and to the message entrusted to him. A major concern of these speeches is the affirmation of Paul's loyalty to Israel's heritage and hope, and of God's faithfulness to the promises given to his people (cf. Acts 23:6; 24:25f.; 26:6f.; 28:20). This picture coincides remarkably with the core of Romans 9–11, and it is tempting to read the end of Acts as God's answer to the wish of Paul to become a sacrifice for his people's salvation (cf. Rom. 9:3).

However, it is by no means clear that this trial of Paul ended with a death sentence. The earliest evidence for his death as a martyr (from late first century AD), 1 Clem. 5:6–7, takes it for granted that the apostle did visit Spain (cf. Rom. 15:24) and thus became 'a herald in the East and in the West' and 'taught righteousness to the whole world' – a righteousness quite different from that which the Roman Empire boasted of. Paul may have lived on until the persecutions in the aftermath of the fire of Rome in AD 64 and died together with hundreds of unknown believers. Thus Paul's last years remain as open to conjecture as several years of his early career before his missionary journeys. In any case, his story did not end with his death but has continued in many chapters of church history in which he plays an important role.

Notes

1 See D. F. Graf, 'Aretas', *ABD* 1 (1992), 373–6.

2 J. B. Green, 'Festus, Porcius', *ABD* 2 (1992) 794–5, gives reasons for assuming the year 59 CE.

3 W. C. van Unnik, *Tarsus or Jerusalem: The City of Paul's Youth* (London: Epworth, 1962).

4 J. Jeremias, 'Paulus als Hillelit', in E. E. Ellis and M. Wilcox, eds., *Neotestamentica et Semitica: Studies in Honour of Matthew Black* (Edinburgh: T. & T. Clark, 1969) 88–94.

5 J. Neusner, *The Rabbinic Traditions about the Pharisees before 70* (Leiden: Brill, 1971): 'The Gamaliel I-materials . . . contain no hint of a relationship to Hillel' (1.295; cf. 376).

6 Ibid., 376.

7 See, e.g., T. L. Donaldson, 'Zealot and Convert: The Origin of Paul's Christ–Torah Antithesis', *CBQ* 51 (1989) 655–82; M. R. Fairchild, 'Paul's Pre-Christian Zealot Associations: A Re-examination of Gal 1.14 and Acts 22.3', *NTS* 45 (1999) 514–32. The relevant traditions have been studied exhaustively by W. R. Farmer, *Maccabees, Zealots, and Josephus* (New York: Columbia University Press, 1956), and M. Hengel, *The Zealots* (1961; ET Edinburgh: T. & T. Clark, 1989).

8 See James D. G. Dunn, 'Paul: Apostate or Apostle of Israel?', *ZNW* 89 (1998) 256–71, 259.

9 The wording is reminiscent of 1 Sam. 26:18, where it is David who addresses the Saul of old.

10 Cf. A. B. du Toit, 'Encountering Grace: Towards Understanding the Essence of Paul's Damascus Experience', *Neotestamentica* 30 (1996) 71–87.

11 *Pace* M. Hengel and A. M. Schwemer, *Paul between Damascus and Antioch: The Unknown Years* (London: SCM, 1997) 155–6.

12 See H. J. Cadbury in F. J. Foakes Jackson and K. Lake, eds., *The Beginnings of Christianity*, vol. 5 (1933) 384–5.

13 Cf. the difference between *Kaisarianoi* for *partisans* of Caesar during the civil war (Appian 3.91) and *Kaisariastai* for people who deemed a Caesar worthy of divine honours (*IGRom* 4.1348).

14 See M. Hengel, *The 'Hellenization' of Judaea in the First Century after Christ* (London: SCM, 1989).

15 R. Aus, 'Paul's Travel Plans to Spain', *NovT* 21 (1979) 232–62 and (independently) R. Riesner, *Paul's Early Period* (Grand Rapids, MI: Eerdmans, 1998) 245–53 have

proposed that Isa. 66:18–21 provided the scriptural basis for Paul's vision of world-wide evangelism.

16 See S. Mitchell, 'Galatia', *ABD* 2 (1992) 870–2: 'There is no evidence in Acts or any non-testamentary source that Paul ever evangelized the cities of N. Galatia by any means' (871).

17 See K. Haacker, 'Gallio', *ABD* 2 (1992) 901–3.

18 See K. Haacker, *Paulus: Der Werdegang eines Apostels*, SBS 171 (Stuttgart: KBW, 1997) 27–44; Riesner, *Paul's Early Period* 147–56.

2 Paul as missionary and pastor

STEPHEN C. BARTON

STARTING POINT: APOSTLE TO THE GENTILES

The foundation of Paul's thought and practice as a missionary and pastor was a life-changing experience of revelation experienced as grace and call.[1] He gives his most direct account in Gal. 1:11–16:

> For I would have you know, brethren, that the gospel which was preached by me is not man's gospel. For I did not receive it from man, nor was I taught it, but it came through a revelation of Jesus Christ. For you have heard of my former life in Judaism, how I persecuted the church of God violently and tried to destroy it; and I advanced in Judaism beyond many of my own age among my people, so extremely zealous was I for the traditions of my fathers. But when he who had set me apart before I was born, and had called me through his grace, was pleased to reveal his Son to [literally, 'in'] me, in order that I might preach him among the Gentiles, I did not confer with flesh and blood.

This first-person testimony is extremely important. It shows us, first, that for Paul the starting point of his Christian self-understanding was a divine gift in the form of a revelation to/in him of Jesus Christ risen from the dead and exalted in glory at God's right hand as his Son (cf. Rom. 1:4; 2 Cor. 3:16–18). Second, Jesus Christ as God's Son risen from the dead is represented by Paul as the 'gospel' (*euaggelion)*, and intrinsic to the gospel is that it is a message to be preached (*euaggelizesthai*).[2] Third, and related, the revelation to Paul was an experience, not only of conversion ('my former life in Judaism'), but also, and above all, of call. The language of Paul in Gal. 1:15–16 is biblical language used in the callings of the prophets,[3] and the sense of call comes through in the climactic purpose clause, '*in order that* I might preach him [i.e. Christ] among the Gentiles'. So whatever we say about Paul as missionary and pastor has to take as its foundation and dual starting point Paul's experience of the risen Christ and his sense of prophetic calling to be an apostle of Christ to the Gentiles. The threefold conversion narratives in Acts point in precisely the same direction (cf. esp. 9:15; 22:15; 26:16–18).

But how are the revelation of Christ and the call to be an apostle to the Gentiles (cf. 1 Cor. 9:1; 15:8–11) related? The most cogent answer, briefly, has to do with eschatology and christology: belief and teaching rooted in the Bible and early Judaism about the presence and action of God in human history for salvation and judgment. Paul's experience of the risen Christ brought with it the recognition that his people's messianic hope was fulfilled, that the new age of the kingdom of God and the resurrection of the dead had begun, and that the time of God's blessing through Abraham to all nations (cf. Galatians 3; Romans 4) had come. His special vocation was to announce this to the Gentiles in order that the full harvest of God's people, Gentiles as well as Jews, might be brought in.[4] We get some idea of the importance to Paul of his eschatological role as apostolic messenger to the Gentiles in Rom. 10.12–17 (see also 1:5; 11:13; 15:15–16):

> For [in the light of the death and resurrection of Christ] there is no distinction between Jew and Greek; the same Lord is Lord of all and bestows his riches upon all who call upon him . . . But how are men to call upon him in whom they have not believed? And how are they to believe in him of whom they have never heard? And how are they to hear without a preacher? And how can men preach unless they are sent? . . . So faith comes from what is heard, and what is heard comes by the preaching of Christ.

Thus, preaching Christ to the Gentiles so that Gentiles (*as Gentiles*) might be 'grafted in' to the tree of God's eschatological people 'Israel' (Rom. 11:17–24) lies at the very heart of Paul's work as missionary and pastor. But what did this mean in practice? What was the scope of Paul's work?[5]

SCOPE AND PURPOSE: APOSTLE AS ENVOY, PLANTER, BUILDER, FATHER/MOTHER/NURSE, PRIEST

Paul does not describe himself as a 'missionary' or 'pastor': and it is important that we do not interpret him in terms drawn from times and institutions which may be close to our own but not native to Paul himself. Rather, we need to note that Paul uses a wide array of rich metaphors, each of which captures something of how he saw his work.[6] Among the most important are the following:

(1) *Metaphors of representation.* Although it is rare in Paul, the ambassadorial metaphor nonetheless captures something very important about his self-understanding.[7] The key text is 2 Cor. 5:18–20 (cf. Phlm. 9; Eph. 6:20):

> All this is from God, who through Christ reconciled us to himself and gave us the ministry of reconciliation; that is, in Christ God was reconciling the world to himself, not counting their trespasses against them, and entrusting to us the message of reconciliation. So we are *ambassadors for Christ*, God making his appeal through us. We beseech you on behalf of Christ, be reconciled to God.

What this tells us is that Paul sees himself in exalted terms as no less than an agent or representative of God, bringing a very important message – that of reconciliation to God through Christ – to all nations. Furthermore, as the bearer of the message, Paul sees himself as actually participating in God's reconciling activity. And, of course, it is precisely reconciliation which he is trying to achieve in his dealings with the church in Corinth. But there is an extraordinary paradox! How does the exalted ambassador of God on behalf of Christ show his credentials? Paul answers: 'through great endurance, in afflictions, hardships, calamities, beatings, imprisonments, tumults, labours, watching, hunger . . .' (2 Cor. 6:4–5). These are hardly ambassadorial credentials in any normal sense. But that is the point: Paul is ambassador on behalf of the one who reconciled the world to God *by his death.* That is, Paul's credentials conform to the credentials of the crucified and reconciling Messiah whom he is called to represent.

What is true of Paul as 'ambassador' is true also of Paul as 'apostle' (*apostolos*), the much more frequent self-designation (Gal. 1:1; 1 Cor. 1:1; Rom. 1:1; etc.).[8] Although the origins of the term are a matter of debate, the central idea is that of the envoy, one who is sent as a representative of a higher authority and who is to be received accordingly (cf. John 13:20; 20:21). In the New Testament, this idea is used very widely: of Christ himself, as the envoy ('sent one') of God; of the Twelve as sent out by Jesus on mission; of Paul as the envoy of God or Christ, proclaiming Christ to the world; of people like Timothy and Titus who serve as envoys of Paul in his dealings with his churches; and of messengers of individual church communities.[9] With respect to Paul, the main point is that 'apostle' conveys his sense of personal authority as apostle *of Christ* ('Paul, a servant of Jesus Christ, called to be an apostle' – Rom. 1:1), and his sense of vocation as one who has been called by God and *sent to the Gentiles* ('Jesus Christ our Lord, through whom we have received grace and apostleship to bring about the obedience of faith for the sake of his name among all the nations' – Rom. 1:4–5). It also conveys the powerful motivation behind his conviction that, in order to fulfil his commission, he has to work on the frontiers, taking the gospel where no one had taken it before (cf. Rom. 15:18–24).

(2) *Agricultural metaphors.* Speaking of himself and Apollos, Paul says to the Corinthian Christians: 'What then is Apollos? What is Paul? Servants through whom you believed, as the Lord assigned to each. I planted, Apollos watered, but God gave the growth . . . For we are God's fellow-workers; you are God's field, God's building' (1 Cor. 3:9). This tells us much about Paul's apostolic self-understanding. First, his authority and calling come from God, and he knows that he is not unique in that respect: he is not a *prima donna*. He and Apollos are both 'servants' (*diakonoi*) of God and 'fellow workers' (*sunergoi*) in relation to each other. Second, and reminiscent of the biblical picture of Israel as God's vineyard (Isa. 5.1–7), Paul sees the church as God's 'field' in which he and other apostles are called to labour. The agricultural metaphor implies that roles of nurture and cultivation – activities which are not just 'one-off', but which involve long-term commitment – are important. Third, as the one who does the 'planting', Paul sees himself as having an initiatory role. This is what we might call 'evangelism': sowing the seed of the gospel (cf. Mark 4:1–20; John 4:34–8) through the preaching of the good news of Christ with a view to making converts. Also, the temporal primacy involved in 'planting' implies for Paul a certain primacy of authority in his relations with his converts, a primacy reinforced by other metaphors, as we shall see.

(3) *Architectural metaphors.* The church at Corinth is not only 'God's field'; it is also 'God's building [*oikodome*]' (1 Cor. 3:9). Indeed, Paul goes further, by specifying what kind of building the church is: 'Do you not know that you [plural] are God's temple [literally, 'sanctuary', *naos*] and that God's Spirit dwells in you?' (1 Cor. 3:16). This allows him to situate himself. He is like a 'skilled master builder'; and it is he who lays the foundation – identified specifically as 'Jesus Christ' (1 Cor. 3:11). As with the 'field' metaphor, the 'temple' metaphor is corporate in scope: in the Bible and the Judaism of Paul's day, it was a metaphor for the people among whom God had chosen to dwell, i.e. Israel.[10]

Thus, in describing himself in his apostolic work as a master builder laying temple foundations, Paul is implying that God has given him a prime role in initiating and establishing a new people of God amongst whom God has chosen to dwell (cf. 2 Cor. 6:16; Eph. 2:21–2). And 1 Corinthians as a whole shows that Paul understood this role, not only in terms of the initial preaching of the gospel, but also in terms of 'building up' (*oikodomein*) the church into a 'temple' whose holy living made it a place fit for God's presence (cf. 6:19; 8:1; 10:23; 14:3, 4, 5, etc.). So the scope of Paul's work was not just evangelism with a view to initial conversion; it was also to do with building and establishing in the faith of Christ. And it was not just oriented towards individuals: it was also and primarily concerned with households, communities, and societies.[11]

(4) *Generative, nurture, and kinship metaphors.* Closely related to the imagery of Paul as 'planter' and 'builder', but more personal and relational in character, is the even more common imagery of parenthood, kinship, and nurture.[12] As applied by Paul to his apostleship, such imagery allows him to communicate to his churches that his relations with them are both reciprocal (believers are his 'brothers and sisters') and unequal (as of a 'father/mother' to his/her 'children'). Common in ancient times, both in Judaism and in the Graeco-Roman world,[13] this was language of leadership and authority both in the public domain of politics and in the more private domain of the household, cult group, and voluntary association. But leadership and the exercise of authority need not be the enemies of love (as modern Westerners may too readily assume): and in Paul, what we see is a missionary and pastor seeking to give firm leadership out of love with a view to the growth to maturity of the fledgling Christians in his care. Thus, the generative dimension of apostleship gives rise to a particular sense of authority and responsibility arising out of the fact that he has 'fathered' his churches: 'I do not write this to make you ashamed, but to admonish you as my beloved children. For though you have countless guides in Christ, you do not have many fathers. For I became your father [literally, 'I fathered you'] in Christ Jesus through the gospel' (1 Cor. 4:14–15; cf. Phlm. 10).[14]

This 'parental' responsibility clearly involves Paul in the continuing nurture of his (adult) 'children' through personal example ('[B]e imitators of me':1 Cor. 4:16), instruction, and correction. Such language and practice have their roots in the biblical wisdom tradition and in the self-understanding of the philosophers, and was taken over by Paul. A classic instance comes in his earliest extant letter, where he says: '[F]or you know how, *like a father with his children*, we exhorted each one of you and encouraged you and charged you to lead a life worthy of God' (1 Thess. 2:11–12). And, in a statement which must temper assumptions we might have about 'fatherhood' as a cover for authoritarianism, Paul also says, in the same context, and using feminine imagery: '[W]e might have made demands as apostles of Christ. But we were gentle among you, *like a nurse taking care of her children*' (1 Thess. 2:6–8).[15] Paul's letters are full of kinship and relational language of this kind. It shows that his missionary and pastoral work sought to create and sustain a new household: the household of God (cf. Gal. 6:10; Rom. 8:14–17; Eph. 2:19).

(5) *Sacerdotal metaphors.* Not unrelated to the way Paul thinks of himself as laying the foundations of a new household and holy people is the way he thinks of himself as playing a priest-like role in his mission to the Gentiles. The main evidence comes in an important statement in Romans, replete with cultic language, where Paul says: 'But on some points I have written to you very boldly by way of reminder, because of the grace given me by God to be a minister [*leitourgos*] of Christ Jesus to the Gentiles in the priestly service [*hierourgein*] of the gospel of God, so that the offering [*prosphora*] of the Gentiles may be acceptable [*euprosdektos*], sanctified [*hagiasmenos*] by the Holy Spirit' (Rom. 15:15–16). This statement helps us to see that Paul understood his missionary work as part of the great drama of creation and salvation in which God is bringing into being a people set apart to offer him worship.

What is radically novel is that, whereas previously the offering of worship had excluded the Gentiles since, as non-Israelites, they were cultically impure, now through the death and resurrection of Christ as preached by Paul, the way was open for Gentiles as well as Jews to share together as one in the worship of the one true God (see also Rom. 12:1–2). As James Dunn puts it: 'The (eschatological) transformation of traditional Jewish categories and cultic distinctives is striking. Not only is the priestly ministry of Paul "out in the world", but the offering breaches the fundamental cultic distinction between Jew and Gentile which prevented Gentiles from even getting near the great altar of sacrifice in the Temple.'[16] Therefore, in so far as Paul contributes, through his apostolic ministry, to making the 'offering of the Gentiles' pleasing to God, he is playing a (radically transformed) priestly role. His missionary and pastoral work contributes to the eschatological coming together of people of all nations to glorify God.

CONDITIONS: APOSTLE AT RISK

But what was it like in practice? What were the conditions in which Paul worked as missionary and pastor? Readers of Paul in the affluent West tend perhaps to assume that Paul was educated, relatively well-off, and 'middle class', someone who made quite an impression as he travelled in the company of his 'co-workers' through the cities of the northern Mediterranean. Indeed, he has often been interpreted in these terms, and there is a lively and continuing debate about Paul's social status.[17] If we look closely at what Paul himself says, what we find is evidence of someone who – whatever his background, upbringing, and education – shared, by virtue of his apostolic vocation, in the indigence and vulnerability of the non-elite majority in the Roman world. The following passages are especially revealing:

> For I think that God has exhibited us apostles as last of all, like men sentenced to death; because we have become a spectacle to the world, to angels and to men. We are fools for Christ's sake, but you are wise in Christ. You are held in honour, but we in disrepute. To the present hour we hunger and thirst, we are ill-clad and buffeted and homeless, and we labour, working with our own hands. When reviled, we bless; when persecuted, we endure; when slandered, we try to conciliate; we have become, and are now, as the refuse of the world, the offscouring of all things. (*1 Cor. 4:9–13*)

> Are they servants of Christ? I am a better one – I am talking like a madman – with far greater labours, far more imprisonments, with countless beatings, and often near death. Five times I have received at the hands of the Jews the forty lashes less one. Three times I have been beaten with rods; once I was stoned. Three times I have been shipwrecked; a night and a day I have been adrift at sea; on frequent journeys, in danger from rivers, danger from robbers, danger from my own people, danger from Gentiles, danger in the city, danger in the wilderness, danger at sea, danger from false brethren; in toil and hardship, through many a sleepless night, in hunger and thirst, often without food, in cold and exposure. And, apart from other things, there is the daily pressure upon me of my anxiety for all the churches. (*2 Cor. 11:23–8; see also 2 Cor. 4:7–12; 6:4–10; Phil. 4:10–13*)

These lists and those like them – referred to by scholars as 'hardship (or *peristasis*) catalogues' – are obviously rhetorical constructions with a view to persuading the Corinthians to change their understanding of what it means to be an apostle of Christ.[18] But it is nevertheless the case that the catalogues would not have been persuasive unless they fairly reflected the nature of Paul's actual experience. We may summarize what they reveal as follows:

(1) *Paul the itinerant.* Paul's apostleship involved frequent journeys by land and sea, taking him a total distance, according to the cumulative evidence of Acts, of some ten thousand miles. Indeed, so inveterate a traveller was Paul that Brian Rapske designates him an 'intrepid professional' – someone who travelled even in the 'doubtful' or 'closed' season.[19] Such travel took Paul through inhospitable wilderness and into unpredictable, often violent cities. This was a perilous business, as the narrative of Acts confirms repeatedly. Particularly compelling is the account of

Paul's journey in captivity to Rome, during which he suffered shipwreck (cf. Acts 27:1–28:16):

> But soon a tempestuous wind, called the northeaster, struck down from the land; and when the ship was caught and could not face the wind, we gave way to it and were driven... As we were violently storm-tossed, they began next day to throw the cargo overboard; and the third day they cast out with their own hands the tackle of the ship. And when neither sun nor stars appeared for many a day, and no small tempest lay on us, all hope of our being saved was at last abandoned. (*Acts 27:14–20*)

This story of the threat to Paul the traveller from the natural environment parallels the threats to his mission from the social and political environment which Acts recounts from chapter 13 on. Such accounts not only give us a picture of the risks which Paul faced on a daily basis: they also have their own theological point. Against those who may have argued that such catastrophes undermined Paul's claim to be a true apostle of Christ, they show that, on the contrary, Paul was doing the Lord's will and, in consequence, was under divine protection (cf. Acts 27:23–4; also 9:15–16; 23:11).[20] In sum, we can be clear that, although Paul made use of his 'co-workers' as intermediaries travelling on his behalf, he also travelled extensively himself, even at the risk of his own life. That was what his calling required. As he says elsewhere: '[F]rom Jerusalem and as far round as Illyricum I have fully preached [literally, 'fulfilled'] the gospel of Christ' (Rom. 15:19). Taking the gospel to the Gentiles was ground-breaking, frontier work. It left Paul physically exposed and vulnerable.

(2) *The working apostle.* Because Paul's apostleship was itinerant, he had to work to support himself (see 1 Corinthians 9).[21] The references to manual labour ('working with our own hands') are not the proud boast of the skilled craftsman working in a 'niche market', as they might be today. Rather, they are an expression of what, in ancient times, was viewed as economic indigence and social humiliation: manual labour was the work of the poor and slaves. Thus, apart from the receipt of occasional financial support from his churches (see 2 Cor. 11:8–9; Phil. 4:15–16), Paul was forced to do 'bit-work' in the leather or tent-making trade in the tanners' quarters, as he moved from one city to the next. The references to 'toil and hardship' and 'hunger and thirst' show how vulnerable, physically, economically and socially, he was. Ronald Hock puts it like this:

> Such, then, was the social world within which artisans plied their trades. Stigmatized as slavish, uneducated, and often useless,

artisans . . . were frequently reviled, abused, often victimized, seldom
if ever invited to dinner, never accorded status, and even excluded
from one Stoic utopia. Paul's own statements accord well with this
general description . . . Making tents meant rising before dawn, toiling
until sunset with leather, knives, and awls, and accepting the various
social stigmas and humiliations that were part of the artisans' lot, not
to mention the poverty – being cold, hungry, and poorly clothed.[22]

But for Paul, such labour had a positive side as well. First, the artisan's
workshop provided a context in which he could communicate the gospel to
any who cared to listen, including the poor, who made up the vast majority of
urban inhabitants. Using the workshop as a setting for intellectual discourse
of one kind or another was not unprecedented. From as early as the fifth
century BC there is the case of Socrates discoursing on philosophy in the
workshop of the Cynic artisan-philosopher Simon the shoemaker.[23] Second,
in an age when self-styled 'sophists' pedalled their ideas for the price of their
next meal, Paul's work was a way of protecting the integrity of the message
that he preached from any accusation that his words were spoken only in
order to please his audience and thereby gain financially (1 Thess. 2:3–6).[24]
Above all, however, Paul's sacrificial practice was a way of representing in
his own life the self-giving of the crucified and risen Christ whom he was
called to proclaim (2 Cor. 4:10–11).

(3) *The suffering apostle.* The texts refer also to hostility and persecution: beatings, stonings, imprisonments, 'danger from my own people, danger from Gentiles . . . danger from false brethren'. Once again the picture is
one of an apostle at risk – this time, not from travel or subsistence-level
work, but from society. Paul was someone who lived on the margins. As
Alan Segal puts it: 'To read Paul properly . . . one must recognize that Paul
was a Pharisaic Jew who converted to a new apocalyptic, Jewish sect and
then lived in a Hellenistic gentile Christian community as a Jew among
gentiles.'[25] As a result, Paul attracted social and political enmity. Some of
this came from his Jewish kinsmen, who viewed him as an apostate, someone whose 'lawless' behaviour, especially his table fellowship with 'unclean'
Gentiles (Gal. 2:11–21), put him beyond the pale. Paul, however, was determined to maintain his Jewish connections in order that continued access to
synagogues would allow him to preach both to his fellow Jews and to Gentile
sympathizers. He did so at a terrible price: expulsion from synagogues and
disciplinary action in the form of severe corporal punishment: 'five times',
he says, 'I have received at the hands of the Jews the [maximum penalty of]
forty lashes less one' (2 Cor. 11:24).[26]

But Paul also provoked enmity from pagans who viewed him as a
troublemaker and threat to political, economic, and household order. This

enmity expressed itself in lynch-mob stoning and 'tumult', judicial beatings, and imprisonment by the Roman authorities (Acts 16:11–40; 23:23–24:27; 28:16–31).[27] The action against Paul and Silas at Philippi, a Roman colony, is a good example (Acts 16:11–40). According to Acts, after considerable provocation, Paul exorcizes a demonized slave girl employed as a sooth-sayer. The story contines:

> But when her owners saw that their hope of gain was gone, they seized Paul and Silas and dragged them into the market place before the rulers . . . [saying] 'These men are Jews and they are disturbing our city. They advocate customs which it is not lawful for us Romans to accept or practise.' The crowd joined in attacking them; and the magistrates tore the garments off them and gave orders to beat them with rods. And when they had inflicted many blows upon them, they threw them into prison, charging the jailer to keep them safely. Having received this charge, he put them into the inner prison and fastened their feet in the stocks. (*16:19–24*)

We have here all the ingredients of a situation of risk and hostility: the apostles seen as outsiders, Jewish preachers of a new 'name' (verse 18) and unlawful customs (verse 21) in a Roman colony; aggrieved Roman citizens of probably slender means who have lost a significant source of income through Paul's intervention; a volatile and xenophobic crowd eager for a piece of the action; magistrates (*strategoi*) taking summary action to humiliate and punish Paul and Silas and so restore order; and incarceration – in part, it seems, for protective reasons (verse 35) – in the 'inner prison' and in stocks, at the hands of a jailer (see also 16:37). What happened at Philippi was not a 'one-off'. Acts tells us of a similar episode at Ephesus incited by the guild of silversmiths whose trade in silver shrines of Artemis Paul was seen as undermining (19:23–41). Thus, if Paul's mission alienated him from his fellow Jews, it brought the opprobrium of many pagans as well.

Paul also attracted enmity from his fellow Christians ('danger from false brethren'), something which his periods of absence on journeys or in captivity must have exacerbated. This comes through in Paul's reference to 'the daily pressure upon me of my anxiety for all the churches' (2 Cor. 11:28). Paul saw his apostleship as bound up with the communities of faith which God, through Paul's gospel preaching, had brought into being. So he goes on: 'Who is weak, and I am not weak? Who is made to fall [away], and I am not indignant?' (verse 29). To understand Paul's apostleship, we have to see Paul in relationship. So closely did he identify with his churches that, in a very real sense, their life was his. If they suffered, he suffered too. The letter we call 2 Corinthians, especially chapters 10–13, is searing testimony both to the heart-ache they caused him and to his refusal to be separated from them.

PRACTICE: 'IN PUBLIC AND FROM HOUSE TO HOUSE'

In conclusion, we should try to sketch a picture of how Paul went about his 'gospelling' work. In the process, one or two widely held assumptions about Paul may come to be seen as open to modification and further exploration.

(1) *The apostle as street-corner preacher?* The portrayal in Acts 17:16–34 of Paul preaching on the Areopagus to the assembled Athenians tends to dominate our perception and our artistic representations of Paul's mission. We think of him as a powerful public speaker addressing the throngs in the main places of public intercourse – the street-corner, the market place, the law court of the Areopagus, and the like. However, while it would be rash to discount this view – Paul being the opportunist that he was (see Acts 17:16–17) – it may be that the Paul of the letters looks a little different from the Paul of Acts and that even Acts points in more than one direction.

First, 2 Cor. 10:10 shows Paul's sensitivity to the accusation that he was not held in high regard as a public speaker (cf. 10:1; also 1 Cor. 1:17), an accusation which, significantly, he does not deny. This seems at odds with the picture of Paul the accomplished orator in Acts 17. Second, the evidence of Paul's letters suggests that his 'preaching' mainly took place either in synagogues (where he became subject to the disciplinary action of the 'forty lashes less one' (2 Cor. 11:24) discussed earlier), or in private houses which then become the nucleus of the churches Paul founds and nurtures (cf. 1 Cor. 16:15,19; Rom. 16:23; Phlm. 2; Col. 4:15).[28] Acts, in fact, often has Paul begin his preaching in a synagogue only to be expelled, in consequence of which he moves into a rented hall or a private house, to continue his preaching and teaching there (see Acts 17:5; 18:7; also 20:20 – 'teaching you in public and *from house to house*'). Third, it has been pointed out that, because Paul was likely to have been at a disadvantage in the public domain, having neither the oratorical skills nor the necessary sponsor to give him an entrée, the private house was well suited to his situation once the synagogue was no longer open to him:

> It is no accident that patrons, households and house churches are so prominent in the letters of Paul the missionary. As a place and social context for preaching the gospel, the private house offered certain advantages over preaching in synagogues and public places. The

problems associated with preaching the crucified Christ in synagogues
are obvious and . . . speaking in public places often required things
which Paul did not possess or would find difficult to obtain, such as an
invitation, a sponsor, an audience and credentials as a certain type of
speaker corresponding to a specific genre of speaking event. Above all,
speakers needed some type of social status or a recognized role. An
invitation to teach in someone's house would provide Paul with all of
these things and give his preaching activity a kind of stability and
security which the explosive situation of the synagogue or the
competition of public speaking could not offer.[29]

So instead of Paul, the 'Billy Graham-style' specialist in mass evangelism, the picture we get is much more local and small-scale, centring above
all on evangelism and nurture in individual households. But this is not a
case of Paul as advocate of the 'small is beautiful' principle of twentieth-
century lifestyle discussion. Not only was the private household (the *oikos*)
an accepted centre in antiquity for teaching and intellectual activity, but
it was also seen as a critical part of the network of structures, roles, and
relations that made up the larger city-state (the *polis*). So the conversion
of households had potentially subversive political implications – an issue
elaborated, for example, in the apocryphal Acts of Paul and Thecla.[30]

(2) *Keeping in touch*. We have seen that Paul was *both* 'missionary'
and 'pastor'. His mission as apostle to the Gentiles had as its purpose, not
only evangelization, but also the founding of churches and their continuing
nurture. These churches were a novelty in social terms, for they brought
together in house-gatherings people who normally kept themselves (or were
kept) apart: Jews and pagans who responded to the apostle's preaching and
teaching in synagogues and private homes (Gal. 3:28; 1 Cor. 12:13). The
novelty generated stresses and strains, so it was important for Paul to keep
in touch. The 'salvation' he sought for his converts was a matter, not just
of their initial conversion, but also of their growth to Christian maturity
(1 Cor. 10:32–3; also 9:22). How, finally, did Paul keep in touch?

First, by his physical presence with his churches, sometimes for quite
extended periods (Acts 18:11) – something made possible by his willingness
to work to support himself. Nor did Paul restrict himself to 'one-off' visits.
He revisited his churches whenever he felt able to do so (1 Cor. 4:19; 2 Cor.
1:15ff.; Phil. 1:24–6). By his presence with them and as their 'father' in the
faith, Paul aimed to embody and inculcate a model of Christian practice for
his 'children' to imitate.[31]

Second, by means of intermediaries, especially the 'co-workers', 'fellow
servants', 'brothers [and sisters]', many of whom formed part of his company

on mission and whom he sent as his emissaries to mediate either within the churches or between the churches and Paul himself (Phil. 2:19–24, 25–30).[32] In passing, it is worth observing, with Margaret Mitchell, that the sending of intermediaries by Paul may not necessarily have been a regrettable second-best. Sometimes it seems to have been politic for Paul to keep his distance and send a co-worker (like Timothy or Titus) in his stead![33]

A third means of contact was by letter (carried by an intermediary). This accounts for the corpus of Paul's letters which make up such an important part of the canon of the New Testament. Their entirely 'pastoral' concern, directed as the letters are to churches already in existence, shows again how integral was the teaching and nurture of churches to Paul's apostolic self-understanding. Intended to be read aloud, they constitute an extension of Paul's gospel preaching and teaching (Gal. 4:20). In most cases, they are addressed to his own churches. The Letter to the Romans, however, is Paul's extended self-introduction to a church not founded by him, the important Christian community in Rome. But in this case also, his motivation in writing is related very clearly to the progress of the gospel (cf. 1:15; 15:22–4).

Fourth, there was the practice of gift giving and receiving as a way of keeping contact.[34] Sometimes the gifts were material, such as financial support for Paul from Philippi (Phil. 4:14–20), or the collection which Paul promoted and raised for the impoverished believers in Jerusalem (1 Cor. 16:1–4; Rom. 15:25–7). Sometimes the gift was spiritual, as when he says to the Christians in Rome: 'I long to see you, that I may impart to you *some spiritual gift to strengthen you*, that is, that we may be mutually encouraged by each other's faith, both yours and mine' (Rom. 1:11–12).

Finally, there was the communication – indeed, the communion – taking place by means of prayer and acts of remembrance: Paul praying for his churches (1 Thess. 1:2–3; 1 Cor. 1:4–9; Phil. 1:3–11) and asking them to pray for him (Rom. 15:30–2; 1 Thess. 5:25; 2 Thess. 3:1–2).[35] This was perhaps the most important way of keeping contact, for it united Paul and his churches in their relations both with each other and with their heavenly Lord. It was this Lord whom Paul served as missionary and pastor.

Notes

1 See the essays in R. N. Longenecker, ed., *The Road from Damascus: The Impact of Paul's Conversion on his Life, Thought, and Ministry* (Grand Rapids: Eerdmans, 1997).

2 An over-literal translation of Gal. 1:11, which brings out this dual aspect of 'gospel' as both message and proclamation, would be: 'For I would have you know, brethren, that *the gospel which was gospelled by me* is not man's gospel.'

3 Compare esp. Jer. 1:5: 'Before I formed you in the womb I knew you, and before you were born I consecrated you; I appointed you a prophet to the nations.' Relevant also is Isa. 49:1–6.

4 Similarly, I. H. Marshall, 'A New Understanding of the Present and the Future: Paul and Eschatology', in Longenecker, ed., *Road from Damascus* 43–61, here 59.

5 See, in general, P. Bowers, 'Fulfilling the Gospel: The Scope of the Pauline Mission', *JETS* 30/2 (1987) 185–98.

6 On Paul's use of metaphors see J. D. G. Dunn, *The Theology of Paul the Apostle* (Grand Rapids: Eerdmans/Edinburgh: T. & T. Clark, 1998) 328–33.

7 See A. Bash, *Ambassadors for Christ* (Tübingen: Mohr Siebeck, 1997).

8 See P. W. Barnett, 'Apostle', in G. F. Hawthorne et al., eds., *Dictionary of Paul and his Letters* (Downers Grove, IL/Leicester: IVP, 1993) 45–51.

9 Especially valuable is M. M. Mitchell, 'New Testament Envoys in the Context of Greco-Roman Diplomatic and Epistolary Conventions: The Example of Timothy and Titus', *JBL* 111 (1992) 641–62.

10 On the temple in early Jewish literature see R. Hayward, *The Jewish Temple: A Non-biblical Sourcebook* (London: Routledge, 1996); on temple imagery in Qumran, see B. Gärtner, *The Temple and the Community in Qumran and the New Testament* (Cambridge: Cambridge University Press, 1965).

11 This social and political dimension is well brought out in M. M. Mitchell, *Paul and the Rhetoric of Reconciliation: An Exegetical Investigation of the Language and the Composition of 1 Corinthians* (Louisville: Westminster/John Knox, 1991).

12 See E. Best, *Paul and his Converts* (Edinburgh: T. & T. Clark, 1988) 29–58.

13 For examples, see ibid., 31–5.

14 Compare Gal. 4:19, where Paul likens himself to a woman in labour: 'My little children, with whom I am again in travail until Christ be formed in you!'

15 On the context of this text in relation to Hellenistic (especially Cynic) philosophy, see A. J. Malherbe, *Paul and the Popular Philosophers* (Minneapolis: Fortress, 1989) 35–48, 67–77.

16 J. D. G. Dunn, *Romans*, WBC 38 (Dallas: Word, 1988) 860–1.

17 See E. A. Judge, *The Social Pattern of Christian Groups in the First Century* (London: Tyndale, 1960) 49–61, and A. J. Malherbe, *Social Aspects of Early Christianity* (Philadelphia: Fortress, 1983, 2nd edn), both now controverted by J. J. Meggitt, *Paul, Poverty and Survival* (Edinburgh: T. & T. Clark, 1998) esp. 75–154.

18 See, for example, J. T. Fitzgerald, *Cracks in an Earthen Vessel: An Examination of the Catalogues of Hardships in the Corinthian Correspondence* (Atlanta: Scholars Press, 1988).

19 B. M. Rapske, 'Acts, Travel and Shipwreck', in D. W. J. Gill and C. Gempf, eds., *The Book of Acts in its Greco-Roman Setting* (Grand Rapids: Eerdmans, 1994) 1–47, here 3–6.

20 So ibid., 43–6.

21 See R. F. Hock, *The Social Context of Paul's Ministry: Tentmaking and Apostleship* (Philadelphia: Fortress, 1980).

22 Ibid., 37.

23 For the details, see ibid., 37–42; also Hock's article 'The Workshop as a Social Setting for Paul's Missionary Preaching', *CBQ* 41 (1979) 438–50.

24 See G. Theissen, *The Social Setting of Pauline Christianity* (Philadelphia: Fortress/Edinburgh: T. & T. Clark, 1982) 27–67; also Best, *Paul and his Converts* 97–106.

25 A. F. Segal, *Paul the Convert: The Apostolate and Apostasy of Saul the Pharisee* (New Haven: Yale University Press, 1990) 6–7.

26 See A. E. Harvey, 'Forty Strokes Save One: Social Aspects of Judaizing and Apostasy', in A. E. Harvey, ed., *Alternative Approaches to New Testament Study* (London: SPCK, 1985) 79–96.

27 See B. Rapske, *The Book of Acts and Paul in Roman Custody* (Grand Rapids: Eerdmans/Carlisle: Paternoster, 1994); also C. S. Wansink, *Chained in Christ: The Experience and Rhetoric of Paul's Imprisonments* (Sheffield: Sheffield Academic Press, 1996).

28 See further, Malherbe, *Social Aspects of Early Christianity* 60–91; also J. Reumann, 'One Lord, One Faith, One God, but Many House Churches', in J. V. Hills, ed., *Common Life in the Early Church* (Harrisburg: Trinity Press International, 1998) 106–17.

29 S. K. Stowers, 'Social Status, Public Speaking and Private Teaching: The Circumstances of Paul's Preaching Activity', *NovT* 26 (1984) 59–82, here 68.

30 Relevant here is D. L. Balch, *Let Wives Be Submissive: The Domestic Code in I Peter* (Atlanta: Scholars Press, 1981).

31 On Paul as a model, especially in the Philippian, Thessalonian, and Corinthian correspondence, see P. T. O'Brien, *Gospel and Mission in the Writings of Paul* (Grand Rapids: Baker Books, 1995) 83–107; also Best, *Paul and his Converts* 59–72.

32 See E. E. Ellis, 'Paul and his Co-Workers', *NTS* 17 (1970–1) 437–52.

33 Mitchell, 'New Testament Envoys'.

34 See G. W. Peterman, *Paul's Gift from Philippi: Contemporary Conventions of Gift Exchange and Christian Giving* (Cambridge: Cambridge University Press, 1997).

35 See W. B. Hunter, 'Prayer', in *DPL* 725–34.

Part two

Paul's letters

3 1 and 2 Thessalonians

MARGARET M. MITCHELL

HISTORICAL CONTEXT

On a day in the late 40s or early 50s, after some years of missionary work in Syria, Arabia, and Asia Minor, Paul sailed from Troas and landed in Europe, acting on his intention to spread his gospel proclamation in territory 'where Christ had not yet been named' (Rom. 15:20). Travelling along the Via Egnatia, the major thoroughfare from the East to Rome, Paul would have encountered a great range of artisans, peddlers, slaves, sailors, traders, farmers, and civil servants, alongside the formidable presence of the Roman military. When he stepped off the highway in Macedonia, first at Philippi and then at Thessalonica, Paul entered cities known for long and fervent associations with the cult of Roma and the Emperor. He came bearing a message crystallized in the proclamation, *Kyrios Iesous* ('Jesus is Lord', 1 Cor. 12:3), a confession destined to collide with the customary acclamation, *Kyrios Caesar*, 'Caesar is Lord' (see Acts 17:7). In this early encounter, the 'living and true God' (1 Thess. 1:9) was preached in the capital of the Roman province of Macedonia, whose local coins a mere half century before had boldly designated Julius Caesar as *theos*, 'god'. Thessalonica's position, as both trade station on the Via Egnatia and chief Macedonian port on the Thermaic Gulf, ensured a rich and cosmopolitan mix of available religious options – the Hellenistic-Egyptian cults of Isis, Osiris, and Sarapis, the local cult of the Kabeiroi, and the Olympian gods Zeus (*Hypsistos*, 'the highest'), Apollo, and Aphrodite, as well as Herakles, the Dioskouroi, and the ever-popular Dionysos.[1] To the eclectic devotees of these gods, who as a matter of course expressed their civic loyalty and gratitude for benefactions through the imperial cult as well, Paul brought an uncommon message. While there was nothing unusual in the idea that the god he spoke of had a son, what would have struck his pagan listeners as peculiar – and incipiently dangerous – was the insistence that this god was the only one to whom worship was due.

This idea was not, of course, a Christian creation. The 'living and true' God whom Paul proclaimed was the God of Israel, the God of the Jews, whose ancient prophets Paul invokes by name (2:15) and by allusion (Isa. 59:17 in 1 Thess. 5:8) in 1 Thessalonians, despite the fact that, rather unusual for the Pauline corpus, the letter is devoid of scriptural quotations. But would Paul's Thessalonian converts have known of the Jewish god before they set eyes on this foreign missionary? According to Acts 17:1–9, when Paul arrived in Thessalonica, 'as was his custom,' he attended the synagogue on three successive sabbaths to engage in evangelization through a christological exposition of the scriptures. But if we had only Paul's first letter to the Thessalonians, we would have no reason to imagine a synagogue mission by Paul in Thessalonica. The different picture that emerges from this letter is that Paul, while working night and day (2:9), preached the gospel of God to potential converts, presumably in his workshop itself, or nearby. While Paul accords with Luke's scenario in representing the means of evangelization as verbal proclamation and argumentation (*logos*; see 1:5; 2:2–4, 9–12, and especially 2:13), he nowhere indicates that scriptural interpretation was a part of that proof. Moreover, Paul insists that preaching was not the *sole* means by which the gospel was communicated, but that the gospel came to them also through the persuasive means of miracle (*dynamis*, also 'power'), the Holy Spirit, and the great conviction of its teller himself, who stood as a living, imitable emblem of the faith he professed (1:5–6; cf. 2:8). In terms of historical reliability we must favour the Pauline picture to the Lukan, though it is not implausible that some of the Thessalonian converts were Gentile 'God-fearers', whose conversion to the living and true God (rendered easier by their preparatory learning in the scriptures) Paul considered completed by their acceptance of the gospel.

The message Paul preached ('our gospel' – 1:5) to these Macedonians was a narrative of 'good news' (*euaggelion*) which he characterizes variously as 'the gospel of God' (1:5; 2:2, 8, 9) and 'the gospel of Christ' (3:2). Both titles are apt, since God and Christ are the two main characters of the story. The basic plot, encapsulated in 4:14 and 1:10, is quite simple: Jesus died, God raised him from the dead, and at some future time Jesus will rescue those who believe in him from 'the coming wrath' at his 'parousia' or advent (2:19; 3:13; 4:15; 5:9, 23), a projected event described in the language of an imperial visit to a provincial city. The gospel story Paul offered the Thessalonian pagans is an updated version of Jewish apocalyptic narratives, known to us from a range of extant writings, both biblical (such as Daniel 7 and 12) and apocryphal (4 Ezra, 1 Enoch, 2 Baruch, Dead Sea Scrolls),[2] which forecast a dramatic divine intervention in human history to exact final judgment on the good and the evil. Paul's is an essentially post-messianic version of that apocalyptic tale (i.e. the Messiah has already come), triggered by his intense expectation that the recent resurrection of Jesus from the dead had already set in motion the events of the last days, whose final scenes will be inaugurated by the Son's return from heaven (1:10).

We do not know how many Thessalonians accepted Paul and his gospel narrative about Jesus the dead and risen Lord who will come from heaven, but according to 2:9 Paul was in that city working and disseminating his gospel for some length of time. Although an itinerant missionary, Paul apparently stayed long enough to get a community started, which involved preaching the gospel and giving spiritual mentorship, including a large component of ethical instruction and encouragement (2:12; 4:1–2, 7). During this time, as Paul tells it, a warm relationship developed between the group of believers and the missionary who had issued God's call to them. Indeed, an index of their faithfulness was their imitation of Paul as their evangelist, like children growing up to look like their father (2:11). The community Paul formed among these Thessalonians called themselves by the language of fictive kinship; Paul addresses them fully fourteen times in this short letter as *adelphoi*, which we translate as 'brothers', or, better, 'brothers and sisters' (since there is no indication that Paul intends the term to exclude women). The outcome of Paul's preaching, as he later recounts it, was a three-fold acceptance: of Paul himself (1:9; 2:1), of the word of God (2:13), and of the Holy Spirit (1:6). 'Turning to' this God of Israel meant that God in return 'gave his holy spirit' to them (1:9; 4:8), presumably in baptism (though Paul does not name the rite specifically in this letter). Then, after the initial period of evangelization by Paul, for a reason not specified here, Paul left Thessalonica, and continued on his way west, on to Athens, from which he apparently wrote this first letter to the Thessalonians.

BACKGROUND TO 1 THESSALONIANS

While likely not the first letter Paul ever wrote to a church, 1 Thessalonians is probably the earliest Pauline letter that was preserved and later published (in which case, it is the oldest writing in the New Testament). As such it is an enormously important document: the first early Christian letter, the inaugural text of a tradition of Christian epistolary literature that extends to the present day.[3] Like all letters, in antiquity as well as today, each Pauline epistle was written to address a specific situation, about which Paul had become informed from a distance. Interpretative method for reading epistolary literature requires us to reconstruct, as best we can, the historical context surrounding the letter, and the issues with which it is concerned. Then on the basis of that reconstruction we attempt to discern how Paul chose to intervene pastorally at that moment through his letter (and the intermediary who carried it), and how he structured and composed his letter to effect his chosen purpose.

We learn from 1 Thessalonians that after leaving Thessalonica Paul, in Athens, has heard about the goings-on in his young church back in Macedonia from two sources: (1) the general rumour mill and (2) and his own trusted envoy, Timothy. As Paul presents it, the news about the Thessalonians on the Christian grapevine that extended through Macedonia, Greece, and beyond (maintained, presumably, by word of mouth among missionaries and business travellers) was quite positive: the report of their faith in God has gone out over the network (1:7–8), as have reports of their loving acts towards fellow Christians in their province (4:10).

But Paul had nonetheless been nervous about the Thessalonians, fearing that they might 'be shaken' in a time of afflictions (exactly what this involved is not specified), and might defect from their loyalty to Paul and his gospel (3:1–5). Paul was worried enough to send Timothy to Thessalonica on a reconaissance and (possibly) recovery mission for the Thessalonians' faith: 'in order to strengthen you and encourage you on behalf of your faith . . . to gain knowledge about your faith, lest somehow the tempter had tempted you, and our labour might be in vain' (3:2, 5). Exactly what this temptation was, which was presumably generated by 'these afflictions' (3:3–4; cf. 1:6), remains uncertain. There are several possibilities: the general pressure on new converts to regress when beset by pressure from non-Christians to conform to the *status quo*; more aggressive, violent acts of persecution (as 2:14 seems to indicate) against the new cult; the arrival of other Christian missionaries after Paul had left who cast doubt on his legitimacy and sincerity; or some combination of these options. Timothy went to Thessalonica from Athens as Paul's representative (3:1–2; if he took a letter from Paul along with him, it is not extant) and, after a visit of unspecified duration, returned to Paul with a report about the Thessalonian Christian assembly: the 'good news' of their faith and love, and their fond memory and devotion to Paul, whom they wished to see face to face (3:6). The personal nature of this report strongly suggests that part of Timothy's mission was to restore the relationship between Paul and his early converts, which had somehow been jeopardized in their separation. The success of Timothy's mission emboldens Paul to write and reaffirm the relationship from his point of view, by stressing his own reciprocal regard for the Thessalonians (3:6, 10) to match the renewed pledge of loyalty to Paul that they had sent through the agency of Timothy.[4] But the restoration of the relationship that Timothy's mission had effected did not in itself resolve all the pastoral issues in the church.

In this now favourable climate, Paul takes up his pen to provide the best possible substitute for the face-to-face contact cherished by beloved friends: a letter that would represent his living presence among the Thessalonians and carry the power to effect fully his pastoral leadership among them. In the letter Paul assumed his familiar fatherly role among his converts, resuming the work he carried out when living there: 'encouraging' the Thessalonians 'how to walk worthily of God' (2:12), only now, at this later stage in their progress, 'encouraging' a mature *increase* in the ethical behaviour they have begun so faithfully (4:1, 10; cf. 5:12–22).

But in addition to this renewal of ongoing pastoral instruction, it is clear that Timothy's report was more mixed than it initially sounds; while the church was progressing nicely in faith, there was a problematic issue that required immediate attention. Some Thessalonians were experiencing grief at the death of fellow Christians before the occurrence of the parousia promised by Paul's gospel. We do not know if these deaths were due to natural causes (such as infant mortality) or if they are to be attributed to some form of sporadic persecution or mob action; in any case, they apparently caused a theological and pastoral crisis. These deaths were taken by some to invalidate Paul's kerygma, consequently sowing doubts about the legitimacy of his claim to speak, not just his own humanly fallible words, but God's own truth (2:3–6, and especially 2:13). Paul judged this to be the sign of a serious problem that required immediate epistolary pastoral attention.[5] But he did not respond to the problem as the Thessalonians might have phrased it themselves ('why are our members dying?'); rather he first subjects it to his own theological diagnosis. Paul determines that the issue is not the deaths themselves (that is why he gives no counsel on matters medical, as if the deaths were biological, or strategic, if due to persecution, and he does not offer the standard arguments of philosophical consolation for loss of loved ones). Instead, Paul's diagnosis is that the problem resides *with the Thessalonians*, and their loss of *hope* (4:13; compare 3:6 and 1:3). His letter, which mediates his pastoral presence from a distance, is meant to offer the Thessalonians the words that will restore their hope.

1 THESSALONIANS

The letter is very carefully composed to effect this purpose. After the epistolary prescript (which, we should note, includes Silvanus and Timothy as co-senders alongside Paul, who nonetheless emerges as the only singular voice – 2:18), Paul transforms the health wish of the everyday Greek letter into a thanksgiving to God for the *spiritual health* of the Thessalonians as he remembers it from their past times together: their work of faith, labour of love, and endurance of hope (1:3). All three elements of this favoured Pauline triad of virtues (faith, hope, and love; cf. 1 Cor. 13:13), he says, were in clear evidence in the halcyon days when the Thessalonians embraced the gospel as he initially proclaimed it to them. By emphasizing their past trust in his gospel, and their broad continuing reputation for faith, Paul lays down the basis for his argument that by wavering because of the death of some of their company the Thessalonians are *de facto* contradicting themselves and their own most fervent commitments (1:6–10; cf. 4:13–14).

Because the Thessalonians' problem is, according to Paul's diagnosis, a theological one, his remedy requires a fresh, revised version of his initial kerygma – which had stressed the expectation that God's Son, Jesus, will come soon from heaven (1:10) – in order to include the fate of the dead. But before he can offer a theo*logical* solution, Paul must first convince the Thessalonians that his *logos* (his word) is indeed trustworthy. Hence in the long section 2:1–3:13 Paul recounts the relationship between himself and the church, using the Thessalonians themselves as his character witnesses, to thwart in principle any doubts that he would 'word-smith' for his own profit (see the language in 2:3–6), rather than promulgate among them 'the word of God' (2:13). He now writes in joy and confidence, he maintains, because of Timothy's positive report, but nonetheless does desire 'to restore what is lacking in their faith' (3:10). This recital of the relationship, and especially its present restored status, leads Paul to break forth in thanksgiving (3:9, for the third time in the letter; cf. 1:2; 2:13) and a blessing formula that urges an increase in love even as it reaffirms the current loving bond between missionary and church (3:11–13). Here, as elsewhere, he reminds the Thessalonians rather pointedly that what is at stake now, as always, is their eschatological salvation at the parousia (3:13), and he confirms that their ultimate destinies are inseparably linked with one another (2:19), even as they have shared in the experience of persecution on earth (2:2, 14–16; 3:3–4, 7).

In 4:1–2, with 'finally, therefore', Paul resumes his pastoral work with instructions for the present, reassuringly grounded in the past. He reminds the Thessalonians that he previously gave them instructions about ethical living ('walking in such a way as to please God'), which they received and acted upon (cf. 4:6, 11). Therefore, he insists, the current letter is not designed as an overhaul of the catechetical curriculum, but is an update to match their current situation as more mature converts. In 4:3–8 he focuses on their 'sanctification' (a recurrent theme in the letter: see also 3:13 and 5:23) in sexual matters, a state which, Paul insists, requires the renunciation of improprieties more associated with idolatry than their new monotheistic faith (4:5). Once again he punctuates this advice with the adamant reminder that the words are not his, but God's (4:8). In 4:9–11 Paul praises the Thessalonians for their 'brotherly love', again encouraging an increase (this is the push and pull characteristic of the paraenesis of this letter – 'you are already doing this, of course, but do it more'), and counsels that 'walking in a seemly fashion' extends also to prudent work habits and self-support.

Paul comes to the heart of the matter in 4:13–5:11, a continuous piece of theological reasoning that is punctuated by the refrain: 'therefore, comfort one another' (4:18: 'with these words'; cf. 5:11). Since it is *words* that Paul offers to resolve the Thessalonians' theological problem, we can appreciate why so much of the earlier part of the letter was spent defending the truthfulness of his word. In 4:13–18 Paul yet again promulgates a word which is not solely his own, but 'a *word* of the Lord' (4:15), which is designed to address the Thessalonians' hopelessness about the fate of the dead and loss of faith in the truth of the gospel. The Thessalonians should not grieve 'like the rest, who do not have hope' (4:13). The basis Paul offers for a recharging of their hope (which was conspicuously absent from Timothy's report about their 'faith and love' in 3:6) is an updated apocalyptic scenario which now includes a special episode about the Christian dead, a topic apparently untreated in the original mission kerygma (cf. 1:9–10): when the Lord returns in his parousia the dead will not be left out, or usurped, but, on the contrary, they will be raised *first* (4:15–16), and only after this will the living join them in eternal union with the Lord in the clouds (4:17).

In 5:1–11 Paul addresses the concomitant misperception that recent events have disconfirmed the 'timetable' inherent in his gospel narrative, by insisting that the Thessalonians should well know that his proclamation did not include a specification of 'the times and seasons', for 'the day of the Lord comes like a thief in the night' (5:2). Hence, he argues, the delay in the parousia does not invalidate the gospel, but is in accord with it. Once again Paul reframes the issue: what is crucially at stake is not 'staying awake' in the euphemistic sense of not 'falling asleep' in death (4:13), but 'remaining soberly alert' against the danger of ethical torpor and sloth while awaiting the second coming (5:4–10). Rather than speculating on the timetable, Paul urges the Thessalonians to continue to play the role assigned to them in the narrative: 'sons of light' (5:5), thereby both keeping to their gospel faith and adhering to the standard of behaviour that will ensure the eschatological salvation God holds in store for them in Jesus. This role requires the appropriate raiment, which Paul prescribes for them by a clever allusion to Isa. 59:17 that corresponds exactly with his rhetorical focus throughout the letter: the breastplate of *faith* and *love* (which they already apparently have, at least to some good measure – 3:6), which must be supplemented by the helmet of 'the *hope* of salvation' (5:8) that it has been the burden of this epistle to fasten tightly on their heads. Paul's own work of encouragement and comfort to the community by his *logos* should now be replicated among themselves (5:11).

As a further aid to this programme of ecclesial reaffirmation, Paul requests the Thessalonians to show appropriate regard to their local leaders, whom they should consider examples of the 'increase in love' to which he had exhorted them (4:10). What this love and the peace that would accompany it (5:13) entail in concrete terms is spelled out in 5:14–22, a final piece of fatherly exhortation that prescribes the ethical and liturgical underpinnings of a group that assembles in the name of 'the God of peace' (5:23). Paul assures his Gentile converts, who had apparently come to doubt their choice to 'turn away' from the gods of their compatriots and friends to worship his strange God, that his God is trustworthy, and will indeed fulfil the promises Paul his spokesman has conveyed about him (5:24). The letter concludes with a call for prayer, greetings, a solemn adjuration for the public reading of the letter, and a final benediction (5:25–8).

BACKGROUND TO 2 THESSALONIANS

The document we call '2 Thessalonians' is among the letters attributed to Paul whose authorship has been disputed by scholars (along with Colossians and Ephesians, the so-called 'deutero-Paulines'). Decisions about the authorship of 2 Thessalonians, or any other letter, drastically affect the interpretation of the setting, purpose, and meaning of the text. Arguments that Paul did not write this letter stem from literary, historical, and theological considerations. It is clear that 2 Thessalonians stands in some type of literary relationship with 1 Thessalonians. Most strikingly, it replicates quite closely the structure of that letter, which is itself unparalleled elsewhere in the Pauline corpus (including a rather odd second thanksgiving formula, blessings which occur both within the letter body and at its conclusion, and the introduction of ethical exhortation with the exclamation, 'Finally'). This similarity extends to vocabulary, with conspicuously parallel phrases such as 'the Lord/God of peace' (2 Thess. 3:16//1 Thess. 5:23); 'in labour and toil night and day working so as not to be a burden on any of you' (2 Thess. 3:8//1 Thess. 2:9); 'may the Lord/our God . . . direct' (2 Thess. 3:5//1 Thess. 3:11, a term found only here in the Pauline letters); 'we ask you, brothers and sisters' (2 Thess. 2:1//1 Thess. 4:1). Both letters share an emphasis on imitation of Paul (2 Thess. 3:7, 9//1 Thess. 1:6).[6] All of these observations lead us to ask why Paul would have written a letter so similar in structure, and with such pronounced thematic and linguistic re-echoing of his prior missive to the same church (yet in a more verbose and elongated Greek style).

These overlaps in diction create an even greater incongruity when we turn to the historical context presumed by the second letter, which would require the Thessalonians to have shifted 180 degrees in their theological outlook: they were now being tempted to believe that 'the day of the Lord had (already) come' (2:2), whereas in the first letter it was the non-arrival of the promised parousia which had caused them such grief. Furthermore, the theological emphasis of 2 Thessalonians itself is not so much upon the assurance of salvation at the parousia for all believers, dead and living, as it is upon God's retributive justice against the enemies of the church at the eschaton (1:5–12; 2:10–12; cf. 1 Thess. 4:6, directed at immoral *insiders*). As part of this development, the God who guaranteed the truthfulness of Paul's gospel (1 Thess. 2:13) is now contrarily portrayed as the purveyor of a deliberate 'act of deception' designed to entrap obstinate unbelievers (2:10–12). The central character of this eschatological vision is not God's Son, but his antitype – a malevolent figure (with multiple names) who will have his due on the public stage of history, but only temporarily, before he and those he led astray are finally vanquished.

To account for these similarities and differences between the two epistles, the best (though still debated) hypothesis is that 2 Thessalonians was not written by Paul, but by a follower of his who deliberately patterned this text on the earlier letter, to provide an answer to an eschatological crisis of a later time that carries the authoritative weight of the now-dead Paul. The actual recipients of 2 Thessalonians, therefore, were not necessarily Thessalonians (of any time period), but were meant to encompass any Christian readers a generation or more after Paul who revered him and the wisdom of his epistles, but were perplexed about how best to interpret his apocalyptic eschatology in their present context. This judgment is confirmed by the same shift in identity of the adversaries; 'those who are afflicting you' (2 Thess. 1:6) in this letter are no longer the specific Macedonian 'compatriots' of the Thessalonians (1 Thess. 2:14), but 'those who do not know God and do not obey the gospel of our Lord Jesus' (1:8), and hence universal 'unbelievers' (2:12).

This thesis is buttressed further by elements in the letter itself that indicate that Paul is no longer alive, but is now available to Christians only through the tradition preserved in his letters. In 2:2 three forms of revelation are named: the spirit, a word, or a letter 'as though written by us'. This indicates that the author of 2 Thessalonians was aware of the possibility, and probably the actuality, of other letters that were being composed in Paul's name during his time (sometime near the end of the first century or beginning of the second, since Polycarp of Smyrna alludes to 2 Thessalonians early in the second century). In 2:15 the readers are urged to stand fast and seize Paul's teachings, as known to them *either* through his word or a letter.

But as the letter closes, the available media by which Paul communicates have been trimmed down to the letter alone (3:14). This relegation of the living voice of Paul to the text suggests that the reference to Paul's personal signature 'which is a sign in every letter; this is the way I write' in 3:17 is an instance of 'he doth protest too much' (cf. 1 Cor. 16:21), a sign of the hand of a pseudepigraphical author.

The author of 2 Thessalonians wrote giving Pauline guidance for subsequent times. As Paul had before him, he carries forward the task of apocalyptic updating to certify the validity of the original scenario, while confirming that recent events are all a part of the divine plan. In particular, the author writes to Christians who are enduring some unspecified form of persecution from unnamed non-Christians (1:4–7; cf. 3:2, 'absurd and wicked people') who reject the gospel (2:10–12) and bring affliction and suffering. This external threat is matched by twin concerns from within the church: a fraudulent teaching masquerading as apostolic tradition (2:2, 15), which has led some church members to disobey Paul's word (3:14–15; cf. 2:14–15). Specifically, the deception has consisted of a false imminentist eschatology ('the day of the Lord has come'), which has concomitantly spurred some to idleness.

2 THESSALONIANS

2 Thessalonians is a remarkable literary composition. Preserving the skeleton of its precursor, 1 Thessalonians, the author begins with the same epistolary prescript (senders, recipients, greeting) and the familiar initial thanksgiving, with echoes of the earlier letter in the expression of gratitude for their faith, love and endurance (1:3–4; cf. 1 Thess. 1:3). The faith of the addressees in the face of affliction is praised by the author, who in turn broadcasts it more widely on the Christian grapevine (2 Thess. 1:4–7, as in 1 Thess. 1:6–8). They are a laudable example for all to follow (2 Thess. 1:5; cf. 1 Thess. 1:7). But, starting with 1:6, the author amplifies the thanksgiving to accentuate the theme of *dual* judgment at the eschaton, and stresses that when the Lord Jesus comes from heaven with the angels, as promised, he will bring severe, unrelenting, and eternal punishment to unbelievers. Believers, who are now being afflicted, in contrast, will at that time receive their due 'rest with us' (1:7), a relatively muted description of eschatological bliss. Their role in the parousia (with no distinction made between the living and the dead) is to serve as witnesses of the retribution against their enemies, and of the glory of the Lord which they hope to share (1:8–12; cf. 2:14).

In 2:1–2 the author addresses his most pressing concern to his readership: 'We ask you, brothers and sisters . . . not to be shaken in mind or upset ... (thinking) that the day of the Lord has come.' The argument of dissuasion that follows (2:3–16) proceeds in a most ingenious manner. The pseudepigraphical author, like Paul his literary and theological model, offers an enhancement of the apocalyptic scenario to provide more detail about the events between the death and resurrection of Jesus, and the parousia. Specifically, he includes a whole embedded narrative of the dark days which will precede the dawn of the parousia. What is most fascinating is that that darkness is cast in terms precisely antithetical to the positive promise of Jesus' parousia expounded in 1 Thess. 4:13–5:12. Whereas there Paul stressed that *first*, before the rapture of believers, the believing dead would be raised, our author insists that *first*, before the *parousia*, there will be an *apostasia* ('apostasy, revolt'). Before the revelation of the Son of God from heaven with his powerful angels (1:7), 'the son of perdition' (a.k.a. 'the man of lawlessness') will be revealed (2:3).

Now the spotlight is on this notoriously wicked figure, 'the man who opposes, and highly exalts himself above everything which is called a god or object of worship' (2:4). He goes so far as to sit in God's temple showing himself off as a god. Our author insists that the appearance of this individual (perhaps a Nero *redivivus* figure known to his contemporaries), though horrifying, in no way discredits the Pauline tradition that has been handed down but rather fulfils it ('I said these things to you when I was with you' – 2:5). The current time with all its trials is the period of 'the mystery of lawlessness' expected to precede the pernicious preliminary parousia of 'the lawless one' (2:8), whose 'revelation' and 'parousia' (which are the public deeds of Satan who supplies his powers – 2:9) will dazzle for just a brief moment, before the Lord Jesus will annihilate him at last in his own competing, and superior, 'epiphany of parousia', which will once and for all separate truth from falsehood.

Like its literary model, this revised apocalyptic vision incorporates new characters into the original plot in order to assure the readers that all is going according to plan. But the apocalyptic scenario of 2 Thessalonians is externally rather than internally directed. It offers comfort to the readers not by poetic description of the bliss they will share with all believers, living and dead (which is briefly stated as a fact in 2:13–14), but through a proleptic enjoyment of the imagined fate that is coming to their enemies. What the readers are called upon to do, in turn, is not merely to 'stay awake' (1 Thess. 5:6–10), but to stand in fidelity to the Pauline tradition, which is as powerful in its present epistolary form as it was in the living voice of Paul (2:15; cf. 3:4, 10, 12, 14).

As in 1 Thessalonians, after a blessing that closes off the first part of the argument (2 Thess. 2:16; cf. 1 Thess. 3:11–13), the author introduces ethical exhortation with 'Finally' (3:1). The readers are asked to pray for the success of the Pauline mission against its detractors, and, even more importantly, to bring it about by practising his commands themselves (3:4). After this authorizing prelude, the author applies this insistence upon the authority of Paul's word and example – by which is meant a complete coalescence of the historical, the epistolary, and the pseudepigraphical voices – to a single contemporary issue: the problem of idleness in the community (3:6–13). The author argues that this behaviour (likely a logical response to the imminentist eschatology) represents an abandonment of the true Pauline tradition which had been handed down to them (3:6), which is here reiterated in no uncertain terms. Just as Paul taught and exemplified, while awaiting the eschaton believers are to work for their living, and quietly engage in a life of good works.

The emphasis on the authority of Paul's word as contained in the letter reaches its culmination in 3:14 with the solemn command, not to read the letter to all the assembly (as in 1 Thess. 5:27), but to use the letter as a disciplinary tool to separate out the dissenters from the true faithful within the church (in a manner highly reminiscent of Paul's 1 Cor. 5:9). However, the author does not want to create enmity among Christians in this way, he urges, but rather mutual admonishment and community correction (3:15).

The letter body ends, like 1 Thessalonians, with a blessing from 'the Lord of peace' (3:16; cf. 1 Thess. 5:23), but this time quite generalized, followed by the rather conspicuous formula of authentic authorship that presumes a wider corpus of Paul's letters (3:17). As a Pauline composition, 2 Thessalonians both certifies the reliability of the letters written by the historical Paul and makes an overt claim to carry forward that tradition with complete fidelity into the writer's own generation, in which the danger is 'apostasy' of a different form – not a return to Roman paganism, but a misrepresentation of the authentic Pauline teaching about the end times and appropriate behaviour in the mean time.

Notes

1 See H. L. Hendrix, 'Thessalonica', *ABD* 6.524–5.

2 See J. J. Collins, 'Apocalypses and Apocalypticism: Early Jewish Apocalypses', *ABD* 1.282–8, and A. Yarbro Collins, 'Apocalypses and Apocalypticism: Early Christian', *ABD* 1.288–92.

3 See H. Koester, 'I Thessalonians – Experiment in Christian Writing', in F. F. Church and T. George, eds., *Continuity and Discontinuity in Church History: Essays Presented to George Huntston Williams on his 65th Birthday* (Leiden: Brill, 1979) 33–44.

4 See M. M. Mitchell, 'New Testament Envoys in the Context of Greco-Roman Diplomatic and Epistolary Conventions: The Example of Timothy and Titus', *JBL* 111 (1992) 641–62.

5 See A. J. Malherbe, *Paul and the Thessalonians: The Philosophic Tradition of Pastoral Care* (Philadelphia: Fortress, 1987).
6 For lists of the structural and lexical parallels between 1 and 2 Thessalonians, leading to opposite interpretations of the implications to be drawn thereby, see G. Milligan, *St. Paul's Epistles to the Thessalonians* (London: Macmillan, 1908) lxxx–lxxxv (authentic); W. Trilling, *Untersuchungen zum 2.Thessalonicherbrief*, Erfurter Theologische Studien 27 (Leipzig: St Benno, 1971) 46–132 (pseudepi-graphical); and further assessment in E. M. Krentz, 'Thessalonians, First and Second Epistles to the', *ABD* 6.520–1.

4 Galatians

BRUCE LONGENECKER

Paul's letter to the Galatian Christians teems with impassioned fervour unequalled in any other Pauline letter. It reveals an embattled Paul in a fierce struggle to preserve his own apostolic credentials, the gospel that he preached, and of course the spiritual health of Galatian communities that he had founded a few years earlier. It contains some of Paul's most bold and impetuous theological reasoning, reasoning that he seems to have adjusted somewhat in content and tone in his later letter to the Roman Christians. In Galatians, we get a glimpse of Paul in a mode of impulsive reflex, assembling theological arguments to influence the corporate and personal life of the Galatian Christians in a situation that deeply disturbed him.

The Christians to whom Paul wrote were Gentiles (4:8) living in churches spread over some distance in the area of Asia Minor known to us today as Turkey. (Scholars continue to dispute the precise location of these churches, whether to the north towards the Black Sea or to the south closer to the Mediterranean.) They had affectionately received Paul and his message at an earlier date (3:1; 4:13–15), sometime in the late 40s. As a consequence of Paul's ministry among them, the Galatian Christians had profound experiences of the Spirit (3:2–5) that instilled in them a hardy sense of Christian identity that continued for some time (5:7a). At some point Paul left these communities to preach the gospel elsewhere. At a later date, he received news that a group of Jewish Christian evangelists had influenced the Galatian Christian communities advocating a gospel that differed considerably from his own. In Paul's opinion, these people were 'trouble-makers' or 'agitators' (1:7; 5:10).

If a profile of the agitators can be reconstructed on the basis of the text of Galatians, three important features seem likely. (1) The agitators were probably highly gifted rhetoricians with impressive skill in interpreting the scriptures of Israel. It is possible that some Pauline interpretations of scripture in Galatians are attempts to provide alternative interpretations of passages favoured by the agitators in support of their gospel.

(2) The agitators might well have claimed the sponsorship of the Jerusalem church, the mother church with substantial regulatory authority over the expanding church in Paul's day. Against this backdrop, Paul, whose relationship with the church in Antioch (and consequently with the established church in Jerusalem) had at one point suffered a rather serious set-back (2.11–14), might have begun to appear like a renegade, with a controversial message bolstering a maverick enterprise. In Galatians 1–2 Paul addresses the issue of authority in ways that seek to invalidate the agitators' claims. So, he highlights the revelatory character of his gospel, tracing its origins to a divine disclosure that by-passed human channels of authority (while also causing great rejoicing in the Judaean churches – 1.11–24). Nonetheless Paul also claims that, even if human channels of authority are to be respected, his mission and theology are not to be perceived as problematic, since the apostolic leaders of the Jerusalem church had already validated his mission and theology at an early period (2:1–10; cf. 1:18–24). The insinuation here is that, if anyone has strayed from the established path, it is not Paul; the precedent for Christian leaders in Jerusalem to depart from the 'truth of the gospel' (2:5) has already been set by Peter, perhaps with the blessing of James (2:11–14).

(3) The agitators preached a form of Christianity that showcased Abrahamic descent in conjunction with the covenantal law of Moses – the celebrated eternal revelation of God confirmed and affirmed by God's Messiah, Jesus. While similar configurations of Abrahamic descent and Mosaic law are attested in Jewish literature of Paul's day, the agitators clearly articulated a message that gave Jesus the Messiah a central role within one such configuration. For them, there was no reason to think that the Messiah had abolished the requirements established by God for all time in the Torah. These requirements included the need for circumcision particularly (e.g. 6:12–13) and perhaps nomistic observance generally (i.e., observance of the law; e.g. 4:21; 5:4). It is these aspects of the agitators' teaching that Paul addresses directly in his letter. While he normally engages with their position by means of sustained theological argument, on at least one occasion he resorts to outright derision, stating that, if they are so interested in cutting, perhaps they should simply castrate themselves and be done with it (5:12).

In view of this profile of the agitators, it is tempting to think that Paul's letter to the Galatian Christians deals primarily with the issue of 'the law', not least since this seems to be the issue that has overwhelmed the Galatian communities. Such an impression, however, requires some qualification. While the Galatian Christians' regard for the law provoked Paul to write much on the subject, his deliberations on nomistic observance are framed within the context of prior convictions about the nature of Christian personal and corporate life. In particular, he surveys the Christian life in relation to two dimensions: a temporal and a qualitative dimension. With reference to the temporal dimension, Paul appraises the Christian life in relation to God's eschatological works and God's previous dealings with Israel; in this context, his case relies on the temporal movement from the 'then' to the 'now'. With reference to the qualitative dimension, Paul demonstrates the Christian life to be intrinsically marked out by Christ-likeness; in this context, his case relies on a portrait of self-giving as the essential component of Christian lifestyle.

Of these two dimensions, it is arguably the qualitative dimension, which focuses on cruciform lifestyle, that forms the backbone of the theological body of the letter. If that claim is over-stated, it is only slightly so. Paul's strategy in Galatians is most effective when he exploits the full scope of the qualitative dimension. Although he employs various arguments concerning the law in Galatians, Paul's finest deliberations on the subject are informed by a belief that cruciform existence is intrinsic to Christian identity and is the most intimate form of relationship with God. Paul's instructions about the law follow in the wake of this pre-determined vision of Christian moral identity. Because he has such a clearly defined conception of the moral quality of the Christian life, he finds that other issues, even the vexed issue of nomistic observance, are consequently resolved. This feature provides Paul with some of his most salient theological resources in Galatians.

This vision of Christian moral identity informs Paul's expectations for his Galatian communities, and impacts on the way that he depicts his own life. In Galatians 1–2, Paul recounts some personal biographical features. These include: his incomparability in traditional forms of Jewish life and his persecution of the church (1:13–14), his experience of having God's Son revealed to him (1:12, 15–16), his visits with Christian leaders in Jerusalem (1:18–24; 2:1–10), and the rupture in his relationship with other Christian leaders in Antioch over the issue of compelling Gentiles to live like Jews (2:1–14). This leads into a crucial paragraph on the salvific sufficiency of Christian faith (2:15–21), a paragraph that climaxes in the claim: 'I have been crucified with Christ, and it is no longer I who live, but Christ who lives in me' (2:19b–20a; further variations on this theme appear in 5:24; 6:14, 17). Paul envisages himself as having died in order that the crucified Christ might live through him.

Paul depicts the Christophany that changed his life in similar terms in 1:15–16, where he writes: 'God . . . was pleased to reveal his son in me.' These verses are frequently translated in such a way as to suggest that God's Son was revealed 'to' Paul. But Paul's Greek construction (*en emoi*, as in 2:20) suggests that God did not simply reveal new information to Paul; instead, God took hold of Paul's life and made it an arena in which Christ himself became embodied. This is not simply enlightenment, but is seen by Paul as 'enlivenment'. Since his encounter with the risen Christ, Paul's own life has become the vehicle for the risen son of God to 'come to life' in ways consonant with Paul's calling.

Paul's depiction of Christ living 'in me' may seem dramatic and bold. As later chapters make clear, however, Paul does not envisage this to be a special privilege distinctive to his own apostleship. Instead, he expects enlivenment of Christ to be characteristic of Christian living in general. So in 3:27, Paul reminds the Galatians of their identity as those 'baptized into Christ' and therefore those who have 'put on Christ'. That is, they are to perform Christ, just as actors in a play perform the character of others. Christian life involves the dramatization of Christ, and a faithful enactment of Christ is expected of all his followers. The same is clear from other imagery that Paul uses in 4:19, where he speaks of his desire that Christ should 'be formed in you'. The metaphor is maternal. As a mother nourishes new life within her womb, so the corporate life of the Galatian Christians is to be the womb that nourishes Christ in order that he might be 'birthed' among them.

Paul puts tight controls on what it means to 'perform' or 'give birth to' Christ. While he thinks of Jesus Christ as the risen and exalted Lord under whose feet all things will be subjected, it is the crucified Christ whom Christians perform. The enlivenment of Christ in Christians does not consist of advantage, ascendancy, or dominance in this life; instead, it involves the patterning of a cruciform lifestyle. Whenever Paul employs enlivenment imagery, he envisages Christian lifestyle giving expression to the pattern of self-giving modelled by Christ. This is clear from 2:20, where Paul's claim that Christ lives in him is immediately qualified by the characterization of Christ as the one 'who loved me and gave himself for me'. Crucifixion is a central reality of Christian experience, since cruciform lifestyle is to be replicated in the lives of Christians. We should not be surprised, then, that the same quality of Christ's life is highlighted at the beginning of the letter (which is where Paul frequently introduces themes that will be elaborated later in a letter's main body). In the opening of Galatians, Christ's life of service is featured alongside his resurrection. So the Christ whom God raised from the dead (1:1) is also the Christ 'who gave himself' for the benefit of others (1:4).

This theological strand animates some of the letter's most significant passages. So, highlighting the sufficiency of Christian faith, Paul speaks of that faith as 'faith working practically [Greek: *energoumenē*] through love'

(5:6), and he defines Christian love as self-giving: 'through love become servants to one another' (5:13). The same definition that Paul gives in relation to Christ's love in 2:20 is replicated here in relation to Christian love, with love being defined in each case as self-giving service for the benefit of others. It is precisely this quality of service that is at the forefront of Paul's mind when 'love' appears as the spearhead of his list of the fruit of the Spirit (5:22–3).

This aspect of Paul's letter deserves to be strongly featured since it serves as a rich vein providing him with fertile theological resources. Four points in particular need mention in this regard. First, Paul's emphasis on cruciform existence demonstrates that moral responsibility retains a central place within his gospel of faith. Since the law placed restraints on human behaviour, and since Paul claims that Christians are not required to observe the law, some of his contemporaries came to the view that Paul's gospel left Christians free from moral restraints of any kind (see, e.g., Rom. 3:7–8; 6:1, 15; see also Paul's correction of Corinthian beliefs in 1 Cor. 6:12; 10:23). Galatians demonstrates that such a view of Paul's gospel is erroneous. While Christians may be free from a nomistic pattern of life, their freedom is for the purpose of obligating them to others in patterns of service. In this regard the whole of 5:13 can be quoted: 'For you were called to freedom, brothers and sisters; only do not use your freedom as an opportunity for self-indulgence, but through love become servants of each other.' If his gospel of Christian freedom appeared to be theologically dangerous or ethically deficient, Paul here is concerned to couple an emphasis on Christian freedom with a counter-emphasis on Christian responsibility.

Second, Paul presents Christian self-giving as itself the fulfilment of the law. So he writes: 'For the whole law is fulfilled in one word: "Love your neighbour as yourself"' (5:14; see also 6:2). In a context where the issue at stake was the doing of the law, Paul points to Christ-like service as the embodiment of everything that the law was seeking to promote. Although Christians are not required to observe the law, Paul claims that Christ-like service is the unsurpassed expression of the law's ultimate interests and intentions. Although Paul attempts to shift the Galatians' interests away from nomistic observance towards self-giving service, he nonetheless retains a place for the law in his imaging of Christian life. But his point is not that Christians should simultaneously serve others and keep the law; instead, he means simply that, through their service to others, the expectations of the law are fully concretized in unrivalled fashion.

Here Paul seems to be making a subtle distinction between 'doing the law' and 'fulfilling the law'. Doing the law is disparaged as ineffectual and non-productive. In 3:10, for instance, Paul writes: 'For all who rely on the works of the law are under a curse; for it is written, "Cursed is everyone who does not remain in all the things written in the book of the law to do them.'" Traditionally this verse has been read to mean that a curse rests on anyone who tries to observe the law as a means of salvation, since no one is able to do the law fully. While this interpretation faces certain historical and theological difficulties, and while recent scholarship has attempted to remove those difficulties through other interpretations, the traditional interpretation is probably correct. Paul thinks of human sinfulness as so overwhelming that attempts to do the law inevitably end in despair (cf. Romans 7). When the Spirit is present, however, a different situation is envisaged. Paul does not suggest that the Spirit enables the full performance of the law – a view that might be similar to that held by those in Galatia who advocated nomistic observance. Instead, he envisages that the Spirit promotes cruciform existence, which in a round-about way is the concrete embodiment of what had been envisaged for Israel in the law.

Third, it becomes clear from Galatians that Christ-like existence is for Paul the realization of an unparalleled intimacy with God. Several of Paul's comments testify to a conviction that the people of Israel had already enjoyed a special relationship with God. So he speaks of the law having been given as a 'pedagogue' (3:24–5), a word difficult to translate into English, but one that would include connotations similar to the term 'child-carer' or 'guardian'. (The NRSV translates it as 'disciplinarian', which captures some of the connotations, but perhaps in overly harsh terms.) In Graeco-Roman society, a pedagogue oversaw the up-bringing of a child. Included in the pedagogue's charge were the supervision, care, guidance, protection, instruction, and discipline of the child. This metaphor of the pedagogue is suggestive of a broader familial relationship, since a pedagogue was employed by a father who wanted his child to be nurtured in accordance with paternal expectations and hopes.

The metaphor of the law as pedagogue is well suited to Paul's temporal argument; just as a pedagogue is relieved of duty once the child comes of age, so the law's function as an overseer of God's people comes to an end with the coming of Christ (3:24 should read 'the law was our guardian until Christ came' rather than 'the law was our guardian to lead us to Christ', as it is sometimes translated). It is with the benefit of Christian hindsight that the experience of being under a pedagogue (the law) can be seen as a form of confinement (3:23), since with the coming of Christ a form of guidance is available that sets people free for service: that is, the guidance of the Spirit. It is the Spirit, rather than the pedagogue, that is to form the character of God's people come of age. The pedagogical role of the law has given way to the guidance of the Spirit. So Paul writes: 'If you are led by the Spirit, you are not under the law ... If we live by the Spirit, let us also be guided by the Spirit' (5:18, 25). The Spirit, who as we have seen produces the fruit of Christ-likeness in Christians, has been sent into the hearts of Christians, reproducing in them Jesus' own intimate cry to God: 'Abba, Father' (4:6). Israel's relationship to God had been a mediated one by means of the law acting as a pedagogue (see also Paul's fairly dense comments in 3:19–20); by contrast, the Christian's relationship to God is one of intimacy, as the Christian enters into the boundaries of Jesus' own cherished and distinctive sonship. While the people of Israel enjoyed a special relationship with God prior to Christ (signalled by the giving of the law), that relationship was of a different order altogether to the kind of unprecedented intimacy that comes in the wake of Christian union with Christ.

Fourth, while Paul parades Christ-likeness as the essential characteristic of Christian living, he characterizes the agitators in terms that run contrary to this model. This is true especially in 4:17 and 6:12–13. In 4:17, Paul writes: 'They make much of you ... so that you may make much of them.' Paul is suggesting that the agitators are seeking to enlist the Galatians as enthusiastic devotees and supporters in order to enhance the reputation and stature of the agitators themselves. In 6:12–13 the agitators are depicted as wanting to 'make a good showing in the flesh ... so that they may boast about your flesh'. Paul's double use of the word 'flesh' (*sarx*) is both intentional and poignant. Circumcision, of course, is carried out in the 'flesh', and the word is used here to signal the agitators' interest in nomistic observance, driven by a zeal for covenant purity among God's people. But to this interest in the circumcised 'flesh' Paul attaches a moral quality, intimating that the agitators' interests are ultimately driven by an ignoble character (cf. 4:17). Their primary motivation, he suggests, involves inflating their own prestige and acclaim (perhaps among their colleagues in the Jerusalem church). Consequently Paul links their programme of nomistic observance with a 'fleshly' demeanour, which is marked out by a vicious cycle of ambitious, cut-throat rivalry and fierce competitiveness (5:15, 26). In the end, Paul perceives the way of life recommended by the agitators as inevitably deteriorating into a morass of corruption and perversity, as featured in his list of the 'works of the flesh' (5:19–21).

This, of course, is an aberrant mutation of the kind of social health and mutuality that Paul envisages the Christian gospel engendering. He maintains that all members are 'one in Christ' despite differences in their respective identities (3:28), and he perceives that a community of this kind can only be sustained as members give of themselves for the betterment of others, all by the power of God. In contrast to this cruciform model of self-giving, however, the agitators are seen by Paul to be promoting a form of human self-centredness. In their hands (he believes), the gospel fails to testify to the power of the sovereign God who is creating a world-wide community of people moulded in the likeness of his self-giving Son. Instead, the gospel has become a means of manipulation in order to augment the agitators' magnificence as they mould others in their own likeness. This is a world away from their own self-understanding and interests. But in Paul's reconstruction, and no doubt to their own astonishment, they are depicted as pedlars of human self-interestedness in the guise of good news.

But if Paul tries to outscore the agitators on the matter of character, he may have had a harder time bettering them as a scriptural interpreter. At various points in Galatians 3–4 especially, Paul engages in scriptural interpretation, seeking to show that scripture itself supports his gospel. This includes his attempt to demonstrate from scripture that Abrahamic inheritance is to be defined in terms of faith (3:6–9; 4:21–31) and that faith is the proper response of those who would be righteous before God (3:10–14). Paul's expertise as an interpreter of scripture is not to be taken lightly, for in these passages he weaves together fascinating webs of textual resonance to support his gospel and mission.

Nonetheless, the impressiveness of Paul's interpretative skill is matched by the somewhat arbitrary manner in which he occasionally extracts meaning from scriptural texts. So, for instance, when speaking about the promises 'spoken to Abraham and to his offspring' in 3:16, Paul introduces a grammatical peculiarity, arguing that the scriptural phrase 'and to his offspring' (cf. Gen. 13:15; 17:8; 24:7) must refer to a single person rather than a collective entity, since the word is singular rather than plural ('offsprings'). In this way, he is able to sideline ethnic definitions of Abrahamic heritage and to focus that concept exclusively on Christ, the single seed.

While the effects of this argument cohere well with Paul's overall concerns in Galatians, his hearers in Galatia might be excused for raising an eyebrow at this point. They would certainly be cognizant of the fact that 'offspring' naturally has a corporate ('descendants') rather than individual referent. Paul knows this too, of course, and uses the word 'offspring' to mean descendants later in the same chapter (3:29; see also Rom. 4:16, 18). But Paul's christocentric reading of the Abraham account is based on this grammatical nicety, a peculiar reading that is far from the most natural reading of the texts in Genesis. Paul might have been wiser trying to earth his christological interpretation of the phrase 'and to his offspring' in a messianic interpretation of 'offspring' in 2 Sam. 7:12–14, but his interpretative procedure is never articulated in this way. Evidently he considered a christological interpretation of 'offspring' to be best defended by a grammatical oddity supporting an interpretation unencumbered by the narrative dynamics of the scriptural text.

Much the same could be said of Paul's interpretation in 4:21–31 of Abraham's two 'women', the 'slave woman' Hagar and the 'free woman' Sarah (not mentioned by name). Paul rather arbitrarily associates Hagar the slave with the law, and Sarah the free woman with the Spirit. Despite his protestations that this is what scripture actually 'says' (4:21, 30), Paul also seems cognizant that his interpretation is somewhat imaginative, calling it an 'allegory' (4:24). Here again, the voice that Paul finds in scripture is one that coheres well with his gospel, but only once it has been significantly dislodged from its original narrative context. In this regard, Paul's term 'allegory' seems to suggest awareness on his part of the interpretative freedom exercised on this occasion. That is, Paul's allegory is not presented as scriptural 'exegesis'. It is more like a call to re-image the scriptural text in accord with prior Pauline convictions. Paul seems hopeful that the Galatians would inherit this playful reconfiguration of the scriptural story, allowing themselves to think of that story along lines that nurture a Pauline perspective rather than disqualify it.

Did Paul expect too much in thinking that the Galatians would be influenced by his rather creative readings of scripture? Perhaps, and certainly the agitators would have been keen to highlight the lack of exegetical rigour in some of Paul's scriptural expositions. Perhaps by the time he wrote Romans Paul was forced to rethink the effectiveness of the arguments set out in Galatians. So in Romans 4, when again discussing Abrahamic descent, Paul follows lines of argument that by-pass those of Galatians 3. When writing Galatians, however, Paul simply assumes that his pondering on scriptural passages will carry weight.

This is a significant assumption, and one that can be adequately explained only with reference to Paul's confidence that Christ was alive in him. Paul envisaged the embodiment of Christ as encompassing every aspect of his life, including his reading of scripture. Conversely, Paul seems to think of the character deficiency of the agitators as an impediment to their ability to interpret scripture for the benefit of Christian communities. Paul's convictions seem to run along these lines: the peddling of 'another gospel' by the agitators can be traced back to their unwise readings of scripture ('unwise' within the cruciform community of Christ), and their unwise readings of scripture can be traced back to a defect in character. Evidently Paul envisaged the working of the Spirit to result in the establishment of a creative context in which scripture is read in such a way as to enhance and enrich the Christian self-giving community, even if those readings are unfettered by the original contours of the scriptural narrative. The freedom brought by the Spirit translates into service of others, and that service of others is, for Paul, the prerequisite for wise Christian readings of scripture. Paul is aware that other interpretations of scripture may qualify as possible explications of texts, but he also seems to assume that valid interpretations of scripture for the Christian community are those that do not trespass or undermine the pattern of cruciformity established in the life of Jesus Christ.

Throughout this chapter I have highlighted the feature of Christian moral identity and cruciform existence as the backbone to the Galatian letter, signalling how other aspects of Paul's letter are animated by it. In the process, those other aspects have not had the attention that they deserve. More would obviously need to be said on a gamut of these and other features. But we cannot attempt in this chapter to discuss every feature of the letter. Our situation is much like that of Rabbi Hillel of the first century who was once approached by a man asking to be taught the whole of the Torah while he (the enquirer) stood on one foot. Hillel's response was simply this: 'What is hateful to you, do not do to your neighbour. That is the whole Torah. The rest is commentary thereon; go and learn it.' In a slightly exaggerated parody, it could be suggested that cruciform character is the whole of Galatians; the rest augments that whole, and perhaps we do well to learn it. In particular, the closing words of Paul's exhortations are propitious: 'So then, whenever we have an opportunity, let us work for the good of all', to which he adds in good Pauline fashion: 'and especially for those of the family of faith' (6:10).

5   1 and 2 Corinthians

JEROME MURPHY-O'CONNOR

Paul's choice of Corinth as his first missionary base reveals much about his character and temperament. A city which took pride in the slogan, 'Not for everyone is the journey to Corinth' (Horace, *Epistles* 1.17.36; cf. Strabo, *Geography* 8.6.20) was above all a challenge. A challenge that Paul was prepared to accept because if he won he would have planted the gospel in the most difficult of all environments, a fiercely competitive commercial centre where material gain was the one true god. To be able to say that Corinthians believed in Jesus would be irrefutable proof of the power of the gospel.

Corinth, moreover, offered Paul superb communications. Its position on the isthmus linking the Peloponnese to mainland Greece gave it command over the north–south trade route as well as over the east–west sea traffic. The taxes it levied made it 'wealthy Corinth' (Homer, *Iliad* 2.570). (For more background on the city see my *St. Paul's Corinth.*[1])

Arriving in Corinth from Athens in the spring of AD 50, Paul found lodging and work with Prisca and Aquila, Jewish Christians who had fled from Rome as the result of reprisals taken by the Emperor Claudius against a turbulent synagogue in AD 41 (many continue to prefer the less probable date of AD 49). Corinth was an ideal city for all three to ply their trade of tentmaking. Corinth was responsible for the Isthmian Games, one of the four great panhellenic festivals, and vast numbers of tents were necessary both for the crowds that flocked to the sanctuary of Poseidon at Isthmia and for the shopkeepers of Corinth who went out to serve them.

Though he was only a despised manual labourer, Paul's fervour was such that his first converts came from what we today would describe as the upper middle class (1 Cor. 1:15–16). Two were pagans, Stephanas, who had the leisure to assume a leadership role, and Gaius, who had a house big enough to host the whole church. Crispus was a wealthy Jew. The whole community numbered between forty and fifty at a minimum and no doubt reflected the makeup of the general population. Some had been born free, others were ex-slaves, and others again were still in servitude. None were great magnates or field slaves.

Paul's experience of persecution at Thessalonica alerted him to the fact that he could not simply found churches and then leave them to their own devices. Some degree of maintenance was necessary. Since he could not always be present, he had to write. This posed no difficulty because as a teenager in Tarsus Paul had been trained to write and speak Greek well. The quality of his secular education has often been underestimated, even though it shows in the rhetorical skill with which he presents his arguments. The first letters he wrote in the exercise of his pastoral responsibilities were to the Thessalonians, and one at least was written from Corinth shortly after he had settled there.

Paul's founding visit to Corinth lasted eighteen months. His departure can be roughly dated by his encounter with the proconsul Gallio in the late summer of AD 51 (Acts 18:12). On his way to Jerusalem Paul stopped at Ephesus, which was to become his second missionary centre. If the churches he had founded in Galatia, Macedonia, and Achaia are thought of as on the periphery of a circle, the capital of Asia was in virtually the exact centre. Clearly he planned to keep in touch with his converts.

After the conference in Jerusalem on the necessity of circumcision for pagan converts, from which Paul emerged victorious (Gal. 2:1–10), and a short period in Antioch when he severed his relationship with that church which had first commissioned him (Gal. 2:11–14), Paul returned to Ephesus in mid to late summer AD 52. He stayed there for two years and three months (Acts 19:8–10), during which he probably wrote letters to Galatia, Philippi, Colossae, Philemon, and Corinth.

FIRST CORINTHIANS

The document that we know as First Corinthians was not in fact Paul's first letter to Corinth. In 1 Cor. 5:9 he mentions a previous letter, which has been lost. It was probably written in response to news about Corinth brought by Apollos when he joined Paul in Ephesus (1 Cor. 16:12), and reflects Paul's concern for the quality of community life. Those whose behaviour reflected the egocentricity of society should be ostracized.

The circumstances surrounding the writing of 1 Corinthians are much more complex, and go a long way to explaining the number of subjects dealt with in what is easily the most dialogical of all Paul's letters. He first got word of problems at Corinth from Chloe's people (1 Cor. 1:11). She had business connections in both Corinth and Ephesus, and her base could have been in either. It is more likely, however, that her people were visitors to Corinth, because they report things that were not problems for the Corinthians. Some of these were so outrageous that Paul could not believe his ears. There must have been some mistake. Just in case, however, he sent his closest collaborator Timothy to check (1 Cor. 4:17). While Timothy was on his way, a delegation from Corinth arrived in Ephesus (1 Cor. 16:17) bearing a letter from the church, in which certain issues were proposed to Paul for his consideration. The delegation could answer all the questions arising out of the report of Chloe's people. Without waiting for Timothy's return – notice his absence in 1 Cor. 1:1 – Paul immediately composed a letter which the delegation took with them on their return.

Paul had three sources of information regarding the situation at Corinth – Chloe's people, the delegation, and the letter. Together these revealed two sets of problems, to which Paul responds in different ways. What the Corinthians saw as problems he discusses calmly and rationally. But in the way he deals with what they failed to see as problems one can detect a latent anger at the blindness of those who flattered themselves on their intelligence. An exasperated 'Do you not know?' occurs again and again.

Divisions within the community (chs. 1–4)

For Paul society was characterized above all by divisions. Even within the great hostile groupings – Jew and Gentile, master and slave, men and women – individuals cut themselves off from their fellows by barriers of fear and suspicion (see, e.g., Rom. 1:29–31). Because of their isolation individuals easily fell victim to Sin, Law, and Death. They unthinkingly accepted the value system of society (Sin), which for Jews meant blind obedience to the commandments of Moses (Law). In both cases the result was a selfish, inward-looking existence (Death).

Not surprisingly the dominant characteristic of the church for Paul had to be unity. It had to be the antithesis of society (Gal. 3:28) if it was to be an instrument of salvation. He was profoundly shocked at the Corinthians' failure to grasp this fundamental truth. They might have given lip service to the ideal, but in practice they were not disturbed by jealousy, strife, and party factions within their ranks (1:12; 3:1–4).

Understandably, therefore, Paul deals first with this crucial issue. The Corinthians had to understand what the church was. He points out that he and Apollos are collaborators, not competitors (3:5–9). Authentic proclamation is not a matter of verbal skill but a demonstration of the power of the Spirit (2:1–5). He evokes the composition of the community as evidence that God's ways are not our ways. If God acted by the standards of the world he would never have chosen the weak to shame the strong (1:18–31). Thus the Corinthians should have realized for themselves that the church is a different sort of grouping from any in society.

Paul's technique in two parts of this opening section, namely, 2:6–3:4 and 4:8–10, is to subvert the terminology of those whom he believes to be at the root of the trouble in the community. The religious perspective betrayed by this terminology is that of Philo (the Alexandrian Jewish philosopher, a recent contemporary), and strongly suggests that Paul has in mind the followers of Apollos, a converted Jew from Alexandria (Acts 18:24–8). For convenience we shall call them the Spirit-people. They must have been deeply wounded by an attack that held them up to ridicule.

The importance of the body (chs. 5–6)

The Spirit-people attached so much importance to mind, wisdom, and spirit that they tended to undervalue the importance of the physical body in religious life. For Paul, however, the body was the sphere in which the following of Christ became real. Moreover, one's behaviour was a public statement, and thus had missionary potential as witness.

Different facets of this approach appear in the three issues that Paul takes up in this section. Both his tone and the way the cases are introduced betray the fact that none of them were problems as far as the Corinthians were concerned!

The Corinthians prided themselves on having an incestuous couple in the church (ch. 5). Why? Paul had demanded that they be different and incest was condemned by both Jews and Gentiles. Paul's fury at such childishness is barely restrained. If the church is to witness to society it must purify itself by withdrawing from all contact with the offender.

Paul condemns the Corinthian practice of going to pagan courts (6:1–11) because he saw it as a lost missionary opportunity. It was not an attempt to hide dirty linen. If Christians were seen to solve problems without recourse to lawyers, it would be a living demonstration of the power of the gospel.

The third case (6:12–20) can be written out as a dialogue because Paul cites the arguments used by some Corinthians to justify sex with prositi-tutes (verses 12a, 13ab, 18b). In essence they denigrate the body; it is morally irrelevant. Paul retorts that since the body is to be resurrected it must be important in God's eyes. Thus certain actions are inappropriate. In the present instance sex with a prostitute must be excluded because no commitment to the other is involved, whereas in the divine plan as revealed in Gen. 2:24 copulation implies a permanent union.

Problems of social status (ch. 7)

One of the problems raised in the letter from Corinth was whether married couples should have sex (verse 1). Apparently some at Corinth were advocating that they should live celibate lives because that was spiritually better (verses 1–9). With this request Paul associates other cases involving a similar type of change in social status, namely, married to single (verses 10–16), slave to free (verses 17–24), and single to married (verses 25–40).

Paul applies a very coherent set of principles to the solution of these problems. (1) God's call comes to people in all walks of life. Hence one's social status is essentially irrelevant. In particular, celibacy is not intrinsically better than marriage (verse 7). Thus in itself no social change will raise one in God's estimation. (2) A change of status may be initiated in order to compensate for human weakness. The 'virgins' in verses 25–40 are those who in one way or another are committed (implied by the mention of 'sin' in verse 36) to celibacy, which is Paul's preference (verse 7). Yet, if they find that they have overestimated their strength, they should marry (verse 36). (3) A forced change of status should be accepted. A spouse has no control over the decision of a partner who desires a divorce (verse 15), and slaves cannot dictate the decision of their masters (verse 21).

Problems arising from the pagan environment (chs. 8–10)

The Corinthians also consulted Paul on the legitimacy of eating meat which had been offered in pagan sacrifices (8:1). Cheap meat became available on great feasts when priests, who received a portion of the sacrifice, had to sell their surplus before it rotted. Some at Corinth saw nothing wrong in buying such meat for consumption at home. They also felt free to participate in banquets held in pagan temples where such meat would certainly be served.

The reasoning of these Christians was very simple. There was but one God. Idols were only inanimate statues. What was offered to them was not changed in any way. It remained just ordinary meat (8:4).

Paul could not disagree with this reasoning, but he took issue with the underlying theistic and individualistic approach. Christians belonged to a community in which the strong had a responsibility for the weak. The latter were recent converts who had not fully relinquished life-long emotional ties to paganism. They felt that they would be dragged down if they touched sacrificial meat. Out of love the strong should recognize such weakness, and not cause pain by their behaviour. The true test of morality was not a theological argument for the legitimacy of a course of action, but the impact of that action on others in the community. Would it edify or destroy them? Theory must be put into practice with extreme delicacy.

Paul merely invites the strong to consider what he says. He does not impose a solution on them. On the contrary, he tells them what he would do. He would sacrifice something to which he had a right in order not to make life difficult for others (8:13). Paul expands this point in ch. 9. Like other apostles he has a right to financial support. But he forgoes any claim on his communities because he is convinced that to preach the gospel free of charge is more effective. If he is not doing it for money, he must be doing it out of sheer conviction of its truth.

In order to break down the sense of security that the strong derived from the strength of their conviction Paul reminds them of the experiences of Israel during the exodus (10:1–13). What had happened to the Israelites, the chosen of God, could happen to the strong. Anyone can make a mistake, particularly through over confidence.

Finally, Paul reminds the strong that, like sex (6:12–20), the physical act of eating and drinking has an objective significance apart from their intention (10:14–22). If the sharing in the Eucharistic bread and wine creates a union with Christ, then, whatever the strong think, participation in pagan rites creates a union with the 'demon', who is the power of the idol. The strong become partners with demons by inducing the weak to act against their consciences (8:7–11) and thereby destroy them.

The weak, for their part, should not go looking for trouble (10:23–30). Unless they were absolutely sure that meat had been offered to idols, they should buy it, and eat it when it was offered, without question. Moreover, the weak should not gratuitously assume that the strong were acting against their consciences when they ate idol meat.

Paul's concern for both weak and strong should be the model of their behaviour because it was the way Christ acted towards the good and sinners to bring them to salvation (10:31–11:1).

Problems arising in the liturgical assembly (chs. 11–14)

From problems arising out of the position of the church in the middle of a pagan city, Paul now moves closer to home and considers a series of problems that have arisen within the community. Only the third, concerning spiritual gifts (chs. 12–14), was raised by the Corinthians. The other two were brought to Paul's attention probably by Chloe's people, who were scandalized by what they saw when they attended the liturgical assembly at Corinth.

The first thing that struck the visitors from Ephesus was the appearance of those who exercised leadership roles in prayer and prophecy (11:2–16). The man had long hair and the woman did not have hers done in the conventional way. In Paul's world long hair on a man was the overt signal that the man was a homosexual. 'Long hair is not fit for men but for voluptuous women' (*Pseudo-Phocylides* 211). Long hair was natural to a woman and unruly hair was not a sign of deviant sexuality. Paul, however, assimilates the two by saying that, if the woman is prepared to be unfeminine, she should go the whole way and look mannish by shearing or shortening her hair as lesbians did. 'A woman with her hair closely clipped in the Spartan manner, boyish-looking and wholly masculine' (Lucian, *Fugitives* 27). The point at issue is the blurring of the distinction between the sexes. Barrett notes perceptively that 'it does seem probable that horror of homosexuality is behind a good deal of Paul's argument in this paragraph'[2].

Once again (cf. 5:1–5) the Corinthians had given one of Paul's statements the most absurd meaning possible. In declaring that the divisions of society were abolished in the church, he had mentioned men and women (Gal. 3:28). The Corinthians took this to mean that the distinction between the sexes was no longer relevant.

To counter this absurdity Paul turns first to Gen. 2:18–23, where God is shown creating man and woman in different ways. This meant that the distinction between male and female was important in the eyes of God. In consequence, a man should look like a man, and a woman like a woman. This is all he draws from Genesis (11:7–10). This text, however, had been used by Jews to prove the inferiority of women. In a brief parenthesis (11:11–12) Paul flatly excludes this interpretation. In the Pauline churches women were fully the equal of men. Secondly, he argues from 'nature' (11:14–15). He is referring in fact to the first-century convention regarding male and female hairlengths. 'In Greece . . . it is usual for men to have their hair cut short and for women to let it grow' (Plutarch, *Roman Questions* 267B).

This interpretation of 11:2–16 is argued in detail in my two articles 'Sex and Logic in 1 Corinthians 11:2–16' and '1 Corinthians 11:2–16 Once Again'.[3] It is not, however, widely accepted. For the majority the references to men are purely hypothetical and serve merely as the backdrop to the censure of (some) women for failing to cover their heads at worship. Loose flowing hair on a woman in public was considered unseemly.[4]

The second problem that scandalized Chloe's people was the treatment of the poor at the Eucharist (11:17–34). They were effectively left to starve, while the rich gorged themselves. This unfortunate state of affairs arose because Christians met in private houses, in which the dining room was not big enough to accommodate everyone.[5] Inevitably the host would make sure that believers of his rank would get there early to have good places in the warmth, and food and drink to entertain them. When those who were not masters of their own time arrived, they were allotted places in the draughty courtyard.

For Paul such discrimination meant that the Eucharist was not really celebrated at Corinth because the sharing was only nominal (11:20). In the intention of Jesus at the last supper the sharing of bread and wine was meant to focus the daily sharing in love which was the message of the death of Jesus, who died for us (11:26). Those who attempted to celebrate the Eucharist without actually loving their fellows were no better than the soldiers who murdered Jesus (cf. Heb. 6:6). Thus the celebration of the Eucharist should be preceded by a self-examination in which each tests his relationship to the body which is the church (11:28–9).

Finally, after dealing with problems that the Corinthians had not even noticed, Paul turns to the question of spiritual gifts (chs. 12–14). It would appear that the Corinthians overestimated the gift of glossolalia (speaking in tongues). They interpreted such unintelligible speech as the sign that the Holy Spirit had taken over the mind of the speaker. In consequence, the gift of glossolalia conferred higher social standing, which, of course, is why it was estimated so highly.

Paul did not share this view. He was quite prepared to believe that individuals were inspired by the Holy Spirit. Some, however, when they tried to express the revelation they had received, could not find the words to do so. To those around them they produced only inchoate speech, meaningless babbling. Paul directed such people to be calm and slow down until they could put their insights into clear words (14:5). Only then would their gift benefit the community.

All gifts were for the sake of the community, not to raise the stature of the beneficiaries. Everybody had something to contribute. Some gifts might appear banal, like administrative ability, but a variety of gifts were necessary. A human body could not just be an eye or a mouth. The big toe is also indispensable. Here Paul develops his understanding of the church as the body of Christ (12:12–31). By this he means that the church is the physical presence of Christ in the world. Christ continues to act in history in and through his church. This church, moreover, is different from all other human groupings. They are functional communities united only in their carefully governed actions to achieve a common goal. The church, in contrast, is a community of being. Its members do not simply cooperate, but share a common existence. They are related to one another like the limbs of a body. The arm is not the leg. They look different and they have different roles. But they belong to the same body. If one or the other is severed from the body, it is no longer an arm or a leg, although it may look like it for a while.

Love is the greatest of all the gifts because it is totally dedicated to the good of the other (ch. 13). It is what makes Christians Christlike. Paul singles out one expression of love for special mention, the gift of prophecy (14:1–25). It is *par excellence* a gift of leadership. It is the gift which most builds up, directs, and sustains the community (14:3). Nonetheless,

Spirit-filled assemblies could be rather chaotic, not least if one believer interrupted another claiming a new revelation. Paul insists that they do not pretend to lose control, that the number of speakers be limited, and that 'the others' should evaluate any prophetic utterance (14:29–32). Common sense remains an invaluable criterion!

In all probability Paul did not write 14:34–5 (though the point is disputed). Not only does it contradict 11:5, but the appeal to the law (possibly Gen. 3:16) is completely unpauline. The injunctions reflect the misogyny of 1 Tim. 2:11–14, and stem from the same patriarchal, postpauline circles which could not accept the full equality of women which Paul espoused (11:11).

The resurrection (ch. 15)

Some at Corinth denied the resurrection (verse 12). These were those who denigrated the body. For them it could not be part of heavenly beatitude. Resurrection is the fundamental truth of the faith, and at least as important as the unity of the community. Why then does Paul leave it to last? Because he was a well-trained orator who knew that the most important points should be dealt with at the beginning and end of a speech. Everyone perks up and pays attention when a speaker says, 'Finally' or 'In conclusion'.

Paul begins by reminding the Corinthians of the precise words in which they had confessed their belief in the resurrection of Jesus (verses 3–5). If they now doubt, they can check its truth by interrogating those who had experienced the crucified Jesus as alive. Paul does not mention the empty tomb because bodies in Jerusalem graves disintegrate in about two months.

His next step is to confront two different theses and to examine their consequences. If the Corinthians are correct that there is no such thing as resurrection (verses 12–19), then Jesus has not been raised, and nothing has been changed. There are no gifts of the Spirit of which they were so proud. If, on the contrary, Paul is right (verses 20–8), then what happened to Christ can happen to all believers. Death is not the end. Christ's power continues to be active in the world until complete transformation signals the completion of his mission.

There is no logic in this. Rather we are faced with the passion of the prophet. But it is not a spurious, theatrical effect. If Paul puts himself at risk every day by preaching the resurrection, it must be because he is utterly convinced of its truth (verses 26–34).

Paul's imaginary interlocutor now changes tack and focuses on the resurrection body (verses 35–49), saying, in effect, 'Let us suppose that the dead are raised. Then they must have bodies. But we cannot have the faintest idea of what such bodies would be like. Hence it is pointless to continue the discussion.' Paul's reply is the essence of common sense. From the seed we could never imagine the tree. Yet they are the same being. One body simply gives way to another. Moreover, we use the word 'body' in a number of different senses. Thus we can at least say what the resurrection body is not. It will lack all the disadvantages of our present bodies. On the positive side, we can say that it will resemble the glorified body of the risen Christ.

Paul fully expected to be alive at the general resurrection (verses 51–8). He and others with him would not have to die, but they would have to be transformed in order to exist in a completely different world.

Conclusion (ch. 16)

Paul concludes the letter with a series of housekeeping issues. He begins with directives as to how money should be collected for the poor of Jerusalem (cf. Gal. 2:10). Clearly each believer at Corinth was capable of making a contribution. Equally for the majority spare cash was limited. If the sum was to do honour to the church it would have to be accumulated gradually.

Paul then outlines his travel plans (verses 5–9), and in the process reveals that he was writing from Ephesus sometime before Pentecost. Other considerations fix the year at AD 54, when Pentecost fell on 2 June. Circumstances beyond his control forced Paul to change these travel plans not once but twice. His adversaries twisted this into an accusation of inconsistency, which Paul has to answer in Second Corinthians.

Paul's affection for Timothy shines through his angry concern that he be received properly at Corinth (cf. 4:17). By insisting that Apollos did not wish to return to Corinth Paul protects himself from the accusation that he prevented him (verses 10–12).

In his gracious compliments to the members of the delegation from Corinth (verses 15–18) Paul unconsciously reveals his concept of authority. He never appointed anyone to a leadership role. He expected leaders to emerge from the community on the basis of their gifts, and then to be recognized by the community (1 Thess. 5:12–13). Spiritual gifts were attested by performance.

Since letters to the same community might be written by different secretaries (cf. Rom. 16:22), Paul was obliged to write one or two sentences in his own hand to authenticate the letter (verses 21–4).

SECOND CORINTHIANS

The unity of 1 Corinthians has never been convincingly questioned. There is wide agreement, however, that 2 Corinthians 1–9 and 2 Corinthians 10–13 cannot have belonged to the same letter. It is psychologically impossible that Paul should suddenly switch from warm, generous celebration of reconciliation with the Corinthians (chs. 1–9) to savage reproach and sarcastic self-vindication (chs. 10–13). The two parts must have been joined when the letters were passed to other communities. For convenience we shall call chs. 1–9 Letter A, and chs. 10–13 Letter B.

Some who accept the division of 2 Corinthians into two letters claim that Letter B was written before Letter A because its severe tone suggests that it should be identified with the now-lost Sorrowful Letter, which is mentioned in 2:4 and 7:8. Close examination, however, shows that the subject matter of the Sorrowful Letter has nothing in common with that of Letter B. As we shall see, it is much more likely that Letter A was written before Letter B. The former was written from Macedonia in the spring of AD 55, while the latter was composed sometime later than summer.

Another controverted issue in the study of 2 Corinthians is the identity of Paul's opponents. Some have argued that they were Palestinian Christians of Jewish origin who insisted that Gentile believers should observe the law of Moses. Others disagree, claiming that they were Hellenistic-Jewish wandering preachers who put a premium on eloquence, ecstatic experiences and the power to work miracles. To opt for one or the other is to ignore important evidence. The truth is a combination of the two.[6]

The Spirit-people at Corinth were alienated by Paul's treatment of them in 1 Cor. 2:6–3:4 and 4:8–10. They prized eloquence and ostentatious religious authority in a leader, and Paul failed on both counts. They gave hospitality to Judaizers from Antioch who were opposed to Paul's law-free mission. The two groups had little in common, apart from hostility to Paul, and had to make concessions to each other. To a limited practical extent the incoming Judaizers were 'Corinthianized' and the local Spirit-people 'Judaized'.

Letter A (chs. 1–9)

After the dispatch of 1 Corinthians Paul's plan for the following summer was a visit to his foundations in Macedonia with a view to arriving at Corinth before the onset of winter (1 Cor. 16:5–6). Timothy's return from Corinth put paid to this project. He brought the bad news that Paul's Judaizing enemies from Antioch had arrived in Corinth. This was a problem that had to be dealt with personally. Paul immediately took ship for Corinth.

There he was insulted by the leader of the Judaizers, and Paul's Corinthian converts did not take his side.[7] They punished him for his treatment of the Spirit-people in 1 Corinthians by remaining chillingly neutral. Paul's anger so inflamed the atmosphere that even he realized that to prolong his stay would be counter-productive. He set out for his aborted visit to Macedonia promising to return to Corinth.

In Macedonia he decided that a letter would be more effective than a return visit. This was the lost Sorrowful Letter (2:4), which he entrusted to Titus to take to Corinth. While he waited with great anxiety to hear about the effect of the letter, Paul moved from Ephesus, first to Troas (2:12), and then to Macedonia, where Titus finally rejoined him, bringing the good news that the Corinthians had repented of their treatment of Paul (7:5–6).

Ostensibly Letter A was written to celebrate this reconciliation, but Paul also had to answer the criticisms of him circulating in Corinth which Titus reported. The result is a much more sophisticated and subtly effective letter than 1 Corinthians.

Chopping and changing (1:12–2:13)

After trying to generate sympathy for himself among the Corinthians by evoking a life-threatening experience in Ephesus (cf. Phil. 1:19–26), Paul asserts that his change of travel plans was not made arbitrarily. His integrity is that of Christ, who had 'christed' him (1:21).

He explains the origins of the Sorrowful Letter (2:1ff.), and reveals his generous heart by asking the Corinthians to cease punishing the one who had offended him. Too much or too long might militate against the desired remedial effect.

Authentic apostleship (2:14–6:10)

Paul's evocation of his successful ministry at Troas (2:12), which he sacrificed out of love for the Corinthians, leads him into a consideration of the true nature of authentic Christian ministry. His presentation is rather disconcerting. He will touch on one point, drift almost imperceptibly to another, slide off to a third, and then circle back disconcertingly.

This is not because Paul is incompetent, either as a thinker or a writer. His treatment of the resurrection in 1 Corinthians 15 reveals his ability to marshal an argument in which all the parts dovetail smoothly with each other. If he here adopts a different tactic, it must be because he has a more complex agenda. In fact, it would appear that he is trying to do three things: (1) to reply to objections to his leadership style by outlining the nature of authentic ministry; (2) to drive a wedge between the Spirit-people and the Judaizers from Antioch; and (3) to win back the Spirit-people by presenting the gospel in terms they will appreciate.

As channels of grace preachers carry an awesome burden of responsibility (cf. 1 Cor. 1:17). Their strength, in consequence, must be God-given. It is he who makes them ministers of a new covenant of the Spirit (3:6).

Those who strive to interpret the new covenant in terms of the letter of the law corrupt the gospel. In order to drive this point home, Paul compares the time of the law and the time of the gospel (3:7–4:6). The most fundamental contrast is between Moses, who dissimulated (3:13), and Paul, who speaks with confident openness. The Spirit-people, of course, would wish to identify with the latter attitude, and Paul reinforces this desire by characterizing his gospel in terms of Spirit and freedom (3:17). He distances them from the Judaizers by transferring the veil of Moses to his law; it is associated with blindness (3:15).

Both the Spirit-people and the Judaizers failed to recognize the essential role played in salvation by Christ, the former by elevating him to the Lord of glory in a way which divorced him from the crucified Jesus (1 Cor. 2:8), and the latter by insisting on the works of the law rather than the following of Christ. In reaction Paul insists that authentic illumination – a concept designed to appear to the Spirit-people – was given only by a gospel that focuses on the glory of God *in the face of Christ* (4:1–6). He is the revelation of the Father. In him the pristine clarity of humanity as the image of God (Gen. 1:26–7) is restored.

The Spirit-people wanted a leader in whose power and presence they could take pride. For Paul the basic responsibility of a minister was to be another Christ (1 Cor. 11:1). Jesus' life, however, was characterized by humiliation and suffering. He lived with the spectre of death hanging over him. Thus it is those who reflect the dying of Jesus in their comportment who manifest the authentic humanity of Jesus (4:7–12; cf. Gal. 2:20). The secure, the safe, the honoured, the merely verbal cannot *be* who Jesus was. The supreme paradox is that only the dying can bring forth life.

As wounds, blows, illness, and fatigue visibly wore Paul down, his faith, hope, and love steadily increased (4:16). He could anticipate a reward that far outweighed his present sufferings. He did not fear death. It was no more than a passage from the transitory realities of this world to the enduring security of the heavenly world (5:1–10). The confusing mix of building and clothing metaphors in this passage reflects different strands of Jewish tradition regarding life after death (cf. 1 Enoch 39:3–4 and 62:15–16). Paul does not take it for granted that beatitude is the normal end of life. 'Naked' connotes punishable guilt (cf. Isa. 47:3), and all have to appear before the judgment seat of Christ, where they will be judged on what has been done in and through the body (cf. 1 Cor. 5–6).

The thought of the final judgment brings Paul back to the false criteria that the Spirit-people employ in judging him (5:11–6:10). They stressed things that are seen (4:18), and looked for ecstatic visions and revelations. As ever for Paul, the true criterion is Christ. The total dedication of Christ to the well-being of others is the decisive influence on Paul's life and the model he strives to imitate. Such altruism highlights the selfishness that is the norm of fallen existence. His 'life' identifies our selfish being as 'death' (5:14).

As a Pharisee Paul believed Jesus to be a false teacher who had led Jews astray (Gal. 1:13; Phil. 3:5). Now he knows this to have been a fleshly assessment. Because of his understanding of the authentic humanity of Christ he now looks at all human beings in a different way (5:16). He judges them by the entirely new criteria given in the self-sacrificing love of Christ. Christ overcame the power of Sin by accepting its consequences (5:21). By accepting the same way of life (6:3–10) Paul prolongs the reconciling mission of Christ both verbally and existentially (6:1).

Paul's relations with Corinth (6:11–7:16)

Having dealt with the theology of reconciliation, Paul now turns to the practicalities of his reconciliation with the Corinthians after the blow-up that led to the Sorrowful Letter (2:4). In language chosen for its Philonic connotations he appeals to the Spirit-people to open their hearts to him (6:11–7:4). In a very childish way they have tried to be followers of Christ while continuing to live by the conventions of society. This led them to misjudge Paul.

Since a letter can be read in different ways Paul had been in a fever of anxiety as to how the Sorrowful Letter would be received (7:5–16). Would it intensify opposition to him at Corinth, or would it win them to his side? When he finally met up with Titus, he learned that the Corinthians had repented. Paul was delighted that they had recognized their guilt. But he could easily undo the good achieved by appearing to take pleasure in their grief. With the prolixity born of embarrassment he launches into a dissertation on 'worldly' and 'godly' grief. The Corinthians experienced the latter. Paul's sense of relief is so great that in verse 14 he forgets what his real attitude had been six months earlier when he wrote the Sorrowful Letter (2:4, 13; 7:5). He feels that he can trust them completely.

The collection for the poor of Jerusalem (chs. 8–9)

In the serene confidence that all was well at Corinth Paul concludes Letter A by reminding believers there of the commitment that they had made a year previously to contribute to the collection for the poor of Jerusalem (1 Cor. 16:1–4).

A large portion of the population of Jerusalem lived principally or exclusively on organized relief or individual alms. As the church drifted away from the synagogue, Jewish channels of relief began to dry up, and the church had to provide for its own (Acts 2:45; 4:34–5). Eventually an appeal was made to the Christian diaspora, which Paul took very much to heart (Gal. 2:10).

It would be self-defeating for Paul to order the Corinthians to be generous (8:8; 9:7). He challenges them by evoking the generosity of the Macedonian churches of Philippi and Thessalonica (8:1–15), and applies not so subtle moral blackmail by raising the spectre of Macedonian mockery if they are not prepared when the northerners come with Paul to Corinth (9:4). To ensure that this will not happen he advises the Corinthians that Titus and two others will assist in the organization of the collection (8:16–9:5). In the last analysis, however, Paul stops trying to manipulate the Corinthians, and concludes with a powerful, theologically motivated appeal for generosity (9:6–15).

Letter B (chs. 10–13)

After Letter A had been sent with Titus in the spring of AD 55, Paul found himself in Macedonia without any problems to deal with. It was a glorious opportunity to become an apostle again. He had not personally founded a new church since Corinth five years earlier. Where was he to go? In all probability he accepted the invitation to the west of the great Roman road, the Via Egnatia. If he had gone all the way he would have ended up in Illyricum (Rom. 15:19).

How much Paul had invested in his plans for the summer of AD 55 can be gauged from the depth of his frustration when news from Corinth forced him to change them. Letter A had succeeded in saving the Spirit-people from the Judaizers. Isolated, the latter intensified their criticisms of Paul. His preaching was uninspired and his presence unimpressive (10:10). He had fled Corinth when challenged by the Judaizers and did not dare to return (2:1). His attitude towards money was highly suspicious (11:7–10; 12:16).

Paul could only take such sniping as a malicious distortion of his motives and actions. Cursed by a personality oversensitive to slights, he explodes in a wild outburst of sarcasm and irony. His self-imposed barriers to the use of rhetoric in ministry (1 Cor. 2:1–5) crumble, revealing the extraordinary quality of his pagan education. His casual mastery of the conventions is manifest in his ability to turn them upside down.

The Fool's Speech (11:1–12:13)

This is particularly evident in the body of this letter, the Fool's Speech. Paul had been forced into a corner and, although he knew it to be foolishness, he had to show that he could beat his opponents at their own game. The rules for a normal speech in self-defence demanded a list of one's achievements moving from the lesser to the greater. The Judaizers had stressed their Jewishness, their achievements, and their visions and revelations.

Paul responds with a perfect parody of this technique. After underlining that he is probably even more Jewish than they because he speaks Aramaic (11:22), he compiles a catalogue of his sufferings, and failures, culminating in his unheroic escape from Damascus like a baby in a basket (11:23–33). As regards his visions and revelations, they did not change him in any way or provide him with information which he could use (12:1–6).

While others boast of their strengths, Paul will boast only of his weaknesses. He singles out one weakness as his 'thorn in the flesh' (12:7). Usually interpreted to mean a psychological or physical illness, this is more likely to be a reference to opposition to Paul within his own foundations (cf. Num. 33:55; Ezek. 28:24). He could never sit back and complacently contemplate a perfect community. This kept him humble. It also made him conscious that it was his weakness that made grace visible (12:9). He lacks everything that in the eyes of the world would make his mission feasible. Yet he has achieved the extraordinary: believing communities exist. All must *see* that Paul is merely the channel of divine power (4:7).

If Paul was merely the mediator of God's power, then the whole question of miracles was irrelevant (12:11–13). His opponents at Corinth had made the ability to work miracles a criterion of authentic religious leadership. With biting irony Paul points out that the purpose of miracles was not to enhance his stature, but to benefit the community. The one true miracle that he wanted to emphasize was the transformation of individuals into other Christs, willing to sacrifice everything in love.

A warning prepares a visit (12:14–13:13)

Paul knew that he would have to go to Corinth to deal with the situation. The Sorrowful Letter (2:4) had successfully been substituted for a visit – or so he thought at the time. Now he knows he should have seen for himself. Letter B was just a stop-gap to give himself time to disengage himself gently from his new converts in Illyricum. Obviously the reception accorded the letter would have an impact on the way Paul would be received at Corinth. Thus he brings the issue out into the open.

He begins by defending himself against the accusation that his refusal to be subsidized by the Corinthians while he lived among them was a sign that he did not love them (12:14–18). Perhaps he was dipping into the collection money. Paul's real reason for refusing was that he did not want his freedom limited by becoming a client of a particular patron or patrons, but he presents it as a gesture of love. The Corinthians should love him in return. Paul's policy, which he should have explained, was to accept financial support only from churches in which he was not living (11:9; Phil. 4:10–20), because individual gifts would be lost in the total sum.

The willingness of the Corinthians to believe the worst of Paul, even though he had taken public precautions to keep everything above board (8:20; 1 Cor. 16:1–4), triggers the memory of other faults (12:19–13:10). The selfish attitudes of many in the community reflect the values of society (12:20; 1 Cor. 3:3). This had better change before he arrives. In 13:2 Paul draws the attention of his readers to the fact that this is the second formal admonition that they have received; the first was given on his second visit (2:1). Thus in terms of the Palestinian interpretation of Deut. 19:15, which is evoked in 13:1, he is free to inflict punishment when he arrives if they have not changed.

But what could Paul actually do? He could not coerce them into goodness (9:7; Phlm. 14). The only course open to him, and he shudders at the thought (13:10), would be to declare that the quality of the lives of the Corinthians did not conform to the gospel, and that they were not in reality Christians. The church at Corinth would cease to exist, and five years of intense love and care would have been wasted.

In fact Paul need not have worried. The fact that the Corinthians subscribed to the collection indicates that he was well received (Rom. 15:26). During the winter of AD 55–6 he wrote Romans in Corinth.

Notes

1 J. Murphy O'Connor, *St Paul's Corinth: Texts and Archaeology* (Collegeville: Liturgical Press, 1992).
2 C. K. Barrett, *1 Corinthians*, BNTC (London: A. & C. Black, 1968) 257.
3 'Sex and Logic in 1 Corinthians 11:2–16', *CBQ* 42 (1980) 482–500; '1 Corinthians 11:2–16 Once Again', *CBQ* 50 (1988) 265–74.
4 G. D. Fee, *1 Corinthians*, NICNT (Grand Rapids: Eerdmans, 1987) 505, 509.
5 For the plan of a typical house, see my *St Paul's Corinth* 162.
6 See in particular C. K. Barrett, *2 Corinthians*, BNTC (London: A. & C. Black, 1973) 28–30.
7 Ibid., 212–13.

6   Romans

ROBERT JEWETT

The longest and most influential of Paul's letters has a complex textual history, with fourteen families of texts featuring varied arrangements of the final chapters. While many earlier scholars tended to view chapter 16 as not originally intended for Rome, recent studies have demonstrated that the original version of the letter contained the material of all sixteen chapters. It is likely, but far from generally accepted, that 16:17–20 and 16:25–57 are interpolations reflecting later interpretations of the letter.

Romans is carefully organized, with an introduction in 1:1–15, a thesis statement in 1:16–17, four proofs (1:18–4:25; 5:1–8:39; 9:1–11:36; and 12:1–15:13), and an elaborate conclusion in 15:14–16:24. From the perspective of classical rhetoric, Romans is an 'ambassadorial' message in the demonstrative genre that seeks to encourage a particular ethos in the audience so they will support a project that Paul has in mind. The introduction and conclusion indicate that the primary purpose of the original letter was to elicit support for Paul's mission to Spain, mentioned in 15:24, 28. Since there was no significant Jewish population in Spain at this time, which eliminated the possibility of starting a mission in the usual manner in a Jewish synagogue, advance preparations were required. A significant series of linguistic barriers needed to be crossed, translating Old Testament and early Christian materials into Latin and then into the Celt-Iberian dialects still employed by most of the population in Spain. Paul needed the assistance of the Christians in Rome in making such preparations, and since he had not founded that church, he had to introduce himself and his gospel in order to persuade the Romans to cooperate in this daunting project.

Romans was sent in the spring of CE 57 with Phoebe, the leader of a church near Corinth and a wealthy patron who had probably agreed to underwrite the Spanish project (16:1–2). After Paul delivers the Jerusalem offering (15:25–32) in the summer of 57, he intends to sail to Rome and then to travel westward to Spain, which was considered to be the end of the known world. But he was imprisoned in Jerusalem, was detained for two years in a Caesarean prison, and arrived in Rome in chains (Acts 21–8), probably suffering execution in CE 62 before being able to carry out the missionary project that this letter was intended to stimulate.

The situation in the Roman churches has been reconstructed from evidence throughout the letter, and especially from the introduction and conclusion. Chapter 16 reflects Paul's knowledge of five groups of believers with differing leadership patterns and orientations, although in view of the large number of martyrs under Nero seven years later (Tacitus, *Annals* 15.44), there must have been many more groups. From inferences in Paul's greetings to a large number of leaders whom he had met during their exile from Rome after the Edict of Claudius (probably in CE 49), it appears likely that the Christian movement began in Roman synagogues sometime in the decade of the thirties.

After the synagogues were closed during the period of the edict (i.e. CE 49–54), the Christian cells probably moved to houses and tenement spaces, and since many of the orginal Jewish-Christian leaders were now absent, new leaders emerged from Gentile backgrounds. Peter Lampe has shown that the densest groupings of early Christian congregations were in two of the worst slums in Rome, where there was the highest density of tenement buildings. This gives rise to the theory of 'tenement churches' that met in living and workshop spaces in insula ('tenement') buildings, in contrast to a 'house church' such as that in the home of Prisca and Aquila (Rom 16:5). Lampe has also demonstrated the fractured nature of Roman Christianity which lacked a central organization. Conflicts between the 'weak' and the 'strong' apparently had arisen over liturgy and ethics, involving social and ethnic tensions between Gentile and Jewish Christians (Romans 14). By reformulating the gospel to find common ground, Paul seeks to overcome such conflicts, which would jeopardize sponsorship of the Spanish mission.

OPENING (1:1–17)

Paul's care to address various groups in Rome is visible throughout the introduction, which features a composite creed (1:3–4) and a threefold address, to the 'called of Jesus Christ', the 'called to be saints', and 'God's beloved in Rome' (1:6–7). Particularly significant is Paul's sense of missionary obligation expressed in 1:14–15, 'both to Greeks and to barbarians, both to the educated and the uneducated' in Rome. Here Paul reverses the most significant barriers of honour and shame in Graeco-Roman culture, indicating that his mission was particularly aimed at an audience such as the barbarians in Spain, who had repeatedly resisted Roman rule and were viewed, along with other barbarians, as a lethal threat to civilization. These references provide the background for the thesis in 1:16–17, which states that Paul is 'not ashamed of the gospel'.

According to the standards of the culture, he should be ashamed of proclaiming the crucified one as the redeemer of the world, including even the barbarians and the uneducated. The gospel is the 'power of God' because it overcomes the hostile boundaries of honour and shame in offering salvation to 'every one who has faith, to the Jew first and also to the Greek'. Paul cites Hab. 2:4 that 'the righteous shall live by faith', which overturns the superiority claims of those who conform to the law or to the high standards of Graeco-Roman culture. This introduction demonstrates that Romans should be interpreted as a missionary document, not as an abstract, theological treatise. It moves from the missionary diplomacy of this introduction to the hope that with the completion of the mission, 'all the peoples' (15:11) will come to praise God in harmony and with 'one voice' (15:5–6), because their lethal competition that threatens the peace of the world has been overcome by the message of Christ crucified for all.

FIRST PROOF (1:18–4:25)

In the first proof Paul confirms the thesis that God's righteousness is revealed in the gospel of Christ crucified. In order to shatter the superiority claims encouraged by Roman culture, which had infected the 'weak' and the 'strong' in their competition with each other, Paul argues that God's wrath stands against those who 'suppress the truth' by 'worshipping the creature rather than the creator' (1:25). The cross of Christ reveals the unacknowledged tendency to stamp out the truth, to wage war against God, so that humans and institutions can maintain their guise of superior virtue and honour.

All groups are involved in this perverse competition, but most of the details in 1:18–32 reflect traditional critiques of Graeco-Roman religion and culture. Sexual perversions, in particular, are depicted as evidence of God's wrath currently visible (1:26–7). A catalogue of antisocial types of persons whose destructive actions are proof of divine wrath completes this paragraph, shattering any claim of Roman cultural superiority (1:29–32). The depiction of Gentiles who 'do what the law requires' because it is written on their hearts (2:14–15) shows that no superiority claim of Jews against Gentiles can be correct. When Paul lists the boasts of Jews in 2:17–20, he is attempting to articulate the kind of pride and arrogance that was surfacing in the Jewish Christians in Rome, not to make a general case against the Judaism of his day. But he goes on to show that the entire human race is 'under the power of sin' (3:9). The claim that 'Jews as well as Greeks are all under sin' (3:9) is followed by a series of scriptural citations that repeat no fewer than eight times that 'no one' can claim righteous status or performance. In the light of the parameters established in 1:14 and developed in 1:18–32, this undercuts the superiority claims of every system of gaining honour through performance or inherited status. It follows that 'from works of law no flesh will be set right before God' (3:20). It is not just the Jewish law that is in view here, but law as an identity marker for any culture. In the face of the impartial righteousness of God, no human system of competing for glory and honour can stand.

In response to this universal distortion, Christ was 'put forward as a mercy seat' (3:25), replacing the Jewish temple with a new institution of atonement that is open 'through faith' to everyone. To be 'made righteous' in the context of the Christ (3:21) means that humans who have fallen short of the 'glory of God' (3:23) have such glory and honour restored, not as an achievement but as a gift. The threefold reference in Rom. 3:24 to divine 'grace', to the 'gift', and to 'redemption' through Christ makes it plain that no one gains this honourable, righteous status by outperforming others or by privilege of birth or wealth. In contrast to the hyper-competitive environment of the Graeco-Roman world, including its Jewish component, this new status is granted by Christ only to those whose shame is manifest. The issue here is not whether individual forgiveness is available but how the universal deficit in honour is overcome by grace. The word 'justification' is inadequate here, because it implies individual alibis and a primarily forensic context; a translation such as 'make righteous' shows the link with the 'righteousness of God' that Paul has in mind. 'Faith' in this context is a matter of accepting the gospel of Christ crucified, which means that all boasting is excluded (3:27). The mainspring of the Greco-Roman and Jewish systems of honour and shame was removed by Christ. Salvation is by grace alone. Henceforth no group can claim priority in God's sight, because boasting has been exposed as an assault on the oneness of God (3:29–30).

If people are made righteous only through faith, what of the promises made to Abraham that his descendants would inherit the earth? In chapter 4, Abraham is shown to be the ancestor of those 'having faith in the One who makes the ungodly righteous' (4:5). The promise was made to him prior to the gift of the law or to his own circumcision, so he becomes the father of both Jews and Gentiles who emulate his faith (4:9–12). The promise was fulfilled only because of Abraham's faith, not because of his conformity to the law. He believed in the God 'who gives life to the dead and calls that which does not exist into being' (4:17), a citation of confessional material which implies that faith in Christ crucified and resurrected is the way to inherit Abraham's promise (4:23–5).

SECOND PROOF (5:1–8:39)

The second proof elaborates and defends the thesis about righteousness through faith, beginning with the admonition 'let us have peace with God through our Lord Jesus Christ' (5:1), which entails abandoning the boasting that amounts to a declaration of war against God. Henceforth Christians are to 'boast in the hope of the glory of God' (5:2), which implies turning away from efforts to claim superior honours. Instead, they are to boast in their afflictions (5:3) because they know in Christ that they will not be 'put to shame' since God's love 'has been poured into our hearts through the holy spirit given to us' (5:5). No matter what tragedies they experience, they are certain of God's love. The traditional forms of boasting are no longer needed to gain and sustain their honour in the face of a hostile world. Christ's blood that was shed for the undeserving fills that need, and its consoling message is conveyed by the Spirit directly to the vulnerable hearts of believers, who thereby are enabled to live in confident hope no matter how badly they are treated. In Christ, adversity has lost its power to shame. Having previously made themselves into 'enemies' of God through their boasting in its various forms, claiming superiority to others in order to overcome shame for themselves, they are now 'reconciled to God through the death of his son' (5:10).

By revealing the truth about the human condition, and by the power of divine love to fill the otherwise insatiable yearning for honour, the death of Christ makes peace possible, both with God and with the human race. To boast 'in God through our lord Jesus Christ' (5:11) is to abandon all human claims of virtue, status, or superiority. And it definitely does not mean boasting that God is on the side of an ethnic group, as in 2:17 ('boasting in God'), because 3:27–31 has closed that door for ever. God is not the possession of either Jews or Gentiles, weak or strong, barbarian or Greek. To boast 'through our Lord Jesus Christ' is to take up the revolution he inaugurated. His blood (5:9) is the source of the grace in which believers stand (5:2), which eliminates all need for boasting, except to boast in the God whose boundless love was expressed in the crucified one. To participate in this revolutionary stance is the 'reconciliation' that believers have 'now received' (5:11), i.e. 'peace with God' (5:1). But the amazing features of Paul's formulation are the future verbs and the modifying phrases, 'we shall be saved by him from the wrath of God...shall be saved by his life'

(5:9, 11). This seems to eliminate the human factor entirely and lacks the eschatological reservation found in other passages. The last judgment will be as much a matter of pure grace as righteousness itself.

At 5:12–21 Paul shows how Christ's life (5:10) defines the future destiny of believers, just as Adam defined the future of his descendants. Having dissociated performance from future salvation in the preceding paragraph, Paul has to provide a new basis for explaining the effect of Christ. This is the purpose of the Adam/Christ comparison; not to develop a 'doctrine' of original sin but to show how the new 'reign' of grace and righteousness extends its influence over 'all people' (5:17, 21). The two realms are antithetical power spheres: the one marked by grace, the free gift, 'rightwising', life, acquittal, obedience, and righteousness; and the other by trespass, judgment, condemnation, death, disobedience, and sin.

This leads to 6:1–14, where Paul describes baptism as participation in Christ's death and resurrection. The syllogism of verses 1–4 shows that grace is not advanced by remaining in sin because baptism marks the death of the sinful self and the beginning of 'newness of life'. The 'obsolete self was crucified' with Christ (6:6) in order to break the reign of sin (6:6, 12–14). To be 'alive to God in Christ Jesus' (6:11) is to be shaped by the reign of grace so that behaviour is no longer determined by conformity to the law and the quest for honour. The mystical relationship between Christ and believers qualifies the entirety of life, removing the members of house and tenement churches from the 'dominion of death' (6:9) enforced by the sinful honour system.

Believers are to allow themselves to be used in the service of Christ, with their bodies dedicated 'to God as instruments of righteousness' (6:13). In contrast to legal compulsion, this is a revolutionary form of enslavement to righteousness (6:15–23) that results in holy behaviour and leads to 'eternal life'. To be 'obedient from the heart' (6:17) is to act in accordance with righteousness because a new motivation has been implanted by grace. Believers are therefore freed from sin (6:18, 22) and from conformity either to law or lawlessness (6:15, 19), not because of their superior virtue or will power but by their involvement in the mystical, all-encompassing realm of holiness inaugurated by Christ (6:18–19). Their salvation remains a matter of receiving the 'free gift of God ... in Christ Jesus our Lord' (6:23).

In Rom. 7:5–8 Paul describes how the 'passions that were sinful because of the law' lead humans to 'death'. Paul goes on to explain how sin invades and corrupts the law. 'I did not know sin except through law. For I was unaware of coveting except that the law said, "You shall not covet." But finding foothold through the commandment, the sin worked in me all covetings' (7:7–8).

When Paul speaks in this passage about actually being 'discharged from the law, having died to that in which we were being held down' (7:6), he is talking about the effect of Christ as he had experienced it. Paul's conversion was directly related to his own conformity to the cultural and religious laws of his tradition. He had acted out of the zealous ideology that gripped a portion of Judaism in the period before the Jewish-Roman War, in which the heroic model of Phinehas in Numbers 25 inspired lynching strategies to eliminate alleged evil-doers. His persecution of the church was in direct proportion to the passion with which he maintained his own conformity to the law. Paul's conversion involved discovering his own hostility to God, for in his zeal for the law, he had ended up opposing the Messiah and his followers; as 7:11 formulates it, 'sin deceived me' by corrupting religion itself.

Paul also discovered the murderous consequences of the law when it was corrupted by the human energy of coveting honour. While he had assumed that righteous violence was ordained by God, he suddenly discovered the dilemma of the frustrated zealot: 'I do not do the good that I want' (7:19), reiterating 7:15b–c, using the language of good and evil. The good that Paul had wished to achieve as a persecutor of the church was to advance the rule of the Torah as a means to usher in the messianic age. He had sought to follow the will of God but discovered through the encounter with the risen Lord that he was in fact opposing the Messiah. What 7:19 describes is not an inability to obey the law as Paul understood it, but rather the failure of zealous obedience to produce the good. The 'sin dwelling in me' (7:23) is a demonic social power deriving from a distorted system of honour and shame that had infected religion as well as the political realm.

In 8:1–17, the nature of the new life in Christ is described in terms of an ongoing tension between the flesh and the spirit, the old law and the new. Under the power of sin and flesh, the law was distorted and became an instrument of gaining honour for oneself and one's group. But in Christ the law regains its proper, spiritual function that leads to genuine life (7:10–14; 8:4). Thus 8:2 refers to the law derived from the 'spirit of life in Christ Jesus', a spiritual law that functions in the domain of Christ, setting believers free from the compulsion to misuse the law as a means of gaining status. Christ 'condemned the sin in the flesh' (8:3), making it possible for believers to fulfil 'the righteous requirement of the law' (8:4). Rather than treating others as means to gain honour, which was the typical style of the old age of the flesh, the community in which divine law is being fulfilled acts out of genuine love.

The agent of this transformation according to 8:3–4 is God, who sent his son to inaugurate a new form of community by his life, death, and guiding Spirit. The 'mind of the flesh' and the 'mind of the spirit' (8:5–9) are antithetical orientations to gaining honour. To gain prestige through performance or by virtue of allegedly superior status is the way of the flesh, shaped by the dominant culture both Graeco-Roman and Jewish. To receive the gift of honour as a result of Christ's dying for the ungodly, without making any claim of merit, is the way of the Spirit that leads to 'peace' (8:6).

As verses 9–11 make clear, the mark of the new community is the Spirit that energizes behaviour in this new direction. Its primary arena of manifestation was social enthusiasm, speaking in tongues, prophecy, and joyous celebration in the context of the common meal that united the formerly shamed from different families and backgrounds into a single family honoured and chosen and hallowed by God. To be led in this new direction is to fulfil the role of sons and daughters of God, living not out of fear that one is unacceptable and must struggle ferociously for honour but in the assurance of the Father's love and acceptance (8:14–16). To be child of God in this new sense is to enjoy a joint inheritance of glory with Christ, sharing the promises of God along with the sufferings that Christ experienced. Although a measure of glorification is currently visible among the saints, in partial and vulnerable forms, those who persist in living according to the Spirit will participate in its fulfilment now and at the end of time. But this is not honour that one has earned and thus can boast about; it comes only as a gift of grace, and only in the context of suffering with Christ.

In 8:18–30 Paul shows that the current suffering of the Roman churches is part of the groaning of creation, yearning for redemption from the burden of sin. The Spirit participates in this vulnerability, interceding for believers (8:26–7) and cooperating with them in the achievement of good (8:28). Paul's wording implies divine and human co-responsibility in the face of adversity, and in the context of this letter, the 'good' to be accomplished by this cooperation includes the daily work and congregational formation in behalf of the Roman house and tenement churches as well as the risky mission to Spain that they are being asked to support. The thrust of the argument is encouraging: despite adversity and the ongoing weakness of the congregation, the Spirit labours alongside believers in such tasks.

The paragraph ends with the startling claim that all such persons whom God made righteous were also 'glorified', using a past-tense verb (8:30). Believers are in the process of being glorified according to the image of Christ, as in 2 Cor. 3:18, made radiant with righteousness. Despite present suffering, their status of being called, rectified, and glorified is already visible. The glory that will yet be revealed in a definitive form in the children of God (8:18–19) will one day overcome the ambiguity of life in a fallen world. But in the work that the Spirit already is accomplishing in Rome, and the work Paul hopes they will contribute to the Spanish mission, this glory has become – and will become – partially visible.

In the final paragraph of the second proof (8:31–9), Paul takes up the question whether anyone is able to impeach believers and thus to disqualify them from participating in the glorious new form of sovereignty over the world. Since God makes them righteous and Christ intercedes for them, Paul puts the vital question in 8:35 whether any person should be able to discredit the status of other groups, on the premise that the elect should be exempt from misfortune. Paul lists seven forms of hardship in this verse, which had been used in the Corinthian crisis to show that he was disqualified from genuine apostolicity. The Corinthian super-apostles had claimed exemption from hardships while arguing that no one whose career was as troubled as Paul's could possibly embody the power of Christ (2 Corinthians 10–13). In Rom. 8:36, Paul cites LXX Ps. 43:23 to prove that the tribulations suffered by believers are for Christ's sake, which makes full sense only if there were voices in Rome that Paul wishes to counter, arguing that sufferings such as those of the Jewish-Christian exiles disqualified them as genuine disciples. Paul contends that if God loves them, no power on earth or heaven can impeach their honour (8:37–9).

THIRD PROOF (9:1–11:36)

The third proof deals with Israel's unbelief and the mystery of divine election. The issue is whether God's promise to Israel has failed (9:6), which in the words of the thesis would imply that the gospel is not 'the power of God for salvation' (1:16). In an extensive midrashic discourse, 9:6–18 cites Gen. 21:12 as the initial text and Gen. 18:10, Gen. 25:23, Mal.1:2–3, Exod. 33:19, and Exod. 9:16 as the supplemental texts. This midrash creates a logical proof of the thesis in 9:6a by developing a distinction between the true Israel and Israel as a whole. Divine selectivity is seen to be at work in the designations of Isaac and Jacob as the recipients of mercy. The objection to the gospel in terms of its alleged allowance of divine 'injustice' implies a curtailing of this divine freedom. Thus the reiteration of God's active 'will' not only stands in contrast to the impotence of human willing (9:16) but also carries forward the logic of 'God's selective purpose' (9:11). When this argumentative thrust is taken into account, it becomes clear that the truly scandalous form of selectivity was that God 'has mercy on whom he wills', namely, on those who did not deserve it. This matter of honour and shame was the nub of the issue, both in Paul's former persecution of the church and in current Jewish repudiations of the gospel. It is also the point repeatedly discussed in this passage, that none of the patriarchs earned the blessing in any way.

In 9:17 Paul applies a widely shared teaching about Pharaoh's hardening in order to make the much more controversial case that God's mercy is sovereign. Paul was convinced that the refusal of this sovereign mercy revealed in the gospel placed his Jewish compatriots in the role of Pharaoh, incredibly reversing their status before God. In 9:19–29 Paul takes up the question that derives from election, namely, whether God can hold anyone accountable for failing to perform. Midrashic citations are employed to show that God remains just and that the potter has a right to mould his clay as he wishes. Citations from Hosea are fused in 9:25–6 to show that the true Israel consists of those now being called from both Jews and Gentiles to participate in the new community of faith. In 9:27 Paul cites an Isaiah text to suggest that the remnant from the 'sons of Israel' are current believers in Christ. The passage ends with an Isaiah quotation showing that the true Israel as the seed of Abraham will pass through judgment and be 'left to us', implying participation through God's mercy in the faith community of Jews and Gentiles embodied in the church.

In 9:30–10:4 Paul discusses the implications of Gentiles gaining righteousness while Israel continued to prefer works over faith. They struck the 'stumbling stone' of Christ because he opposed the religion of works. Paul explains that non-believing Israel demonstrates 'zeal for God but without knowledge', which alludes to the idealization of Phinehas and Elijah as paragons of Jewish zealotism in the kind of Judaism that Paul had favoured prior to his conversion. Zeal refers to the intensity with which believers maintain their allegiance to God and, especially in the period of the Jewish resistance movement, to the Torah. The lack of 'knowledge' refers to a failure to acknowledge the way God's righteousness is embodied in Christ. Paul's fellow Jews were 'seeking to validate their own righteousness'(10:3), implying a competitive stance in which one's 'own' accomplishment is being compared with others. Although this is usually taken in a strictly individualistic manner, it also refers to the sense of ethnic or sectarian righteousness boasted by various groups in the Mediterranean world. The words 'Christ is the goal of the law' (10:4) serve to explain the misunderstanding about the purpose of the law manifest in the phenomenon of competitive zeal. In Christ righteousness can be gained without conforming to the mores of any culture. Christ thus reveals and accomplishes the original goal of the law, which had been subverted by competition for honour and by ascribing shame to outsiders. Salvation is open to 'all who believe' in the gospel, which transcends the ethnic boundaries between Greeks and Jews and barbarians that have been mentioned repeatedly in the letter.

In 10:5–13 the discussion of how to 'bring Christ down' and 'bring Christ up' indicates that the motivation of zealous obedience in the first century was to usher in the messianic age. Paul's basic critique is that this motivation is now outmoded, since Jesus came as the Christ, proven by the resurrection, and revealing the central problem with religious zeal through his death on the cross. The shamed, crucified one is confessed here to be the Lord (10:9–10), and it was precisely the demand for religious and moral conformity that led to his death. In his crucifixion the entire realm of gaining honour through meeting the conditions of approved behaviour and belief was overthrown.

The threefold reference to 'heart' in 10:8–10 shows that for Paul faith is more than a set of beliefs. It is related to the condition of the heart, that motivating centre of mind, emotion, experience, and purpose. This is a realm ordinarily dominated by shameful secrets that faith in Christ crucified has the power to expose. As this text proclaims, the redeeming '"word is near you, on your lips and in your heart", that is, the word of faith that we proclaim' (10:8). Paul knows that the Romans have been living out this faith, that it is deeply anchored in their converted hearts, and thus that they will recognize its consistency with the 'word of faith' that the letter to the Romans proclaims. He gives priority here to the message fastened deeply in the heart; it is already 'near' them. This correlates closely with the following section, which celebrates the preaching of the gospel despite its rejection by a portion of Israel (10:14–21). Since 'faith comes from what is heard' (10:17) and is destined to 'go out to the ends of the world', a citation from Ps. 18:5, the mission to Spain has scriptural warrant and could stimulate the ultimate conversion of Israel itself (10:19).

In 11:1–24 Paul deals with whether God responds to Israel's reluctance by abandoning her. A faithful remnant currently being saved 'by grace' (11:5–6) and the hardening of others are temporary matters that should not engender feelings of superiority on the part of Gentile Christians (11:17–22). God has the power to 'graft' the distant Israelites back into 'their own wild olive tree' where they belong (11:23–4). In 11:25–32, he sets forth the 'mystery' that Israel's zeal for salvation will be provoked by the conversion of the Gentiles so that ultimately 'all Israel will be saved' (11:25–6). No arrogance is warranted on either side, because 'God consigned all persons to disobedience, in order to have mercy on all' (11:32). This is followed by a hymn to the mysterious mind of God (11:33–6) that incorporates citations from Isa. 40:13 and Job 41:3 showing that while no human can have perfect knowledge, God alone deserves to be glorified. It is well that the third proof ends on this theme, because in fact Paul's prediction of Israel's conversion to Christianity did not prove to be accurate.

FOURTH PROOF (12:1–15:13)

The fourth proof urges an ethic based on righteousness through faith, including a new basis of tolerance within a diverse conununity. To respond appropriately to the 'mercies of God' requires a living sacrifice of bodily service that is not 'conformed to this world' (12:1–2). The 'renewal of the mind' evokes the recovery of righteous rationality, implying a complex of assumptions and mental abilities characteristic of a group rather than an individual. The focus on group decision-making in this introductory paragraph is sharpened by the unequivocal phrasing 'that you [plural] may ascertain what is the will of God' (12:2). The spiritual and moral resources required for this task are described in 12:3–8, beginning with a wordplay on avoiding the superiority claims popularized by society: 'do not be super-minded above what one ought to be minded, but set your mind on being sober-minded, according to the measuring rod of faith that God dealt out to each'. By referring to the unique experience of faith that each person and group possess in Christ, Paul defines 'sober-mindedness' as the refusal to impose the standard of one's own relationship with God onto others. This had a direct bearing on the conflicts between the 'weak' and 'strong', in which each side was attempting to compel the other to accept its views.

In 12:9–21 Paul sets forth guidelines for 'love without pretence', stressing the ongoing need to distinguish between good and evil (verses 9, 21) in terms of a new system of honour within the community of faith. In place of competition between house and tenement churches, they are to treat each other 'with brotherly love, taking the lead in honouring one another' (12:10). By mutual sharing of both resources and troubles (12:13–15) and by 'being drawn toward lowly people' (12:16) rather than, as the society preferred, toward the elite in one's own group, they will experience the genuine solidarity of love. This will also lead to a new relationship towards outsiders, blessing persecutors (12:14), refusing to repay evil for evil (12:17), living at peace with hostile enemies (12:18) and leaving vengeance up to God (12:19–20).

In 13:1–7 Paul urges voluntary submission to local governmental authorities on the premise that the God who grants such authority is not Mars or Jupiter, as in the Roman civic cult, but the God embodied in the crucified Christ. While opposing resistance and urging payment of taxes, this passage nevertheless constitutes a massive act of political co-optation. That the Roman authorities were appointed by the God and Father of Jesus Christ turns the entire Roman civic cult on its head, exposing its suppression of the truth. Nothing remains of the specious claim in the civic cult that the empire had been given to Rome because of its superior virtue and piety, an implicit claim that had been demolished by 1:18–3:20. What remains is the simple fact of divine appointment, a matter justified not by the virtue of the appointee but by the mysterious mind of God, who elects whom God wills as the agents of divine purpose (9:14–33; 11:17–32). Submission to the governmental authorities is therefore an expression of respect not for the authorities themselves but for the crucified deity who stands behind them.

In 13:8–10 Paul goes on to urge that social obligations are to be transcended by mutual love, which alone fulfils the law. This short paragraph concludes with a saying that requires accurate translation to reflect Paul's use of the article and the chiastic sequence: 'the love does no evil to the neighbour; therefore law's fulfilment is the love'. The logical social corollary to 'the love' in this verse is the agape meal otherwise known as the love-feast, the common meal shared by most sectors of the early church in connection with the Lord's Supper. The reference to 'law's fulfilment' reflects that fact that the greatest barrier to intercommunion in the Roman situation was the insistence on conformity to various forms of law, which divided the weak from the strong and prevented the celebration of the love-feast together.

These often raucous celebrations provide the context for the following paragraph, warning against unseemly behaviour. Whereas the Greeks divinized Dispute or Emulation as energizing powers and the Jewish nationalists advocated zealotism, the early Christian revolution in the honour and shame system turned these virtues into vices, viewing 'strife' and 'zealotry' as factors of the old age (13:13), as deeds of darkness that eroded the equality of believers and destroyed the faith community.

In 14:1–15:13, Paul counters the competition for honour between the Roman churches. His basic point is that to despise and judge fellow Christians is to lose sight of who the Lord is. If God has 'welcomed' one's opponent (14:3) and if God is the one before whom competitors 'stand or fall' (14:5–6), then the continuation of hostilities constitutes an assault on God. Mutual welcome is therefore appropriate (14:1; 15:7), whose social context in the situation of the Roman churches would be shared invitations to love-feasts. While insisting that 'nothing is profane in itself, except that if a person reckons it profane, it is profane for that one', Paul goes on to argue that 'if your brother is grieved by food, you are no longer walking according to love' (14:14–15). His protection of the 'weak' is balanced by protecting the integrity of the strong (14:16). This is a revolutionary form of social tolerance that allows differences to stand while reaching out to accept others as equal members of the body of Christ. To build up 'one another' (14:19) clearly implies that both the weak and the strong are to undertake this task of edifying the other side. Then by citing LXX Ps. 68:10 in Rom. 15:3, Paul suggests that the contempt and judging within the Roman congregations add to the shameful reproach that Christ bore on the cross for the sake of all. This lends force to the admonition that the competing house churches should seek to 'please the neighbour' in 15:2, adding to the other group's honour and integrity rather than participating in mutual shaming. By overcoming these conflicts, the Christians in Rome will be enabled to join their voices in praise of the same God (15:6) and to participate credibly in augmenting the global chorus that will one day unite the warring world (15:9–13).

PERORATION (15:14–16:24)

The peroration urges participation in Paul's missionary endeavours and mutual welcome by various house and tenement churches in Rome. Following the guidelines of classical rhetoric, this section provides an emotional appeal in support of the missionary goal that Paul wishes to advance. His mission has already extended as far west as Illyricum (15:19), and Paul plans to conclude his work in the east and move to Spain, thus completing the circle of the known world. He explains his final errand to deliver the Jerusalem offering (15:25–32) and then asks the Roman house and tenement churches to extend greetings to each other's leaders and to 'greet one another with a holy kiss', acknowledging that both the weak and the strong have a legitimate right to be considered part of the Christian family.

To greet and welcome one another into their fellowships, which would have consisted of celebrations of the sacrificial death of Christ and his enlivening presence among them, is to participate in the 'grace of our Lord Jesus Christ', which concludes the letter in 16:24. In order for the revolution of divine grace through Christ to be extended in a credible manner to the barbarians at the end of the known world, it must first be embodied in transformed relations between the Christians themselves, riven by ethnic and theological conflict. Only in this way can the thesis of Romans be fully demonstrated, that the 'gospel is the power of God for salvation to every one who has faith' (1:16).

7 Philippians

MORNA HOOKER

Written to a Christian community with whom Paul has had a long and happy relationship, the letter to the Philippians is characterized by joy – a remarkable fact, since it was sent from prison, where its author was held on a capital charge. The letter expresses confidence about Paul's own future since, whether he lives or dies, Christ is with him (1:19–26), and about the Philippians, whom he describes as his joy and his crown (4:1), concerning whom he will boast on the day of judgment (2:16).

CONTEXT

Paul's authorship of this letter has rarely been doubted. It was written to Christians in Philippi, a fairly small city of about 10,000 inhabitants in eastern Macedonia. In the first century AD, Philippi was important as an agricultural centre; it was a Roman colony, which meant that its citizens enjoyed considerable legal and property rights, and the city's administration was modelled on that of Rome. Communications were reasonably easy by the standards of that time, since the city was conveniently placed on the Via Egnatia, along which one could travel westwards to the Adriatic coast, while the port of Neapolis lay ten miles to the south.

Although there would have been a considerable nucleus of Roman citizens living in Philippi – many of them Italian by birth – most of the inhabitants would have been Greeks. Of those mentioned by name in Philippians, three – Epaphroditus (2:25), Syntyche, and Euodia (4:2) – have Greek names, and one – Clement (4:3) – a Latin name. There is no archaeological evidence that Jews lived in the city, and Luke makes no reference to a synagogue there in his account of Paul's visit to Philippi in Acts 16. His reference to a 'place of prayer' outside the city, apparently attended only by women, suggests a minimal Jewish presence: the vast majority of Paul's converts would have been Gentiles.

Paul writes the letter from prison (1:7,12–18) – but where was that prison situated? The traditional answer to this question has always been

'Rome', where (so Luke tells us) Paul was held for at least two years (Acts 28:16, 30) and where – again according to tradition – he was finally executed. Some scholars object that the distance between Rome and Philippi – some 800 miles – means that the various journeys implied by Phil. 2:25–30 (at least five) would have taken too long. The length of Paul's imprisonment, together with the strategic siting of Philippi, is sufficient answer to this objection. Another difficulty with locating the writing of the epistle in Rome is the fact that in 2:24 Paul expresses the hope that he will visit the Philippians on his release, whereas his original plan had been to visit Rome on the way to Spain (Rom. 15:22–9). But if he is indeed now in Rome, then several years have elapsed since he wrote Romans, and he has come to Rome as a prisoner: he could well have changed his mind about his future plans.

According to Acts, Paul was also imprisoned in Caesarea for two years (23:35; 24:27), but he was never in imminent danger of execution there, as he clearly was when he wrote Philippians (1:19–26); moreover, the objections brought against Rome as the place of composition apply equally to Caesarea. Paul himself speaks of many imprisonments (2 Cor. 11:23), without indicating where these may have been. References to an occasion when his life was in danger in Asia (2 Cor.1:8–10) and to fighting with wild beasts at Ephesus (1 Cor. 15:32 – though this is clearly metaphorical) have led some to suggest that he was imprisoned in Ephesus, but there is no evidence that he was held there on a capital charge. Assuming the letter to have been written from Rome, we may date it in the early sixties.

OCCASION

Paul seems to have had several reasons for writing this letter. One was to tell the Philippians how he was faring in prison (1:12–26). Another was to explain why he was sending Epaphroditus, who had been seriously ill, back to Philippi. Epaphroditus had been sent by the church to minister to Paul in prison, but his illness had caused such concern in Philippi that Paul felt it necessary for him to return home to allay the community's fears. Some tact was needed on Paul's part: Epaphroditus had been the Philippians' representative, and Paul was anxious not to give the impression that he had rejected his services, or that Epaphroditus had failed to carry out his mission. The return of Epaphroditus to Philippi meant that Paul was able, thirdly, to seize the opportunity to give pastoral advice to the community, urging them to stand firm in the face of adversity and to be loving and unselfish in their behaviour towards one another, while dealing in particular with a problem of personal rivalry that had come to his attention (4:2–3). A fourth possible reason is not so clear. In 4:10–20 Paul refers to a gift that the Philippians have sent him: if this has just arrived, then the chief purpose of the letter must be to express his thanks. But it is possible that Paul is simply taking the opportunity here to refer once again to a gift for which he has already given thanks in an earlier letter. We shall look at this question again under 'Structure'.

Yet another reason often suggested for this letter is the possible existence of opponents who were undermining Paul's work in the Philippian church; it is suggested that this explains his constant stress on the need for unity. Various groups of opponents are, indeed, mentioned, but it is doubtful whether there was any opposition to Paul's teaching within the Christian community in Philippi. In prison, Paul was aware of some Christians outside who were personally opposed to him, but he still regarded them as fellow evangelists (1:12–18). In Philippi, there were those outside the Christian community who were persecuting the church (1:27–30). The clearest warnings against those who might have been perverting the Christian gospel are found in 3:2 and 3:18–19, but in the former Paul urges the Philippians to be on their guard against Judaizers, and in the second he tells them of the existence of people whose lifestyle shows them to be 'enemies of the cross': there does not appear to be any imminent danger from either group.

The emphasis on unity is a common one for Paul, and there are good reasons – both the rivalry that he is himself experiencing and that he has been told exists in Philippi and the persecution that the Philippians are enduring – why it should be stressed in this letter.

STRUCTURE

To a large extent the letter follows the normal pattern of Pauline epistles: the opening address and greeting (1:1–2) are followed by a prayer of thanksgiving (1:3–8), which merges into a prayer of intercession (1:9–11). As usual, the introductory thanksgiving touches on topics that are going to be elaborated in the epistle: these are the Philippians' participation in the gospel; Paul's confidence that God will continue his work among them until its completion; and his own imprisonment and defence of the gospel. The fact that Paul describes himself and Timothy as *douloi* (literally 'slaves') of Christ Jesus in the opening greeting rather than as 'apostles' is perhaps also a deliberate pointer to what is going to be an important theme in the epistle.

The first section of the epistle deals with the theme of Paul's imprisonment and its possible outcome (1:12–26). Paul then turns to the Philippian community, and urges them to live in a manner worthy of the gospel

(1:27–2:18). Within this section, 2:6–11 are remarkable, since they form an unusually lengthy and rhythmic passage extolling Christ, a passage which may perhaps have been composed earlier, either by Paul or by someone else. Whatever its origin, the passage is undoubtedly part of the Philippian letter, firmly embedded in its context, and its ideas are expounded in a typically Pauline way.

In the next section, Paul explains his plans to the Philippians – plans concerning Timothy, himself, and Epaphroditus (2:19–30).

At this point there is an abrupt jump in the argument (3:2), which some scholars believe indicates the piecing-together of two separate letters. The Greek of 3:1 is unfortunately ambiguous, but one possible translation is 'Finally . . . farewell', which certainly suggests that Paul is nearing the end of his letter. Though this theory suggests an attractive solution to the problem of the sudden change in topic in 3:2, it raises others: why should an *editor* join two such disparate passages? What happened to the end of the first letter and the beginning of the second, and why were they not preserved? Moreover, the Greek of 3:1 is, as we noted, ambiguous, and should perhaps be translated 'And so . . . rejoice.' In fact, both the language and the logic of 3:2–4:1 echo that of 1:27–2:18, suggesting that the two passages belong to the same letter.

The section 4:2–23 forms the conclusion to the letter as we have it, with various exhortations (4:2–9) being followed by a personal note of thanks (4:10–20) and closing greetings. Again, questions have been raised about the integrity of the letter: if Philippians was a letter of thanks, was it not discourteous to delay thanking the Philippians till the very end? Could this passage, then, be part of an earlier letter? But messages have been going to and fro (2:25–6), suggesting that Paul has already expressed his thanks and is here repeating them. Moreover, there are again echoes in 4:10–20 of the vocabulary used in 1:3–11, forming an *inclusio*. There are good reasons, then, for accepting the integrity of Philippians as it stands.

THE CHRISTIAN COMMUNITY IN PHILIPPI

One unusual feature in the opening verses of the letter is the fact that it is addressed to 'bishops and deacons' in addition to those who are called 'the saints in Christ Jesus'. In fact, this translation of the Greek is misleading. The word *episkopos* originally meant 'overseer', the word *diakonos* 'servant'. Elsewhere in the New Testament, *episkopoi* seem to be equivalent to *presbuteroi*, 'elders' (see Acts 20:17, 28; Titus 1:5–7). Paul uses *diakonos* with reference to his own ministry (1 Cor. 3:5; 2 Cor. 6:4), and in Rom. 16:1 he refers to Phoebe as a *diakonos* of the church in Cenchreae.

Who, then, were these two groups? Did the *episkopoi* and *diakonoi* have different functions? The fact that Paul and Timothy are described as *douloi* in verse 1 shows that we are not dealing with any kind of hierarchy: the words are not yet technical terms. Nevertheless, Paul clearly has office-bearers of some sort in mind, and some kind of structural organization appears to be emerging among the Philippian Christians, possibly reflecting the ordered structures of the Roman colony in which they lived. The *episkopoi* probably exercised some supervisory role, while the function of the *diakonoi* was above all to act as ministers to the Christian community.

Why were these people singled out here by Paul for special mention? In linking the community in general with its leaders in his opening greeting, he was in fact following the pattern of many contemporary letters. It is possible that Paul mentions these leaders here because they had particular responsibility for sending the gift which the Philippian community had sent to Paul in his imprisonment.

This gift was not the first that the Philippians had sent to Paul; in 4:15–16 he refers to the way that they – alone among the churches – had supported his missionary work. It may seem strange that Paul was prepared to accept this assistance, since we know that he adamantly refused financial support from other churches (1 Cor. 9:15–18; 1 Thess. 2:9). What Paul refused, however, was financial aid from those among whom he was working, lest he appear to be profiting from the gospel (2 Cor. 11:7–10); what the Philippians did was to support his missionary endeavours *elsewhere*, and he refers to their 'sharing in the gospel' (1:5), as well as to their sharing 'in the matter of giving and receiving' (4:15). Now they have shared in his distress (4:16). If he describes them in 1:7 as those who 'share in God's grace with me', that suggests that he has in mind the way they have aided him, both in his 'imprisonment and in the defence and confirmation of the gospel'. This aid included sending Epaphroditus – a very practical aid, since prisoners were often dependent on friends and relatives for the necessities of life. Paul's regard and affection for the Philippians – whom, he says, he loves and longs for (4:1) – is not surprising.

PAUL'S IMPRISONMENT AND THE PROGRESS OF THE GOSPEL

Following the opening thanksgiving and intercession, Paul gives the Philippian community news of his own situation, in order to reassure them. He cannot, indeed, assure them that he will be released, since he is far from confident about this, but he is, nevertheless, confident that, whatever happens, Christ will be glorified. Paul tells the Philippians nothing about the conditions of his imprisonment or about how he is being treated, but a great deal about what that imprisonment is achieving, and about how the possible verdicts at his trial might serve the gospel. His imprisonment 'has actually helped to spread the gospel', since the whole imperial guard is talking about his case, and so learning about the Christian faith, while fellow Christians are emboldened to make a similar stand. Paul's own experience of opportunity through suffering is thus a proclamation of the gospel of crucifixion-resurrection.

As far as the possible outcome of his trial is concerned, Paul does not know whether to hope for deliverance – which will mean the opportunity to go on preaching the gospel – or death – which will mean being 'with Christ'. Either way, Christ will be exalted (1:20). Yet he feels that the church needs him still (1:24), and therefore hopes to see the Philippians again (1:26; 2:24).

Paul's overwhelming concern for the gospel and for the welfare of the Christian community, not for his own well-being and safety, is an indication of the sincerity of his declaration that the one prize he values is to gain Christ and to be found in him, to know him and to share his sufferings (3:8–10). Being 'in Christ' means for Paul conformity to his death, in hope of resurrection (3:10–11). No wonder, then, that he declares in 4:11–13 that he has learned to be content, whatever he has! He can cope with any and every circumstance through the risen power of the one who suffered humiliation and death.

What Paul tells us here about his own circumstances and attitudes suggests a conscious attempt to proclaim the gospel in his life by modelling himself on the actions of Christ. This is most clearly expressed in chapter 3, where Paul also tells us something about his origins. He was, he tells us, thoroughly Jewish by birth and upbringing (3:5–6). He had been a Pharisee, zealous for the law, to the extent that he had persecuted the church, and had considered himself a blameless upholder of the law. Yet he regarded these enormous privileges as worthless in comparison with the great gain to be found by being 'in Christ' (3:7–11), and abandoned 'law-righteousness' for the righteousness which comes through Christ. And though he has not yet reached the goal – resurrection from the dead – he is pressing towards it (3:12–16).

Throughout this chapter there are interesting echoes of the language of 2:5–11, suggesting that Paul saw his own Christian discipleship as conformity to the pattern of Christ's self-emptying and exaltation, which had brought glory to God. It is not surprising, then, that he interpreted all his suffering 'for [literally 'in'] Christ' (1:13) as a means of proclaiming the gospel.

THE CHRISTIAN LIFE

At the centre of this letter lies Paul's appeal to the Philippians to stand firm against opposition and to live in a manner that is worthy of the gospel (1:27–2:18; 3:1–4:1). The opposition may well have come from those in Philippi who thought that Christianity threatened their customs and liveli- hood (cf. Acts 16:16–24). Far from suggesting that the Philippians 'grin and bear' their suffering, Paul urges them to see it as an opportunity to do some- thing 'for Christ': God has given to them – as to Paul himself – the privilege not simply of believing in Christ but of suffering for him (1:29–30).

Belonging to Christ may involve suffering: it certainly involves mem- bership of the community of believers – those whom Paul describes as being 'in Christ' (1:1). Paul is well aware that tensions within the Christian com- munity can create as many problems as those caused by opponents from outside! If Christians are to stand firm and uphold the gospel they must obviously be united (1:27). This unity is not simply pragmatic, however, but flows from the attitude (or 'mind') of Christ, an attitude which should pervade the whole Christian community (2:3, 5). Those who are 'in Christ' (2:1) should share the love, compassion, and sympathy that come from him, and behave in the appropriate way towards one another. Those who share his mind will do nothing from selfish ambition or conceit, but behave with humility and with concern for the interest of others (2:3–4).

At this point Paul introduces the christological passage in 2:6–11 with the enigmatic command 'think this among you which also in Christ Jesus'. Older translations (e.g. the AV) understood verse 5 as a command to follow the example of Jesus: the Philippians should have the mind (or attitude) 'which was also in Christ Jesus'. Recent exegetes (pointing to the absence of the verb 'was' in the Greek, and the use of the phrase 'in Christ Jesus') have argued that it is an appeal to the Philippians to have the attitude which belongs to them 'as those who are in Christ'. They argue that 2:6–11 are a pre-Pauline summary of the kerygma, and that verse 5 is thus a command to 'be what you are – in Christ', as the result of what God has done through him.[1]

Arguments about whether or not this passage is pre-Pauline centre on its christology, poetic structure, and vocabulary. What is important for us is the way in which Paul uses the passage. As so often happens in theological controversy, each view contains some elements of truth. In this case, the attitude that Paul is urging the Philippians to adopt is the attitude shown by Christ himself, and if one wishes to know what behaviour is appropriate for the Christian community one should look at him. But Paul is not simply urging the Philippians to imitate Christ, for in reminding them of the way in which Christ 'emptied' himself he is reminding them also of the events which made them what they are – the people who are 'in Christ'. The link between Christ's attitude and theirs is a causal one, since it is because of what Christ did that they are members of God's people. As those who are 'in Christ' they can – and must – show the attitude that was shown by Christ Jesus, and which should now belong to them.[2] Paul's ethical teaching is rooted in theology.

The christological passage itself, often referred to as the Philippian 'hymn', falls into two main sections. Instead of Paul's normal pattern of crucifixion followed by resurrection, we have what we would call 'incarnation' (leading to crucifixion) followed by exaltation. Nevertheless, there are parallels to many of the ideas found here elsewhere in Paul: Rom. 8:3 and Gal. 4:4 speak of Christ being born as man (though sent by God); 2 Cor. 8:9; Gal. 2:20 and 3:13 describe Christ's own self-giving, Rom. 5:18–19 his obedience.

The possible background for the ideas being used in this passage is a matter of considerable debate. Some argue that this is to be found in Isaiah 53, but the term 'servant' used there is a title of great honour, whereas the word used of Christ in verse 7 ('slave') indicates total loss of rights and status, and there are no real parallels in thought or vocabulary. Far more probable are the ideas surrounding Adam, a figure already used by Paul, notably in Rom. 5:12–19. There is an obvious contrast between Adam's disobedience and attempt to become like God and Christ's self-emptying. Again, it is objected that the vocabulary used of Adam in Gen. 1:26 differs from that used in Phil. 1:6 of Christ, and that there is no real parallel between the actions of the man Adam and those of one who, being in the form of God, *became* man, i.e. took on the likeness of Adam. In fact, however, Paul never thinks of Adam and Christ as equals, as is plain in Rom. 5:15–17, which stress the superiority of what happens in Christ to what happened in Adam (cf. 1 Cor. 15:45). If Christ emptied himself in order to become man, then being 'in the form of God' is clearly superior to being created in God's image; yet paradoxically, by emptying himself and being born in human likeness, the one who was in the form of God was acknowledged as the true revelation of God's being and his equal.[3]

The meaning of the passage – and, indeed, of almost every phrase in it – has been a matter of considerable debate. It seems clear that it is about one who was pre-existent. But what is meant by 'the form of God'? Recent research suggests that the word *morphē* ('form') refers to something visual, and that the phrase indicates that the pre-existent Christ shared the characteristics of God.[4] But did he possess 'equality with God'? The word *harpagmos* has often been translated as 'something (not yet possessed) to be grasped', often as 'something to be clung to'.[5] The suggestion that the word means 'something to be exploited' opens up a new possibility: equality was something which belonged to Christ by right, but which he chose not to use.[6] This refusal to exploit his rights is in keeping with his action in making himself nothing (verse 7). The common translation of this phrase as 'emptied himself' (Greek *ekenōsen*) has led many to ask 'of what?', and this question led to the development in the nineteenth century of the 'kenotic theory', which held that Christ emptied himself of the attributes of divine omnipotence and omniscience. But the emphasis in Philippians 2 seems rather to be on Christ's willingness to abandon the status and privileges that belonged to him by right for the form of a slave, without rights or privileges of any kind.

To do this, he was born in the likeness of man, and then humbled himself still further by becoming obedient to the most appalling and shameful of all deaths, crucifixion, the punishment meted out to rebellious slaves. The contrast between the opening and closing phrases of this section could not be greater.

The second part of the so-called 'hymn' sets everything in reverse. The triumphant opening 'Therefore' (because of everything Christ had done) introduces God's action in exalting Christ to the heights. The preposition *hyper*, found here in the Greek verb *hyperupsōsen*, implies something that excels or surpasses. Does the phrase mean simply 'he highly exalted him', or does it imply that God gave to Christ a status he had not enjoyed before? If verse 6 is understood to mean that Christ enjoyed equality with God, no higher elevation is possible. But if, as suggested above, he never claimed the equality with God that was his by right, then at this point he is *acknowledged* as having that equality. This, in fact, is spelled out in the final lines of the passage, since now Christ is given the name that is above every name (which must be the divine name of 'Lord' (verse 11)) and accorded the worship that in Isa. 45:23 is described as belonging to God (verses 10–11). Yet even this is said to bring glory to God the Father! The one who is in God's form reveals the character of God by his actions, and so brings him glory.

In verse 12 Paul makes sure that the Philippians understand the implications of Christ's actions: 'Therefore you too must be obedient.' The way in which Christ's actions are a model for Christians is demonstrated in Paul's own abandonment of status and privilege in order to be found 'in Christ' and share his sufferings (3:4–10). In 3:17 the behaviour of Paul and others becomes, in turn, a model for the Philippians, while they are warned against those who by their selfish behaviour live as 'enemies of the cross'. Following Christ's example is not simply a matter of human endeavour, however, since it is God who is at work in believers, transforming their lives (2:13), and it is Christ who will finally transform them into his own likeness, through the power bestowed on him at his own exaltation (3:20–1). We find here the pattern of 'interchange' so common in Paul (cf. Gal. 3:13–14; 4:4–5; 2 Cor. 5:21; 8:9): Christ shares the human condition (Phil. 2:6–8; cf. Rom. 8:3), in order that believers may share what he is (Phil. 3:21; cf. Rom. 8:29–30).[7]

THE CHRISTIAN HOPE

The transformation of believers will take place when Jesus Christ appears from heaven (3:20). He will then be acknowledged as 'Saviour' and 'Lord' – titles at present used in Roman Philippi for the Emperor. There are several references in Philippians to the Day of Christ (1:6,10; 2:16) and to the coming judgment (1:28; 4:3). Perhaps Paul's own critical situation makes him particularly aware of the nearness of the End (cf. 4:5). In 1:19–26, where Paul contemplates his own possible execution, he declares that 'to live is Christ, to die is gain' (verse 21), since to die is to 'be with Christ' (verse 23), but he makes no reference to the coming Day of the Lord. Logically, these two eschatological expectations might seem incompatible, but each expresses different aspects of the Christian hope: on the one hand the conviction that finally everything will be set right and justice will be done; on the other, the belief that death cannot destroy the union of believers with Christ. Paul is confident that his own death will mean being 'with Christ' in an even closer way than in life.

In chapter 3, also, Paul speaks of future hope in two ways – first, as resurrection (verse 11), then as the return of Christ, which will mean the transformation of believers (verses 20–1). However this hope is expressed, Paul speaks of it in terms of arriving at his goal and obtaining the prize (verses 12–16), which is to be made like Christ, not simply in death (verse 10) but in glory (verse 21). When that happens, the believer will share to the full in the pattern set out in 2:6–11.

Notes

1 Notably E. Käsemann, 'Kritische Analyse von Phil 2:5–11', *ZTK* 47 (1950) 313–60; ET 'A Critical Analysis of Phil 2:5–11', *JTC* 5 (1968) 45–88.

2 Cf. M. D. Hooker, 'Philippians 2:6–11', in E. E. Ellis and E. Grässer, eds., *Jesus und Paulus*, FS W. G. Kümmel (Göttingen: Vandenhoeck & Ruprecht, 1975) 151–64; reprinted in M. D. Hooker, *From Adam to Christ* (Cambridge: Cambridge University Press, 1990) 88–100.

3 Cf. M. D. Hooker, 'Adam *Redivivus*: Philippians 2 Once More', in S. Moyise, ed., *The Old Testament in the New Testament*, FS Lionel North, JSNTS 189 (Sheffield: Sheffield Academic Press, 2000) 220–34.

4 See M. Bockmuehl, '"The Form of God" (Phil. 2:6): Variations on a Theme of Jewish Mysticism', *JTS* 48 (1997) 1–23.

5 For the many various possible translations, see N. T. Wright, '*Harpagmos* and the Meaning of Philippians 2:5–11', *JTS* 37 (1986) 321–52; reprinted with revisions in N. T. Wright, *The Climax of the Covenant: Christ and the Law in Pauline Theology* (Edinburgh: T. & T. Clark, 1991) 62–90.

6 R. W. Hoover, 'The HARPAGMOS Enigma: A Philosophical Solution', *HTR* 64 (1971) 95–119.

7 See, in particular, M. D. Hooker, 'Interchange in Christ', *JTS* 22 (1971) 349–61, reprinted with other essays on the same theme in Hooker, *From Adam to Christ* 13–25.

8 Colossians and Philemon

LOREN T. STUCKENBRUCK

COLOSSIANS: GENERAL SITUATION

Author and readers

Colossians purports to be written as a letter by the apostle Paul, along with Timothy (1:1), through the services of a scribe (4:18). This letter is addressed to the Christians in Colossae, a city in Phrygia located inland from Ephesus on the south side of the river Lycus in western Asia Minor. Paul himself did not found the Colossian church (2:1); the letter suggests that his link to the Christians there may have developed through Epaphras, who had worked among them (1:7–8) and from whom he sends them greetings (4:12). According to the text, Paul composed the letter while in prison (4:3, 18; see 4:10; 1:24).

Date

If the letter was composed or endorsed by Paul, then it was written during one of Paul's imprisonments, that is, either in Ephesus (during the mid 50s CE) or in Rome (which would imply a date around 60 CE, just prior to the earthquake which struck the Lycus region in 60–1 CE). If the letter was composed after Paul's death, then its composition may have occurred sometime between the recovery of Colossae and a date near the end of the first century.[1]

Occasion of the letter

At least four reasons which led to the writing of the letter may be identified. Firstly, the author wishes to respond to problems which he has heard have become the source of conflict and uncertainty among members of the Christian community at Colossae. These problems are initially introduced suggestively in 2:4 ('that no one might deceive you through plausible arguments'; cf. 'philosophy', verse 8), and then openly confronted in 2:8–23 (specific issues raised: verses 11, 13 – circumcision; verses 16, 21 – dietary laws; verse 16 – calendrical regulations; verse 18 – 'worship of angels'; verses 18, 20–3 – ascetic practices).

Secondly, Paul uses the letter as an opportunity to have Tychicus, who is to deliver the letter, report to the Colossians about his and Epaphras' condition (2:1; 4:18) and to communicate their concern for the Colossians (4:10; cf. 2:1–5). Thirdly, the letter is sent through Tychicus as he returns with a certain slave Onesimus, who is from Colossae (4:7–9). This purpose links Colossians to Paul's letter to Philemon, in which Paul sends a covering letter to accompany Onesimus as he is returned to his owner (see under Philemon below). Finally, to a certain extent the letter was not only addressed to the Colossians, but was also meant to be read aloud before the Christian community in Laodicea (cf. 2:1) to whom a separate letter (not preserved) had also been sent (4:16). This may suggest that the author did not regard the problems he addressed in the letter as solely relevant to a particular situation in Colossae.

Structure

The letter is broadly structured in much the same way as other letters attributed to Paul. It is framed on the one side by an opening address with greeting (1:1–2), and on the other by a series of personal greetings (4:7–18). In between, the letter proceeds with an extensive thanksgiving and prayer (1:3–23), statements affirming Paul's commitment to the gospel and to the Colossians, Laodiceans, and others who have not seen him (1:24–2:5), and the main theme of the letter (2:6–4:6). The structure includes two main features which seem to depart from what one may have expected of a letter from Paul:[2] (1) the surprising length devoted to the introductory matters before the main theme of the letter is articulated (1:1–2:5); and (2) the inclusion of a series of household codes in the otherwise customary exhortations at the end (3:18–4:1). Can these features be explained as departures introduced by Paul himself in response to special circumstances in Colossae, or do they represent the influence of another hand in the writing of the letter?

The question of authorship

The extent to which Colossians reflects the theology of Paul the apostle is closely related to the question of whether the letter may be said to have been written by him. Since the second half of the nineteenth century, a number of scholars have doubted the authenticity of this letter, preferring to argue that it was written by a devotee or disciple of the apostle after his death.[3] Several reasons for this, based on general and specific observations, have been advanced. These include the following considerations: the widespread practice of pseudonymity in Graeco-Roman antiquity; stylistic differences between Colossians and Paul's 'undisputed' letters (especially in vocabulary, style of argument, and use of tradition); a more fully developed church order in Colossians (1:18, 24; 2:19; 3:15; cf. Eph. 4:15–16); and differences in theological perspective (e.g. regarding christology, eschatology, and ethics).[4] The strength of this position has been most frequently noted in relation to an apparent inconsistency between the eschatology of Colossians and that of Paul. Whereas several passages in Colossians emphasize a more 'realized eschatology', in which, for example, the baptized believer can be said to share the resurrection existence of Christ (so 2:12–13; 3:1,10), Paul's thought regarding baptism is elsewhere far more tentative with respect to whether such a state can already be achieved (so especially Rom. 6:1–11).

Other scholars, however, have found such arguments unconvincing.[5] For example, it has been counter-argued that since pseudonymous works in antiquity were nearly always attributed to revered figures from the *distant* past, the composition of a letter in the name of the *recently* deceased apostle would have been highly unusual. Furthermore, the language, style, and theology of Colossians are sometimes not regarded as decisive. A comparison with Paul's letters to the Philippians and Philemon suggests, firstly, that Philippians likewise uses vocabulary frequently not found in the other 'authentic' Pauline letters and, secondly, that Colossians would not have been alone as a letter of Paul which does not contain any formal citation of the Jewish scriptures. In fact, the use of tradition in Colossians would not seem to depart substantially from what we know from the undisputed correspondence of Paul. As in Paul, the letter draws heavily on traditions which may go back to liturgical practice or theological reflection on baptism (so 2:20; 3:1–5, 9b–12; cf. Rom. 6:4–5; Gal. 3:27–8; 1 Cor. 12:12–13). Finally, Colossians, as among the undisputed letters of Paul, retains a certain eschatological reserve, so that the 'resurrection life' attributed to the Christian is not yet one in which 'glory' has been achieved; the believer's life 'is hidden with Christ in God' and 'Christ who is your life' is yet to be revealed (3:3–4). As in Romans 6, the ethical exhortations derive their force from a reminder that those being addressed have not yet tangibly attained the sort of life promised to them when they were baptized. One could further argue that the special character of the language, instead of stemming from another author, can be explained as Paul's attempt to come to terms with the particular situation in Colossae (see below).

In the end, none of the considerations for or against the Pauline composition of Colossians is decisive. However, it may not be necessary to decide between the alternative views which, respectively, regard the letter as either 'Pauline' or 'post-Pauline';[6] given the strong personal stamp on the letter, the use of a secretary, the possible involvement of Timothy, and the undoubted influence of the apostle's ideas therein, it is likewise possible that the letter was composed during Paul's lifetime by someone closely associated with him.

The nature and extent of Paul's influence, however, whether Paul was immediately or remotely responsible for the content of the letter, remain unclear. In general, much of the debate surrounding the authenticity of Colossians (and Ephesians) depends on assumptions about what latitude may be allowed for the consistency of the apostle's thought. Nevertheless, it is hard to ignore the strongly christocentric ecclesiology of the letter, in which Christ is unequivocally designated as 'the head of the body, the church' (1:18; cf. 1:24). This goes beyond the apostle's comparable statements in 1 Cor. 12:12–27. It is impossible to determine whether this represents a genuine development of thought in Paul, whose ideas in the letter were being elicited by problems to which he was responding, or was the result of someone else's attempt to address problems in Colossae while appealing to Paul or a received pool of Pauline tradition. In the end, while the notion of Colossians as a letter composed during the lifetime and at least under the influence of the apostle cannot be dismissed, it would be misleading to use the letter as a starting point for reconstructing central features of Paul's theology.

Trouble at Colossae

Whatever one says about its authorship, Colossians is clearly addressed to a Christian community undergoing what the writer regarded as a theological crisis. The problems in Colossae have been generated by teachings that have threatened to undermine the readers' Christian identity. The document does not tell us whether those responsible for these teachings originated from within the community of Colossae, from a rival local Jewish or pagan religious group, or from the outside. It is not clear, for instance, whether Archippus, who in 4:17 is urged to 'complete the task' he has received in the Lord, is being challenged as one who in some way exemplifies the troubles introduced by the opponents or as one who is simply being encouraged to follow through with his calling. Thus, in the absence of any data arising from persons mentioned in the letter, we are left to infer a profile of the opponents on the basis of ideas attributed to them in the text. In addition to clues from the letter, any portrait of the opponents must, of course, be consistent with what can be known about the local religious environment, on the one hand, and – because of the references to 'circumcision' (2:11, 13), 'feasts, new moons, and sabbaths' (2:16) and 'worship of angels' (2:18) – with what can be known about possible expressions of Jewish tradition in Asia Minor, on the other.[7]

Since the information about the opponents is conveyed through a series of hostile statements, features of their ideas should be reconstructed with caution. Nevertheless, several clues may be identified from the text. On a general note, the author characterizes the opponents' instructions as a deceptive 'philosophy' based on 'human tradition according to the elemental spirits of the universe' (2:8; cf. 2:22). More specifically, the teaching is said to advocate an adherence to dietary regulations, the observance of religious feasts, 'new moons', and 'sabbaths' (2:16), and a submission to a strict form of physical asceticism (2:20b–22). The vocabulary used in 2:16 and the author's reference to 'circumcision' in 2:11 suggest that the Colossian community was being confronted with ideas and practices which, if not immediately derived from Jewish practices, were at the very least significantly shaped by Jewish tradition.

Perhaps the most important text for determining the profile and nature of the opponents is the enigmatic reference to 'angels' in 2:18, the meaning of which has been subject to vigorous scholarly debate. The text of 2:18 may be translated as follows: 'Do not let anyone disqualify you, insisting on humility [or self-abasement] and worship of [or together with] angels, which things he has seen when entering, puffed up without cause by the mind of his flesh.' Traditionally, it has been supposed that the author is here vilifying those who were encouraging others to offer worship to angelic beings or deities in a cultic setting. By taking the Jewish dimension of the opponents' views seriously, some have argued that the author was attempting to refute a rigorous form of Judaism,[8] perhaps Essenism,[9] in which there must have been a questionably high regard for angelic intermediary figures.

However, given the absence of evidence of any outright 'angel cult' in Judaism,[10] a number of interpreters have argued instead that the proper background for this description is to be found in pagan mystery cults. In line with this background, the phrase 'worship of angels' is thus interpreted as the worship of 'cosmic deities' – these are represented in 2:8 as the 'elemental spirits of the universe' – by those who have been initiated into the cults.[11] Although this explanation reflects a commendable interest in finding local factors behind the controversy in Colossae, the evidence produced is largely limited to a single word in 2:18, and the inscriptions from Claros used to illuminate this background date from the middle of the second century. Thus the viability of this portrait of the opponents has been questioned.

Still another view has preferred to speak of a religious 'syncretism' behind 2:18, in which the notion of local religious influences at Colossae is combined with the possibility of a Jewish presence.[12] One reconstruction of the opponents that has won considerable support in recent years has placed the opponents' teachings against the backdrop of a more thoroughgoing Jewish apocalyptic form of asceticism. According to this view, the 'worship of angels' is to be interpreted as a reprehensible aspiration to participate in angelic worship, while the ascetic practices of 'humility' and dietary regulations are considered as ways of preparing for visionary experiences in which these angels are observed.[13] The advantage of this view is primarily twofold. In the first place, the motifs of 'humility' and 'worship with angels' occur together in the context of visionary accounts in the contemporary Jewish apocalyptic literature.[14] Secondly, and more importantly, this proposal offers a coherent way of explaining why the teachings of the opponents might have appealed to the Colossians as a viable expression of Christian faith. On the basis of the false teachings, some in the community may have found themselves thinking, rather plausibly, that if Christ's resurrected state is a heavenly one, then in order to achieve Christian maturity, it is necessary to do so as tangibly as possible, that is, by engaging in rigorous ascetic practices which, in turn, would have paved the way to a mystical participation in angelic worship of God.

Although perhaps the most coherent hypothesis, this understanding of the opponents does nevertheless encounter difficulties with regard to 2:18, especially as not only the 'worship of angels' but also the 'humility' is described as what has been 'seen'. If ascetic practices are meant to be preparatory for visionary experiences, then how is it that these activities are to be 'seen' in the same sense as the angelic worship which is observed in the visions themselves? Moreover, some Jewish apocalyptic documents not only refer to angelic worship of God but also, at the same time, mention the veneration of angels[15] even while cautioning against the danger that seers may be tempted to direct worship of angels within the context of their visionary experiences.[16] Therefore, perhaps a more satisfactory way of dealing with the problem is to understand the verb 'to see' less in its literal sense than in a derived connotation, namely, in the sense of 'to experience within the context of seeing'. This understanding does not require that ascetic practices be the object of visionary experiences, nor does it require that 'worship of angels' mean either 'worship with angels' or 'worshipping the angels'; these are not mutually exclusive alternatives.

Taken together, these considerations allow for the following profile of the opponents: (1) They were Christians well acquainted with Jewish practices and ascetic-mystical traditions, and thus perhaps Christian Jews. (2) They advocated a series of practices through which one could identify and measure spiritual maturity: circumcision, observance of special days of the calendar, dietary regulations, and participation in visionary experiences in which angels played a significant role.

From the opponents to a theological response

The author discourages the Colossian Christians from becoming involved in a series of practices which he regards as superfluous to one's basic identity in Christ. The desire to participate in angelic worship is dangerous because it detracts from the all-sufficiency of Christ, in whom the fullness of God resides (2:9). The ascetic preparations for mystical visions, the quasi-angelic existence achieved through participation in heavenly worship, and the possibility of becoming infatuated with the angels themselves all threaten to diminish the completeness of God's self-disclosure through the person of Christ. One may infer that the opponents thought of maturity as a new level of spirituality and knowledge which went beyond 'Christ'. They may have modelled Christian faith on Christ's heavenly state, finding therein a warrant to consider any physical, or terrestrial, activity as inferior to that which is heavenly.

In stark contrast, the author is convinced that the opponents and those who are influenced by them have sacrificed the all-encompassing significance of Christ to a dualistic worldview that breeds a false sense of superiority (2:18b). In reality, the practices required by those troubling Christians in Colossae do not lead to spiritual maturity and 'wisdom' at all (2:23), but are rather a shadowy illusion (2:17; cf. 2:4b). For the opponents, living in the 'flesh' is to be denounced as a yielding to base human appetites. For the author, however, the problem of the 'flesh' is reconceived from above; fleshly living is the result when, fuelled by spiritual arrogance, the opponents ignore the salvific importance of life in the body.

The author rejects a cosmology that subordinates life below to a heavenly state of spiritual maturity; Christ is not to be placed in the service of cosmology (2:20) or philosophy (2:8). Thus for him Christ *is* cosmology (1:15–20), Christ *is* wisdom (2:3), and Christ *is* spirituality, the beginning and end of religious maturity (1:28; 2:6–7; 3:1–4). This redefinition of values on the basis of christology is an important reason why the author urges his Colossian readers to continue to remain loyal to the tradition they received when they became Christians (2:6–7).

Hence it is not surprising that once the author has vehemently condemned the opponents' views, his exhortations to the Colossians are decidedly christocentric in character: the Colossians are to seek 'the things that are above, where Christ is' (3:1); 'let the peace of Christ rule in your hearts' (3:15); 'let the word of Christ dwell in you richly' (3:16); do 'everything in the name of the Lord Jesus' (3:17); 'serve the Lord Christ' (3:24); and recognize that there is 'a Master in heaven' (4:1). The opponents, on the other hand, have not held fast to the head, that is, they have not persisted in finding wisdom from its real source. Their claim to a heavenly spirituality beyond Christ is misguided because Christ himself, who is seated at the right hand of God (3:1b), has been exalted to the pinnacle of reality. If Christ is the measure of all reality, then the 'things that are above' cannot by definition lie outside or, better, above Christ. And because the structure of the universe, whether heaven or earth, has been fashioned through the agency of Christ in creation (1:15–20), the state of being 'raised with Christ' and being devoted to 'things that are above' (3:1–2) require that one take seriously the created order as a whole. Hence attentiveness to what is 'above' finds legitimate expression, not in asceticism of the body or through participation in angelic life, but in love, mutual support, and ordered behaviour within the framework of existing relationships in the Christian community (3:5–14) and of existing social structures in the world (3:18–4:1).

The Colossian hymn

Although statements about Christ in Colossians were no doubt formulated in such a way as to respond to the issues posed by the opponents, the author also may have drawn on tradition to support his position. This is likely in the case of the Christ-hymn of 1:15–20.[17] The hymn, which shows no signs of a polemic against opposing views, makes a grand claim in the way it links Jesus' death by crucifixion to cosmology. Inspired by reflection on the reconciling significance of Jesus' death for both earthly and heavenly spheres of creation (verse 20), the tradition begins with the conclusion that the crucified Christ, God's Son (verse 13), must therefore have been God's agent through whom all of creation, whether visible or invisible, came into being (verse 16). The former claim is reminiscent of Pauline statements about the death of Jesus as a conciliatory event (cf. Rom. 5:10; 1 Cor. 7:11; 2 Cor. 5:18–20), while the latter recalls Paul's statement in 1 Cor. 8:6 (cf. further Heb. 1:3 and John 1:1–3). Here, however, the explicit link between the pre-existent agency of Christ as God's Son and the death of Jesus is more clearly articulated in the hymn than before (cf. Phil. 2:6–11; 2 Cor. 8:9).

The content of the hymn in its entirety would have been without religious-historical precedent, especially outside the early Christian communities. Nevertheless, the sapiential background to the hymn is important; some early Jewish documents suggest how much the hymn's claims about Christ build on the notion of 'wisdom' that could be described as if a personified being alongside God. Like Christ, 'wisdom' could be regarded as 'firstborn' in creation (Prov. 8:22, 25; Philo, *Ebr.* 30–1; *Quaest. Gen.* 4.97), being 'before all things' (Sir. 1:4), holding 'all things together' (Wis. 1:6–7), being the 'image of the invisible God' (Wis. 7:26), and as having participated in the fashioning of 'all things' (Prov. 3:19; 8:22–31; Ps. 104:24; and esp. Wis. 7:22; 8:2, 4–5; 9:2).[18] If the troublemakers in Colossae were laying claim to a superior wisdom and to a level of experience that goes beyond Christ, then the transfer of functions from 'wisdom' as a divine attribute to Christ in the hymn would, on the grounds of a Christ-cosmology, have rendered this claim categorically impossible from the start.

Elsewhere in the letter, the author creatively adapted language from the hymn to emphasize how a proper understanding of Christ makes the opponents' teachings superfluous. Firstly, whereas the hymn refers to Christ as 'the head of the body, the church' (1:18), the author both retains this notion (3:15) and goes beyond it by identifying the 'body' more directly with Christ (1:22, 24; 2:16, 19), whose body, in turn, is identified as the church (2:16; cf. verse 19). Any life inside the church that does not immediately derive from and reflect the pre-eminence of Christ is thus precluded (3:15–17).

Secondly, the emphasis of the hymn on Christ's agency in the creation of 'all things' and sustenance of 'all things' in him (verses 16–17) provides the author, no doubt aware of the wisdom motif behind the tradition, with a warrant to claim that in Christ 'are hidden all the treasures of wisdom and knowledge' (2:3; cf. 1:9). Moreover, if in Christ the fabric of the cosmos is held together, then it is only in Christ as head (2:19), life (3:4), and source of wisdom and knowledge (2:6) that the Christian community as a whole will grow into maturity (2:6, 19) and social relationships among its members will be properly ordered (3:18–4:1). Thus the code governing social relationships laid out in 3:18–4:1 is not simply reflections of a *status quo*; it is qualified at every opportunity by the author's appeals to Christ through phrases such as 'in the Lord' (3:18, 20), 'fearing the Lord' (3:22), 'as to the Lord' (3:23), 'you serve the Lord Christ' (3:24), 'you also have a Master in heaven' (4:1).

Thirdly, the hymn's emphasis that thrones, dominions, rulers, and powers were – along with everything else – created through the agency of Christ 1.1322(1:16) helps the author diminish the importance being attached to the angelic and elemental powers which the readers are being tempted to adhere to (2:8, 18, 20).

Fourthly, in addition to Christ's pre-eminence over creation, the hymn identifies Christ as 'firstborn from the dead' (1:18), a clear reference to his resurrection. This death and resurrection motif is transferred by the author into statements about the Christian community. The Christ event not only has brought forgiveness of sins and reconciliation (1:13, 20, 21; 2:13), but is the very framework within which the readers are to structure their lives. Through baptism they have been initiated into the triumph of Jesus' death over the legal demands and inimical powers (2:14–15) and they have already been 'raised with Christ' (2:13; 3:1), whereby they may 'put on' a new form of life in which ethnic, social, and religious distinctions no longer count in the same way as before (3:9–11, 12–14). Hence it is imperative that the readers realize not only what their identity is in relation to the Christ event, but also that this be the sole basis on which they grow into maturity (2:6–7, 19). It is in Christ that they are to convert their identity into appropriate ethical and social behaviour (3:5–8; 3:18–4:1); in Christ spirituality and life in the community have their foundation; and in Christ the 'glory' destined for God's people will become fully manifest (1:26–7; 3:4).

The household code

In addition to ideas contained in the Christ-hymn, the author seems to have drawn on some form of tradition in formulating rules for the household in 3:18–4:1. Formally, these instructions might not seem to provide a necessary part of the argument in the letter, as the exhortation to be devoted to prayer and thanksgiving in 4:2 could easily be read as if it immediately followed upon the exhortation to 'do everything in the name of the Lord Jesus, giving thanks to God the Father through him' in 3:17. Moreover, the rules are paralleled by similar collections of codes adapted by other early Christian writers (especially Eph. 5:22–6:9; 1 Pet. 2:18–3:7),[19] which, in turn, reflect the importance attached by Graeco-Roman philosophers, historiographers, and Hellenistic Jewish writers to 'household management' as integral to the proper ordering of society.[20] Some have interpreted these regulatory codes as a means of coping with a delay of the parousia or of dealing with overly non-conformist spiritual enthusiasts. Whatever the merit of these reasons, it is at least likely that they reflect a broad concern to give Christian instructions a profile in relation to widespread ideals concerning social behaviour (wives and husbands, parents and children, masters and slaves).[21]

Within the context of Colossians, the regulations serve a double function. On the one hand, over against the opponents, they assist the author in arguing that spiritual maturity should not be looked for outside the network of social structures of the present world, a network which he takes for granted. On the other hand, the entire system of social relationships is relativized or even held in check; submission in each of the relationships is to be adhered to *in accordance with* what is 'fitting in the Lord' (3:18 – wives to husbands), 'pleasing in the Lord' (3:20 – children to parents), and showing respect and rendering service to 'the Lord' (3:22, 23, 24 – servants to masters). Slave-owners are reminded that they are no different from slaves before God, who is impartial (3:25) and to whom they must answer as their 'master in heaven' (4:1). Although the household rules are one way the author responds to the opponents' teachings, they are nevertheless placed 'under the critical distance of the gospel'.[22] The code in Colossians, therefore, shows how instructions in relation to social institutions functioned as a means of articulating a Christian social identity by an author who is delicately negotiating between specific internal and broader external issues encountered by the community.

PHILEMON: GENERAL SITUATION

Senders and recipients

The letter to Philemon distinguishes itself not only as the shortest of Paul's letters (335 words in total) but also as the only one addressed primarily to an individual. It claims to be written by Paul during his imprisonment (verses 9, 13) together with Timothy (verse 1; cf. 2 Cor. 1:1 and Col. 1:1) and is addressed to a certain Philemon whose house is the gathering point for a church (verses 1–2). The inclusion of Apphia (Philemon's wife?), Archippus, and Philemon's house church in the address (verse 2) suggests that the letter was not ultimately intended to be private. The concerns expressed in the letter are thus placed within a context of social relationships within the Christian community. The letter not only involves a matter between Paul and Philemon: the way Philemon responds to what Paul writes will have implications for his church.

Location and the link to Colossians

Several names in the letter link Philemon above all with the letter to the Colossians: in addition to Archippus (cf. Col. 4:17), Paul mentions Epaphras (verses 23; cf. Col. 1:7–8; 4:12–13), Mark (verse 24; cf. Col. 4:10), Aristarchus (verses 24; cf. Col. 4:10), Demas and Luke (verse 24; cf. Col. 4:14), and Onesimus (verse 10; cf. Col. 4:9), through whom the letter is being delivered (verse 12). Since the author of Colossians regards Archippus, Epaphras, and Onesimus as from Colossae, there is no reason to doubt that Philemon and his house church were located there.

Just how the letters to Philemon and Colossians are linked has been the source of considerable debate; while the authenticity of Philemon has recently not been subject to doubt,[23] much has rested on whether or not the authenticity of Colossians as a letter of Paul can be upheld. If Paul wrote Colossians, then it is possible that Philemon was sent by the apostle as a letter (delivered by Onesimus) addressing a personal matter alongside a letter (delivered by Tychicus) that was dealing with broader issues being faced by the Christian community in Colossae as a whole.[24] Conversely, if

Colossians was written some time after Paul's death, then Philemon would have provided the author of Colossians with a likely source of references to the individuals mentioned in a bid to enhance the authenticity of the letter.

Both ways of construing the relationship between the letters are problematic. In the former instance, it would have to be asked why prominent persons in one letter – that is, Tychicus in Col. 4:8–9 (he is one of the main members of the party sent with the letter) and Philemon himself – are left unmentioned by Paul in the other. In the latter case, it remains puzzling why Philemon would have been omitted or Tychicus added in a letter which otherwise is supposed to depend on Philemon.[25] A search for an explanation of the differences in names between Colossians and Philemon leads to a third possibility, namely, that the two letters were composed relatively close to one another in time, but that someone other than Paul (Timothy?) was immediately responsible for Colossians.[26] Though this hypothesis seems to fit best with the evidence, it is nevertheless far from certain; scholars are not as yet in a position to resolve the matter with confidence.

Date and place of writing

The question of when Philemon was composed is bound up not only with how one relates it to Colossians, but also with which of Paul's imprisonments it has to do with. Scholars today are divided about whether Paul the prisoner was writing from Ephesus (presumably sometime during the mid 50s CE), Caesarea, or Rome (during the early 60s). Although the Ephesian imprisonment of Paul is hypothetical – it is not mentioned in Acts but has been inferred from 2 Cor. 1:8 and 11:23 – it commends itself for two main reasons. Firstly, the distance between Ephesus and Colossae to be covered by Onesimus in having come to Paul is far more realistic than a journey all the way to Rome and back. Secondly, Paul's declared wish that he might soon come to Philemon (verse 22) is more understandable if he were in Ephesus than far away in Rome.[27]

Genre and structure

The letter, which displays considerable diplomatic and rhetorical skill, adheres closely to the pattern of ancient Hellenistic letter writing, in particular letters of recommendation.[28] With this pattern in mind, one may divide Philemon into four sections: (1) the opening greeting (verses 1–3); (2) the thanksgiving and prayer for Philemon (verses 4–7); (3) the main body: Paul's appeal on behalf of Onesimus (verses 8–22); (4) the closing greetings (verses 23–4).

THE PURPOSE AND ARGUMENT OF THE LETTER

Purpose

Determining the occasion of Philemon depends largely on how the events leading up to the letter are reconstructed behind Paul's artful rhetoric. According to the text, Onesimus, a slave (verse 16), 'was separated' from his master, Philemon (verse 15), and had found his way to the imprisoned Paul (verses 11,13). While with Paul he had become a Christian (verse 10); in fact, Paul himself had developed affection for him (verse 12) and was now apparently benefiting from his service (verse 13). The tone and diplomatic language of the letter make it certain that the separation of Onesimus from Philemon did not occur under lawful circumstances and that Onesimus owed Philemon money (verse 18: 'if he has wronged or owes you . . . ').[29] Hence Paul's own involvement with Onesimus required explanation and, in view of the breach, the status of Onesimus' legal relationship with Philemon needed to be resolved. However, it is not merely a matter of legal reciprocity between Paul and Philemon. Although Paul formally offers to remunerate Philemon for any loss incurred through the absence of Onesimus, he still writes as one who, assuming that he is in a superior position in the Christian community, can 'command' Philemon to exercise his duty (verse 8) and expect him to be obedient (verse 21). Philemon, then, provides an example of how responsibilities in the legal and Christian spheres of life interfaced and, moreover, how Paul attempted to deal with such a situation.

The text does not specify the circumstances under which Onesimus came to Paul. Was Onesimus, as has traditionally been thought, a fugitive slave, or did he leave his master in order to seek out Paul? If Onesimus had been a fugitive in the Roman legal sense, then it is not clear why he came to Paul, who was a friend of Philemon.[30] Running away from his or her owner would have incurred severe penalties for a slave, and much the same applied to those who harboured such slaves. In the case of fugitive slaves who were caught, for instance, punishments could involve anything from beatings to crucifixion. For this reason, fugitives were likely to escape to far away places where they were unknown, or they sometimes sought asylum in temples where they asked for help in finding a new owner.[31] Though the matter addressed in the letter to Philemon is delicate, nothing in the letter itself indicates that such legal implications underlie Paul's attempts to persuade Philemon to welcome Onesimus back. Instead, Roman jurisprudence foresaw cases in which a slave having problems with his or her owner could engage a third person to act as his or her advocate, especially as the owner was likely to be angry. The slave's aim, in this scenario, is not to run away or escape, but rather, with better conditions in sight, to be readmitted to the owner's household. Despite a remaining uncertainty about whether Roman law would have been perceived as applying to Onesimus as Philemon's slave, it is this construal which seems to conform best to the genre of epistle adopted by Paul (see above).

Argument

Paul makes clear that, whatever the relationship between Philemon and Onesimus has been in the past, things have changed. What was once a legal matter in which an inferior slave was subject to some form of punishment by the owner has been radically altered by Onesimus' conversion. To be sure, Paul still recognizes Philemon's right to interpret Onesimus' actions as legal wrongdoing (verse 18). In the mode of a diplomat, however, Paul does not attempt to put a spin on a past event which cannot be changed. Now, Paul calls not only Philemon a 'brother' (verses 7, 20) but also Onesimus (verse 16 – 'a *beloved* brother'). As a believer, Onesimus is now 'more than a slave' (verse 16). Onesimus' conversion and the change of relationship it implies are expressed by word play in verses 10–11: the name 'Onesimus', one commonly given to slaves of this period, itself means 'useful' or 'beneficial' (it has the same root as *onaimen*, 'let me benefit', in verse 20); and Paul declares that whereas he was once 'useless' (*achrestos*) to Philemon, Onesimus has now become 'useful' (*euchrestos*) to them both. Paul expects that Philemon will on his own be able to discern the consequences of this and do 'what is good' without being under constraint (verse 14). Paul even expects Philemon to welcome Onesimus back just as he would Paul himself (verse 17). And what does Paul expect for himself from Philemon's hospitality? According to verse 22, it is a guest room! Whereas the situation has begun by Onesimus being in debt to his master (verse 18), Paul's argument, on the basis of Onesimus' conversion, turns the tables: Philemon is, in fact, the one who is indebted to Paul (verse 19).

By carefully negotiating his argument between demand and constraint, on the one hand, and by appealing to Philemon's honour and goodwill, on the other, Paul reconfigures a once problematic relationship between master and slave into what he hopes will become a relationship in which the master has not so much lost a slave as gained a brother (verses 15–16). Paul's rhetoric is, therefore, deliberative; for all the freedom accorded to Philemon, diplomacy and rhetoric are mustered to persuade Philemon that there is only one appropriate course of action towards Onesimus, an action which is ultimately to his own benefit as well. Implicit may be Paul's hope that Philemon will now grant Onesimus manumission,[32] though the text itself does not specify that this is precisely what Paul has in mind (cf. 1 Cor. 7:21).

Notes

1 See variously V. P. Furnish, 'Colossians, Epistle to the', *ABD* 1.1094-5; J. D. G. Dunn, *The Epistles to the Colossians and to Philemon*, NIGTC (Grand Rapids/Carlisle: Eerdmans/ Paternoster, 1996) 39–41.

2 See Dunn, *Colossians and Philemon* 41–2.

3 On the history of this discussion, see, e.g., W. G. Kümmel, *Introduction to the New Testament* (ET Nashville: Abingdon, 1975) 340–6.

4 For the basic arguments, see E. P. Sanders, 'Literary Dependence in Colossians', *JBL* 85 (1966) 28–45; E. Lohse, 'Pauline Theology in the Letter to the Colossians', *NTS* 15 (1969) 211–20; Furnish, 'Colossians' 1092–4.

5 So, e.g., Kümmel, *Introduction*; P. T. O'Brien, *Colossians, Philemon*, WBC 44 (Waco: Word, 1982) xli–xlix; and L. T. Johnson, *The Writings of the New Testament* (Philadelphia: Fortress, 1986) 357–9.

6 See Dunn, *Colossians and Philemon* 38–9 and references in n. 47 there.

7 The religious background to the opponents' teaching in Colossians has been variously characterized:
  (a) mystery religions – e.g. M. Dibelius, 'Isis Initiation', in F. O. Francis and W. Meeks, eds., *Conflict at Colossae* (Missoula: Scholars, 1973) 61–121;
  (b) proto-Gnostic syncretism consisting of pagan and Jewish elements – e.g. G. Bornkamm, 'The Heresy of Colossians', in Francis and Meeks, *Conflict* 123–45; Furnish, 'Colossians' 1092;
  (c) Jewish syncretism – e.g. E. Schweizer, *The Letter to the Colossians* (London: SPCK, 1982) 131–3: 'Jewish Pythagoreanism'; C. E. Arnold, *The Colossian Syncretism* (Grand Rapids: Baker, 1996);
  (d) some form of Judaism – e.g. F. O. Francis, 'Humility and Angel Worship in Colossae', in Francis and Meeks, *Conflict* 163–95; O'Brien, *Colossians, Philemon* 141–5; Dunn, *Colossians and Philemon* 29–35.

8 So, e.g., A. L. Williams, 'The Cult of Angels at Colossae', *JTS* 10 (1909) 413–38; J. J. Gunther, *St. Paul's Opponents and their Background* (Leiden: Brill, 1973) 173–7.

9 J. B. Lightfoot, *St Paul's Epistles to the Colossians and to Philemon* (London: Macmillan, 1879) 71–111.

10 E.g. L. W. Hurtado, *One God, One Lord: Early Christian Devotion and Ancient Jewish Monotheism* (Philadelphia: Fortress, 1988) 23–35, followed with some reservations by L. T. Stuckenbruck, *Angel Veneration and Christology*, WUNT 2.70 (Tübingen: Mohr Siebeck, 1995).

11 Dibelius, 'Isis Initiation'.

12 See n. 7 above, categories (b) and (c).

13 The position originally argued by Francis, 'Humility and Angel Worship in Colossae', has been followed by, e.g., C. A. Evans, 'The Colossian Mystics', *Biblica* 63 (1982) 188–205; O'Brien, *Colossians, Philemon* xxx–xxxviii; C. Rowland, 'Apocalyptic Visions and the Exaltation of Christ in the Letter to the Colossians', *JSNT* 19 (1983) 73–83; T. J. Sappington, *Revelation and Redemption at Colossae*,

JSNTS 53 (Sheffield: JSOT, 1991) 150–70; and Dunn, *Colossians and Philemon* 180–2.

14 Dan. 9:3; 10:2–3; T. Isaac 4:1–6; 5:4; 4 Ezra 5:13, 20; 6:35; 9:23–5; 2 Bar. 5:7–6:4; 9:2–10:1; 12:5–13:2; 43:3; 47:2–48:1; Apoc. Abr. 9:7–10 and 12:1–2. See also Philo, *Som.* 1.36; *Vit. Mos.* 2.67–70; *Sacr.* 59–63.

15 This is a possibility acknowledged by Francis ('Humility and Angelic Worship' 129). See Tobit 11:14–15 (both recensions) alongside 12:16; *Songs of the Sabbath Sacrifice* from Qumran (4Q400 2.1–2 and 4Q403 1 i.32–3).

16 The *Ascension of Isaiah* is an interesting case in point: it combines two cautions against inappropriate worship and honour, respectively, towards angels (7:21; 8:4–5) with the notion of angelic beings being venerated (e.g. 7:15). Cf. L. T. Stuckenbruck, 'Worship and Monotheism in the *Ascension of Isaiah*', in C. C. Newman, J. R. Davila, and G. S. Lewis, eds., *The Jewish Roots of Christological Monotheism*, JSJS 63 (Leiden: Brill, 1999) 70–89.

17 The extent to which the author has composed part or even all of the hymn is open to question. What is significant is that the wording of the hymn does not in itself seem to have been formulated with the specific troubles in Colossae in mind.

18 Also significant are early Jewish texts which refer to a personifying 'logos' to which, as if a divine agent, similar functions could be attributed; see Sir. 43:26; Philo, *Som.* 1.622–64; *Heres* 23, 188; *Fuga* 112; *Vit. Mos.* 2.133; *Quaest. Exod.* 2.118.

19 In the New Testament see 1 Tim. 2:8–15; 6:1–2; and Titus 2:1–10. See also Didache 4:9–11; 1 Clement 21:6–9; Ignatius, *Polycarp* 4:1–5:2; Barnabas 19:5–7; and Polycarp, *Philippians* 4:2–3.

20 Concerning these sources and their significance, see esp. J. Crouch, *The Origin and Intention of the Colossian Haustafel*, FRLANT 109 (Göttingen: Vandenhoeck & Ruprecht, 1972) 74–101; D. Balch, 'Household Codes', in D. E. Aune, ed., *Greco-Roman Literature and the New Testament* (Atlanta: Scholars, 1988) 25–50; J. D. G. Dunn, 'The Household Rules in the New Testament', in S. C. Barton, ed., *The Family in Theological Perspective* (Edinburgh: T. & T. Clark, 1996) 43–63.

21 See Dunn, *Colossians and Philemon* 244–5.

22 So Johnson, *Writings of the New Testament* 365.

23 F. C. Baur's conclusion in the nineteenth century that Philemon is a non-Pauline 'Christian romance' (*Paul: The Apostle of Jesus Christ* (1845; ET 2 vols., London: Williams & Norgate, vol. 2, 1875) 144) is simply untenable on grounds of vocabulary, style and the structure of the argument; see esp. S. S. Bartchy, 'Philemon, Epistle to', *ABD* 5.306.

24 So, e.g., F. F. Bruce, *The Epistles to the Colossians, to Philemon, and to the Ephesians*, NICNT (Grand Rapids: Eerdmans, 1984) 177; Johnson, *Writings of the New Testament* 353–4.

25 See Dunn, *Colossians and Philemon* 37–9.

26 Ibid., 38–9 and bibliography in n. 47 there.

27 See esp. the thorough discussion in O'Brien, *Colossians, Philemon* xli–xliv.

28 See esp. C. H. Kim, *Form and Structure of the Familiar Greek Letter of Recommendation* (Missoula: SBL, 1972); S. K. Stowers, 'Letters (Greek and Latin)', *ABD* 4.290–3.

29 Verse 18 does not make clear whether Onesimus' financial obligation to Philemon was due to an act of stealing or to the removal of himself as a possession from Philemon's household.

30 This question is raised by P. Lampe, 'Keine "Sklavenflucht" des Onesimus', *ZNW* 76 (1985) 135–7, whose alternative to the 'fugitive' hypothesis has influenced this discussion.

31 See further the helpful discussions, with relevant bibliography, in Bartchy, 'Philemon' 307–8 and Dunn, *Colossians and Philemon* 303–7.

32 J. A. Harrill, *The Manumission of Slaves in Early Christianity*, HUT 32 (Tübingen: Mohr Siebeck, 1995). See S. S. Bartchy, 'Slavery (Greco-Roman)', *ABD* 6.71.

9 Ephesians

ANDREW T. LINCOLN

Among the major distinctives of Ephesians within the Pauline letter collection, there are two that make the most immediate impression. In terms of content, the concentrated attention it gives to the phenomenon of the church stands out, so that it is not at all surprising that this letter has been a key resource for theological reflection on the corporate nature of Christian existence. In terms of form, it is noticeable that discussion of the church appears in both halves of a document that does not have the usual Pauline letter body. Instead, between its letter opening (1:1, 2) and closing (6:21–4), Ephesians is divided into two lengthy parts – an expansion of the usual thanksgiving section that runs from 1:3 to 3:21, and an extended paraenesis or section of ethical exhortation that stretches from 4:1 to 6:20. In the former the letter's recipients are reminded of the privileges they enjoy as believers in Christ and members of the church and of their significant role in God's plan for the cosmos. In the latter they are summoned, in the light of their privileged status, to conduct their lives in an appropriate fashion in the church and in the world.

Ephesians is also distinctive as the most general of the Pauline letters. Since the usual strategy for interpreting Paul's letters builds on the recognition that he carries out the pastoral application of his gospel in interaction with the particular circumstances and needs of his readers, Ephesians proves initially frustrating. It gives us extremely little information about its recipients or their specific circumstances. Even its title is misleading at this point, because 'in Ephesus' was not included in 1:1 in the earliest manuscripts. Once the superscription 'to the Ephesians' became attached to the letter on the basis of the tradition of Paul's stay in that city and the surprising lack of any other letter from the apostle to the Christians there, the place name was also later inserted in the address. This should not be taken to mean, as is frequently suggested, that the original letter was a circular with a blank left for a place name. There are no examples of such practice in the extant letters from the ancient world.

The reading of 1:1 in the best manuscripts is difficult to translate because of a very awkward *kai* ('and'), but is usually rendered 'to the saints who are also faithful in Christ Jesus'. This is quite unlike the addresses in other Pauline letters. The most economical explanation of the textual data is the hypothesis that the letter was originally addressed to two churches, so that the address read 'to the saints who are in x and in y, faithful in Christ Jesus'. This would also be more in line with the form of other addresses. What then happened was that, in the interests of the catholicity of the Pauline correspondence, the two place names were deleted by a scribe who somewhat clumsily left the 'and' between them in the text.

If the search for the whereabouts of the readers is unpromising – the usual guess, partly on the basis of the later association with Ephesus, was that the readers were somewhere in Asia Minor – can we at least discover from what the writer says about them who they were and how he perceived their needs? In three places the letter is explicit that its addressees are Gentile Christians. 'So then, remember that at one time you Gentiles in the flesh, called the "uncircumcision" by those who are called the "circumcision"' is the way that 2:11 begins, without any indication that this presupposes a change of audience. The readers are addressed again in 3:1 as 'you Gentiles' and later in 4:17 exhorted to 'no longer live as the Gentiles live' with the obvious implication that, although they are ethnically Gentiles, their previous lifestyle, that of Gentile non-believers, must now cease.

If what is said to these former Gentiles does indeed reflect their perceived needs, then the initial eulogy in 1:3–14 and the depiction of the contrast between their past and present that shapes both 2:1–10 and 2:11–22 suggest that they need reminding of the privileges of their salvation. They also need to recall the debt that they owe to Paul's unique ministry (3:1–13). The intercessory prayer reports in 1:17–23 and 3:14–19 indicate that they require greater insight into and further knowledge of what their salvation entails, particularly of the power of God that is available in Christ and of the love of Christ. The content of 4:1–16 shows that the recipients need to recognize the church's unity and to play their part in maintaining that unity and enabling the church to grow to maturity. The topics dealt with in the exhortation of 4:17–5:20 suggest that more attention ought to be paid to the quality of their behaviour in such areas as dealing with anger, edifying speech, forgiveness, sexual purity, worship, and thanksgiving. They need also to bring distinctively Christian motivation into play in their conduct in the household (5:21–6:9) and to resolve to stand firm by availing themselves of Christ's strength and God's armour (6:10–20). By this means we can build up a picture of the readers as those whose main problems, in the writer's view, are powerlessness, instability, and lack of resolve, stemming from an insufficient awareness of their true identity as Christians.

Such a picture is sufficiently general to fit a group of Christians in a variety of times and places. But some features make sense in a setting after the death of Paul, a setting that is increasingly recognized to be the most likely for Ephesians. There are four main grounds that are part of the cumulative case for holding that its writer was a follower of Paul rather than the apostle himself. In contrast to the more direct and incisive style of the undisputed letters, Ephesians is written in long sentences with numerous relative and participial clauses, strings of prepositional phrases, and the piling up of synonyms. There are changes in emphasis in the thought of this letter in comparison with the undisputed ones, so that the focus is more on Christ's exaltation and cosmic lordship than on his death, on realized eschatology rather than an imminent parousia, on the universal church rather than the local assembly. Further, Ephesians reflects a setting later than Paul's time. Gone are Paul's struggles over the admission of Gentiles, and instead 2:11–22 looks back on an achieved unity between Jews and Gentiles with the abrogation of the law and the creation of a new humanity that transcends the old ethnic categories. The digression of 3:1–13 with its depiction of Paul as 'the very least of all the saints' in order to magnify the grace of God in his life reads like a retrospective estimate of Paul's place in the schema of salvation. Finally, Ephesians appears to have been familiar with and made use of Colossians. When an examination of the similarities and differences between the words, phrases, and themes of the two letters is considered in the light of the fact that those themes follow the same sequence, the most likely explanation is that the writer of Ephesians knew Colossians well enough to employ it creatively in his own fresh reinterpretation of the Pauline gospel.

If then Ephesians is pseudonymous, a setting after Paul's death would help to explain why churches of the Pauline mission would need to have underlined for them what Paul's ministry achieved and how much they owed to the apostle. With his death there would also have been a loss of a unifying human source of authority and a consequent lack of a sense of cohesion and unity on the part of the churches of the Gentile mission. This would make sense of the letter's insistence that its readers are part of the universal church, its appeal for the maintenance of unity, and its emphasis on the apostolic tradition and the role of teachers in passing on that tradition. In addition, the death of Paul would have brought home the fact that the parousia was not going to be quite as imminent as the Pauline churches had once expected and that they needed help in facing a more long-term coexistence with the surrounding society without simply accommodating themselves to its values. So, while Ephesians addresses less specific and explicit needs than the undisputed letters of Paul, it is not simply a general theological treatise. In fact, it can be seen as continuing Paul's tradition of rehearsing the gospel message in a way that is geared to the needs of readers, this time by updating the Pauline gospel for the needs of his churches in the generation after his death.

The writer's rhetorical strategy in attempting to build up his readers' sense of identity and unity begins with writing in the name of Paul, in order both to signal the source of the authoritative tradition he is passing on and to reproduce the apostolic presence with its sense of immediacy. He then employs the language of worship, of thanksgiving, of prayer, of the reminder of the contrast between past and present, and of doxology in chapters 1–3. This consolidates the writer's and readers' common relation to God and Christ and their shared values and taps into the readers' religious sensibilities and their emotions. By means of participation in thanksgiving and doxology, their confidence in the Pauline gospel's alternative vision of existence is bolstered. They celebrate a reality in which Christ has triumphed over hostile cosmic powers and has given to the church all necessary resources for living.

In this way the writer provides an effective springboard for the second part of his message. Its ethical exhortation builds on and arises out of the motivation generated by the sense of gratitude evoked through praise. This pastoral strategy reflects a theology in which Christian living is first of all a response to God's gracious initiative in Christ. The term that best represents the writer's own perspective on Christian identity is 'calling', and this term is employed in a way that sums up his related purposes in the two parts of the letter. What he wants the readers to grasp is described in the prayer report in 1:18 – 'that you may know what is the hope of your calling'. And how he wants them to behave is encapsulated in the very first verse of the paraenesis, 4:1 – 'I, therefore, the prisoner in the Lord, beg you to lead a life worthy of the calling to which you have been called.'

As was noted at the beginning of this chapter, distinctive to Ephesians' elaboration of the notion of calling is its stress on the corporate aspect – belonging to the church. There are nine uses of the term for the church (ekklesia), and their reference, as in images for the church such as 'the body of Christ', is not primarily to local churches, as in the undisputed letters, but to the universal church, the empire-wide community of Christian believers seen in its totality. The first use of the term in 1:22 dominates the closing of the initial thanksgiving period and sets the tone by emphasizing, in the wake of Christ's exaltation, the exalted status of the church, since Christ's supremacy over the cosmos, his headship over all things, is said to be exercised for the benefit of the church. In 3:10 the church is again assigned a highly significant role at the heart of the disclosure of the mystery of God's purpose for the cosmos. It is in fact the means by which God makes known the divine wisdom to the principalities and authorities in the heavenly places. Then in the only doxology in the New Testament to refer to the church, glory is ascribed to God not only in Christ but also first in the church (3:21). In this striking formulation the church is seen as the community within humanity whose existence is meant to redound to the glory of God. The remaining uses of the term *ekklesia* are clustered within the writer's creative elaboration on the household code (5:23, 24, 25, 27, 29, 32), where the relationship of union between Christ and the church is made the model for Christian marriage.

Ephesians employs a variety of images for the church. So, for example, it is one new person, a new humanity created to replace the division and enmity between Jew and Gentile in the old order (2:15). It is God's household or family (2:19). It is Christ's fullness (1:23), that which is filled by Christ, the present focus for and medium of his presence. And it is to grow into and appropriate that fullness (4:13). The church is Christ's bride (5:23–33), reminding the readers that in their intimate union with the exalted Christ they are to live holy lives, since the goal of Christ's love for the church in his sacrificial death was the presentation of the bride to himself in glory and moral perfection. It is the new temple with the exalted Christ as the keystone holding it all together, with Christian apostles and prophets as the foundation, having given the original interpretation of the gospel, and with believers as the bricks that are being built together into this temple that is God's dwelling place in the Spirit (2:20–2).

The dominant image, in that it is used ten times in the letter, is that of 'the body of Christ' (1:23; 2:16; 3:6; 4:4, 12, 16(twice); 5:23, 29, 30). In a variation on Jewish notions of representative solidarity, it entails that believers are seen as having been incorporated in Christ. The image is employed to help the readers to view themselves as a compact whole in relation to the exalted Christ as their head. In relation to Christ as head, the church as body can be depicted as both submitting to (5:23, 24) and receiving its life from Christ (4:15, 16). Elsewhere the force of body imagery is to stress that the church is one and indivisible (2:16; 3:6; 4:4). Yet in 4:7–16 the body of Christ as a structured unity is depicted as also containing the diversity of the contributions of every individual member and the special functions of the ministers of the word who act as ligaments, providing the connections between the various parts. The writer underscores that it is this interdependence of the various parts of the body that is necessary if there is to be proper corporate growth.

The body of Christ imagery serves as a reminder that Ephesians is supremely concerned about the unity of the church. The seven basic unities on which the existence of the church depends are set out in 4:4–6 – one body, one Spirit, one hope, one Lord, one faith, one baptism, one God and Father. Believers are urged to expend every effort (4:3) to maintain the unity the church already possesses and are instructed that the essential ingredient for achieving this is love (4:2, 15, 16). For the writer, the quality and unity of the church's corporate life has everything to do with the fulfilment of its calling in the world. He has already made clear in 1:10 what is the hope of that calling, what is the goal of God's purposes in the world, namely, the summing up of all things in harmony in Christ, a unified and reconciled cosmos. It is the emphasis on the church's unity that clarifies what he says later in 3:10 about its significant role in God's cosmic purposes. It discloses God's wisdom to the cosmic powers not by its preaching or by its worship but by its very existence as the one new humanity out of Jews and Gentiles. In its overcoming of the divisions of the old order the church reveals to the hostile powers that their fragmenting and alienating regime is at an end. For Ephesians the church in its unity is meant to serve in this world as a tangible pledge of the overcoming of all divisions when the cosmos is restored to harmony in Christ.

There can be little difficulty in seeing how the Nicene Creed's 'We believe in one holy catholic and apostolic Church' can be derived from Ephesians or why this letter has figured prominently in ecumenical discussion. It is also not surprising that Ephesians has been recognized as giving a catholic or universal impulse to Christians' view of the church, one that can serve to prevent a proper emphasis on being the church in a particular locality from becoming parochial or sectarian. Indeed the Second Vatican Council's *Constitution on the Church* caught the vision of Ephesians in depicting the church as 'the sacrament of intimate union with God and of unity for the whole human race'.

Its language of worship and prayer, its profound grasp of God's initiative in salvation, and its perspective on the church provide the context in which Ephesians encourages the moral formation of its readers. The patterns of behaviour that are in line with their new identity can be summed up as justice and holiness (4:24) or love (5:2). Practising these patterns is seen as learning Christ (4:20) and requires appropriating their new humanity and having their minds renewed (4:23, 24). Two major and overlapping areas are given special treatment – speech and sexual morality. Sins of the tongue are seen as detrimental to the work of a Holy Spirit who binds the community together. Since the readers are members of the body of Christ, they are to avoid lying, anger, and destructive and unwholesome words, all of which endanger harmonious relationships (4:25–5:2). Talk about fornication, obscenity, and coarse joking are also to be avoided. The writer believes that talk about sexual sins can lead to a tolerance of their practice, and so warns that fornicators, the impure, and the covetous will not inherit the kingdom. But in any case believers have a new identity as children of light with its connotations of holiness and, as they live in conformity with such an identity, this light that has Christ as its source is able to expose and transform the darkness of the surrounding society and its values (5:3–14).

The readers are to live responsibly in that society. Taking up the standards of proper household management in the Graeco-Roman world, the writer instructs his readers to bring to bear within the structures of the patriarchal household with its husband–wife, parent–children, master–slave relationships the Christian motivations of love and service (5:21–6:9). His distinctive contributions to early Christian treatment of this topic are twofold: his exhortation to all household members to submit to one another, which for him is quite compatible with the following instructions about particular subordination within the three relationships; and his extended discussion of the marriage relationship, which he compares to the union between Christ and the church. Within the household social differences remain but are transformed through the distinctive motivation that comes from believers' recognition of the lordship of Christ. Justified twenty-first-century sensitivities about the accommodation to patriarchy and slavery ought not to lead to an overlooking of the fact that this household code challenges the Graeco-Roman notion of household management as a constituent part of the state, replacing the rationale of loyalty to the state with that of submission to Christ.

Ephesians' vision of the church as having a special role in God's purposes can run the danger of triumphalism. It should be remembered, however, that for its original readers such a vision was provided not to confirm or boost their already arrogant view of themselves or their powerful status within society, but rather to strengthen an insufficient sense of their identity. For them and for later readers there are also two major constraints within the letter that do not permit any spirit of self-congratulation or complacency. It is made clear throughout that Christian believers owe their privileged status and special role to God's gracious initiative in Christ. Nowhere is this more forcefully stated than in 2:8–10 – 'For by grace you have been saved through faith, and this is not your own doing; it is the gift of God – not the result of works, so that no one may boast. For we are what he made us, created in Christ Jesus for good works, which God prepared beforehand to be our way of life.' It is noticeable that, whatever its range of meaning in the undisputed Paulines, where it is characteristically employed in the expression 'works of the law', here, removed from the context of polemic with other Jewish Christians, 'works' stands for human effort. Such effort is precisely what is ruled out as the cause or source of salvation in order that there should be no grounds for boasting. Even faith is held to be God's gift, and even believers' good works are to be seen as prepared by God for them in advance. Everything about Christian existence is to be attributed solely to God's grace.

The other constraining factor emerges especially in the summarizing exhortation of 6:10–20, which calls on the readers to view their role as part of a cosmic battle. God's purpose of harmony for the cosmos in the face of divisive powers may have the church as its present exhibit, but the letter concludes with a strong reminder that such evil powers still attempt to thwart that purpose. The battle imagery also becomes a vehicle for a final formulation of the writer's two earlier concerns – about the readers' identity and about their corresponding conduct. As regards their identity, they are to see themselves as Christ's salvation army, soldiers fitted out in God's full armour and having available to them all the resources of power that God has provided through the salvation accomplished in Christ. As regards their conduct, the first four items of the armour represent the virtues they must demonstrate – truthfulness, righteousness or justice, living out the peace produced by the gospel, and faithful reliance on God's resources in Christ. But above all, what is necessary in this battle is to stand firm. The call to stand is given three times (6:11, 13, 14). This exhortation to appropriate the resources for firm resolve in the face of the fierce forces of evil entails that what characterizes the church's role in the world is a confident realism rather than any naive optimism.

From the vantage point of the concluding exhortation the basic dynamic in the thought of Ephesians can be seen to be reflected in its use of the three verbs, 'to sit', 'to walk', and 'to stand'. The first part of the letter treated its readers' identity in terms of their status and privileges, and one of the most striking formulations of this perspective was the assertion that they had been seated with Christ in the heavenly places (2:6). The second part of the letter treated what it meant to live out this identity in the world, and each major section of its paraenesis contained the verb 'to walk' (4:1, 17; 5:2, 8, 15). Now the final call for firm resolve combines the emphases of sitting and walking in its exhortation to the readers 'to stand', that is, to maintain their position of strength in Christ as they live worthily of their calling in the world in the midst of opposition from hostile evil powers.

10 The Pastoral Epistles

ARLAND J. HULTGREN

The term 'Pastoral Epistles' applies to a group of three letters within the New Testament, namely, 1 Timothy, 2 Timothy, and Titus. Already in the thirteenth century Thomas Aquinas (1225–74) referred to 1 Timothy as 'a pastoral rule, which the apostle [Paul] committed to Timothy'.[1] The designation of all three letters as the 'Pastoral Epistles', however, came much later. That is usually attributed to the German scholar Paul Anton (1661–1730), who used the term collectively in lectures and writings in the eighteenth century. The term is descriptive of the aim and contents of the three letters. Among other things, they provide instructions for pastoral oversight of congregations, and they speak of the qualities and duties of church leaders.

THE PASTORALS IN THE EARLY CHURCH

Each of the Pastorals begins by identifying Paul the apostle as its author. Each one goes on to represent itself as a communication from Paul to either Timothy or Titus, persons entrusted with obligations to teach and provide leadership within churches committed to their care. The letters provide further instructions in carrying out those obligations in the present and on into the future.

In spite of the fact that the letters themselves designate Paul as their author, the Pastorals are not actually attributed to him by known external sources until the second half of the second century. The well-known heretical teacher Marcion, who taught in Rome and founded churches ca AD 130–60, seems to have known nothing about the Pastorals; when he made a collection of the writings of Paul, he did not include the Pastorals among them.[2] Furthermore, the earliest known manuscript of Paul's letters in codex (= book) form – Papyrus 46, which is usually dated from as early as AD 200 – does not contain the Pastorals. To be sure, the document has some leaves (pages) missing at the front and back. But the missing leaves are not likely to have provided space to contain the Pastorals.[3]

On the other hand, the early Roman document known as the Muratorian Canon, from ca AD 175–200, includes the Pastorals among the letters of Paul.[4] Moreover, the Pastorals are mentioned as letters of Paul by late second-century writers, such as Irenaeus (ca AD 130–200), Clement of Alexandria (ca AD 150–215), and Tertullian (ca AD 160–225).[5] From that time on, the Pastorals are regularly included in lists of Paul's writings.

The lack of evidence for the existence of the Pastorals (and thereby their lack of attribution to Paul) prior to the second half of the second century is puzzling. It prompts a number of questions, including questions about their authorship and origins.

AUTHORSHIP AND ORIGINS OF THE PASTORALS

Questions about the authorship and origins of the Pastorals have occupied scholars for a long time. Their authorship by Paul has been questioned mainly on the basis of five factors.

(1) The lack of universal knowledge of the Pastorals among the letters of Paul in antiquity is significant for questioning their having been written by Paul. It is not by itself decisive, but it is one factor within a larger complex of more compelling ones.

(2) One of the most compelling arguments is that the Pastorals contain terms and expressions that are not found in the undisputed letters of Paul. If all the Greek words used in the Pastorals are listed, the total amounts to 901. Of these 901, 52 are proper nouns (names of persons and places, such as Adam, Jesus, Paul, Ephesus, and Crete). Once these are set aside, there are 849 different words used at least once in the Pastorals.

Of the 849 words used, no fewer than 306 (or 36 per cent) are not found in the ten other letters attributed to Paul in the New Testament. Of these 306, as many as 121 (14 per cent of the 849 words) appear in the writings of the second-century Apostolic Fathers and Apologists. And if one sets aside three of the ten Paulines which, on various grounds, are disputed in terms of authorship (Ephesians, Colossians, and 2 Thessalonians), the number of words not found among the seven undisputed letters rises to 326 (38 per cent of the 849).

Another item to consider in regard to terms and expressions is that there are many expressions within the undisputed Pauline letters that do not appear in the Pastorals. These belong to Pauline style, the 'connective tissue' of his habits of expression. There are 77 such words and phrases. Two examples are given here. First, there are two ways to express 'with' in Greek. That is either by use of *syn* followed by a noun in the dative case or by use of *meta* followed by a noun in the genitive case. Paul uses both (the former 28 times, the latter 37 times) in his undisputed letters. But the writer of the Pastorals uses only the latter (18 times). A second example is that Paul uses the Greek conjunction *hoste* ('so that') 37 times in the seven undisputed letters to introduce a clause expressing a result, but the author of the Pastorals never uses it at all.

(3) Theological terms and concepts known from the undisputed letters of Paul are either missing or used differently in the Pastorals. The concept of an imminent parousia (coming) of Christ, for example, is present in Paul's letters (1 Cor. 15:51–2; 1 Thess. 4:15–18), but not in the Pastorals. Missing also is the familiar Pauline expression of the believer's living 'in Christ' (Rom. 6:11; 8:1; 1 Cor. 1:30; 2 Cor. 5:17; etc.). The term 'faith' always means 'the Christian faith' in the Pastorals (1 Tim. 1:2; 3:9, 13; 4:1; 2 Tim. 4:7; Titus 1:13; etc.) or a Christian virtue (1 Tim. 1:5, 19; 4:12; 6:11; 2 Tim. 2:22; Titus 2:2; etc.), whereas in Paul's letters it more commonly has the basic meaning of 'trust', which is placed in God, Christ, or the gospel. The term translated 'godliness' (NRSV) is found ten times in the Pastorals as an important virtue (1 Tim. 2:2; 3:16; 4:7, 8; 6:3, 5, 6, 11; 2 Tim. 3:5; Titus 1:1), but never in the undisputed letters of Paul.

(4) The form of church order found in the Pastorals – with bishops, presbyters, and deacons as the norm – does not appear in the undisputed letters of Paul. What one finds in the Pastorals is more like church orders found in the writings of the Apostolic Fathers than in the writings of Paul.

(5) There is great difficulty fitting the Pastorals into the career of the apostle Paul as we know it from other sources (Acts and the undisputed letters). In order to do so, one has to assert that they fit into Paul's life after events narrated at the close of the book of Acts. According to those who make such a claim, Paul was released from prison, travelled to Spain, returned to Rome, wrote 1 Timothy and Titus while still free, was arrested and imprisoned again in Rome, wrote 2 Timothy while in prison, and then was executed. Such a construction, however, is based on an account from the fourth century, written by Eusebius, that does not stand up to critical scrutiny.[6]

While no one of the five points discussed here is decisive by itself, the cumulative weight of them suggests strongly that the Pastorals, as we have them in their present form, do not appear to be the work of the apostle Paul as we know it from other sources. Although some scholars contend for the authenticity of the Pastorals, a wide range of scholars consider them pseudonymous. There have been attempts by others to argue for a mediating position. Some account for the differences between the Pastorals and the undisputed letters by suggesting that the former were dictated in the main by Paul but written up in their final form by a secretary who worked with considerable freedom. Others have suggested that the Pastorals, though written after the death of Paul, contain some genuine fragments or authentic materials from him. It can be said, however, that neither of the last two proposals has been widely received as persuasive, and in either case the Pastorals, as we have them in their present form, are not strictly 'Pauline' in the sense of the seven undisputed letters.

The conclusion drawn here is that the Pastorals were written after the close of Paul's career. They were most likely written at the end of the first century or at the outset of the second by a writer who was devoted to Paul and sought to represent him in a time and situation that called for an authoritative, apostolic voice. The place of composition is debated. The usual suggestions are Ephesus or Rome.

The matter of pseudonymity has received increased attention in modern studies. The discussion cannot be surveyed here. Suffice it to say that pseudonymous writings were produced in both Jewish tradition and Graeco-Roman cultures prior to the rise of Christianity. That there could be pseudonymous writings in the New Testament is not surprising. In each case the author sought to represent the views of the person to whom the writing was attributed, had that person been living and working at the time of the actual author. Pseudonymous writings were received as authoritative by the early church if they were sufficiently in keeping with what was already known about the persons to whom they were attributed, and if they were of theological and pastoral importance for the church itself.

THE THEOLOGY OF THE PASTORAL EPISTLES

The Pastorals set forth theological claims that belong to the common Christian tradition of the first century and to the New Testament as a whole. But they also have some distinctive theological concerns of their own. Three of these will be discussed.

God and Creation

God the Father, who is one, has created all things and has created them good (1 Tim. 1:2; 2:5; 4:3–4; 2 Tim. 1:2; Titus 1:14–15). He has not withdrawn from the world but 'gives life to all things' (1 Tim. 6:13) and 'richly provides us with everything for our enjoyment' (6:17).

In light of these assertions and others, it is likely that the goodness of the creation was being challenged. Within the second century the challenge was particularly strong in the teachings of Marcion and among the Gnostics. The Gnostic attitude is expressed most emphatically within the apocryphal *Gospel of Philip*, according to which 'the world came about through a mistake' (75.2–3). Although the teachings of Marcion, the *Gospel of Philip*, and the full-blown Gnostic systems arose after the composition of the Pastorals, it is likely that early forms of Gnosticism already existed by that time, and in those early manifestations of Gnosticism the world was despised, and life was to be ascetic.

Over against such views, the Pastorals stress the goodness of marriage and having children (1 Tim. 3:2–5; 5:10, 14; Titus 2:4), the legitimacy of secular authority (1 Tim. 2:1–2; Titus 3:1–2), the care of the elderly (1 Tim. 5:4), compassion for those in need (Titus 3:2, 8, 14), and courtesy towards all people (Titus 3:2). Stress is placed on living in accord with values that are consistent with the Old Testament and common Christian teaching, summed up in the word 'godliness'. Likewise, certain vices are to be avoided, such as the love of wealth (1 Tim. 6:9–10; 2 Tim. 3:2). On balance, then, the Christian is not to flee from this world, but is exhorted to live within it in a manner that is consistent with being a Christian – in other words, a life of good works (1 Tim. 2:10; 2 Tim. 2:21; 3:17; Titus 3:1), moderation (1 Tim. 6:8), and generosity (1 Tim. 6:17–18).

Christology

Four christological titles appear in the Pastorals: 'Christ', 'Lord', 'Saviour', and 'Mediator'. Surprisingly, the title 'Son of God' – used so often in the undisputed letters of Paul – does not appear at all. On the other hand, and even more surprising, at one point the exalted Christ is even called 'God': Christians await their 'blessed hope, the appearing of the glory of our great God and Saviour Jesus Christ' (Titus 2:13). The term 'God' is applied elsewhere in the New Testament to Jesus only at John 20:28 (and perhaps at Rom. 9:5[7]). The degree to which the term should be pressed in the Pastorals, however, is a subtle matter. Elsewhere in the Pastorals a distinction is made between Christ and God (1 Tim. 1:1; 2:5–6; 5:21; 2 Tim. 4:1; Titus 1:4; 3:4–6). Lurking behind the application of the term 'God' to Christ in the Pastorals may well be the ease of applying it to major, heroic figures, particularly in Graeco-Roman ruler cults, in which the ruler was thought to manifest, or even embody, the divine. In any case, for the writer of the Pastorals, God and Christ are intimately related, so much so that at his parousia Christ will bear the divine glory to complete the saving work of God, and in that sense he will be 'God and Saviour'.

The titles 'Christ', 'Lord', and 'Saviour' affirm the majestic, even divine, status of Christ. On the other hand, his true humanity is maintained (1 Tim. 2:5; 6:13; 2 Tim. 2:8), and his death is acknowledged (1 Tim. 2:6; 2 Tim. 2:11; Titus 2:14). When he is spoken of as 'Mediator' (once only, 1 Tim. 2:5), the term does not speak of his nature (divine/human) so much as his function in giving himself as a 'ransom' for the salvation of humankind. His exaltation to heaven and his reign is affirmed (1 Tim. 3:16; 2 Tim. 1:10; 2:12). Finally, it is expected that he will appear at the end of time (1 Tim. 6:14; 2 Tim. 4:8), when he will judge both the living and the dead (2 Tim. 1:18; 4:1, 8).

Interpreters disagree on the question whether the Pastorals affirm the pre-existence of Christ and his incarnation. Those who say No on the matter point to the fact that nowhere do these letters speak of an eternal Son of God or 'logos' (= 'word') existing before the creation of the world. On the other hand, other interpreters point to an implicit affirmation of Christ's pre-existence and incarnation in certain passages. For example, the writer speaks of the 'grace ... given to us in Christ Jesus before the ages began, but ... now ... revealed through the appearing of our Saviour Christ Jesus' (2 Tim. 1:9–10; cf. Titus 2:11). And again, if Christ was 'manifested in the flesh' (1 Tim. 3:16, RSV), they would say, his pre-existence (in a 'not-in-the-flesh' state) is presupposed, for incarnation implies pre-existence.

The christological accent of the Pastorals, however, is not to be found so much in the titles used or in answering the question whether the categories of pre-existence and incarnation apply. Instead, the accent is upon the appearances (epiphanies, manifestations) of Christ at two points – in time past, and at the end of time. Jesus Christ has appeared as the earthly, visible manifestation of the grace, goodness, and loving kindness of God (2 Tim. 1:9–10; Titus 2:11; 3:4), and he will appear at the end of time bearing the divine glory (Titus 2:13; cf. 1 Tim. 6:15–16).

Humanity and its salvation

According to the Pastorals, the whole human race is composed of 'sinners'. Furthermore, 'Christ Jesus came into the world to save sinners' (1 Tim. 1:15). But how do the Pastorals portray the general human condition? And what role does Christ have in the process of salvation?

The Pastorals lack the profound Pauline view that 'sin' is a power that exercises dominion over all persons (Rom. 3:9; 5:12, 21; 7:14; Gal. 3:22) prior to and apart from the saving work of God in Christ. Instead the Pastorals speak of 'sins' (plural) that people commit (1 Tim. 5:22, 24; 2 Tim. 3:6). Yet the distinction should not be overdrawn, for the cause of those sins is a life that is disoriented, serving the self and its passions (Titus 2:12; cf. 2 Tim. 3:2–5). And that is a life that leads away from eternal life and towards judgment and eternal death.

Salvation in the Pastorals consists primarily of the divine rescue of persons from mortality – with its sins, ignorance, and unbelief – for life in the eternal and heavenly kingdom of God (2 Tim. 1:10; 4:18). Christ plays out the rescue operation on behalf of 'God our Saviour, who desires everyone to be saved and to come to the knowledge of the truth' (1 Tim. 2:3–4; cf. Titus 2:11). The way he does that is fourfold. First, he came into the world and manifested the grace, goodness, and kindness of God, thereby eliciting obedience from all who will hear his gospel, and providing for them a model of the godly life. Second, he gave himself as a ransom for all (1 Tim. 2:6). In that act he bore the divine judgment against sins for the benefit of others (cf. Titus 2:14). Third, being raised from death, he 'abolished death and brought life and imperishability to light' (2 Tim. 1:10), bringing it out into the light of day for all to see as a possibility for themselves. And, finally, he will come as our 'great God and Saviour' once again to rescue his people at the end of time and save them for his heavenly kingdom (2 Tim. 4:18).

On the human side, salvation involves accepting the gospel as true and thereby gaining eternal life. To accept the gospel of Christ is to 'take hold of' eternal life (1 Tim. 6:12, 19) and to live the life characterized by godliness, enduring until the end of this life (2 Tim. 2:10, 12). The steadfast and obedient believer enters into the eternal kingdom through his or her own 'departure' (2 Tim. 4:6) or else at the parousia of Christ (Titus 2:13), if that should take place prior to one's own death. To be sure, salvation can be spoken of as a present reality (2 Tim. 1:9; Titus 3:5), but it is essentially future. In their present life Christians are 'heirs in hope of eternal life' (2 Tim. 3:7; cf. 1:2), expecting salvation as a future reality (1 Tim. 4:16).

CHURCH ORDER IN THE PASTORAL EPISTLES

The community envisioned by the writer of the Pastorals was to be, or was already, ordered more explicitly than any others reflected in the writings of the New Testament. Offices are mentioned into which persons are inducted (1 Tim. 3:10; 4:14; 5:22; 2 Tim. 1:6), and the persons so inducted are to be respected, as office bearers, for the sake of their work (1 Tim. 5:17). Three main offices are mentioned.

Presbyters are mentioned in two passages (1 Tim. 5:17–19; Titus 1:5). The term is customarily translated 'elders' in English versions (KJV, RSV, NEB, NIV, NRSV). The Greek term in the singular is *presbyteros*, which can refer simply to an older person in ordinary, secular Greek, but in the Pastorals (as in Jewish and Christian usage already; cf. Matt. 16:21; Acts 15:2; 16:4), it is the title for an office that exists (1 Tim. 5:17–19) or at least ought to (Titus 1:5). Age is not a consideration for being a presbyter, for in the Pastorals it is assumed that the incumbent will have children at home (Titus 1:6). The presbyters form a council (1 Tim. 4:14; *presbyterion* in Greek, literally the 'presbytery', as in the KJV, but translated as 'council of elders' in RSV and NRSV; NEB has 'elders as a body', and NIV has 'body of elders'). These persons have a 'ruling' function, and some are engaged in preaching and teaching (5:17). The English word 'priest' is derived from an abbreviation of the term 'presbyter'.

Deacons are mentioned in one passage (1 Tim. 3:8–13). The Greek term (the singular again) is *diakonos* and can be translated as 'servant' or 'minister' as well, but it is usually translated 'deacon' in English versions at this place (KJV, RSV, NEB, NIV, NRSV). Deacons are selected on the basis of personal qualities, but their duties are not spelled out. Most likely, as made clear from other (but admittedly later) sources,[8] they served under the bishop in charitable work and temporal concerns.

An officer called a *bishop* is mentioned in two passages (1 Tim. 3:1–7; Titus 1:7–9). The Greek term is *episkopos*, meaning 'overseer'. Although the terms 'episcopal' and 'bishop' do not have an obvious relationship, their relationship becomes clear when the beginning and ending of the Greek term are dropped, leaving 'piskop' as the basis for 'bishop'. On the basis of reading all three Pastorals together, it appears that all ministry carried on in the community – both ministry of the word and ministry of service – is under the supervision of the bishop.

There is disagreement among interpreters on the relationship between bishop and presbyter in the Pastorals. Some have concluded that the two titles are equivalent, as they appear to be in some other ancient sources.[9] On the other hand, it is striking to observe that whenever the terms are used in the Pastorals, the term 'bishop' is always in the singular, whereas the term 'presbyter' can be in the plural. On the basis of that phenomenon, interpreters have more commonly concluded that the bishop was the leading office bearer, who may or may not have arisen from the circle of presbyters,[10] and who provided primary oversight for a congregation or a cluster of congregations. In any case, the bishop has three main functions. First, working with the presbyters and deacons, the bishop supervises the life of the community as though it were an extended household (1 Tim. 3:5), caring for all matters, whether spiritual, temporal, or organizational. In all of this, he must be a model of Christian virtue (1 Tim. 3:2–7; Titus 1:6–9). Second, he combats false teaching and preserves what is sound (Titus 1:9). Finally, since he must be an apt teacher (1 Tim. 3:2; Titus 1:9), we can conclude that a major function of the bishop was teaching – and, with that, preaching as well (cf. 1 Tim. 5:17).

There are passages in the Pastorals that refer to women who carry on certain activities in the community. Within the passage speaking about the qualifications of deacons (1 Tim. 3:8–13) there is reference to 'women likewise' (3:11). In certain translations (KJV, NEB, GNB, and NIV) the Greek term translated here as 'women' is translated as 'wives', as though the passage speaks about the wives of deacons. But most likely that can be excluded, since no possessive pronoun ('their') is used, which would be expected in that case. The term in question is translated simply as 'women' in other English versions (RSV, NRSV). Some interpreters have contended that the term, in this context, refers to women who are deacons (as in the case of Phoebe at Rom. 16:1). Perhaps the most that can be said is that the term 'deacon' clearly applies to men (for in 1 Tim. 3:12 it is said that deacons must be 'the husband of one wife'), but that there were women in diaconal service as well, whether or not they bore the formal title.

Another passage speaks of women who are 'widows' (1 Tim. 5:3–16). Those who are 'true widows' can be enrolled (5:9, 11) – thus formally 'rostered' and recognized as a distinct group – if they are at least sixty years of age and lack children or grandchildren to support them (5:4, 8, 16). They are supported by the community (5:5, 16), and their primary functions must have been extensions of the things they were noted for already when they were enrolled: being constant in prayer (5:5), and diligent in charitable work (5:10) on behalf of, and at the expense of, the community. Since a procedure for 'enrolment' was in operation, it is appropriate to ask whether an 'office' or 'order' of widows existed. The question is debated. As in the case of whether women were recognized as deacons, so here the issue is the degree to which a function or status must become formalized to be considered an office. Perhaps the most that can be said is that in the Pastorals there is evidence for the beginning of what would later be a recognized office, as reflected in the writings of Ignatius and Polycarp of the second century and in other sources from the third century.[11]

READING THE PASTORAL EPISTLES

1 Timothy

The letter is addressed to Timothy, who is at Ephesus (1:3). Paul has departed from there to Macedonia (1:3). He intends to return, but he may be delayed (3:14), so he sends instructions to Timothy and expects him to carry them out during his absence. Although the letter is addressed to Timothy alone, rather than to a community, the author in actual fact 'talks past' Timothy on certain occasions to persons who are to hear of its contents. Members of the community, for example, are to hear the exhortation to honour those elders who rule well and teach (5:17), and slaves are obviously to hear the exhortation dealing with them (6:1–2).

After the opening of the letter, Paul calls upon Timothy to oppose false teachers and to be an example for believers (1:3–20). That is followed by a series of instructions on prayer and worship (2:1–15) and a sketch of the pattern of life expected of bishops and deacons (3:1–13). Near the mid-point of the letter the author speaks about the church, 'the pillar and bulwark of the truth', and its confession (3:14–16).

Instructions continue. First, the duties of ministry in the church are surveyed (4:1–5:2). The author says that one should expect false teaching and apostasy. But those engaged in ministry must remain faithful, avoiding false teachings and training themselves in godliness. Furthermore, such persons must set an example in speech and conduct, read the scriptures at public worship, pay attention to their teaching, and treat young and old with respect.

Order and duties in the congregation are important and in need of attention (5:3–6:2a). The matter of enrolling and supporting widows and specifying their duties is spelled out, and that is followed by instructions on the selection, compensation, and disciplining of elders (presbyters). Christian slaves are told to honour their masters, especially if they are Christian masters.

The body of the letter ends with a discussion of true and false teaching (6:2b–21a). False teaching has serious consequences for conduct. Timothy is exhorted again to remain faithful in his own teaching and conduct. The wealthy are called upon to be generous.

The letter closes with a benediction (6:21b).

2 Timothy

This letter differs from the other two in that it has nothing to say about ecclesiastical offices and has a 'thanksgiving' section at the outset, a feature existing in all of the undisputed letters of Paul, except Galatians. The thanksgiving follows after the brief opening, in which Paul addresses Timothy as his 'beloved child' and speaks of him as one whom he has ordained (1:6). This letter begins and unfolds as the most intimate of the three. In its references to Paul and his suffering, it appears to have been written, at least in part, to elicit sympathy for the apostle.

The ostensible circumstances of the letter are that it was written by Paul while he was imprisoned at Rome (1:16–17) to Timothy, who is presumably located at Ephesus (1:18; 4:12). Luke is with Paul (4:11), and Paul asks Timothy to come to him (4:9).

After an opening (1:1–2) and a statement of thanksgiving (1:3–7), the writer addresses Timothy, calling upon him to join Paul in suffering (1:8–10). Paul is a model, who was abandoned by many but is being refreshed by Onesiphorus (1:11–18).

A relatively long exhortation to Timothy is given (2:1–26). He is encouraged to be strong, to endure, to remember the gospel of Christ and Paul its apostle, to tend the congregation, to avoid senseless controversies, and to treat all with kindness, including opponents. The characteristics of apostasy are reviewed (3:1–9), and Paul is portrayed as a suffering, persecuted apostle, a credible teacher, whose teachings Timothy is to remember as he studies and teaches the scriptures (3:10–17).

The body of the letter closes with a final exhortation to preach the word (4:1–8), followed by a lengthy closing section (4:9–21) and benediction (4:22).

Titus

This letter, the shortest of the three, contains the longest opening of the Pastorals (1:1–4). It speaks of Titus as Paul's 'loyal child' in the faith shared between them. It is purportedly addressed to Titus on Crete (1:5); Paul has left Crete and is now at some undisclosed location, but he will eventually be on his way to Nicopolis (western Greece), where Titus is to meet him (3:12).

Following upon the opening, the author speaks immediately concerning the appointment of elders (presbyters) in all the towns of Crete and then delineates the qualifications of a bishop (1:5–9). The ordering of the church is important to combat false teachers, whose teaching and conduct are described (1:10–16).

Much of the letter is concerned with the creation of a Christian ethos (2:1–10) and a discussion of life under grace (2:11–3:11). In the case of the former, the writer gives instructions for the conduct of elderly men and women, young men (for whom Titus is to be a model), young women, and slaves. In regard to the latter theme, the writer describes the transforming power of grace, speaks eloquently of baptismal regeneration, and tells how believers should be devoted to good works.

The letter comes to an end with further instructions to Titus (3:12–14), followed by greetings and a benediction (3:15).

THE PORTRAIT OF PAUL IN THE PASTORAL EPISTLES

The apostle Paul is portrayed in ways that resonate in part with his self-portrait in his letters. As in the undisputed letters, here Paul is identified as an apostle in the opening of each (1 Tim. 1:1; 2 Tim. 1:1; Titus 1:1), and there are references to his suffering and experiencing persecution both in the undisputed letters (2 Cor. 11:23–7, especially) and several times in one of the Pastorals (2 Tim. 1:8, 12; 2:9–10; 3:10–11; 4:6–8, 16). But while there are similarities, there are differences as well. Five of the more obvious ones are presented here.

(1) Within the Pastorals Paul is called a 'teacher of the Gentiles' (1 Tim. 2:7) or a 'teacher' of the gospel (2 Tim. 1:11). Although Paul would most certainly not have found these terms objectionable, he did not use them for himself in his undisputed letters. In fact, they fall far short of his own understanding of his role. Paul refers to himself as an 'apostle to the Gentiles' (Rom. 11:13) and, by using that term, he understood himself as having been called to evangelize Gentiles, incorporating them into the people of God, and thus having a part in the fulfilment of the divine promises, as set forth in parts of the Old Testament (especially in the Psalms and Isaiah). That is a much more dynamic role than being a teacher.

(2) As a teacher, the Paul of the Pastorals transmits Christian tradition consisting of 'instruction' (1 Tim. 3:14), sound doctrine (Titus 1:9; 2:1), and a deposit of truth (1 Tim. 6:20; 2 Tim. 1:12, 14) that can be 'entrusted' to someone else (2 Tim. 2:2). To be sure, Paul could speak of traditions which he had received and handed on (1 Cor. 11:23–7; 15:3–7). Yet it is fair to say that he was above all a proclaimer of the gospel, and that he employed traditions primarily for kerygmatic (proclamatory) purposes, not so much for doctrinal instruction.

(3) That Paul had been a persecutor of the church is acknowledged in the Pastorals. His activity as a persecutor is mentioned near the beginning of one of the letters (1 Tim. 1:13), but at that place it is virtually excused, since it is attributed to sheer ignorance on his part. In his own writings, however, Paul speaks in extremely regretful tones of himself as having persecuted the church, attributing it to his great zeal for his ancestral faith. He had acted, in fact, as one who had advanced in that faith beyond his peers (Gal. 1:13; 1 Cor. 15:9; Phil. 3:6). According to him, it was out of knowledge of, and conviction for, that ancient faith that he was a persecutor of the church, not out of ignorance of the Christian gospel.

(4) The Paul of the Pastorals is a superb example to all, and especially to leaders of the church. To Timothy he says, 'Now you have observed my teaching, my conduct, my aim in life, my faith, my patience, my love, my steadfastness, my persecutions, and my suffering the things that happened to me in Antioch, Iconium, and Lystra' (2 Tim. 3:10–11). Paul is portrayed here as an example in virtually all things that are related to the faith and life of the Christian. While it is true that the apostle Paul could say to his readers, 'Join in imitating me, and observe those who live according to the example you have in us' (Phil. 3:17), there is nothing like the appeal to himself as an

example comparable to the one cited in the Pastorals. At another place, Paul writes, 'Be imitators of me, as I am of Christ' (1 Cor. 11:1). The latter phrase is important, for by means of it Paul points beyond himself to Christ as the one who is ultimately to be imitated.

(5) As seen above, the Paul of the Pastorals is very much concerned about the ordering of the church and its offices. The concern for order within the church – or, better perhaps, an ordering of the life of the church in such a way that it builds up each of its members – is by no means lacking in Paul's undisputed letters, as a reading of 1 Corinthians demonstrates. And there are expressions of concern for effective leadership in congregations, a leadership that is to be respected (cf. 1 Thess. 5:12–13). But there is nothing in those letters that begins to match the level of concern for actual offices, and for the status of persons inducted into them, that is evident in the Pastorals.

The portrait of Paul in the Pastorals is an idealized one. Lacking altogether are those statements of Paul that reflect his sense of frustration and anguish for his churches – actual congregations whose leaders called upon him for help – and that speak of his weaknesses, ailments, incapacities, and failures, as one finds in his undisputed letters (e.g. 1 Cor. 2:4, 10–13; 2 Cor. 10:10; 11:6, 22–9; 12:7–9; Gal. 4:13–14; 6:17). In the Pastorals he is the ideal Christian and apostle. And the reason for that must be that such a Paul was needed. He was needed as a teacher of the truth, standing over against those who were teaching an incipient Gnosticism, a religious development that was 'anti-body' in a double sense: (1) it denigrated the created world and the human body, calling for asceticism; and (2) in its calling for a radical individualistic spirituality, it did not care about preserving the church as the body of Christ, a community of mutual care and love.

THE ENDURING MESSAGE OF THE PASTORAL EPISTLES – AND ENDURING QUESTIONS

Clearly the Pastorals, in their strong affirmation of God as creator and the goodness of creation, have had importance in the subsequent history of Christianity for giving shape to Christian attitudes. They were important early on in the church's defence of itself over against Gnosticism. Moreover, they have been important for providing liturgical materials for the church, such as in their instructions for intercessory prayers in 1 Tim. 2:1–2 and words about baptism in Titus 3:5–7. Echoes of these passages are found in books used for public worship throughout history and around the world. And the Pastorals have been important for the formation and nurture of a Christian ethos for life in the world.

It is the latter impact, however, that has been perceived as a problem as well. The author of the Pastorals takes it for granted that some Christians are slaves (1 Tim. 6:1–2; Titus 2:9–10), and that some Christians are slave-owners (1 Tim. 6:2). Clearly, the Pastorals simply assume that the institution is to be preserved intact. Persons in each group – slaves and slave-owners alike – are exhorted to be respectful of one other.

Another area of controversy is the role assigned to women. The role is familiar to many in certain traditional cultures even today, but for others it is much too restrictive and offensive. The prohibition against women as teachers is dispensed with today in many churches. Part of the argument put forth is that the Pastorals are only one part of the scriptural voice. Paul, for example, speaks rather routinely of women as prophets in the church (1 Cor. 11:5) and refers to a woman who is an apostle (Rom. 16:7) and to another who is a deacon (Rom. 16:1).

Like other books in the New Testament, the Pastorals exist within a constellation of claims, exhortations, and instructions concerning Christian faith and life. Study of the New Testament in depth exposes the differences among them and poses the question, then, of what is of first importance. The Pastorals do not stand alone, and few would grant them the last word on all matters they take up. But the beauty of their expressions concerning God, their strong affirmations of the divine love, will, and grace for human redemption in Christ, and their passion for sound teaching and honourable living in the world have won their acceptance, and their importance, within the canon of Christian literature.

Notes

1 Thomas Aquinas, *Epistola I. ad Timotheum*, lectio 2.
2 Epiphanius, *Panarion* 42.11.9–11.
3 For discussion, see B. M. Metzger, *The Text of the New Testament: Its Transmission, Corruption, and Restoration*, 3rd edn (Oxford: Oxford University Press, 1992) 37–8.
4 For the text of the Muratorian Canon, see H. Bettenson, ed., *Documents of the Christian Church*, 2nd edn (London: Oxford University Press, 1963) 28–9.
5 Irenaeus, *Against Heresies* 3.3.3; cf. 3.3.4, at which a saying in Titus 3:10–11 is attributed to Paul; Clement, *Stromateis* 1.59.2; 2.29.4; 2.52.5; and 3.53.4, at which sayings in all three epistles are attributed to Paul; Tertullian, *Against Marcion* 5.21. At *Stromateis* 2.52.6 Clement says that the heretics regard the letters to Timothy as inauthentic.
6 Eusebius, *Ecclesiastical History* 2.2. For a review of this and other related points, see A. T. Hanson, *The Pastoral Epistles*, NCBC (London: Marshall, Morgan & Scott, 1982) 14–23.
7 The issue at Rom. 9:5 is how the wording of the clause in which it appears is to be punctuated. Is it a relative clause, whose antecedent is Christ (as in KJV, JB, NIV, NRSV), or is it an independent doxology (as in RSV, NEB, GNB)?

8 Ignatius, *Magnesians* 6.1; *Trallians* 2.3; Hippolytus, *Apostolic Tradition* 9.

9 1 Clement 44.4–5; Irenaeus, *Against Heresies* 3.3.4; 4.26.2. see also Acts 20:17, 28 and 1 Pet. 5:1–2, where the terms appear to overlap.

10 That the bishop may have arisen from the circle of presbyters is based on Titus 1:5–9: the qualifications of a bishop are listed in connection with the selection of presbyters. The reason for that is that any presbyter chosen may in time become a bishop.

11 Ignatius, *Smyrnaeans* 13.1; *Letter to Polycarp* 4.1; Polycarp, *Philadelphians* 4.3. B. B. Thurston, *The Widows: A Women's Ministry in the Early Church* (Minneapolis: Fortress, 1989) 92–105, presents information on widows from the third century.

Part three

Paul's theology

11 Paul's Jewish presuppositions

ALAN F. SEGAL

METHODOLOGICAL PRESUPPOSITIONS

Despite the objections of a small but vocal minority, it seems certain that Paul was not only Jewish but also a Pharisee, just as he himself claims:[1]

> If any other man thinks he has reason for confidence in the flesh, I have more: circumcised on the eighth day, of the people of Israel, of the tribe of Benjamin, a Hebrew born of Hebrews; as to the law a Pharisee, as to zeal a persecutor of the church, as to righteousness under the law blameless. But whatever gain I had, I counted as loss for the sake of Christ. Indeed I count everything as loss because of the surpassing worth of knowing Christ Jesus my Lord. For his sake I have suffered the loss of all things, and count them as refuse, in order that I may gain Christ and be found in him, not having a righteousness of my own, based on law, but that which is through faith in Christ, the righteousness from God that depends on faith; that I may know him and the power of his resurrection, and may share his sufferings, becoming like him in his death, that if possible I may attain the resurrection from the dead. *(Phil. 3:4b–11)*

Paul tells us himself that he was a Pharisee and that in his previous, pre-Christian life being a Pharisee was a prestigious attainment, which gave him the respect of his brothers in faith. He also says that he was a zealous Pharisee, pursuing or even persecuting the early Christian church, and that while he was a Pharisee, he felt himself to be blameless and righteous. As is quite clear from his rhetoric, he has thrown this all over to be *in Christ* and this is a mark of derision, and now he thinks of his previous life as encompassed by sin. Instead he now sees his salvation as coming from his faith *in Christ*, in whose sufferings he has shared and through whose sufferings he may attain the resurrection.

At the very least, this makes Paul a radical convert to the new faith in the crucified Messiah.[2] This means that whatever else we may suspect or divine about Paul we know he has left the security of Pharisaism for the insecurity of the new sect which would soon be known, not as those 'in Christ' or in 'the way', as he styled them, but as 'Christianity'. A great many of Paul's assumptions about Judaism will, in effect, stay the same, but a few crucial ones, namely, those that seem to him to contradict his new-found 'Christian' commitment, will be revalued to make sense of his new social and religious surroundings.[3]

Besides his Christian confession, about which a great deal has been written, the few biographical details he gives us here have been the subject of relatively little discussion because there is so little to go on. But one thing seems sure in the mystery which is Paul's life: he was a member of a client group beholden to but quite different from the Roman administration. As we know from modern examples, this predicament yields a very complex and difficult kind of doublemindedness, a combination of pride and shame at one's past, depending on the context.[4]

Paul tells us only a few other details about his former life:

> For you have heard of my former life in Judaism, how I persecuted the church of God violently and tried to destroy it; and I advanced in Judaism beyond many of my own age among my people, so extremely zealous was I for the traditions of my fathers. (*Gal. 1:13–14*)

Again he tells us that, as a Pharisee, he persecuted the church and tried to destroy it. We can confidently assume that in this passage when Paul tells us that he was zealous and that he advanced in Judaism beyond many of his own age, he means that he has received a Pharisaic education and that he was quite zealous and convinced of its truth before he converted to Christianity, convinced enough that he became a strict guardian of its truth and persecuted those who he felt had impugned or violated it. His conversion made him just as convinced of his previous zeal's mistake and just as zealous for his new Christian commitment. Several scholars have pointed to the 'mirror-image' character of his radical conversion.

The question that immediately arises is: what does Paul's Pharisaism tell us about Paul that we do not know from this precious and small autobiographical fragment? It used to be confidently assumed that Paul's Pharisaic past made him a member of the party that uniquely valued the law. Now we know that all the organized parties of the Jews valued the law and that all committed Jews saw their programme for living outlined in it.[5] Even the Sadducees, who apparently minimized the authority of the Torah and maximized their own abilities to acculturate to Hellenistic lifestyles, apparently granted the Torah primary authority in areas where it spoke directly to issues. What differentiated the Pharisees from the Sadducees was the

Pharisaic desire to extend the Torah into contemporary areas that were not obviously covered in ancient scripture. We tend to give the Pharisees primacy since their lessons are subsumed in their later successors, the rabbis, whose literature has come down to us in the rabbinic canon of contemporary Judaism. But it seems clear now from the Qumran community, whose writings were lost until recently, and the scholarly reconsideration of Jewish life attendant on those discoveries, that the primacy of Torah in the lives of all the organized sects or parties of Judaea is assured. Since Paul continued to see himself as Jewish after his conversion to Christianity, it is at least conceivable that he continued to value Torah in some way after his conversion. Paul's question about the law, as was the question for all the Jewish sects, was *how* the Torah was to be interpreted, as much as what its authority was. Paul was convinced that the prophetic promises of the Torah continued to be true because God was faithful to his people Israel. The only question for him was in what way the Torah needed to be practised by Christians.

However, it is also no longer easy to assume that Pharisaism is the same thing as the Judaism found in the Mishnah. Many fundamental rabbinic traditions can no longer be assumed to date to the time of Jesus, though many purport to be considerably more ancient.[6] Although rabbinic Judaism claims the Pharisees as forebears, the differences between the rabbis and the Pharisees are great. The Pharisaic movement was but one amongst a variety of sects in the first century, while rabbinic Judaism matured beginning about 220 CE with the publication of the Mishnah. Furthermore, the Pharisaic traditions evidenced in the Mishnah are of uncertain date. Since they were preserved in oral form, they may have originated in the first two centuries or much earlier, as the traditions often claim. As in any oral literature, they may have been significantly altered in transmission and especially by their rabbinic editors in the middle and end of the second century. In any event, rabbinic documents unconsciously transform evidence of the Pharisees from their first-century position of shared power into statements of comfortable community leadership in the second, third, and fourth centuries.

Thus, rabbinic literature may naturally and unconsciously distort the plethora of Jewish traditions in the first century, making Paul's contemporary writings an important supplement to our rabbinic witness and key for understanding how the rabbinic movement developed out of it. Nor is this a matter of concern to scholars alone. A new historical understanding of the development of rabbinic tradition threatens contemporary Jewish assumptions about the divinely inspired continuity of the Jewish legal system. Ironically, the New Testament gives us evidence of Jewish thought and practice in the first century, helping in some places to establish the authenticity of mishnaic reports. And Paul is almost certainly the only New Testament writer to represent Pharisaic Judaism, though he gives us the view of someone who left it unconditionally. Such are the stakes if we recognize that Paul is the only identifiable Pharisee anywhere to leave us any autobiographical writings. (In his autobiographical *Life*, the Jewish historian Josephus claims to have styled his life as a Pharisee because he wanted a public career; but this is hardly the same thing as being a Pharisee and learned in the Torah, as was Paul.)

The issue is not so much whether Paul was a Pharisee, which seems beyond rational dispute, but what his Phariseeism tells us about him and Judaism. Most New Testament scholars have freely borrowed from rabbinic tradition to fill in the many gaps in Paul's life and to characterize the religion from which he came. However, as we have seen, methodologically this move is just as suspect as thinking that only the Pharisees valued Torah. Form-critical understanding of the development of rabbinic tradition, besides calling the truth and the dating of rabbinic tradition into doubt, has also cast into serious doubt two centuries of Christian scholarship, which too blithely used the Mishnah and Talmud as its main source for understanding the Jewish background to the New Testament. The exact converse methodology actually seems more reliable. Study of the New Testament, an undeniably first-century source, has proven to be quite useful for validating and dating mishnaic recollections of first-century Jewish life. But such comparisons are in their infancy.

The New Testament and especially Paul gives us a helpful alternative view of the rise of rabbinism, even when Paul is being hostile to it. But it also inevitably calls New Testament understandings of rabbinism into question as well. Take the most famous example of Christian scholarship on rabbinic Judaism: Strack–Billerbeck, *Kommentar zum Neuen Testament aus Talmud und Midrasch*,[7] which lists important midrashic and mishnaic traditions for each New Testament passage. In spite of its sometimes unappreciated erudition, its methodology is now obviously entirely suspect. Rather, we should write a commentary to the Mishnah, using the New Testament as *marginalia* which give us important evidence about the antiquity of each tradition.

Paul then becomes an extremely important person in the study of Judaism. Second to Luke he wrote the largest section of the New Testament. But Jewish historians have been very wary about using him. Why should we believe what an apostate tells about Judaism? The answer is, of course, that we, as historians, should never flatly believe anything in the historical record. But equally true methodologically is that if we want to be historians we must also be responsible for weighing every piece of evidence, no matter how biased, and seeing what it does tell us about rabbinic Judaism. Under the circumstances it seems prudent for Jewish historians to look at Paul's witness to Pharisaism, skewed by conversion though it certainly is, to discover what he does tell us about it. And at the same time, then we will come to see a bit of Paul's Pharisaic presuppositions to his Christianity.

In my book *Paul the Convert*, I suggested that the key to understanding the depiction of Pharisaism in Paul is to begin with Paul's conversion, since conversion is the most salient religious event in his life.[8] From this key moment we can make some reasonable guesses both forward and backward in his experience. This means that although the conclusions of Paul's arguments are distinctly Christian (and, indeed, Christian in a particularly radical variety) and his understanding of Pharisaism is that of someone who left it unconditionally, Paul's methods for demonstrating religious truth and his treatment of scripture are still distinctly Pharisaic. In short, Paul left Pharisaism for his own brand of Christianity, but he did not leave Judaism and he did not forget his Pharisaic training. Instead, he brought it to benefit his new Christian affirmation. Furthermore, Paul's critique of his former life in Pharisaism is not necessarily and in every respect to be generalized to include a total condemnation of Judaism or Jewishness. Nor is it the case that his critique of Pharisaism is complete and unconditional. Converts change a major and important aspect of their belief structures, but they do not overthrow everything. In fact, it is quite common to see converts bring their skills and accomplishments and put them to good use in their new religious community. And Paul is no exception. He uses his rabbinic training to demonstrate the truth of the Christian message. And, lest it be forgotten, Paul's critique of Pharisaism is clear to him only after he has converted to Christianity, certainly not before, when it must have been in many ways a satisfying life. There will be more to say about this at the end of this chapter.

To be sure, from the perspective of his new faith commitment, he offers several very scathing critiques of Pharisaism. In the following, he mentions only Jews, but it is clear that the more educated Jews are the ones whom he most singles out as guilty of the crime of hypocrisy which he outlines:

> But if you call yourself a Jew and rely upon the law and boast of your
> relation to God and know his will and approve what is excellent,
> because you are instructed in the law, and if you are sure that you are
> a guide to the blind, a light to those who are in darkness, a corrector of
> the foolish, a teacher of children, having in the law the embodiment of
> knowledge and truth – you then who teach others, will you not teach
> yourself? While you preach against stealing, do you steal? You who
> say that one must not commit adultery, do you commit adultery? You

who abhor idols, do you rob temples? You who boast in the law, do you dishonour God by breaking the law? For, as it is written, 'The name of God is blasphemed among the Gentiles because of you.'

Circumcision indeed is of value if you obey the law; but if you break the law, your circumcision becomes uncircumcision. So, if a man who is uncircumcised keeps the precepts of the law, will not his uncircumcision be regarded as circumcision? Then those who are physically uncircumcised but keep the law will condemn you who have the written code and circumcision but break the law.

For he is not a real Jew who is one outwardly, nor is true circumcision something external and physical. He is a Jew who is one inwardly, and real circumcision is a matter of the heart, spiritual and not literal. His praise is not from men but from God. (*Rom. 2:17–29*)

This is a critique of the hypocrisy that comes from pride of position – and some of it, like circumcision most obviously, applies to all Jews – but it seems clear that the critique is all the more cogent when applied to some learned Jews like the Pharisees, Paul's own previous community in Judaism, to whom he constantly ascribes the greatest intellectual authority and from whom, it appears here, he has received a serious rebuke. It seems clear, then, that Paul's rhetoric is one of polemic and assumes another side, which Paul himself does not describe exactly, beyond his own conviction that they, who call him and his converts sinners, are no better at best and often much worse. This appears to apply not to all Judaism but to a particular group who are critical of his behaviour and that of his churches. Interestingly enough, the group may just as easily be Christian as well as Jewish.

What follows is some exemplars of the techniques and expectations that Paul takes from Pharisaic tradition. I cannot be exhaustive in such a short chapter, though I hope that my examples will be illustrative of the characteristics which Paul takes from his Pharisaic past. Methodologically, the characteristics will be taken from an informal list of known characteristics of rabbinic exegesis, which I find in similar form in Paul's writing, with allowances for the fact that Paul writes in Greek and the rabbis in Hebrew and Aramaic, making necessary some judgments of parallels through translation.

THE PRIMACY OF SCRIPTURE INTERPRETATION

The first characteristic of Pharisaism which Paul illustrates in his writing is demonstration by appeal to scripture. Since he also seems to have a good deal of familiarity with Greek philosophy, this is all the more remarkable. He uses scripture to understand the promises of God and to confirm that his arguments about the significance of the crucified Messiah are correct. Of course, this technique does not uniquely describe Pharisaism. All the sects of Judaea used specific methods of scriptural interpretation to demonstrate the beliefs and practices of their members. And Paul does use *pesher* and *allegory*, literary techniques closer to the Qumran community and Philo respectively. What makes Paul so interesting is that he also uses *midrash* extensively to demonstrate his Christian arguments, even when speaking to an audience that probably had little appreciation for his rabbinic erudition. But, of course, wherever he uses his rabbinic exegetical skills, he is also trying to demonstrate the power of the gospel which has led a member of the most prestigious of the educated orders of Jews to give up his earned position to testify to the truth of the Christian message.

A good example of Paul's use of midrash might be Gal. 3:6–14:[9]

> Thus Abraham 'believed God, and it was reckoned to him as righteousness'. So you see that it is men of faith who are the sons of Abraham. And the scripture, foreseeing that God would justify the Gentiles by faith, preached the gospel beforehand to Abraham, saying, 'In you shall all the nations be blessed.' So then, those who are men of faith are blessed with Abraham who had faith.
>
> For all who rely on works of the law are under a curse; for it is written, 'Cursed be every one who does not abide by all things written in the book of the law, and do them.' Now it is evident that no man is justified before God by the law; for 'He who through faith is righteous shall live'; but the law does not rest on faith, for 'He who does them shall live by them.' Christ redeemed us from the curse of the law, having become a curse for us – for it is written, 'Cursed be every one who hangs on a tree' – that in Christ Jesus the blessing of Abraham might come upon the Gentiles, that we might receive the promise of the Spirit through faith. (*Gal. 3:6–14*)

Paul uses scripture to demonstrate something which no Pharisee would have argued. Paul argues from scripture that the Gentiles are included in God's plan for salvation. Now this in itself is not entirely without precedent in Pharisaic Judaism. Tosefta Sanhedrin 13:2 records an important argument between two second-century rabbis:

> Rabbi Eliezer said: 'All the nations will have no share in the world to come, even as it is said, "the wicked shall go to Sheol, and all the nations that forget God" (Ps. 9:17). The wicked shall go into

Sheol – these are the wicked among Israel.' Rabbi Joshua said to him: 'If the verse had said, "the wicked shall go into Sheol with all the nations", and had stopped there, I should have agreed with you, but as it goes on to say "who forget God", it means there are righteous people among the nations who have a share in the world to come.'

This second-century argument is certainly from a generation or two after Paul. It shows the argumentative technique so characteristic of the rabbis. And here the text shows us that there were rabbis who certainly granted that non-Jews could be righteous. According to rabbinic law these Gentiles are those who practise the Noahide Commandments, normally seven commandments which the rabbis assumed were given to all humanity before Moses and thus were incumbent on all humanity. This concept can be found even in Jubilees, which is surely pre-Christian (second century BCE). But what is interesting is that this passage assumes that the Gentiles will be saved by Torah, by law, though the Torah which they must keep only contains seven commandments, let us say, rather than the traditional 613 which Jews must keep. The numbers are later adumbrations, but the conceptualization is clear. God created the world by Torah, and the difference between Gentile and Jewish responsibility is that Jews must practise far more because they are God's priests.

Paul, on the other hand, uses his midrashic technique to drive a wedge between faith and Torah, a distinction which would never have occurred to a Pharisee. To Pharisees, the passage from Deuteronomy which Paul quotes in Galatians would demonstrate just the converse of what Paul claims. Those who live by the Torah will be blessed and those who break it will be cursed. That is the plain meaning of scripture at that point. Paul uses Christ's death on the cross, something ostensibly anomalous to scripture and something whose anomalousness Paul emphasizes, to argue for an entirely new conclusion – namely, that Christ's death removes the curse of the law to bring the blessing of faith to the Gentiles. This suggests that Paul is not merely making up this exegesis, rather that he is countering a Jewish criticism of Christianity: namely, that Jesus cannot be the Messiah promised by scripture since he died under a curse. The death of the Messiah might have been sufficient to cast doubt on the Christian message, as Paul himself testifies: 'We preach Christ crucified, a stumbling block to Jews and folly to Gentiles' (1 Cor. 1:23). Death in a manner cursed by scripture seems more even than midrash could accommodate. Paul rises to the occasion by giving us a *tour de force* of midrash, showing that the nations will be saved by faith and that this faith is the same principle of salvation on which the Torah itself is based. It is no accident that Paul uses the example of Abraham, the father of all converts, to demonstrate his point.

What would drive Paul to make this exegesis? The critique of Christianity by some other Jews, using this same scripture, for sure. But just as the exegesis is based on Paul's own experience of salvation in Christ, so is his exegesis not based on specific rabbinic teaching but on his conviction and experience in preaching to Gentiles, that the redemptive death of Christ also guarantees the justification of Gentiles through their faith and not by comparing their practice to that of Jews. These are important facts of Paul's experience which change his orientation towards scripture. Once that reorientation has taken place, then Paul can use the techniques he learned as a Pharisee to demonstrate the truth of his new religious experience. For Jews it is right action which brings righteousness. For Gentiles, it is their faith in the promises of Christ's resurrection and return. Doing the law or not doing the law is therefore unimportant. It is important to note that this is not an argument for Jews not to do the law; it is a statement that justifies Gentiles' chance to be redeemed even though they do not do the law. That is the same as the position of the liberal Pharisees, one which he surely encountered but one which it is hardly likely that he advocated while he was a Pharisee. If that is correct, then most Christians have over-interpreted Paul's writing because they have not adequately understood Paul's presuppositions.

THE IMPORTANCE OF RESURRECTION AND THE MESSIAH

Indeed, it is Paul's experience of conversion, whether one accepts the stories in Acts or assumes that the biographical facts of the conversion are lost to history, which makes all the difference for Paul's exegesis. The Pharisees believed that the righteous survive death. This is clear not only from rabbinic writings but also from the Jewish historian Josephus.

> Of the two first-named schools, the Pharisees are those who are considered the most skilful in the exact explication of their laws, and are the leading school. They ascribe all to fate and to God, and yet allow that to do what is right, or the contrary, is principally in the power of men, although fate does cooperate in every action. They say that all souls are imperishable, but that the souls of good men only pass into other bodies while the souls of evil men are subject to eternal punishment. (*Josephus, War 2.162–3*)

> They [the Pharisees] also believe that souls have an immortal power in them, and that under the earth there will be rewards or punishments,

depending on whether they have lived virtuously or viciously in this life. The latter are to be detained in an everlasting prison, but the former shall have the power to revive and live again. (*Josephus, Antiquities 17:14*)

To be sure, the Pharisees seem to have believed in resurrection rather than immortality of the soul, as Josephus describes it. But most scholars understand that Josephus is formulating the Jewish notion of resurrection in Graeco-Roman philosophical garb, since resurrection would have been virtually unintelligible to Josephus' Roman readership.

At the same time, it is also true that many other groups besides the Pharisees enjoyed the hope of resurrection. It is characteristic not merely of Pharisees but of a number of other groups, most particularly apocalypticists like the Qumran group. Since there is no doubt that Paul is himself an apocalypticist, this raises an interesting issue for us. Did Paul learn his apocalypticism from his Pharisaic past or from his opposition to the apocalyptic faith of those he opposed when he was zealous for the law, or was it something that came later from his Christian faith?

Since both groups enjoyed a hope in resurrection, there is no definite proof either way. But one thing seems to show that Paul's hope came from his Pharisaic past. That is his formulation of the resurrection body in 1 Corinthians 15. Here he understands a resurrection body which is not precisely flesh but perfected flesh, something consonant with Josephus' description of the Pharisees in some contradiction to the later explicit description of the fleshly resurrection of Jesus (Luke 24:39):

> So is it with the resurrection of the dead. What is sown is perishable, what is raised is imperishable. It is sown in dishonour, it is raised in glory. It is sown in weakness, it is raised in power. It is sown a physical body [*soma psychikon*], it is raised a spiritual body [*soma pneumatikon*]. If there is a physical body [*soma psychikon*], there is also a spiritual body [*soma pneumatikon*]. (*1 Cor. 15:42–4*)

Paul's description of the resurrection assumes that we live as creatures of body and soul (*soma psychikon*) and will inherit a more spiritual body (*soma pneumatikon*). This is not easily reconciled with the later gospels' description of Jesus' bodily presence, as in Matthew and Luke and even John. But it is consonant with the Pharisaic ambiguity over the terms of the resurrection. That is hardly a proof, but it is suggestive, and it is suggestive of the ways in which Paul remains difficult for later Christians. The Pharisees were sure of resurrection, indeed they were sure that resurrection was prophesied in scripture, but they were unsure exactly how resurrection would be accomplished. Paul seems to me closer to the Pharisaic conception than to the later, more polemical, and hard to justify Christian notion in the later gospels that Jesus' resurrection was fleshly and that his body was reanimated and recognizable to the disciples.

The same might be said in reverse about the expectation of the Messiah. The coming of the Messiah is surely a cornerstone of mature rabbinic Judaism, just as the rabbis cautioned against too easy belief in the Messiah's arrival. And belief in the coming of the Messiah is evidenced throughout the later midrash. Strangely enough, however, the Mishnah of Rabbi Judah the Prince carries scarcely a mention of the Messiah. Was this because the rabbis feared repercussions from the Romans or because they feared a further outbreak of messianism of the type that produced Christianity? In any event, it is not clearly present in the earliest rabbinic document.

So then did Paul become messianic because he became a Christian or was messianism a part of his Judaism before his conversion? It seems to me quite improbable that the Pharisees before the Amoraim were devoid of messianism and that Paul found it only when he became a Christian. Paul, then, is again the earliest Pharisaic evidence of the existence of messianic beliefs among the Pharisees, even if that belief was perhaps greatly augmented and quickened by his later Christian faith. The messianic beliefs and the eschatology of the Pharisees have never been seriously in doubt, and no one seriously doubts that the messianic beliefs and the eschatology of Christianity came from its Jewish past, yet were greatly augmented by their experience of the resurrection of Jesus. But it is hardly noted that the best proof of messianic beliefs in the Pharisees in the first century comes from Paul.

THE MYSTICISM OF PAUL

Paul's Christ mysticism is one of the most interesting and important aspects of his religious life:

> And we all, with unveiled face, beholding the glory of the Lord, are being changed into his likeness from one degree of glory to another; for this comes from the Lord who is the Spirit . . . In their case the god of this world has blinded the minds of the unbelievers, to keep them from seeing the light of the gospel of the glory of Christ, who is the likeness of God. For what we preach is not ourselves, but Jesus Christ as Lord, with ourselves as your servants for Jesus' sake. For it is the God who said, 'Let light shine out of darkness', who has shone in our hearts to give the light of the knowledge of the glory of God in the face of Christ. (2 Cor. 3:18; 4:5–6)

Paul here interprets the appearance of 'the Glory of the Lord' in Exod. 33:21 as a type of the revelation vouchsafed to the Christian community. The Christian community even surpasses those who stood at Sinai, for they behold the Glory of the Lord and are transformed into his divine likeness. To me this suggests that Paul has received a theophany of the human figure of the Lord YHWH, the so-called angel of the Lord. Yet there are several unique aspects to this vision. For one thing, Paul identifies the Glory of the Lord, the angel of the Lord, or the angel of his presence, as having the features of the face of Christ (4:6). For another, for Paul this is the signal that the resurrection of the end time is beginning, that those alive and dead are being transformed into the body of Christ. This is quite a bit like the later Jewish mysticism of ascent and transformation which we know in the Hekhaloth literature, the mysticism we know as *merkabah* mysticism. The version that Paul tells us is more primitive and less developed, much closer to the transformation that is related of Enoch in 1 Enoch 71. But, if this is true, Paul's experience is again the first place we see Jewish mysticism. So not only is it important that Paul's religious life begins in Pharisaic Judaism, but it is also important that he witnesses a number of religious phenomena that we suspect were present in the Pharisaic community of the first century but cannot otherwise demonstrate.

WHAT KIND OF PHARISEE WAS PAUL?

Paul, like everyone of his day, testifies that the Pharisees were known to be expert interpreters of the *Torah*, and that they were zealous about the performance of the *Torah*. He says the same about himself when he was a Pharisee. But his insistence that he was very zealous and that he pursued the Christians, even to violence, suggests that he was an extremist as a Pharisee, not so much a Pharisee like Rabbi Eliezer, but one who was committed to stamping out those who disagreed with him. Terence Donaldson makes a very good case that Paul was not among the tolerant and universalizing part of the Pharisaic movement but among those who distrusted Gentiles, and disliked any deviation as heresy.[10] There is much to this argument. Indeed, Paul's critique of the Jews (not the Pharisees explicitly) in Romans 10 seems to smack of criticism of himself when he was a Pharisee:

> I bear them witness that they have a zeal for God, but it is not enlightened. For, being ignorant of the righteousness that comes from God, and seeking to establish their own, they did not submit to God's righteousness. (*Rom. 10:2–3*)

This is certainly a critique of the kind of person who Paul claims to have been before his conversion. And it illustrates the kind of social space that Paul inhabited. As part of the Hellenistic diaspora, Paul lived in two worlds simultaneously. Even if not from Tarsus, as Luke claims, he certainly learned to read and write Greek, and he spent his Christian career preaching the gospel to the diaspora communities of Greece and Asia Minor. He has to keep two different and often opposing cultures in his mind at once – Judaism and Hellenism. Not only can they be at political odds, but they can be at ideological and cultural odds too. At first his solution was to deny the validity of the outside world and retreat to a kind of fanatical Pharisaism. Luckily for him, he was able to throw this away for a different and more tolerant position. But whether he was able to achieve true toleration is a matter of interpretation of his Christian position, a subject beyond the scope of this chapter. Let us hope that his conversion and mission not only allowed him to see the error of his previous intolerant ways but also showed him how to treat all the world's inhabitants with justice and respect.

Notes

1 Otherwise H. Maccoby, *The Mythmaker: Paul and the Invention of Christianity* (San Francisco: Harper and Row, 1986).

2 See also D. Boyarin, *A Radical Jew: Paul and the Politics of Identity* (Berkeley: University of California Press, 1994). But note that Boyarin seems to see the distinction between Paul's Judaism and his Christianity to lie in his law-free gospel and jump to an intolerant universalism. I do not see that Paul necessarily preached the end of the law, or that he jumped to a universalism. He seems to believe that these categories have no ultimate meaning. But like gender they are quite significant on the unredeemed earth.

3 See A. F. Segal, *Paul the Convert: The Apostolate and Apostasy of Saul the Pharisee* (New Haven: Yale University Press, 1988).

4 For more modern examples, see G. Viswanathan, *Outside the Fold: Conversion, Modernity, and Belief* (Princeton: Princeton University Press, 1998); H. K. Bhabha, ed., *Nation and Narration* (London: Routledge, 1990); H. K. Bhabha, *The Location of Culture* (London: Routledge, 1994). Each of these two authors explores identity in the context of doublemindedness between British and South Asian culture.

5 See A. F. Segal, 'Society in the Time of Jesus', *Rebecca's Children* (Cambridge, MA: Harvard University Press, 1986) 38–67.

6 See the work of Jacob Neusner on this subject. Of his many publications, two of particular interest in this context (because they summarize his form-critical approach) are *The Rabbinic Traditions about the Pharisees before 70*, vols. 1–3, *The Masters, The Houses*, and *Conclusions* (Leiden: Brill, 1971); also *Judaism: The Evidence of the Mishnah* (Chicago: University of Chicago Press, 1981).

7 (Munich: C. H. Beck'sche Verlagsbuchhandlung, 1928).

8 Segal, *Paul the Convert.*

9 See the most incisive treatment by J. D. G. Dunn, *Jesus, Paul and the Law: Studies in Mark and Galatians* (London: SPCK, 1990).

10 T. L. Donaldson, *Paul and the Gentiles: Remapping the Apostle's Convictional World* (Minneapolis: Fortress, 1997).

12 Paul's gospel

GRAHAM N. STANTON

Paul uses a cluster of related terms to refer to his initial missionary preaching and to the proclamation at the heart of his letters. The nouns 'gospel' (*euaggelion*), 'word' (*logos* or *rhēma*), 'preaching' (*akoē*), 'proclamation' (*kērygma*), and 'witness' (*martyrion*) are often used almost synonymously, as are the corresponding verbs.

The most important of these terms is undoubtedly the noun 'gospel', which is used 48 times in the undisputed letters; the verb 'to proclaim good news' is used 19 times. Paul probably inherited the distinctive early Christian use of 'gospel' from those who were followers of Jesus before his own call or conversion. Indeed the noun may well have been used by Greek-speaking Jews in Jerusalem and Antioch very soon after Easter.

The noun 'gospel' is rarely used in the Old Testament, and never in a religious context with reference to *God's* good news. So early Christian use of this noun must be understood against the backdrop of current usage in the cities in which Christianity first took root. Literary evidence and inscriptions both confirm that the term 'gospel' was closely associated with the imperial cult in the cities of the eastern Mediterranean. One particular inscription provides striking evidence. In 9 or 10 BC a decree in praise of Caesar Augustus was erected in the market-place in Priene and in numerous other cities of Asia. The birthday of Augustus, 'our most divine Caesar', is equated with 'the beginning of all things', for he gave 'a new look to the entire world'. His birthday 'spells the beginning of life and real living'. 'The birthday of our God signalled the beginning of Good News [*euaggelia* – plural] for the world because of him.'

In this inscription, and in the other non-Christian examples, the noun 'gospel' is used in the plural. In the first century, the accession of each individual Roman Emperor was regularly considered to provide new hope, the dawn of a new era, 'good news'; hence there could be more than one set of 'glad tidings' or 'gospels'. For Paul, and in all NT usage, the noun is always used in the singular: the life, death, and resurrection of Jesus was God's 'once for all' disclosure of 'a glad tiding'.

The use of the verb 'to proclaim good news' in Isa. 52:7 and 61:1 may well have encouraged Paul and his predecessors to develop the distinctive Christian use of the noun 'gospel' in counterpoise to usage in the imperial cult. In Rom. 10:15 Paul cites Isa. 52:7 (LXX) in summary form, 'how beautiful are the feet of those who bring (God's) good news, (who announce salvation)'. Paul immediately equates his use of the noun 'glad tiding' with the verbal form 'those who proclaim glad tidings' used in this quotation (Rom. 10:16).

What were the central themes of Paul's 'gospel'? At some points in his letters certain theological themes are prominent, but those very themes are conspicuous by their absence elsewhere. This phenomenon has often prompted the observation that Paul's gospel is like a chameleon: it changes colour and shape according to the background against which it is set. As we shall see, however, there is a set of convictions concerning the gospel from which the apostle never wavered, even though the circumstances of the recipients of his letters elicited varying emphases.

PAUL AND HIS PREDECESSORS

In 1 Cor. 15:1–3 Paul acknowledges that the central themes of the gospel he had passed on to the Corinthians were transmitted to him by his Christian predecessors: 'For I handed on to you as of first importance what I in turn had received.' In verse 1 Paul uses the noun 'gospel' and the verb 'to proclaim good news' together, as he does at 1 Cor. 9.18; 2 Cor. 11:7; Gal. 1:11. In verse 3 Paul uses two verbs for the transmission and reception of the gospel (*paradidōmi* and *paralambanō*) which recall the semi-technical terminology used for the careful transmission of teaching from one generation of Jewish teachers to another. The gospel which the Corinthians had received from Paul is the very gospel which he in turn had received from his Christian predecessors.

The content of that gospel is set out in 1 Cor. 15:3–7 in a series of short statements. The first set of four are all introduced by 'that' (*hoti*), giving them the ring of a credal formula: '*that* Christ died for our sins in accordance with the scriptures, *that* he was buried, and *that* he was raised on the third day in accordance with the scriptures, and *that* he appeared to Cephas, and then to the twelve'.

In a number of other passages in which Paul refers to his proclamation or gospel, the turns of phrase or the theological concepts are not typically Paul's own, so there are often good grounds for concluding that he is drawing on and sometimes adapting earlier traditions. In this respect,

1 Thessalonians, Paul's earliest letter, is particularly instructive. In 1 Thess. 1:9–10 Paul records succinctly the main features of the Thessalonians' response to his initial missionary preaching in Thessalonica. A sharp contrast is drawn between 'the living and true God' Paul proclaimed and the idols from which the Thessalonians have turned. The language used is drawn from scripture and from traditional Hellenistic Jewish polemic against idols; it is not distinctively Pauline. The reference to the Thessalonians' eager awaiting of God's Son from heaven is the only reference in Paul's writings to Jesus as God's Son in the context of the parousia. The use of the verb *hruomai* ('deliver') rather than Paul's usual *sōzō* ('save') to refer to the deliverance from the coming wrath is a further probable example of non-Pauline language. Hence these two verses may contain several traces of the content of early missionary proclamation to which Paul himself was indebted. The absence of a reference to the death of Christ gives some support to this view.

In 1 Thess. 4:13 Paul turns to the Thessalonians' anxieties concerning their fellow believers who have died. As part of his assurance that 'through Jesus, God will bring with him those who have died', Paul quotes a credal summary: 'we believe that Jesus died and rose' (4:14). Since Paul does not use the verb *anistēmi* (rise) in this sense elsewhere, he may be quoting here a short, early summary of the content of the gospel, as he does at 1 Cor. 15:3–8.

In the immediate context it is the resurrection which is the focal point of the credal 'formula'. In the credal summary in 1 Thess. 5:9–10, however, Paul spells out the significance of the death of Christ: Christ died for us, for our salvation, so that we may live with him now and after death. Similar phraseology is used in 1 Cor. 15:3; Rom. 5:6; and 8:3. In all these passages Paul is probably drawing on and expanding an early formula: 'Christ died for our sins.' The profound exposition of the significance of the death of Christ in Rom. 3:25–6 probably also draws on earlier traditions.

In Rom. 1:2 Paul refers explicitly to 'the gospel'; the summary of its christological content includes several 'un-Pauline' turns of phrase. In his insistence that God sent his Son for redemption (Gal. 4:4–8; Rom. 8:3) Paul may be drawing on a very early soteriological 'sending' formula which is found quite independently in the Johannine writings (John 3:17; 1 John 4:9).

These examples (and more could be added) confirm the extent to which Paul is indebted to his predecessors for the central themes of his gospel. Nonetheless Paul develops and applies those themes in his own distinctive ways.

THE GOSPEL AS GOD'S INITIATIVE THROUGH HIS SON

Paul repeatedly insists that the gospel is God's initiative, the good news of God's fulfilment of his plan and his purposes for humankind: its focal point is Jesus Christ, God's Son. Paul comments fully and forcefully on the nature of the gospel as *God's initiative* in Rom. 1:16–17: 'For I am not ashamed of the gospel; it is the power of God for salvation to everyone who has faith, to the Jew first and also to the Greek. In the gospel the righteousness of God is revealed through faith for faith ...' Here Paul sets out two programmatic statements about the gospel which resonate throughout the remainder of the letter, and which echo or develop several passages in his earlier letters. So these two verses are a succinct compendium of the central themes of Paul's gospel.

Paul's reference to the gospel as *God's* effective saving power echoes 1 Cor. 1:18: 'the message [*logos*] about the cross is foolishness to those who are perishing, but to us who are being saved it is the power of God.' Its availability to Jew and Gentile alike and without distinction is underlined explicitly in Gal. 3:28 – indeed it is the central argument in Galatians. Paul's reference to the appropriation of the gospel through faith or by believing recalls Gal. 2:16; 3:2, 5: 'a person is reckoned as righteous not by works of the law but through faith in Jesus Christ'.

Rom. 1:17 explains why the gospel is effective for salvation: it is *God's* disclosure or unveiling of his righteousness, his 'rightwising' activity through Christ,[1] a theme we shall discuss further below. The reader already knows from 1:3–4 that Paul's gospel is *God's* declaration concerning Jesus Christ as his Son.

Paul had made precisely the same points concerning *God's* gospel in his earlier letter to the Galatians. In the opening chapter of Galatians Paul emphasizes emphatically that the gospel is *God's* disclosure of Jesus Christ as his Son. In 1:1 Paul notes that the gospel is *God's*, a key point which is filled out in Paul's threefold denial in 1:11c and 12 that his gospel has merely human origins; here he is probably responding directly to the jibes of his opponents. Paul's positive statement about the origin of his gospel at the end of verse 12 is one of the most important in the whole letter. Paul insists that he received the gospel 'through a revelation (*apokalypsis*) of Jesus Christ'. This NRSV translation preserves the ambiguity of the Greek, which can be construed either as 'Jesus Christ's disclosure of the gospel' or as 'God's disclosure of Jesus Christ as the content of the gospel'. The latter is preferable, especially in view of Paul's further comments in 1:15–16, which emphasize God's initiative in the revelation or disclosure of his Son.

The key noun in verse 12, *apokalypsis*, is usually understood in the light of Jewish first-century apocalyptic writings, where it often refers to the unveiling of something or someone previously hidden; hence the gospel is God's 'revelation' or 'disclosure' of Jesus Christ.

As noted above, Paul's use of the noun 'gospel' in the singular underlines its eschatological character. In contrast to repeatable 'glad tidings' concerning the Roman Emperor, *God's* 'glad tiding' is his 'once for all' disclosure of Christ. This is so axiomatic for Paul that although it is implied in the passages from Galatians 1 and Romans 1 just referred to, it is rarely spelled out. Gal. 4:4–5, however, is notable. In this rich christological statement Paul develops the theme of God's sending of the prophets to Israel: God's Son is sent 'in the fulness of time', to fulfil 'once for all' his purposes for redemption, so that all who are 'in Christ Jesus' (cf. Gal. 3:26–9) might receive adoption as God's children.

Paul refers to Christ as God's Son in only fourteen passages. In half of those passages, the reference is linked to Paul's gospel or proclamation (Rom. 1:3–4 (twice); Rom. 1:9; Rom. 8:3; 2 Cor. 1:19; Gal. 1:16; Gal. 4:4). However, Paul also uses other christological titles and phrases to emphasize that Christ is the focal point of his gospel. In 2 Cor. 4:4, for example, Paul notes that the gospel is about the glory of Christ, and then adds a powerful explanation: Christ is the image (*eikōn*) of God (cf. also Phil. 2:6; Col. 1:15; 1 Cor. 15:49). As R. P. Martin notes, this means 'that Christ is not only the full representation of God, but the coming-to-expression of the nature of God, the making visible of who God is in himself'.[2] For a further discussion of Paul's christology, chapter 13 should be consulted.

CHRIST CRUCIFIED AND RAISED FOR OUR SALVATION

We noted above that 'Christ crucified and raised' was at the heart of the gospel transmitted to Paul by his predecessors and cited at 1 Cor. 15:3–7. Paul makes the same point himself in several important passages in his letters.

In 1 Cor. 1:17 Paul emphasizes that he had not been sent to baptize but to proclaim the gospel. Here Paul uses the verb *euaggelizomai*, 'to preach good news', though he might well have used the noun *euaggelion* with a verb such as *kērussō*, 'to announce' (like a herald), which he uses elsewhere (e.g. 1 Thess. 2:9; Gal. 2:2). Paul's message or gospel is about 'the cross of Christ', 'Christ crucified' (1:17, 18, 22). Here *ho logos* is synonymous with *to euaggelion*, as also at 1 Thess. 1:6; 1 Cor. 2:4; 15:2.

There is a striking similarity between 1 Cor. 1:18, 24 and Rom. 1:16, Paul's programmatic statement about the gospel. In both passages 'the word' or 'the gospel' is God's powerful, dynamic act in Christ for salvation for Jew and Gentile alike. As in the credal summary of the gospel in 1 Cor. 15:3–8, 'Christ crucified for our salvation' is the central theme of Paul's gospel.

The precise sense of the words 'Christ died *for our sins*' (1 Cor. 15:3) has been much discussed. C. K. Barrett plausibly suggests that a hint of a double meaning may be conveyed here: 'Christ died on our behalf, that is, to deal with our sins.'[3] The theme is referred to in 1 Thessalonians, Paul's earliest letter (5:10; cf. 4:14). It is stated boldly in the opening greetings of Galatians (1:4), and it is expounded much more fully in Romans, especially at 3:21–6 and 5:6–11.

In the summary of the gospel Paul cites in 1 Cor. 15:3–7, the death and the resurrection of Christ are both said to be 'in accordance with the Scriptures', but we cannot be sure which scriptural passages are being alluded to. The more important point is that the gospel is not a human invention, but fully in accord with God's will as set out in scripture. In Gal. 3:8 Paul makes a similar point: 'Scripture, foreseeing that God would justify the Gentiles by faith, declared the gospel beforehand (*proeuēggelisato*) to Abraham.'

Paul's gospel includes God's raising of Jesus on the third day. Reference to the burial of Christ is included in the summary of the gospel quoted in 1 Cor. 15 to underline the reality of his death and to confirm that the appearances of the risen Christ were neither hallucinations nor the mere revival of memories of Jesus before his death. The sequence 'died', 'buried', 'raised', 'appeared' implies that on the third day, the tomb was empty. The passive verb 'was raised' implies God's involvement. As we have noted at several points, the gospel is *God's* dynamic, salvific act through Christ.

Rom. 10:8 also confirms that the resurrection is an integral part of the gospel. Here Paul refers to 'the word of faith that we proclaim' (i.e. the gospel) and then expounds its central themes: confession of Jesus as Lord, and belief that God raised Jesus from the dead. Acceptance of that proclamation leads to salvation. What is striking here is that salvation is linked to the resurrection, not the cross, as is more usually the case. But this is not the only passage which makes that point. In 1 Cor. 15:14 the validity of Paul's proclamation and of the Corinthians' faith is based squarely on the conviction that Christ has indeed been raised from the dead by God. And in Rom. 4:24–5 the raising of 'Jesus our Lord from the dead' was 'for our justification' and the handing over of Jesus to death was 'for our trespasses'; here salvation is linked both to the death and to the resurrection of Christ.

JUSTIFICATION

For Luther, as for many other interpreters of Paul, 'justification by faith' is seen as *the* hub of Paul's gospel: all Paul's other theological convictions are said to be linked to this over-arching theme. Luther believed that Paul was attacking Jewish legalism, which maintained that one's standing before God, one's righteousness, was grounded on careful observance of the law. Luther used his interpretation of Paul to attack the Catholicism of his day and the general belief that one could earn salvation by one's own efforts: for Luther's Paul, justification of the individual was by faith in Christ, not by carrying out the requirements of the law.

Over the last two or three decades this interpretation of Paul's gospel has been repudiated firmly by most scholars. What accounts for this volte-face? The traditional interpretation has been undermined by two main lines of argument. In 1977 E. P. Sanders developed considerably the work of earlier scholars. He insisted that with the exception of 4 Ezra, in the Old Testament and in later Jewish writings Israel's covenant relation with God was basic: obedience to the law was never thought of as a means of *entering* the covenant, of *attaining* that special relationship with God. Carrying out the requirements of the law ('the works of the law') maintains one's position in the covenant, but it does not earn God's grace as such.[4] In 1983 Sanders clarified his position: 'The question is not about how many good deeds an individual must present before God to be declared righteous at the judgement, but...whether or not Paul's Gentile converts must accept the Jewish law in order to enter the people of God.'[5]

This radical reinterpretation of Jewish teaching and of Paul's gospel coincided with the re-emergence of what had long been a minority interpretation of Paul's theology. Several scholars insisted that Paul's doctrine of justification by faith is not the heart of his gospel, for it is found only in passages in which Paul is engaged in polemic with Jewish Christians, that is, in Galatians and in Romans (and in passing, as it were, in 1 Cor. 6:9 and in Phil. 3:9). In 1977 K. Stendahl expounded this point of view vigorously and insisted that justification by faith was hammered out by Paul for the specific and limited purpose of defending the rights of Gentile converts to be full and genuine heirs to the promises of God to Israel.[6]

This volte-face is often now referred to as 'the new perspective' on Paul. The broad outlines of this approach are widely accepted. However, some scholars question Sanders' claim that observance of the law was for Jews not an entry requirement, but only a means of *maintaining* one's standing before God. While one cannot deny that Paul's teaching on justification is more prominent in Galatians and Romans than in his other letters, in both these letters it is closely associated with Paul's gospel. Hence it can hardly be sidelined as a peripheral theme in Paul's theology.

This becomes clear in Paul's account of his dispute with Peter at Antioch (Gal. 2:11–14). Paul insists that nothing less than 'the truth of the gospel' was at stake (2:14; see also 2:5). The strong language Paul uses in his vigorous repudiation of Peter's decision to stop eating with Gentiles confirms that Paul and Peter were at odds over fundamental issues. In 2:16, one of the most important verses in Paul's letters, the apostle expounds the central theological issue: 'a person is justified not by works of the law but through faith in Jesus Christ' (2:16). In this verse the phrase 'works of the law' is used three times and contrasted sharply with 'faith'. Paul is refuting the claim made by the agitators in Galatia (and implicitly by Peter when he 'compelled Gentiles to live like Jews', verse 14) that one's standing before God is dependent on carrying out the requirements of the Mosaic law. 'Works of the law' is taken by some scholars to refer particularly to the Jewish 'identity markers' of sabbath, circumcision, and dietary laws, rather than to the Mosaic law per se, but the negative comments on the law which follow in Galatians 3 suggest that the latter is more likely.

Paul insists that a person is 'reckoned as righteous' by God (NRSV footnote) on the basis of 'faith in Christ'. The meaning of the latter phrase is keenly discussed. Although some scholars insist that Paul is referring to Christ's *own* faithfulness to God, as in the NRSV footnote, the traditional view that it refers to the believer's faith *in* Christ is preferable.

Paul probably formulated his convictions about 'justification by faith' in the light of his dispute with Peter. But this is not the only facet of Paul's gospel which was first honed in the course of polemic or dialogue with those with whom Paul disagreed. What is clear from Galatians is that Paul's primary concern is not so much the individual's standing before God, as God's acceptance of Gentiles on the basis of their faith in Christ: Gentiles need not be circumcised, that is, become Jews, in order to be accepted by God.

These themes recur in Rom. 1:16–17 and 3:21–31; in both passages Paul insists that God accepts freely both Jews and Gentiles on the same terms, that is, faith in Christ. There is a long-standing debate over the interpretation of the phrase 'the righteousness of God' in Rom. 1:17 and 3:21. Does it refer to a quality to be attributed to God, that is, is Paul stating that God acts towards humankind on the basis of his own righteousness? Or does this phrase refer to God's justifying or rightwising activity,[7] that is, God's deliverance and provision of salvation for all who believe? Several OT passages in which righteousness is almost synonymous with salvation suggest the latter, though some scholars insist that in his use of this phrase Paul is holding together both lines of thought.

For Paul, justification is more than mere acquittal of the guilty sinner. In Rom. 3:26, for example, the verb 'to justify' is used: God declares that the one who has faith in Jesus is justified. For Paul this involves God's act of restoring people to their proper relationship with him; it is very closely related to God's act of forgiveness, as Rom. 4:6–8 makes clear.

RECONCILIATION

Paul's teaching on reconciliation is a further example of a basic theme of his gospel which is expounded in detail in only two letters, in 2 Cor. 5:18–21 and Rom. 5:8–11.[8] Reconciliation is on God's initiative: God has replaced enmity between himself and humanity with peace; hence Paul's use of 'peace' is closely related (cf. Rom. 5:1). Reconciliation takes place 'in Christ', that is, through the sacrificial death of God's Son (Rom. 5:9–10; 2 Cor. 5:14–15).

The word-group has its roots in the Greek world rather than the OT scriptures. S. R. Porter has recently shown that Paul is the first attested Greek author to speak of the offended party (God) initiating reconciliation, using the verb in the active voice.[9] As with a number of his key words and phrases (including 'gospel'), Paul has taken a concept familiar in the Greek world of his day and filled it with 'biblical' content.

Reconciliation is closely related to justification, as Rom. 5:8–11 confirms. As with justification, the initiative in reconciliation is God's: he proves his love towards us in that while we were yet sinners, Christ died for us (verse 8). In verses 9 and 10 both justification and reconciliation are effected through the death of Christ; both have salvation (here in the future) as their outcome.

In the other sustained exposition of reconciliation, 2 Cor. 5:18–21, additional key points are made. God who reconciled the world to himself through Christ has entrusted to us (to Paul and his co-workers, or more probably, to all believers) 'the word (*ho logos*) of reconciliation'. As we have seen, Paul often uses 'the word' synonymously with 'the gospel', so we need not doubt that reconciliation is a central strand in Paul's gospel.

In 2 Cor. 5:20a Paul refers to himself and others as 'ambassadors' for Christ. The word-group was widely used in the Greek-speaking eastern provinces of the Roman Empire to refer to the 'ambassadors' or legates of the Roman Emperor who were entrusted to convey imperial propaganda. Christ and Caesar are set strikingly in parallel: both have their ambassadors. However, the message of Christ's ambassadors, 'be reconciled to God (5:20)', is not one heard from the lips of Caesar's ambassadors.

To whom is this gospel of reconciliation addressed (5:20)? Opinion is divided. Some writers insist that Paul and the Corinthian believers are being entrusted to take to the world at large the 'missionary' call, 'be reconciled to God'. If so, we would then have here a rare example of *the content* of Paul's initial gospel preaching. Others claim that Paul and his apostolic circle are appealing to the Corinthians themselves to be reconciled to God. A decision is difficult, for the context does not readily settle the matter. In any case it would be rash to differentiate the gospel Paul proclaimed to unbelievers from the gospel he addressed to his house-church communities.

THE GOSPEL CAME IN POWER, AND IN THE SPIRIT

At several points in the preceding pages we have noted that the gospel is the glad tidings of God's once for all dynamic salvific act through Christ. The gospel is not merely a set of statements to be affirmed in response to the rhetorical persuasion of a street-corner philosopher: at the opening of his most sustained exposition of his gospel Paul emphasizes that the good news he proclaims is '*the power of God* for salvation to everyone who has faith' (Rom. 1:16).

Paul had already made this point in his earliest letter, 1 Thessalonians. In the opening thanksgiving Paul stresses that his initial proclamation of the gospel in Thessalonica was not 'in word only, but also *in power, in the Holy Spirit, and with full conviction*' (1:5; see also 1 Thess. 2:3–7). Here Paul carefully chooses a triad of terms to balance the triad 'faith, love, hope' in the same sentence. In this thanksgiving (as in many other passages in his letters) Paul's own rhetorical skills are on display. There is an obvious irony in this, for Paul is using rhetoric to emphasize that the gospel did not make its impact on the basis of his own powers of rhetorical persuasion, but through the power and conviction of God's Spirit.

Paul comments much more fully on the dynamic power of the gospel in the opening chapters of 1 Corinthians. In 1 Cor. 1–4 Paul repeatedly distances himself from those who rely on rhetoric to make their appeal. He opens his discussion of this point by noting that Christ did not send him to proclaim the gospel 'with eloquent wisdom' (1:17). By comparison with the wisdom of the wise, Paul's proclamation (*kērygma*) (of the gospel) is foolishness, but it is God's wise plan for salvation (1:18, 21), for Christ is the power of God and the wisdom of God.

Paul reminds the Corinthians that his initial preaching in their city was not 'with plausible words of wisdom, but with a demonstration of the Spirit and of power' (2:4). Why does Paul seem to harp on this point? He is doing this, he insists, so that the faith of the Corinthians might rest not on wisdom but on the power of God (2:5; see also 2:13). At the climax of this section of his letter Paul repeats his key point: 'the kingdom of God depends not on talk but on power (4:20)'.[10]

In the preceding pages some of the most prominent strands in Paul's gospel have been discussed. We have repeatedly noted that the gospel is *God's* initiative, and suggested that this emphasis was made in deliberate counterpoise to the contemporary association of the 'gospel' word-group with the imperial cult. The gospel is about God's provision of salvation for Jew and Gentile alike, not the hoped for beneficence of the Roman Emperor towards his subjects. The gospel is both God's powerful activity (through the Spirit) which elicits faith and also a set of traditions about Christ transmitted from Christian to Christian.

The focal point of Paul's gospel is the death and resurrection of Christ. The death of Christ is salvific, that is, Christ was crucified 'for us', 'for our salvation'. This is an important theme already in 1 Thessalonians, Paul's earliest letter; it echoes throughout Paul's other letters, in several of which it is developed much more fully. As we noted, soteriological significance is also attached to Christ's resurrection: 'Jesus our Lord was raised from the dead for our justification' (Rom. 4:25).

The 'reconciliation' word-group is prominent only at 2 Cor. 5:18–21 and Rom. 5:8–11, but since related themes are found elsewhere, too much should not be made of this. The same is true of 'justification' and 'righteousness': while this word-group is much more prominent in Romans and Galatians than in the other letters, we should not rush to conclude that Paul developed this facet of his gospel only in disputes with 'Judaizing' opponents. This word-group is also related to several other prominent Pauline themes. And we should not forget that Phil. 3:9 (and its immediate context) contains a succinct exposition of Paul's teaching on righteousness: it does not come from the law, but from God, on the basis of faith. Nor should we forget that our knowledge of the content and contours of Paul's proclamation is more limited than we would like, for his letters are not treatises on the gospel.

Discussion of Paul's gospel should not be confined to his usage of the noun and the related verb. We have found that several other terms, especially 'the word', are used in contexts where Paul is undoubtedly expounding his gospel. Although Paul varies his emphases from letter to letter in line with the needs of the recipients, there is a set of convictions concerning the gospel which run like a thread from 1 Thessalonians to Philippians, probably his first and final letters. The gospel is the good news of God's once for all disclosure of Jesus Christ as his Son, sent for our salvation so that 'we might receive adoption as God's children' (Gal. 4:4–5).

Notes

1 The Anglo-Saxon verb 'rightwise' conveys the gist of the Greek better than any current English word.

2 *2 Corinthians*, WBC 40 (Waco, TX: Word, 1986) 79.

3 *The First Epistle to the Corinthians* (London: A. & C. Black, 1968) 338.

4 *Paul and Palestinian Judaism* (London: SCM, 1977).

5 *Paul, the Law, and the Jewish People* (London: SCM, 1983) 20.

6 *Paul among Jews and Gentiles* (London: SCM, 1977).

7 See n. 1 above.

8 The use of the word-group in Col. 1:20–2 and in Eph. 2:16 is slightly different.

9 S. E. Porter, 'Katalasso', *in Ancient Greek Literature, with Reference to the Pauline Writings* (Cordoba: Ediciónes El Almendro, 1994).

10 D. Litfin, *St Paul's Theology of Proclamation* (Cambridge: Cambridge University Press, 1994) 195 notes that the verbs Paul uses to describe his public speaking, such as *euaggelizō, kērussō, kataggellō,* and *martureō,* are not verbs used by contemporary rhetoricians. 'His [Paul's] assignment was simply to make Christ known, non-rhetorically, and the Spirit of God would take care of the rest' (196).

13 Paul's christology

L. W. HURTADO

Paul's beliefs about Jesus were at the centre of his religious commitment, and any attempt to understand Paul's religious thought (or 'theology') has to make central what he believed about Jesus Christ. If considered apart from his religious life, however, these christological beliefs can come across as lifeless intellectual categories or even historical curiosities. In a proper portrayal, his christology should be seen in the context of his religious life, within which a passionate devotion to Christ is central.

One cannot read passages such as Phil. 3:7–11, for example, without sensing the depth of religious feeling towards Christ that seems to have characterized Paul's Christian life. In this passage, Paul compares unfavourably all of his pre-conversion religious efforts and gains over against 'the surpassing value of knowing Christ Jesus my Lord'. He then posits as his aims to 'gain Christ' and 'to know Christ', amplified here in terms of intense aspirations to know 'the power of his resurrection and the sharing of his sufferings by becoming like him in his death'.

Other passages confirm Paul's deep devotion to the person of Jesus Christ. For example, in Gal. 2:19–21 he describes himself as having been 'crucified with Christ', his life now so fully dedicated to Christ that 'it is no longer I who live, but it is Christ who lives in me'. Paul now lives 'by faith in the Son of God who loved me and gave himself for me'. In 2 Cor. 5:14–15, Paul refers to himself and his colleagues in the gospel as powerfully gripped (*synechei*) by 'the love of Christ' (which here means Christ's love), whose redemptive death for others now obliges them to live 'no longer for themselves but for him who died and was raised for them'. In short, Paul's christology, the body of specific beliefs about Christ, forms part of what we may call his Christ-devotion, which in turn shaped his whole religious life.

Moreover, although the christological titles and key terms Paul used to express Christ's roles and significance (so characteristically the focus of scholarly study) are important, and enabled him to declare Christ's significance to others verbally, in order for us to obtain a full estimate of the place

of Christ in Paul's religious life and thought, we also have to take account
of a wider range of verbal and non-verbal expressions of his devotion to
Christ. In this limited discussion we shall concentrate on key features of
Paul's Christ-devotion and identify some key issues in modern scholarly
study of this subject.

KEY FACTORS

In approaching the question of the place of Christ in Paul, we must
keep three crucial factors in view. Before we look at the particulars of
Paul's beliefs, therefore, it is well to note these factors, which condition
and shape everything. First, Paul came to his Christian faith as a deeply
religious Jew zealous for the distinguishing features of his Jewish tradition
(e.g. Gal. 1:13–14; Phil. 3:4–6), among which a strong conviction about the
uniqueness of the God of Israel (which we often refer to as 'monotheism')
was central. However profound the effects of his conversion from opponent
to advocate of the gospel of Christ, the Christian Paul continued to assert an
exclusivistic monotheistic stance, and it shaped and nourished his devotion
to Christ (e.g. 1 Cor. 8:4–6). Paul consistently referred to and defined Jesus
with reference to the one God of the Bible. For Paul, Jesus is God's Son
whom God gave over for the redemption of the elect (e.g. Rom. 8:32) and
raised from death to heavenly glory for their salvation (e.g. Rom. 4:24–5;
8:34). God has put all things in subjection to Jesus (1 Cor. 15:27–8), who
nevertheless will demonstrate his subordination to God in the eschatological consummation (1 Cor. 15:28). God has given Jesus a uniquely high status
as *Kyrios* that requires universal acknowledgement, and which at the same
time redounds to the glory of God (Phil. 2:9–11). Paul can refer to the central
cognitive content of the gospel as 'the knowledge of the glory of God in the
face of Jesus Christ' (2 Cor. 4:6), phrasing which both illustrates the central
role of Jesus and at the same time shows how Jesus is defined with reference
to God.

Whatever other devout Jews who did not follow Paul in embracing the
Christian gospel may have thought of his post-conversion beliefs, it is clear
that Paul thought of himself as faithful to the God of his ancestors and
that he reverenced Jesus as the crucial part of his Christian obedience to
the one God of Israel. As has been noted often, this is clearly illustrated
in 1 Cor. 8:4–6, where Paul is dealing with unavoidable questions of what
kinds of religious activities his Gentile converts can continue to engage in
as Christians. Here Paul refers derisively to pagan religious practices as the
worship of 'idols' and makes an adaptive allusion to the traditional Jewish
confession of the uniqueness of the God of Israel (the *Shema*, taken from

Deut. 6:4), insisting that there is only one true God, and 'one Lord, Jesus Christ'.

To be sure, the inclusion of Jesus with God in this confessional passage is a bold and unparalleled step in comparison with anything we know about other devout Jews of Paul's time. But everything indicates that Paul (with other Christian Jews of his time) saw this stunning prominence that they gave to Christ as fitting within a faithful commitment to one God. The negative attitude towards pagan religion here and elsewhere in Paul's letters means that his reverence for Christ cannot easily be seen as indicating a more open attitude to the pagan pattern of reverence for many divine figures. That is, Paul's christology did not involve any conscious abandonment of the monotheistic stance that he inherited from the Jewish tradition. He would not for a moment have assented to being characterized as a Jewish apostate. For Paul, Jesus was not another god and Paul's reverence for Jesus certainly did not represent any weakening of his devotion to the one God or any diminution of the supremacy and sovereignty of 'the God and Father of our Lord Jesus Christ' (e.g. 2 Cor. 1:3).

Yet it is also clear that Paul accommodated an amazingly exalted view of Christ and an equally striking devotion to him within this monotheistic stance. As Neil Richardson observed, Paul defines Christ consistently with reference to God, and also defines God with reference to Christ. After taking account of Paul's references to God and Christ, Richardson concluded, 'We are justified, therefore, in speaking of a distinctively Christian expression of Jewish monotheism.'[1] Scholars have debated whether Paul's devotion to Christ amounted to a breach of Jewish monotheism, but it is probably better to think of it as representing a form of monotheism apparently new and unparalleled in the Jewish tradition of the time. In Paul and the Christian devotion represented broadly in the New Testament, we have what some scholars have called a 'binitarian' form of monotheistic belief and devotional practice in which two distinguishable figures, God and Jesus, are programmatically treated as recipients of devotion by people who continue to see themselves as monotheists.

Paul shared this monotheistic stance with all other devout Jews, including Christian Jews, and with the Gentile-Christian converts of his time; but Paul was apparently unique among known members of the early Christian movement of his day in at least two ways. These two distinctives constitute the remaining two important factors to take account of in understanding Paul's christology.

First, prior to his profession of Christian faith Paul had been a vigorous opponent of it. Several times in his letters he refers to his persecution of, and efforts to destroy, 'the church of God' (Gal. 1:13; Phil. 3:6; 1 Cor. 15:9).

He characterizes his pre-conversion motivation as religious 'zeal' (Phil. 3:6; Gal. 1:14), which alludes to the Old Testament account of Phineas (Num. 25:6–13), who took violent action against Israelite apostasy, and in Gal. 1:13 Paul describes his own former actions as amounting to exceedingly strong persecution and an effort to stamp out the church.

Furthermore, in all three passages where Paul refers to his previous persecution of Jewish Christians, he indicates that his shift from opponent to advocate of the Christian message involved, indeed resulted from, a major reappraisal of Jesus that struck him as coming from God as a 'revelation'. As noted previously, in Phil. 3:7–11 Paul contrasts his previous religious orientation with his post-conversion devotion to Christ, for whose sake he willingly surrendered all his previous religious aspirations. Paul's reference to his former persecution in 1 Cor. 15:9 is in the context of Christ's post-resurrection appearances to a list of people, among which Paul includes his own encounter with Christ (15:8). Most explicit, however, are Paul's references in Gal. 1:11–17 to 'a revelation of Jesus Christ' (1:12) and to God revealing 'his Son to me' (1:15–16) to describe the nature of the experience that turned him around in religious orientation.

Paul did not come to the christological affirmations reflected in his letters from some neutral or uninformed standpoint. Prior to his conversion he had obviously developed sufficient familiarity with Jewish Christians to become convinced that they were a very dangerous sect and that resolute efforts to destroy it were demanded. It is, therefore, reasonable to suggest that Paul's basic christological beliefs were very likely reflective of the beliefs he had previously opposed. Scholars have concluded that in a number of places Paul recites traditional formulations that probably illustrate the beliefs of those whom Paul had persecuted, beliefs that he then accepted as a convert (e.g. Rom. 4:24–5; 1 Cor. 15:1–7; 1 Thess. 1:10).

In other passages, many scholars believe that we may have echoes of Paul's pre-conversion negative attitude toward Jesus and the christological claims of the Jewish Christians whom he then regarded as deserving stern opposition. For example, Paul's reference to Christ as 'becoming a curse for us – for it is written, "Cursed is everyone who hangs on a tree"' (Gal. 3:13) may be his adaptation of his own pre-conversion view of Jesus as a false teacher whose crucifixion reflected his status as accursed by God. Likewise, in 2 Cor. 3:7–4:6, many scholars see Paul's references to the veiled minds of non-Christian Jews, the illumination that comes 'when one turns to the Lord', and the spiritual blindness of those who cannot see 'the glory of God in the face of Jesus Christ' as likely Paul reflecting his own personal history of opposition to the gospel. It is also possible that we have an allusion to the contrast between his own pre-conversion and post-conversion stances toward Jesus in 1 Cor. 12:3, where Paul counter-poses the phrase 'Jesus be cursed' (*Anathema Iesous*) with the confession inspired by the Spirit, 'Jesus is Lord' (*Kyrios Iesous*).

Yet, on the basis of easily attested experiences of converts to various religious movements of the past and present, it is also reasonable to suspect that Paul may have considered his Christian convictions with a greater degree of reflection than in the case of believers who had not come to their faith from such an opposed posture. As someone who had renounced his former opposition to the Christian movement, he likely pondered more extensively the christological claims he felt compelled to embrace. This may well account for the sense that in Paul's letters we are dealing with a theological thinker. Paul certainly seems to have had some ability in reasoning and rhetorical presentation of his views. But we should also allow for his own, somewhat distinctive, personal movement from persecutor to participant in the Christian movement as an important factor in promoting the development of his thought.

There is a final distinctive feature of Paul to take account of as well. Paul refers to himself as uniquely called by God to win 'the obedience of the Gentiles' to the gospel (e.g. Rom. 1:5; 15:17–19). In phrasing that seems inspired by accounts of God calling prophets in Isa. 49:1–6 and Jer. 1:5, Paul writes of God having destined him before his birth to be called to proclaim Christ among the nations (Gal. 1:15–16). In his description of a conference with leaders of the Jerusalem church (Gal. 2:1–10), Paul claims that they recognized his own special mission from God to bring the gospel to 'the uncircumcised' (2:7–9), implicitly setting his special status alongside (and in distinction to) that of Peter.

It is clear from his letters that Paul understood his calling as requiring him to make obedience to the gospel of Jesus Christ the sole condition of the salvation of Gentiles and of their admission as fully fledged participants in the Christian movement. Over against some other Christian Jews who believed that Gentiles should also have to take up observance of the law of Moses (Torah), Paul insisted that Christ was the sufficient basis of their redemption (e.g. Gal. 2:15–21; 5:1–6) and that Holy-Spirit-empowered obedience to Christ was the defining criterion of their ethical obligation (e.g. Gal. 5:6, 13–26). Paul's conflicts with those Christian Jews who insisted on Gentile observance of the Torah (especially clear in Galatians) show that his own stance was not obviously compelling to all other Christians of his time, and was indeed a controversial stance that demanded justification.

In fact, given Paul's own pre-conversion dedication to Torah-observance (e.g. Phil. 3:5–6; Gal. 1:14), Paul himself must have required some considerable justification of the position he came to advocate as apostle to the

Gentiles. In light of his earlier zeal for Torah, it is understandable that he refers to his gospel of Gentile freedom from Torah-observance as having come to him with the force of a 'revelation' (Gal. 1:12), and not through the teaching of other Christians. But, even if he felt compelled by some experience of revelatory effect to posit Christ as replacing Torah as the criterion of salvation, he must have found it necessary for his own religious integrity (not to say sanity!) to reflect on how this could be so. He must have needed to satisfy himself that he could integrate such a high view of Christ into a (howbeit reformulated) continuing commitment to the God of Israel who had given the Torah through Moses.

So, whether, as he claims, Paul received as a 'revelation' a basic conviction that the Gentiles were to be included into the elect through faith in Christ without Torah-observance, and then had to think through how this could be so, or (as some scholars have suggested) he came to his conviction about the conditions for Gentile salvation by reasoning through implications of Christ's redemptive death and resurrection at some point after his own conversion, either way Paul's mission to the Gentiles necessitated and probably helped to shape the development of his christology. Paul says that the basic belief that 'Christ died for our sins' was part of the Christian tradition that he received as a new convert (1 Cor. 15:3), a christological conviction likely shared by Paul and other Jewish Christians, including those who pressed for Gentile observance of Torah. But for Paul to make faith in Christ sufficient for Gentile salvation either demanded or rested upon the sort of rich elaboration of the implications of Christ's redemptive death that Paul presents in passages such as Gal. 3:1–29 and Rom. 3:9–31. And in these passages Paul seems to be emphasizing his own reflections rather than simply reciting christological tradition. Particularly in his views of how Christ is to be understood in relation to the Torah, it is likely that Paul's christology shows the effects of his special mission to the Gentiles.

MAJOR CHRISTOLOGICAL BELIEFS

Although several frequently studied passages are commonly thought to be especially important as conveying Paul's beliefs about Jesus, nowhere in Paul's letters do we have a programmatic presentation of his christology. Except for the places (such as Gal. 3:10–4:7) where he finds it necessary to unpack the implications of Christ for his Gentile converts, in general Paul seems to presuppose the christological beliefs that he affirms as shared with his readers, and so in many cases his christological statements are brief and expressed in terms of shared Christian traditional formulations. So, any discussion of Paul's christology requires us to offer some sort of organization of his beliefs. For the purposes of the present discussion, we can consider Paul's christological beliefs under two headings: (1) Jesus' relation to God and (2) Jesus' significance for Christians.

(1) Jesus' relation to God

As noted already, Paul characteristically defines Jesus' significance in relation to God 'the Father'. In fact, all of the christological titles that Paul uses and all of the claims that Paul makes about the efficacy of Jesus' re-demptive work on behalf of the redeemed either explicitly or implicitly involve God as well. To speak of Jesus as 'Christ' (which Paul does so fre-quently that the term practically functions as a name for Jesus) is to claim that he is God's uniquely anointed/chosen one through whom the promises of eschatological redemption are fulfilled (Rom. 9:4–5).

Perhaps the most explicit and direct way that Paul links Jesus with God is to refer to Jesus as God's Son. Although Jesus' divine sonship is not referred to frequently in Paul (only fifteen times in the undisputed Pauline letters, and also in Eph. 4:13 and Col. 1:13), it is an important feature of his christology. As indicated earlier, Paul can refer to the divine action that turned him from opponent to advocate of the gospel as a revelation of God's Son (Gal. 1:15–16), and summarizes his message as 'the gospel concerning his [God's] Son' (Rom. 1:3).

Paul's references to Jesus as God's Son are concentrated in Romans and Galatians (eleven references), where Paul is in most intense and sustained dialogue with the Jewish tradition. This makes untenable the view that Paul's assertions of Jesus' divine sonship derived from pagan ideas of divine sonship and were intended primarily to legitimate Jesus as object of worship to Paul's pagan converts in terms that they could readily appreciate from their pre-Christian religious background. In fact, Paul does not refer to Jesus as divine Son in contexts where Christian worship is in view (1 Cor. 8–10) or in any statements that call for worship of Jesus or contrast Christian worship with pagan worship of gods and demi-gods. Instead, the Pauline references to Jesus' divine sonship are in contexts that emphasize Jesus' unique and intimate relationship to God, God's direct involvement in Jesus' redemptive work, and Jesus' paradigmatic and foundational role for the redeemed.

A survey of references will illustrate these points. Paul's gospel is con-cerned with God's Son (Rom. 1:3, 9; 2 Cor. 1:19), who has been shown to hold this status 'in power' through his resurrection, which always in Paul is God's act of vindication (Rom. 1:3–4). Though enemies of God, humans were reconciled to God through the death of his Son (Rom. 5:10), whom God sent forth as a human agent to redeem the elect (Rom. 8:3; Gal. 4:4). In an apparent allusion to Abraham's offering of Isaac (Genesis 22), Paul refers to God as having not withheld 'his own Son', giving him up 'for all of us' (Rom. 8:32). The redeemed are also to become sons of God, patterned after Jesus the paradigmatic Son (Rom 8:29). God now gives to the redeemed 'the Spirit of his Son', through whom they too can now address God as 'Abba, Father' (Gal. 4:6; cf. Rom. 8:14–17). Christians have been called by God 'into the fellowship of his Son, Jesus Christ our Lord' (1 Cor. 1:9), and now await their eschatological salvation from heaven in the future appearance of God's Son whom God raised from death and who thus 'rescues us from the wrath that is coming' (1 Thess. 1:10). As God's Son and Christ (Messiah), Jesus has been raised from death and exalted by God to have dominion over all things; yet the Son's exaltation will ultimately issue in his self-subjection to God 'so that God may be all in all' (1 Cor. 15:20–8).

These references to Jesus as God's Son seem often to allude to the Old Testament portrayal of the Davidic king (e.g. Ps. 2:7; 2 Sam. 7:14). Jesus' resurrection and exaltation to heavenly rule at God's 'right hand' (Psalm 110) are thus to be taken as the enthronement of Jesus as king, the king who rightly rules at God's own appointment. This is particularly clear in 1 Cor. 15:20–8, where Christ's resurrection is said to have involved God installing him as the royal ruler ('he must reign', 15:25) to whom all things are to be made subject. In Col. 1:13–14, God is said to have 'rescued us from the power of darkness and transferred us into the kingdom of his beloved Son'.

In other passages Paul refers to Christ as the glorious 'image of God', the glory of God being revealed 'in the face of Jesus Christ' (2 Cor. 4:3–6). A similar theme runs through a frequently studied passage in Col. 1:15–20. Here, Christ is referred to as 'the image of the invisible God', in whom 'all the fullness [of God] was pleased to dwell'.[2] The meaning of this idea of Christ as God's 'image' (*eikon*) in whom God's glory is reflected seems to be drawn from ancient notions of the function and significance of the images of gods that were characteristically the visible objects to (and through) which one reverenced the gods. The effect is to describe Christ in amazingly exalted terms.

Paul also appears to link Christ with God in creation as well as redemption. In 1 Cor. 8:5–6, all things are from and for God and are through Christ. Most scholars take the 'all things' here as referring to the creation of the world, Christ thus somehow seen as the agent through whom 'all things' came to be. Once again, Col. 1:15–20 echoes this theme. Here Christ is explicitly said to be the one 'in whom all things in the heavens and upon the earth were created' (1:16).

In another passage that has generated considerable scholarly attention, Phil. 2:6–11, Paul refers to Christ as having been 'in the form of God' (*en morphe Theou*) and as having chosen not to regard 'equality with God as something to be exploited' for his own advantage (2:6). Though some scholars have argued that 'form of God' alludes to the Gen. 1:26–7 reference to the human creature as made in God's image, most see the descriptions of Christ and his actions of self-humbling in Phil. 2:6–8 ('emptied himself . . . being born in human likeness') as perhaps the earliest extant evidence of the Christian belief that the man Jesus somehow had divine and heavenly origins, a belief usually referred to by scholars as Christ's 'pre-existence'. As we will note later, the question of whether Paul attributed a heavenly 'pre-existence' to Jesus is a disputed point in current Pauline scholarship.

(2) Jesus' significance for Christians

If Paul always implicitly or explicitly expresses Jesus' status and significance by reference to God, it is also true to say that Paul's christology emphasizes Jesus' significance in relation to the redeemed, the believers who make up the churches. For example, Paul's many references to Jesus as 'Christ' (anointed one) designate Jesus both as God's anointed agent of redemption and as the figure through whom the redeemed come to salvation, the 'Messiah'. Scholars have in fact noted that Paul's uses of the term 'Christ' are mainly in statements referring to Jesus' redemptive death and resurrection (e.g. Rom. 3:21–6; 5:6–8, 15–17; 6:4; 1 Cor. 15:3), which in the gospel that Paul preached were the key events that made redemption possible. In this emphasis upon the death of 'Christ/Messiah' Paul shows both the early Christian appropriation of religious categories from the Jewish tradition and the distinctive adaptation of these categories in the light of the figure of Jesus. The early Christian conviction that God had raised Jesus from death and that he was the Christ/Messiah led them to see his crucifixion as an event in the plan of God, producing the distinctive notion that the death of the Messiah was a crucial and central part of his messianic work for the redeemed. All this seems to have happened so quickly and so early that Paul received these beliefs as sacred tradition when he became a member of the Christian movement in the very earliest few years of its existence (ca AD 30–5), as he indicates in 1 Cor. 15:1–7. Moreover, as emphasized early in this chapter, Paul not only believed that Jesus' death was redemptive, but he was also gripped by it as an act of love for him and for all the redeemed that called for their greatest devotion in return (e.g. Gal. 2:19–20; 2 Cor. 5:14–15).

The other most common Pauline title for Jesus is 'Lord' (*Kyrios*), which Paul applies to Jesus about 180 times (excluding the Pauline epistles widely thought to be pseudepigraphical) and which in various contexts carries several connotations. In fact, about one hundred times in the undisputed letters Paul uses the expression 'the Lord' without any other title to designate Jesus. One of Paul's most striking uses of 'Lord' with reference to Jesus is in several citations of Old Testament passages where the Greek term *Kyrios* represents the Hebrew name of God (usually vocalized by scholars as *Yahweh*; e.g. Rom. 10:13 (Joel 2:32); 1 Cor. 1:31 (Jer. 9:23–4); 10:26 (Ps. 24:1); 2 Cor. 10:17 (Jer. 9:23–4)). This application of Old Testament 'Yahweh texts' to Jesus surely connotes a remarkable association of Jesus with God.[3] The logic behind this may be the idea reflected in Paul that God has given Jesus the name and status of 'Lord', 'the name above every name' (as in Phil. 2:9–11, another christological passage that alludes to an Old Testament passage, Isa. 45:23, where God (*Yahweh*) is the original referent). Paul also appropriates the Old Testament expression 'the day of the Lord [*Yahweh*]' to refer to the eschatological victory of Jesus (e.g. 1 Thess. 5:2; 1 Cor. 5:5), in some cases modifying the phrase to make explicit the application of it to Jesus (e.g. 1 Cor. 1:8; 2 Cor. 1:14). Jesus thus seems to be the divinely authorized figure who accomplishes the eschatological salvation that 'day of the Lord' came to signify.[4]

Kyrios (Lord) is also the characteristic term used in various credal and liturgical expressions in Paul's letters, expressions thought by scholars to be Paul's use of formulae whose origin was in the worship practice of early Christian groups. In 1 Cor. 12:3, for example (in a lengthy passage concerned with early Christian worship), the Holy Spirit is said to prompt in believers the acclamation 'Jesus is Lord.' Virtually the same acclamation appears in Rom. 10:9–10, and again the context indicates a worship-setting for the acclamation. The references in 10:12–13 to 'calling upon' (the name of) the Lord, an Old Testament expression for worship, indicate worship actions such as ritual invocation and confession. The slightly fuller form of the confession, 'Jesus Christ is Lord', appears in Phil. 2:11, in a passage that projects a future universal acknowledgement of Jesus. Phil. 2:6–11 is widely thought to be Paul's adaptation of an early hymn sung in Christian worship, where the ritual invocation of Jesus as 'Lord' was done in anticipation of this future acknowledgement by all creation. The term 'Lord' appears also in the confessional statement in 1 Cor. 8:5–6, where, as noted already, Paul declares Christian devotion to be restricted to the 'one God' and the 'one Lord'.

In another liturgical context, 1 Cor. 11:17–34, Paul repeatedly refers to Jesus as 'Lord' in his discussion of the Christian common meal that was a central feature of worship in his churches. It is 'the Lord's supper' (verse 20), about which Paul has instructions 'from the Lord' (verse 23). The meal proclaims 'the Lord's death until he comes' (verse 26). Believers eat the bread of the Lord and drink his cup (verse 27), and unworthy behaviour in the meal can make them 'liable for the body and blood of the Lord' (verse 27), who may chasten them to prevent their ultimate condemnation (verse 32).

Paul also designates Jesus as 'the Lord' (the title used either by itself or with other identifying terms) in contexts where he wishes to emphasize Jesus' authoritative status in questions of Christian behaviour. In Rom. 14:1–12, for example, Paul urges tolerance among believers about differences of scruples over foods and special days, emphasizing that believers live and die 'to the Lord' (and note especially verse 9, where Paul uses 'Christ' in referring to Jesus' death/resurrection and 'Lord' to refer to the status he holds as a result of these redemptive events). In 1 Cor. 6:13–7:40 Paul deals with a number of sexual issues, repeatedly referring to Jesus as 'the Lord' to whom believers are responsible and from whom authoritative teaching comes (e.g. 7:10–11; cf. 7:25). In 1 Thess. 4:1–12, Paul refers to 'the Lord Jesus' (verses 1–12) or simply 'the Lord' (verse 6) in exhorting believers to follow the ethical instructions given in this epistle.

Another type of statement in which Paul refers to Jesus as 'Lord' has to do with eschatological matters. As example, although Paul refers to awaiting God's Son in 1 Thess. 1:9–10, note the several references to Jesus as 'Lord' in this epistle in statements dealing with Jesus' eschatological return (2:19; 3:13; 4:15–17; 5:2, 23). In 1 Cor. 1:7–8, believers are described as awaiting the eschatological revelation and 'day of our Lord Jesus Christ', and in 4:1–5 Paul refers to Jesus as 'the Lord' whose coming will render judgment. The phrase 'the Lord is near' in Phil. 4:5 refers to the same expectation. The Old Testament expression 'day of the Lord', mentioned earlier as taken over in early Christian circles to refer to Jesus' eschatological coming, likely influenced Paul's tendency to use 'Lord' in references to Jesus' eschatological return. It is clear that for Paul, Jesus is the eschatological deliverer awaited by believers and through whom God's triumph over evil is accomplished.

MAJOR ISSUES

Several issues feature prominently in scholarly investigation and continuing debate about Paul's christology. Space permits only a brief introduction to them.

(1) Paul and the earthly Jesus

The Jesus whom Paul proclaims and serves was obviously the resurrected and glorified Son of God, but what was Paul's acquaintance with, and attitude toward, the earthly Jesus who went about in Galilee? In a few places Paul cites words of Jesus, perhaps quoting from some written collection of Jesus' teachings or from oral tradition (e.g. 1 Cor. 7:10–11; cf. Mark 10:2–9), and he can refer to Jesus' behaviour as an inspiring example for believers (Rom. 15:3, 7–9; Phil. 2:6–8). But he does not convey very much of what we find in the gospels about Jesus' ministry. Some scholars have cited 2 Cor. 5:16 as indicating that Paul had little interest in the earthly Jesus, but this is a misunderstanding of the verse. Here, Paul's reference to knowing Jesus or anyone else 'according to the flesh' means holding views that are merely based on human perceptions (such as Paul's former rejection of Jesus as accursed by God) that are not shaped by God's 'new creation', in which 'everything old has passed away and all things have become new'.

(2) Incarnation?

Though most scholars see in Phil. 2:6–8 and in other passages such as Gal. 4:4–6 and Rom. 8:3–4 (also Col. 1:15–20 if this epistle is taken as from Paul) indications that Paul saw Jesus as in some way having had a heavenly 'pre-existence', as mentioned earlier some scholars dispute this.[5] They see these passages as simply rhetorical references to Jesus' human birth and subsequent exemplary obedience to God's will. It bears noting that Paul seems to presume acquaintance with what he is asserting in these passages and does not feel the need to defend his statements. If, thus, these passages do express the notion of Christ's pre-existence, this notion may well not have originated with Paul. There is some evidence that in Jewish traditions of the time 'pre-existence' was attributed to some figures, and signified their centrality in God's purposes.

(3) 'Binitarian' devotion?

Scholars recognize that the reverence for Christ reflected in Paul's letters amounts to a notable pattern of beliefs and devotional practices for which we have no real parallel in Roman-era Jewish tradition. Some scholars[6] conclude that we can speak of a novel 'binitarian' devotional pattern evident in the Pauline letters, Christ included with God as recipient of devotion in early Christian circles, albeit Christ always functionally subordinate to God 'the Father'. But some other scholars[7] contend that this is an exaggeration of things and that the reverence of Christ in Paul, though impressive, does not amount to worship and was not then seen as quite the innovation in monotheistic commitment that is alleged by other scholars. In either view, however, the devotion to Christ manifest in Paul's letters is a major development in religious history.

(4) Paul as innovator?

Some scholars[8] portray Paul as very much an innovator in his christology, but others note how little evidence there is in his letters that his christological views were contentious to other Christians. To be sure, there is evidence that Paul was controversial, as shown particularly in the epistle to Galatians. But here and elsewhere in his epistles (e.g. 2 Corinthians 11) the controversies have to do basically with his validity as an apostle and whether, as Paul proclaims, Gentiles are excused from Torah-observance. To other Jewish Christians Paul defends his Gentile mission by invoking christological convictions that are shared by them (e.g. Gal. 2:11–16). Certainly, it appears that he drew implications from these shared convictions that were not seen so readily by others. But, apart from the defence of his gospel of Gentile salvation, Paul shows little indication that his christological convictions were innovative or controversial among the Christians he knew. If this is correct, then his letters are in a sense all the more historically important as reflections of christological convictions widely characteristic of his churches and of at least a good many other Christians as well.

CONCLUSION

In Paul's epistles we have not only his testimonies of his christological beliefs and the piety in which they fitted, but also invaluable historical evidence of the rapid christological developments that characterized the Christian movement in the earliest years. By the time of Paul's undisputed letters, written some twenty to thirty years from the death of Jesus, a veritable explosion in christological convictions had taken place. In his conversion to the Christian movement, Paul not only assented to a set of christological beliefs, but became a passionate advocate of them. His epistles are remarkable evidence of the intensity of the Christ-devotion that Paul practised himself and promoted among his churches.

Notes

1 Neil Richardson, *Paul's Language about God*, JSNTS 99 (Sheffield: Sheffield Academic Press, 1994) 272.

2 The Pauline authorship of the epistle to the Colossians is doubted by some scholars. But, whether by Paul or written posthumously by one of his followers, this passage echoes here christological themes found also in the undisputed epistles.

3 See D. B. Capes, *Old Testament Yahweh Texts in Paul's Christology*, WUNT 2.47 (Tübingen: Mohr Siebeck, 1992).

4 L. J. Kreitzer, *Jesus and God in Paul's Eschatology*, JSNTS 19 (Sheffield: Sheffield Academic Press, 1984).

5 E.g. J. D. G. Dunn, *Christology in the Making*, 2nd edn (London: SCM, 1989); J. Murphy-O'Connor, 'Christological Anthropology in Phil. 2.6–11', *RB* 83 (1976) 25–50.

6 E.g. L. W. Hurtado, *One God, One Lord: Early Christian Devotion and Ancient Jewish Monotheism* (Philadelphia: Fortress/London: SCM, 1988; 2nd edn, Edinburgh: T. & T. Clark, 1998); A. F. Segal, *Paul the Convert: The Apostolate and Apostasy of Saul the Pharisee* (New Haven: Yale University Press, 1990); C. C. Newman, *Paul's Glory-Christology: Tradition and Rhetoric*, NovTSup 69 (Leiden: Brill, 1990).

7 E.g. J. D. G. Dunn, *The Theology of Paul the Apostle* (Grand Rapids: Eerdmans/Edinburgh: T. & T. Clark, 1998) 252–60; P. M. Casey, 'Monotheism, Worship and Christological Developments in the Pauline Churches', in C. C. Newman, J. Davila, and G. S. Lewis, eds., *The Jewish Roots of Christological Monotheism*, JSJS 63 (Leiden: Brill, 1999) 214–33.

8 E.g. S. Kim, *The Origin of Paul's Gospel* (Tübingen: Mohr Siebeck, 1981).

14 Paul's ecclesiology

LUKE TIMOTHY JOHNSON

Addressing Paul's understanding of the church (*ekklēsia*) means raising other difficult questions that a brief essay cannot adequately answer. The most critical question concerns which of the letters ascribed to Paul should be considered. Ephesians and 1 Timothy, for example, provide fuller information on aspects of the church than do some undisputed letters. But they are commonly regarded as pseudonymous. Should they be excluded altogether, read as a faithful continuation of themes in the authentic letters, or adjudged betrayals of the authentic Paul's spirit? In order to maintain conversation with the dominant scholarly position, this essay will discuss the evidence of the undisputed letters before that in Colossians, Ephesians, and the Pastoral Letters, even though there are strong reasons for accepting all thirteen letters attributed to Paul as authored by him through a complex process of composition. The present analysis does, however, emphasize thematic links between the disputed and undisputed letters, in order to respect the genuine lines of continuity among them and the marked diversity within even the collection of undisputed letters.

Another procedural question concerns consistency and variation among the expressions of Paul's thought. Which images and understandings are of fundamental character, and which are only brought to the surface by the peculiar circumstances that Paul faces in a specific community? Is it accurate, for example, to call Paul's basic outlook 'charismatic' if he deals extensively with the spiritual gifts in only one letter (1 Corinthians 12–14) – cautiously – and briefly in two others (Rom. 12:6–8; 1 Thess. 5:19–21)? Is Paul's commitment to an egalitarian membership (Gal. 3:28) absolute, or a function of his concern about competitiveness? This question reminds us of the occasional character of the Pauline correspondence. By no means are his letters simply spontaneous outpourings of the moment; recent analysis has confirmed how pervasively Paul used the conventions of ancient rhetoric in his letters. They are, however, genuine letters that respond to situations – sometimes critical – in Paul's own ministry or in the life of his communities.

We never find Paul's thought on any subject laid out systematically, therefore, but only as directed to a specific occasion.

Finally, it is difficult to assess the impact of social realities on Paul's statements concerning the *ekklēsia*. The basic structure of the Graeco-Roman club or society, already substantially appropriated by the Hellenistic Jewish synagogue, was immediately available for Paul's congregations as he worked in the diaspora. And the fact that his churches met in the *oikos* (home) of leading members (e.g. Rom. 16:5; 1 Cor. 16:19; Col. 4:15; Phlm. 2) had a number of implications, supplying a range of metaphors, a model of leadership functions as well as a source of leaders, and a source of tension in deciding the appropriate social roles for women and men in the assembly. This short essay cannot take up these disputed questions, but can remind the careful reader to assess the following summation, which is necessarily general, in light of the complex and diverse witness of the letters themselves.

PAUL'S ECCLESIAL FOCUS

The main point on the topic of Paul's ecclesiology can, nevertheless, be stated clearly and emphatically: the central concern in Paul's letters is the stability and integrity of his churches. He was the founder of communities (1 Cor. 4:15; Gal. 4:13; 1 Thess. 1:5), and expended his energies on their behalf. He lists his 'daily care for the churches' in climactic position in his list of tribulations (2 Cor. 11:28). When absent from his churches, Paul sought to visit them (e.g. 1 Cor. 4:18; 1 Thess. 2:17–18). When he was not able to visit, he stayed in contact through the sending of his delegates (e.g. Phil. 2:19; 1 Thess. 3:2) and the writing of letters. It is significant that all but one of Paul's letters are to be read in churches. The only truly private letter is 2 Timothy. Although addressed to an individual, Philemon includes members of the local church in its greetings (Phlm. 3); 1 Timothy and Titus, as *mandata principis* ('commandments of the ruler') letters, have a semi-public character. Paul's primary concern in his letters, furthermore, is not the individual but the community as such. He appeals to all the members of the church as his readers, and in the letters to his delegates, his focus is on their administration of a local community in Paul's absence. Paul characteristically addresses his readers as 'brothers' in the plural (e.g. Rom. 1:13; 1 Cor. 2:1), and his instruction is directed to their life together, rather than to the good of any individual. As a moral teacher, Paul seeks to shape communities of character. The intrinsic legitimacy of certain practices – such as circumcision, visions, or spiritual gifts – is less his concern than the possible divisiveness such practices might generate within communities through rivalry and competition. Ecclesiology is as central to Paul as soteriology. Indeed, it can be argued that for him soteriology *is* ecclesiology: all of his language about salvation (*sōtēria*) has a communal rather than an individual referent (e.g. Rom. 1:16; 8:24; 11:11, 14).

The Pauline church resembled other *ekklēsiai* such as the many clubs and philosophical schools of the Hellenistic world in its basic structure, its location in the household rather than the cult shrine, and its patterns of mutual assistance. Paul is also capable of presenting himself in terms used by Graeco-Roman philosophers (1 Thess. 2:4–12; Gal. 4:14). The inherently fragile nature of the *ekklēsia* as an intentional community – that is, one dependent on the commitment of its members rather than natural kinship – helps account for Paul's constant concern for 'building up' the church by mutual exhortation and example (1 Thess. 5:11; 1 Cor. 8:1; 14; Eph. 4:12, 16). Paul shows himself willing to exclude or even dismiss those in the church whose behaviour threatens the stability or integrity of the church (e.g. 1 Cor. 5:1–5; 2 Thess. 3:14–15; Gal. 4:30).

Paul's understanding of his own work and that of the church owes more, however, to the symbolic world of Torah and the heritage of Judaism. He speaks of his own role as an apostle in terms reminiscent of the call and work of God's prophets (Gal. 1:15), who were sent out to speak God's word. He refers to the church in terms of God's 'call' (*kalein, klēsis*; Rom. 11:29; 1 Cor. 1:26; 1 Thess. 2:12), giving the noun *ekklēsia* some of the resonance of God's *qahal* (assembly) in scripture (Deut. 23:1–2; Josh. 9:2; Ps. 21:22). Thus, members of the community have not simply chosen to belong to the church as another club; rather, God has called them out of the world. Even with his Gentile communities, Paul can employ the narratives of Torah concerning the people of Israel as exemplary for the church (1 Cor. 10:1–13; 2 Cor. 3:7–18; Gal. 4:21–31). Similarly, the church is to be characterized, as was ancient Israel, by holiness: 'this is the will of God, your sanctification' (1 Thess. 4:3). The boundary between those in the church and outside it is marked by a ritual act (baptism), but is defined by moral behaviour rather than ritual observance (Rom. 6:1–11). Formerly, members lived in the vice typical of those who are 'without God in the world' and given to idolatry (1 Thess. 1:9; Rom. 1:18–32). But by the ritual washing of baptism (Eph. 5:26), they have been cleansed morally, and now are called to holiness of life. This basic distinction is expressed by Paul as the contrast between 'the world' and 'the saints' (*hoi hagioi*, the holy ones; 1 Cor. 6:2).

ISRAEL AND THE CHURCH

In some real sense, therefore, Paul sees his churches as continuous with Israel, considered not simply as an ethnic group but as God's elect people. But three elements in Paul's experience introduced an element of discontinuity with the Jewish heritage as well. The first (in chronological order rather than order of importance) was his own life-experience as one who had persecuted the church precisely out of zeal for Torah (Gal. 1:13–14; Phil. 3:6). The appeal to Deut. 21:23 ('Cursed be every one who hangs upon a tree'), as a rebuttal to those who would claim Jesus as the righteous one, may well have been Paul's own before his encounter with the risen Jesus (Gal. 3:13). His statement, 'no one in the Holy Spirit can say, "Cursed be Jesus"' (1 Cor. 12:3), may well have an autobiographical basis. For Paul the Pharisee, if one held to Torah as absolute norm, then one could not claim Jesus as Lord. It was the experience of Jesus as the powerfully risen Lord that put Paul in a state of cognitive dissonance. If Jesus is the righteous one, then Torah cannot be an absolute norm: God is capable of acting outside God's own scriptural precedents.

The second element follows the first: Paul perceives the resurrection of Jesus as something more than the validation of a Jewish Messiah in the traditional sense of a restorer of the people. The resurrection of Jesus is more than a historical event like the exodus. It is an eschatological event that begins a new age of humanity. Indeed, the resurrection is best understood as new creation: 'If anyone is in Christ, there is a new creation. The old things have passed away. Behold, everything is new' (2 Cor. 5:17).

The third element is Paul's sense of his own mission and its consequences. If Paul was sent to the Gentiles with the good news of what God had done in Jesus (Gal. 1:16), and if Gentiles were to be included in the church without the requirement of circumcision (Gal. 5:1–6), then the perception that the resurrection is a new creation and Jesus is a new Adam is confirmed (1 Cor. 15:45; Rom. 5:12–21). If, as he had done, Paul's fellow Jews reject that proclamation despite their zeal for Torah (Rom. 9:30–10:3), and if, as he had done, Paul's fellow Jews even resist and persecute the proclaimers of the good news (2 Thess. 2:13–16), then there is some real rupture within God's people that must be reconciled. For Paul, then, the relationship between the church and Israel is not simply a matter of continuity or of discontinuity; it must rather be seen in terms of a dialectic within history.

In Paul's undisputed letters, the various sides of this dialectic are expressed in several ways. An obvious example is the way Paul appeals to the principle that 'in Christ there is neither Jew nor Greek, male nor female, slave nor free' (Gal. 3:28), thereby rendering the three great status markers dividing people (ethnicity, gender, class) nugatory for those in the church ('in Christ'). Paul makes this appeal most emphatically in the context of resisting those within a Gentile community who seek to be circumcised, and who would thereby make the church a community in which Jews and males have higher status than Gentiles and women. Note that at the end of Galatians he puts two statements in tension, saying first, 'neither circumcision counts nor uncircumcision, but a new creation' (Gal. 6:15), but then also, 'peace upon the Israel of God' (Gal. 6:16). In Galatians, Paul's polemic would lead one to conclude that the 'Israel of God' was made up only of Gentile believers, so severe are his characterizations of the law (3:19–22) and of 'the present Jerusalem' (4:25). Indeed, in his more negative moments, reacting against the resistance or harassment of fellow Jews, Paul even designates them as 'false brethren' (2:4), unbelievers who are perishing, blinded by 'the god of this world' (2 Cor. 4:3–4), unable to understand even their own scripture, and subject to the wrath of God (1 Thess. 2:16).

On the other side of the dialectic, Paul confirms the truth of Torah's narratives (Rom. 4:1–25) and the words of the prophets (11:8–27; 15:4), recognizing moreover that, unlike Gentile idolaters, the Jews had not only the 'words of God' (3:2) but also the knowledge of God's will (2:18). Thus, although he insists that Jew and Gentile stand in fundamentally the same relationship before God both in their sin and in their capacity for faith (3:9, 22), he also acknowledges that the Jew has a considerable advantage because of the knowledge of God's revelation (3:1–4).

The full dialectic is worked out in Romans 9–11, the climax of Paul's most extended reflection on his mission to the Gentiles. Beginning with three unshakable convictions – his solidarity with his fellow Jews (9:1–3), God's election and blessing of the Jews (9:4–5), and the infallibility of God's word (9:6) – Paul engages in a midrashic reflection on scripture impelled by the implications and consequences of the Gentile mission. He interprets the present situation (9:30–10:4) in terms of a longer history of election and rejection (9:6–29), and understands himself with other believing Jews as a faithful remnant (11:1–6). Jews who now stumble over the crucified Messiah will perhaps, out of jealousy for the favour God is now showing to those who formerly were 'no people', also in the end be rejoined to the increasingly Gentile church, and 'thus all Israel will be saved' (11:13–32). While passionately committed to the cause of the mission to the Gentiles, Paul remains as unswervingly devoted to his own people and to the fidelity of the God who had elected them.

MISSION OF THE CHURCH

Paul never describes the church's mission in terms of a specific task that it is to perform, but in terms of a character of life that it is to exhibit. It is to 'walk worthily of its call' (Eph. 4:1). At the most obvious level, this involves a life of righteousness before God (Rom. 6:13, 18). Just as it is not

physical circumcision but the circumcision of the heart expressed in obedience to the commandments that identifies the genuine Jew (Rom. 2:25–9),
so within the church, it is not a matter of circumcision or not but of 'keeping the commandments of God' (1 Cor. 7:19). Like Jesus and James, Paul
identifies the love of neighbour as the perfect summation of God's commandments, because 'love does no harm to the neighbour' (Rom. 13:8–10).
Paul thus emphasizes a communal understanding of righteousness; it is not
only a matter of being right with God but also a matter of being in right
relationship with others (1 Cor. 8:1–3; Rom. 14:17). Here it is impossible
not to detect the influence of the story of Jesus on Paul's understanding
of the church. In 1 Cor. 1:18–2:5 Paul challenges the arrogance and rivalry
of his Corinthian readers by appealing to the message of the cross, which
demonstrates how God's power works through weakness and God's wisdom through foolishness. The cross that reverses human valuations is the
paradigm for those in the church who 'have the mind of Christ' (2:16): they
are to live together, not in competition but in cooperation, not in rivalry but
in mutual edification.

Paul shows little or no concern for the perfection (*teleiōsis*) of individuals, but is constantly concerned that his churches mature as communities
of reciprocal gift-giving and fellowship. And the norm is the human Jesus:
'Little children, how I am in labour until Christ be formed among you' (Gal.
4:19). Paul understands Jesus as the one 'who loved us and gave himself
for our sins' (Gal. 1:4). Jesus' kenotic (self-emptying) and faithful obedience
towards God, which implied the rejection of any competitive claim towards
God (Phil. 2:5–11), and which established the possibility for all to be righteous through sharing his faithful obedience (Rom. 5:18–21), is also the
perfect expression of Jesus' love for humans, and therefore the model for
relations within the church. Those who 'put on the Lord Jesus Christ' (Rom.
13:14) are able to 'welcome one another as Christ has welcomed [them]'
(Rom. 15:7). Those who 'bear one another's burdens' also 'fulfil the law
of Christ' (Gal. 6:2). Those who are guided by love are willing to give up
their rights for the sake of 'the brother for whom Christ died' (Rom. 14:15;
1 Cor. 8:11). Paul considers attitudes of envy and rivalry to threaten such
relationships (Gal. 5:16–21). Envy and rivalry foster a spirit of competition
that seeks the good of the individual at the expense of the community (Gal.
5:13). Paul therefore advocates another spirit, that of fellowship or reconciliation (Gal. 5:22–4; Phil. 2:1–4). In his view, the paradigm of God's saving
action as revealed in the faith and love of Jesus demands of the strong in
the community not to dominate or assert their will, but in service and humility to place themselves at the disposal of the weak (1 Cor. 8:7–13). As he
measures the integrity of his own mission by this norm of reconciliation

(2 Cor. 5:12–21), so does he measure the integrity and maturity of his churches (2 Cor. 13:1–11). The task of collecting money from gentile churches for the impoverished church in Jerusalem, a task to which Paul committed himself in agreement with the Jerusalem leaders (Gal. 2:10) and to which he devoted – with varying degrees of success – his best energies (1 Cor. 16:1–4; 2 Cor. 8–9), and for which he was willing to risk even his life (Rom. 15:24–32), becomes the body-language of the church's identity as a place of reconciliation.

THE CHURCH IN METAPHOR

Paul's understanding of the church is expressed as much by a series of metaphors as by propositions. Metaphors, especially root metaphors, are much more than rhetorical ornaments; they structure a perception of reality. The metaphors that Paul employs for the church combine elements of a living organism and structure. The simplest metaphors of this kind are agricultural and used only once, perhaps because of Paul's limited ability to handle horticultural terms. The church is a field that Paul has planted and Apollos has watered, but God gives the growth (1 Cor. 3:6–9). Similarly, God's people is a domestic olive tree (the Jewish people) that, although pruned, is 'holy in root and branches' (Rom. 11:16). God has grafted the branch of a wild olive (Gentile believers) onto it, and is capable of grafting the domestic olive on again (Rom. 11:16–24) – a clumsy metaphor indeed. These agricultural metaphors were probably derived from the imagery of the prophets.

A much more complex metaphor drawn from Paul's Jewish heritage is that the church is a family. The note of continuity with Judaism is found in the designation of Abraham as 'our father' (Rom. 4:1) and the affirmation that the Gentiles are the 'children of Abraham' through faith and thus part of Israel, indeed more so than those Jews who are not believers (Galatians 3–4). Also in continuity with Judaism, Paul calls the creator God 'Father' (Gal. 1:1; Rom. 1:7). But Paul connects God's fatherhood directly to 'our Lord Jesus Christ', whom he recognizes as 'Son of God' (e.g. Rom. 1:4; 2 Cor. 1:19). Jesus, however, was intended by God to be 'the first-born of many children' (Rom. 8:29). Believers become children of God through 'the spirit of adoption' that they receive at baptism (Rom. 8:15; Gal. 4:6). The metaphor is made more complex by Paul's speaking of himself as the father of a community through his preaching of the gospel (1 Cor. 4:15). The church is therefore a fictive family in that it is not made up of biologically related people, but because of Paul's realistic sense of the Holy Spirit as 'indwelling' humans (Rom. 8:11), the bonds connecting members of the community are not, for him, simply imaginary. When Paul addresses his readers as 'brothers' (*adelphoi*) or refers to co-workers as 'brother' (*adelphos*) or 'sister' (*adelphē*) (Rom. 15:14; 16:1; 1 Cor. 1:11), this kinship language works powerfully to strengthen community identity and unity. And since in antiquity the relationship between brothers is the supreme paradigm for fellowship (*koinōnia*), kinship language also encourages the patterns of equality and reciprocity that are Paul's moral concern.

A third metaphor is found in only two of the undisputed letters (1 Cor. 12:22; Rom. 12:4–5) but is attested also in two of the disputed letters (Col. 1:18; Eph. 4:12). Although it derives from Graeco-Roman politics rather than Torah, Paul's use of it is distinctive. In this metaphor, the church is the body of the Messiah. The metaphor of the body combines the sense of a living organism and an articulate, many-membered structure. Paul's use emphasizes the legitimacy of many gifts in the community (1 Corinthians 12) and the need for those gifts to be used for the 'building up' (*oikodomē*) of the community as a whole (1 Cor. 14:26). Once more, however, Paul's perception of the community's life as one that is literally given by God through the Holy Spirit (Rom. 5:5) and shaped by transformation into the image of Christ (2 Cor. 3:17–18) gives the metaphor both depth and complexity. Since Paul can speak of the resurrected Jesus as 'life-giving Spirit' (1 Cor. 15:45), and can declare, 'we have all drunk of the one spirit' (12:13), it appears that the metaphor of the body may better be called a symbol in the strict sense, that is, a sign that participates in that which it signifies. Such participation seems demanded by Paul's language concerning the implications of eating the body of the Lord (10:16–22), and the ambiguity of reference present in his statement concerning 'disregarding the body' at the Lord's Supper (11:27–30). When, in the same letter, Paul says of the community (using the plural), 'and we have the mind of Christ' (2:16), it is legitimate to ask whether Paul might truly understand the church as the bodily presence of the resurrected Jesus. Such a mystical understanding – supported by a variety of other expressions (e.g. Gal. 2:20; 1 Cor. 6:17) – may also in turn undergird his statements concerning the disposition of the physical body (as in sexual relations) by members of the church (1 Cor. 6:15–18; 7:14).

The previous two metaphors reveal the important roles Paul assigns to the Holy Spirit in his ecclesiology as the source of its (divine) life and as mediator of its (Christic) identity. The spirit 'dwells in' the community (Rom. 8:9, 11). As a result, Paul also speaks of the community as being 'in Christ' (Rom 6:11; 1 Cor. 1:2) and 'in the Lord' (1 Cor. 7:22; Gal. 5:10), as short-hand for the sphere of influence (or energy-field) that is the community. As with the contrast between the saints and the world, these designations serve to remind members powerfully of their special identity: they are 'in Christ' as 'the body of Christ', and they are 'in the Lord' because they 'belong to the Lord' (1 Cor. 6:13). It is impossible to avoid the conclusion that Paul's understanding of the church involves a deep and mystical identity between this community and the risen Jesus mediated by the Holy Spirit.

Another metaphor is the church as a building (*oikodomē*; 1 Cor. 3:9). Once more, the image combines unity and multiplicity, and has roots in Torah, in Graeco-Roman political philosophy, and in the social situation of early Christians whose *ekklēsia*, in fact, met in the houses of wealthier members. The house is a root metaphor that generates a number of other images: Paul and his associates are household managers (*oikonomoi*; 1 Cor. 4:1–2) who dispense the mysteries of God; members of the community whose speech and actions serve to strengthen the community are said to 'edify' the church (*oikodomein*, to build a house; 1 Cor. 8:1; 1 Thess. 5:11). Paul's distinctive version of the metaphor once more comes from his sense that the community derives from and is ordered to God. The church is therefore 'God's house'. Given Paul's sense of the community as enlivened and guided by the indwelling Holy Spirit, furthermore, it is but a short step to a refinement of the house metaphor, the church is God's temple (1 Cor. 3:16–17). This image combines the elements of unity and multiplicity together with a profound sense of the divine presence within the community, and supports as well the mandate to holiness of life within the church.

ORGANIZATION IN THE LOCAL CHURCH

The notion that Paul's churches either were directed exclusively by the apostolic authority of Paul himself or were charismatic organisms guided exclusively by the Spirit without any human organization is contradicted both by sociological logic and by evidence in the undisputed letters. Paul's frequently expressed frustration reveals how his own visits, the sending of his delegates, and even his letters failed to enable him to resolve even the larger crises of his churches, much less the everyday affairs (*ta biōtika*, 1 Cor. 6:3–4) that require attention in every community. Intentional communities do not survive without mechanisms that enable them to carry out common tasks and make decisions. On the one side, they need to settle disputes; on the other side, they need to provide hospitality, organize fellowship, care for the sick, even receive and read letters from the apostle. They can take communal action in such matters as the collection (1 Cor. 16:1–4) or providing supplies requested by Paul's agent for a future mission (Rom. 15:24; 16:1–2). Pauline churches had available to them from the start, moreover, the simple and flexible structure of the Graeco-Roman *ekklēsia* and the Jewish synagogue. The diaspora synagogue had a board – often made up of wealthy benefactors of the community – that administered finances and settled disputes and oversaw the study and teaching of Torah, as well as the system of organized charity to the needy within the community.

The undisputed letters provide sparse but significant evidence that some such simple structure was present also in Pauline churches from the beginning. Paul can speak of those in the Thessalonian church – presumably in existence for a very short time – who preside over others and exhort them (1 Thess. 5:12). Paul is angry at the Corinthians for picking inadequate members to settle disputes over *ta biōtika* in that church (1 Cor. 6:18). In 1 Cor. 12:28 he lists 'governing' as one of the gifts of the Spirit (see also Rom. 12:8), and instructs the Corinthian church to 'be submissive' to such benefactors (and householders) as Stephanas and Achaicus (1 Cor. 16:15–18). Galatians recognizes that there are those who instruct others in the word who should receive financial support in return (Gal. 6:6). The letter to Philemon assumes that the addressee has some authority over the *ekklēsia* that meets in his house (Phlm. 1–3, 21–2). Finally, Paul addresses the *episkopoi* (supervisors) and *diakonoi* (helpers) in the Philippian church (Phil. 1:1). These brief notices support the conclusion that Paul's churches had local leadership. Equally significant is the fact that Paul treats such leadership in purely functional terms, without providing any theological legitimation in its support.

THE CHURCH IN COLOSSIANS AND EPHESIANS

The letters to the Colossians and Ephesians form a set within the Pauline corpus much like Galatians and Romans. In addition to sharing substantially in diction and style, the two letters work at similar themes from slightly different perspectives. As the position worked out polemically in Galatians is shaped by Romans into a magisterial argument, so also is the position worked out polemically in Colossians shaped by Ephesians into a magisterial reflection. Neither Colossians nor Ephesians adds significantly to our knowledge of structure in the Pauline church, although Ephesians does include a list of ministries (Eph. 4:11). But both letters share Paul's focus on the *ekklēsia* as a community of mutual upbuilding and reconciliation. Their distinctive contribution is to heighten the sense of mystical identification between Christ and the church found also in the undisputed letters.

In Colossians, Paul opposes those who seek to measure maturity by the addition of circumcision (2:11), ascetical observances (2:21–2), and even mystical experiences (2:18), by appealing to the adequacy of the Gentiles' experience of God through baptism into Christ (2:9–15). Against the individualism inherent in the competition for higher status within the community (2:16, 23), Paul calls for a new sense of humanity that unites rather than divides persons on the basis of their status (3:11), and for a maturity based on an ever deeper insight into the mystery of Christ, spelled out in attitudes of mutuality and cooperation (3:5–17). To support the 'fullness of God' that is made accessible through baptism into Christ (2:9–12), Colossians emphasizes the primacy of Christ over both creation and the church (1:15–20). In this letter, the church is the body, but Christ is its head (1:18, 24; 2:19).

Ephesians, which may well have been a circular letter, lifts the local concerns found in Colossians into a reflection on the nature and mission of the church which is the fullest and most mature in the Pauline collection. Virtually every ecclesial theme of Paul's other letters is brought together in Ephesians in a manner so metaphorically complex as to deflect easy summation. In brief, Paul portrays God's will in terms of an *oikonomia* (household administration, 1:10; 3:2) that has cosmic range: God seeks the reconciliation of all humans (1:9–14). The need for reconciliation between God and humans because of sin is expressed socially in alienation among humans. The prime example is the enmity between Jews and Gentiles (2:11–12). Jesus' death and resurrection had the goal of reconciling humans to God and humans to each other in a new humanity that is created in his image in the Holy Spirit (2:13–18). Eph. 2:1–11 elaborates these points through extraordinarily complex metaphors of body, house, and temple that make it clear that as the Jewish temple symbolized lack of access to God for all humanity and with it the enmity between Jew and Gentile (2:14–15), the church is to be the new house of God in the Spirit where all have equal access to God (2:19–22). The church is the place in the world where this mysterious plan of God is being revealed (3:9–11). The nature and mission of the church is therefore the same: to be the symbol of the world's possibility by being the place in the world where human differences do not separate but provide the basis for a deeper unity in the Spirit (4:11–16). The measure of the community's life is therefore 'the bond of love in the Spirit' (4:3), and every behaviour that falls short of 'doing the truth in love' (4:15) must be rejected. If the church fails to be a community of reconciliation, it has no reason to exist. Positively, the love between female and male in marriage (5:22–31) points to the reconciliation possible between Jew and Gentile: 'This is a great mystery, by which I mean, Christ and the church' (5:32).

THE CHURCH IN THE PASTORALS

The letters to Paul's delegates Timothy and Titus are regarded by the majority of scholars as inauthentic and as representing a development of Pauline ecclesiology in the direction of institutional complexity. Whether the judgment concerning authenticity is correct or not, it is not substantially supported by differences in ecclesiology. Indeed, it is a mistake in method to combine these three letters as though they were uniform. 2 Timothy focuses completely on the character and behaviour of Paul's delegate in contrast to the practices of false teachers (2 Tim. 2:14–4:5). The church enters the discussion only implicitly when the author develops the metaphor of the great house in which some vessels are destined for honourable use and others for shameful (2:20–3), as an encouragement to become a 'proven workman for the Lord' within the community of faith (2:15). In Titus, the only explicit mention of ecclesial organization comes in the instruction to establish elders/supervisors in every church, with a short list of qualities desirable in the supervisor (Titus 1:5–9). Otherwise, Titus concentrates on the threat that is implicitly posed to the church by the disruption of households by those challenging the adequacy of grace and advocating observance of the law (1:10–16).

It is 1 Timothy that provides a fuller view of the church, most obviously in its description of the moral and intellectual qualities desired in those who hold the positions of supervisor (*episkopos*, 3:1–7), helper (*diakonos*, 3:8–10, 12–13), and female helper (3:11). Although these descriptions are not found in the undisputed Pauline letters, we have seen that the titles themselves occur in Philippians. Since there is no description of the duties attached to these offices, furthermore, it is only by inference that we conclude that they involved oversight of the community's finances, teaching, settling disputes, and adminstration of charity – the same functions that we infer fell to those designated as 'standing over' others in the undisputed letters. Most strikingly there is also no theological legitimation of these positions. As in the other Pauline letters, the positions are assumed to be in existence and are regarded in purely functional terms.

1 Timothy shows Paul excommunicating those upsetting the community (1:20) and refusing women permission to speak in the assembly (2:11–15), but these reflexes are also found in the undisputed letters (1 Cor. 5:1–5; 14:33–6). Of the major Pauline metaphors for the church, 1 Timothy develops only that of the household (*oikos*). Management ability in one's household is a good indicator of leadership ability in the *ekklēsia* (3:4; cf. 1 Cor. 16:15–18). False teaching draws attention away from 'God's ordering of things' (*oikonomia theou*), to which faith responds (1:5). And in an explicit

development of the metaphor, good behaviour in the *ekklēsia* enables one to be a 'pillar and support of the truth' within the 'household of faith, which is the church of the living God' (3:15).

CONCLUSION

There is great diversity within the Pauline collection concerning the images used for the church or the precise aspect of the church under discussion. But the letters are remarkably consistent in their basic understanding of the church as a community defined by its relationship with God through the risen Lord Jesus Christ, and called to be a community of moral character, recognizable for its patterns of mutual support and fellowship.

15 Paul's ethics

BRIAN ROSNER

Throughout his career Paul was confronted with a number of complex moral and practical problems in the fledgling Christian communities which threatened their very survival. The early church regularly struggled with questions concerning Jews and Gentiles, male and female roles, sex and marriage, rich and poor, church order and worship, politics and slavery. To put it simply, the study of Paul's ethics considers his responses to these issues. These can in the main be found in the form of three types of paraenesis or moral exhortation scattered throughout his letters: traditional paraenesis, involving general moral themes such as holiness and love (e.g. Rom. 12:1–13:14); situational paraenesis, consisting of advice and exhortation on specific matters of pressing concern (e.g. 1 Cor. 5:1–11:1); and ecclesiastical paraenesis, directed to the institutional needs of the church and the ministry (e.g. 1 Cor. 11:2–14:40).[1]

Paul's moral teaching, however, cannot be isolated from the rest of his instruction. Doctrine and ethics are intimately related in Paul's letters. It is commonly observed that some of the letters exhibit a basically two-fold structure (e.g. Romans, Galatians, Colossians, Ephesians), the first predominantly pertaining to matters of belief, the second primarily to Christian conduct. However, this is an oversimplification, for application is not postponed until the second half of Romans, for instance, being implicit in the exposition in chs. 1–2 and explicit in chs. 6 and 8. Likewise, the ethical sections of all of Paul's letters refer frequently to gospel verities. In dealing with litigation between members of the Corinthian congregation (1 Cor. 6:1–11), for example, Paul refers to the last judgment and the inheritance of believers in the kingdom of God.

Nonetheless, several factors suggest that it is not illegitimate to concentrate attention on the question of conduct in Paul's thought. Though intimately related for Paul, doctrine and ethics are not inseparable. In the first century there was a widespread Jewish concern with the interpretation of the Pentateuch, including legal decisions on conduct according to the law. This points to an interest in the broad category of moral teaching in Paul's day as a distinct concern. And various forms of moral exhortation, such as catalogues of virtue and vice (e.g. Rom. 1:29–31; 13:13; 1 Cor. 5:9–11; 6:9–10) and household codes (collections of admonitions addressed to husbands, wives, children and slaves; e.g. Col. 3:18–4:1; Eph. 5:22–6:9), were in common use in many circles in the ancient world.

Paul's desire to teach 'how one ought to walk and please God' (1 Thess. 4:1) was central to all of his activities and plays a major role in each of his letters. If Paul is a missionary, his goal is not only to save the lost (1 Cor. 9:22) but to present every person mature in Christ (Col. 2:28). If Paul is an apostle, it is with the purpose of bringing Gentiles into full allegiance and obedience to God (Rom. 15:19). If Paul is a theologian, his vision of the divine/human relationship is never without practical implications. His constant concern was to exhort the churches to conduct their common life 'in a manner worthy of the gospel' (Phil. 1:27). He spoke of 'the daily pressure upon me of my anxiety for all the churches' (2 Cor. 11:28). In relation to those faith communities which he founded Paul compares himself to a father (1 Cor. 4:15; 1 Thess. 2:11; Phil. 2:22; cf. Phlm. 10; Titus 1:4) and a mother (1 Cor. 3:1–3; Gal. 4:19; 1 Thess. 2:7), caring for the welfare of his converts in the fullest sense. As J. D. G. Dunn notes, 'Paul never spoke other than as a pastor.'[2] Indeed, the study of Paul cannot avoid the subject of Paul's ethics.

To list the main themes of the Pauline corpus only with reference to matters of belief, such as justification, the place of Israel in God's purposes, christology and eschatology, is to ignore the original settings and purpose of his correspondence. His treatment of the great themes of theology is never in abstraction but always with an eye on the practical implications of sound teaching for right conduct. And usually it was in Paul's mind false doctrine or a misunderstanding of doctrine which had led to false practice in the first place. Without exception, Paul's letters were motivated by ethical concerns. All thirteen letters traditionally attributed to him bear this out. Galatians, 1 and 2 Corinthians, and Romans were written in order to heal potential or real divisions in the churches. 1 and 2 Thessalonians clarify matters of conduct in anticipation of Christ's return. Ephesians and Colossians endeavour to foster a lifestyle consistent with salvation in Christ. Philippians discusses the support of ministry and seeks to calm quarrels in the church. Philemon considers a case of slavery. And the Pastoral Epistles deal with false teaching by commending not only sound doctrine but godliness and church order. The challenge for every student of Paul is to discover in Paul's thought not only theological coherence but ethical integration.

Research into Paul's ethics has approached the subject from a number of angles. Scholars investigate the social conditions of the Graeco-Roman world in which Paul and the early Christians lived. Such historical-descriptive work takes seriously the distance between our world and Paul's and takes pains to describe the law courts, meat markets, artisans, and benefactors, and notions of honour, friendship, enmity and so on which form the ancient setting of Paul's instructions.[3] The social scientific approach also studies Paul's ethics not so much as a history of ideas as a history of communities. It employs models and concepts to analyse the group dynamics of the early church with which Paul interacted.[4] The hermeneutical task confronts the question, how do we appropriate Paul's ethical teaching as a word addressed to us? Needless to say, widely divergent answers are defended.

Two other frequently discussed questions are: what role do the law and scriptures of Israel play in Paul's ethics? And how do Paul's ethics relate to his theology? This essay will explore these two fundamental areas before looking at two case studies in Romans and 1 Corinthians.

BIBLICAL ROOTS

In Paul's day Jewish moral teachers assumed without question the authority of Torah and sought in one way or another to apply its instruction to the problems of everyday life. Even if the rabbis, Philo, Josephus, and Qumran adopted different exegetical practices, treating scripture as fixed law, divine narrative, and living prophecy, Jews universally regarded the law of Moses as God's will for his people. Given his undoubted Jewish pedigree, how then does scripture function in Paul's ethics?

According to many scholars, for Paul the Mosaic law is irrelevant to Christian conduct. Paul makes some very negative statements about the law, implying that it is of no value for Christians. According to Paul the law 'works wrath' (Rom. 4:15), 'increases sin' (Rom. 5:20; 7:5, 8–11, 13) and even 'kills' (Rom. 7:5, 8–11, 13; 2 Cor. 3:6). Christians are no longer 'under the law' (Gal. 3:23–5; 4:4–5, 21; 1 Cor. 9:20; Rom. 6:14–15), having through Christ's death been released from it (Rom. 7:1–6). The Mosaic law has in fact come to an end (2 Cor. 3:7–11; Rom. 10:4). Furthermore, he explicitly sets aside several of its key requirements, namely, circumcision (1 Cor. 7:17–20; Gal. 5:2–6), food laws (Rom. 14:1–4, 14, 20), and the sabbath (Rom. 14:5; Gal. 4:9–11).

On the other hand, even though Paul rarely treats scripture as a rule book or applies Torah casuistically, there is good evidence that the Old Testament was a crucial and formative source for his ethics. Paul's critique of the law relates for the most part to its abuse by sin and the pride and presumption it sometimes instilled in his kinsfolk when it marked them out from other nations. He continued to affirm its role in defining sin and condemning transgression. Scripture was according to Paul a fundamental source of teaching (*didaskalia*) and moral exhortation (*paraklēsis*) for Christians (Rom. 15:4), 'written for us' (1 Cor. 9:9) and 'for our instruction' (1 Cor. 10:11).

A survey of his letters indicates that he used the Jewish scriptures in at least four different ways when regulating conduct in the churches.[5] First, Paul sometimes read scripture as a word of God spoken directly to the church. He was not averse to asking, 'What does scripture say?' (Gal. 4:30). Concerning the temptation to take personal revenge when wronged, he quotes Prov. 25:21–2: 'If your enemies are hungry, feed them' (Rom. 12:20–1). With respect to the question of the financial support of ministers of the gospel he cites Deut. 25:4, a text where God, he believes, 'speaks entirely for our sake' (1 Cor. 9:10): 'You shall not muzzle the ox while it is treading out the grain' (1 Cor. 9:9).

Secondly, scripture was often for Paul the implicit source for particular norms. He takes for granted in Rom. 13:8–10, for example, that adultery, murder, theft, and covetousness are wrong because of the Decalogue. Even when not made explicit, the ultimate basis for his moral judgments on a host of matters is instinctively scripture. The language and arguments used in his condemnation of idolatry in Romans 1, 'the works of the flesh' in Gal. 5:19–21, and incest in 1 Corinthians 5 indicate that his moral vision is informed by scripture.

Thirdly, Paul regularly drew attention to scriptural narratives for moral examples. He viewed the experience of Israel as paradigmatic for the church. In 1 Corinthians 10, for example, he refers to Israel's wilderness wanderings and sin with the golden calf in order to warn the church against idolatry, sexual immorality, putting Christ to the test, and murmuring against God. What is striking is that in exhorting this predominantly Gentile church on this basis he describes the events as those of '*our* fathers' (10:1). The church is to perceive itself as part of Israel's story, to hear the resonances between it and their own situation, and to shape their lives accordingly. Similarly in 2 Cor. 8:7–15 Paul encourages the church to take part in the collection for the poor in Jerusalem by referring to Israel's experience of God's provision of manna in the desert (Exod. 16:18 is quoted in verse 15).

Fourthly, in dealing with moral problems scripture is consistently for Paul the narrative framework for the identity of the community. His ethical judgments, as we shall see below, are inseparable from his sense of the vocation of God's people. When Paul writes to the churches in need of moral discernment he reminds them on the basis of scripture of who they are and where they stand in relation to God's purposes. As Richard Hays contends, Paul, with frequent reference to the promises to Abraham and the prophecies of Isaiah, uses scripture to 'provide an overarching proleptic vision of God's design to redeem the world and situates the community of believers within the unfolding story of this dramatic redemption. Every ethical guidance that Paul gives to his churches finds its ultimate warrant in this narrative framework.'[6]

What of other sources for Paul's moral teaching? Paul undoubtedly drew from other sources, especially traditions about Jesus and even at times Graeco-Roman philosophy. That he was familiar with the larger world of Graeco-Roman culture is given striking testimony in 1 Cor. 15:33, where he alludes to the Greek poet Menander. He alludes to Greek games (1 Cor. 9:24–7), employs Hellenistic concepts such as 'conscience' and 'freedom', and recommends certain Hellenistic virtues.[7] However, stark differences distinguish Paul from the pagan moral philosophers, and some 'Greek' influence may have come indirectly to him through Jewish sources.

With respect to Jesus tradition, there are three explicit citations of sayings of Jesus (1 Cor. 7:10–11; 9:14; 11:23–5) and at least eight or nine allusions to or echoes of Jesus' teaching in Paul's letters.[8] Three prominent ethical examples are: Luke 6:27–8/Matt. 5:44 in Rom. 12:14 concerning non-retaliation; Mark 7:15 in Rom. 14:14 concerning (non-)defilement of unclean food; and Mark 9:50 in 1 Thess. 5:13, which has to do with living at peace. It is noteworthy that the first two cases revolve around biblical interpretation (of Lev. 19:18 and the food laws in Leviticus respectively) and the third echoes a biblical theme. It is mistaken to pit Paul the Jew against Paul the follower of Jesus as if they represent rival conceptions of the making of Paul. When it comes to ethics, both Jesus and Paul stand in the biblical and Jewish tradition.

GOSPEL ORIENTATION

In a nutshell, Paul's approach to questions of conduct is to ask, what does the gospel call Christians to do? Paul's moral judgments cannot be understood apart from his theological convictions. In effect, his ethics make no sense without his eschatology, soteriology, and ecclesiology.[9] For Paul, the church has already entered the eschatological age, even though the present evil age lingers on with its characteristic sin and suffering. Believers wait for the day of the Lord, but in the mean time the ethical life is seen as part of God's work of preparing the community for that day: 'You know what hour it is, how it is full time for you to wake from sleep. For salvation is nearer to us now than when we first believed; the night is far gone, the day is at hand. Let us then cast off the works of darkness and put on the armour of light' (Rom. 13:11–12).

For Paul, the cross is not just the way of salvation and the supreme demonstration of God's righteousness and love, but the paradigmatic pattern for the life of Christians. This is evident in numerous texts which point to the death of Jesus as the ultimate act of loving self-sacrifice and obedience. In Rom. 15:1–3 he expects 'the strong' to put themselves out for the sake of 'the weak' in imitation of Christ. In Phil. 2:1–13 selfless obedience is similarly endorsed: 'Let this mind be in you that was also in Jesus Christ . . . who became obedient unto death, even death on a cross.'[10]

For Paul, Christian living is no private matter; God saves and transforms a people, the body of Christ, not autonomous individuals. Paul's overriding concern is the edification of the community, and much of his energy is spent restoring unity to the church. Modern readers often mistakenly read Paul's admonitions as if they are addressed to them individually. Most of the address and images are in fact corporate. Believers in Rom. 12:1 are to present their bodies (plural) as a living sacrifice (singular). In 1 Cor. 12–14 spiritual gifts are for the common good. And the 'new man' (*anthrōpos*) to be put on in Eph. 4:24 refers to redeemed corporate humanity and its attendant values and behaviour rather than 'the new nature' (RSV) individuals possess. The marked social dimension of Paul's teaching is no mere convenience but a theological necessity.

The interdependence of doctrine and ethics for Paul is nowhere better seen than in the close relationship between the so-called indicative and the imperative in his thought. Paul customarily rests his moral imperatives on the basis of God's prior action on behalf of believers in Christ. The ethical injunctions and prohibitions are rooted in the redemptive acts of God. As well as providing the overall orientation of Paul's ethics, the close relation of the indicative (what God has done) to the imperative (what believers must do) can even be seen within the compass of a single verse:

(1) 1 Cor. 5:7 – 'Cleanse out the old leaven [imperative], as you already are unleavened [indicative]';
(2) Gal. 5:1 – 'It is for freedom that Christ has set us free [indicative]. Stand firm then and do not let yourselves be burdened by a yoke of slavery again [imperative]';
(3) Gal. 5:25 – 'Since we live by the Spirit [indicative] let us also walk by the Spirit [imperative].'

In each of these verses, and throughout Paul's letters, the identity of believers is to inform their behaviour. They are to become what they already are by the grace and in the eyes of God.[11]

CASE STUDY ONE: ROMANS 12

The two samples from Paul's letters to follow cover the three types of paraenesis mentioned above, namely, traditional and ecclesiastical paraenesis in Rom. 12:9–21 and 12:4–8 respectively and situational paraenesis in 1 Corinthians 5. The aim is not to offer a verse-by-verse exegesis so much as to attempt to characterize the kind of conduct Paul recommends and to explore the theological basis and motivation of his instruction.

Rom. 12:1–2 signal the beginning of explicit exhortation in Romans, following a long theological exposition in chs. 1–11, which extends through to 15:13. If chs. 12–13 present injunctions relating to Christian conduct in general in the light of the gospel, chs. 14–15 relate more specifically to a problem in the Roman churches. Yet the switch to ethics is hardly abrupt, as it picks up thoughts from earlier parts of the letter. Paul bases his appeal on the mercies of God, which are ringing in the hearers' ears from chs. 9–11, where mercy is a key term. His call for reasonable worship and mind renewal brings ch. 1 to mind with its false and foolish worship and corrupted minds. And the presentation of the believers' bodies reiterates and expands the same call in 6:13 and 19. Total dedication to God is not some after thought, but the climax to which Paul has been building.

The first thing Paul emphasizes in spelling out the implications of the gospel for Christian conduct is charismatic ministry within the body of Christ in humility and mutual service (12:3–8). The transformed way of life finds true expression in community. The rhythmic nature of the section suggests that it was not the first time Paul gave such instruction, a supposition which 1 Corinthians 12 and Eph. 4:11–17 support, where similar teaching can be found. In verses 6–8 seven representative gifts are named, with the emphasis on the manner of their exercise. The stress on unity throughout anticipates and prepares for chs. 14 and 15 and shows how Paul puts even general advice to specific use.

In 12:9–21 the central demand of love is announced and teased out. A puzzling grammatical feature of these verses has led a number of scholars to speculate about the source of the teaching. Intriguingly, Paul uses the participle with imperatival force seventeen times in 12:9–19, something which occurs only occasionally in Ephesians, Colossians, and 1 Peter elsewhere in the New Testament. David Daube suggested that the imperatival participle construction was due to Hebrew or, less probably, Aramaic influence. He noted that the New Testament usage occurs solely in regulations covering social behaviour within community and family, which is one way in which post-biblical Hebrew also used the participle in rabbinic literature.

W. D. Davies concluded on this basis that 'wherever in the Epistles of Paul we find the participle used instead of the imperative there Paul is certainly using material derived from Jewish sources, probably from some kind of Jewish codes of rules that had established themselves within Judaism as useful for the purpose of moral education'.[12] The fact that in 1 Thessalonians 5 Paul delivered many of the same commands using an imperative which he employed in Romans 12 using the participle counsels caution in making such claims. Nonetheless, it does serve as a reminder that while Paul brought much that is distinctive to his ethics, much of what he says was commonplace in both form and content, at least in Jewish circles.

Paul's injunction to non-retaliation in 12:17–21 reflects the realism of his outlook. Some will oppose believers with implacable hostility. His advice to leave vengeance to God and to overcome evil with good has as its motivation, although not spelled out here, the way of the cross.

CASE STUDY TWO: 1 CORINTHIANS 5

In this passage Paul deals with a disturbing report that has come to his attention. The Corinthians are tolerating in their midst (literally 'among you') the presence of a man who is openly sexually immoral. Paul is incredulous and could not be more vehement in his opposition. His dismay reveals a profound sensitivity to the holiness of God and a related concern for the holiness of God's people. It is striking that Paul is so disturbed not by the Corinthians' actions, but by their inaction.

The offence concerned *porneia*, a flexible term meaning 'prohibited sexual relations', which is in this context specifically incest. 'A man has his father's wife' tells us something of the case, the details of which were only too well known to the Corinthians. The present tense 'has' makes it clear that is was an on-going sexual relationship, but not necessarily a marriage. And the phrase 'father's wife', reflecting the language of Lev. 18:8, indicates that the relationship was with his step-mother; Lev. 18:7 forbids sexual relations with one's 'mother' using a different term. That the woman is not a believer is clear since she receives no rebuke from Paul (cf. verse 12: 'what business is it of mine to judge those outside the church?').

In verse 1–2 Paul rebukes the Corinthians for their inaction and tells them in no uncertain terms to remove the offender. Verses 3–5 supply authoritative support for this action, namely, Paul's presence in spirit and the name of the Lord Jesus, and tell them how to carry out the expulsion. Verses 6–8 attempt to offer further motivation, appealing to the spiritual self-interest of the Corinthian church; whereas to remove him will benefit them, not to remove him will harm them. With this Paul supplies a theological basis for the expulsion. Verses 9–11 further facilitate his removal by correcting a misunderstanding; discipline only applies to so-called brothers. Verses 12–13 assert the Corinthians' responsibility to act, and close the section with a weighty command from scripture. Paul's judgment on the case of the incestuous man in the Corinthian church is simple and to the point: the man must be removed. The command to expel the sinner occurs no fewer than six times: it is presented metaphorically in verses 5a, 7a, and 8, in a general context in verse 11 and literally, its strongest form, at the beginning and very end of the passage, verses 2c and 13b.

What motivated the incestuous relationship is open to speculation. It may have been entered for financial reasons, either to stop the step-mother remarrying, and thus keep his father's inheritance, or to keep the mother-in-law's dowry from returning to her father, which would occur if she remained unattached.[13] The fact that 'the greedy' are listed next to the 'immoral' in the vice lists of verses 10–11 takes on new significance with this view. The simpler explanation of personal attraction cannot, of course, be ruled out. There is evidence that step-mothers 'were often closer in age to the man's children than to the man himself'.[14]

Incest of any sort, whether with one's mother or with the wife of one's father, is prohibited in the OT and early Judaism and was sufficient cause for discipline. Many commentators on 1 Corinthians 5 mention Lev. 18:8 and 20:11 as the critical background to Paul's decision to expel the sinner, noting the shared terminology *gunaikos* and *patros*, 'woman' and 'father' (verse 2). Sexual intercourse with the 'wife' of one's father is also condemned in Gen. 49:4 (see 35:22) and Ezek. 22:10–11. However, two verses in Deuteronomy are just as likely to have influenced Paul. First, Deut. 27:20, 'cursed is the man who sleeps with his father's wife', is perhaps the reason Paul 'curses' the sinner in 1 Corinthians 5. Secondly, Deut. 23:1 (22:30), 'a man is not to marry his father's wife', may have been the impetus for Paul to quote the Deuteronomic expulsion formula in verse 13. A variation of that formula appears in Deut. 22:22 ('If a man is found sleeping with another man's wife . . . you must purge the evil from Israel'; cf. 22:24) and is presumably the penalty for the incest prohibited in Deut. 23:1 (22:30). In quoting the Deuteronomic formula in 5:13, Paul, it appears, is simply following Torah.

The main subject of 1 Corinthians 5 is not, however, incest, but exclusion from the community. That Paul's instructions have links with his scriptural inheritance is clear from the use of Passover/unleavened bread imagery in verses 7–8 and from the quotation of the Deuteronomic expulsion formula in verse 13b and is evident in his concern to expel the man for the sake of the church, as an example to dissuade further disobedience.[15]

The passage reflects Paul's characteristic gospel reasoning on ethical matters. The main motivation for the drastic course of expelling the man is the identity of the community as God's sanctified people, his holy temple (see 3:16–17), a status achieved by the work of Christ: 'Cleanse out the old leaven . . . for Christ, our paschal lamb, has been sacrificed.'

What does the incident tell us, then, about the church in Corinth which Paul seeks to correct? Gerald Harris, employing with due caution a sociological model of reaction to deviance developed from an article by H. Himmelweit,[16] suggests that the case of the incestuous man tells us three things about the church, which are confirmed by other indications in the letter. First, the failure to condemn the man would be typical of a group that lacks cohesion, for the more cohesive a group, the stronger the demand for conforming behaviour. Secondly, the incident suggests a church that has a relatively non-authoritarian structure. That the church stood in opposition to and even resented Paul's authority is evident in both 1 and 2 Corinthians. And thirdly, the church's acceptance of the man points to a group that is secure in its cultural setting, for the more threatened a group feels, the greater its rejection of deviant members. Paul's instructions lay down firm boundaries for the group, stress the group's distinct identity from those outside, and call upon its members to act as one.

Indeed, it is striking that Paul's instructions are not directed to the sinner himself but exclusively to the believers in Corinth as a group. Paul addresses the church as a body throughout (the second-person plural pronoun occurs nine times). He wants the discipline to be carried out when they are assembled (5:4) and rebukes them in 5:2, 6 as a group. The metaphor of cleansing by the removal of leaven is applied in a corporate fashion; the Corinthian Christians are to be 'a new lump' (5:7), not new lump*s* of dough. As Wayne Meeks states, Paul 'does not construe the action primarily as an action against the offender, but as a way of purging the community'.[17] That the Corinthians are implicated in the offence of the immoral man is suggested by the instruction to 'mourn' in verse 2. Paul's approach to this crisis is far from any brand of Christian individualism. The church, it seems, stands or falls together.

CONCLUSION

To study Paul's practical teaching is to notice his profound indebtedness to his Jewish inheritance, his historical setting in the Graeco-Roman world, his fervent passion for the gospel, and his unwavering commitment to the welfare of the church. This introduction to the subject has concentrated on the descriptive task involved in the careful reading of the texts. However, as Hays notes, there are three other aspects to the study of Paul's ethics which go beyond purely academic investigation and consider Paul's legacy for the church today: the synthetic task, which places the Pauline texts in canonical context; the hermeneutical task, which relates the texts to our own situations; and the pragmatic task of enacted application involved in living the text.[18]

Notes

1 J. I. H. McDonald, *Kerygma and Didache: The Articulation and Structure of the Earliest Christian Message* (Cambridge: Cambridge University Press, 1980) 89. As is the case with most forms, some flexibility and overlap are evident.

2 J. D. G. Dunn, *The Theology of Paul the Apostle* (Grand Rapids: Eerdmans/Edinburgh: T. & T. Clark, 1998) 626.

3 See, e.g., B. S. Rosner, ed., *Understanding Paul's Ethics: Twentieth-Century Approaches* (Grand Rapids: Eerdmans, 1995), part 2 and the essays by E. A. Judge and B. W. Winter.

4 See, e.g., ibid., part 3 and the essays by G. Theissen and G. Harris.

5 See R. B. Hays, 'The Role of Scripture in Paul's Ethics', in E. H. Lovering and J. L. Sumney, eds., *Theology and Ethics in Paul and his Interpreters: Essays in Honor of Victor Paul Furnish* (Nashville: Abingdon, 1996) 30–47.

6 Ibid., 34–5.

7 See further V. P. Furnish, *Theology and Ethics in Paul* (Nashville: Abingdon, 1996) 44–51; J. P. Sampley, *Walking Between the Times: Paul's Moral Reasoning* (Minneapolis, Fortress, 1991) 94–8. Cf. A. J. Malherbe, *Paul and the Popular Philosophers* (Philadelphia: Fortress, 1989) 68: 'There can no longer be any doubt that Paul was thoroughly familiar with the teaching, methods of operation and style of argumentation of the philosophers of the period.'

8 See Dunn, *Theology of Paul* 650–1.

9 Cf. R. B. Hays' theological framework for Pauline ethics: new creation, cross, and community, *The Moral Vision of the New Testament: A Contemporary Introduction to New Testament Ethics* (San Francisco: HarperCollins, 1996/Edinburgh: T. & T. Clark, 1997) 19–36.

10 See further Rom. 6:1–14; 8:17, 29–30; 1 Cor. 10:23–11:1; 2 Cor. 4:7–15; 12:9–10; Gal. 2:19–20; 5:24; 6:14.

11 The logic of the indicative and the imperative is a distinguishing mark not only of Paul's ethics but of biblical ethics in general. Throughout the Bible human behaviour is always considered in the context of the underlying and overarching relationship with God.

12 W. D. Davies, *Paul and Rabbinic Judaism: Some Rabbinic Elements in Pauline Theology* (London: SPCK/Philadephia: Fortress, 1948) 131.

13 See A. D. Clarke, *Secular and Christian Leadership in Corinth: A Socio-Historical and Exegetical Study of I Corinthians 1–6* (Leiden: E. J. Brill, 1993); and J. K.

Chow, *Patronage and Power: A Study of Social Networks in Corinth* (Sheffield: Sheffield Academic Press, 1993) 130–41.

14 W. Deming, 'The Unity of 1 Corinthians 5–6', *JBL* 115 (1992) 1294.

15 See B. S. Rosner, *Paul, Scripture and Ethics: A Study of 1 Corinthians 5–7* (Grand Rapids: Baker, 1999) ch. 3.

16 G. Harris, 'The Beginnings of Church Discipline: 1 Corinthians 5', *NTS* 37 (1991) 7–10.

17 W. A. Meeks, *The First Urban Christians: The Social World of the Apostle Paul* (New Haven: Yale University Press, 1983) 130.

18 Hays, *The Moral Vision* 3–7.

Part four

St Paul

16 Paul in the second century

CALVIN J. ROETZEL

Ernst Käsemann once remarked that in the generations after his death Paul was 'for the most part unintelligible'.[1] But even when he was intelligible he was often either misunderstood or despised. In the late first or early second century, for example, the letter of James challenged Paul's gospel of justification by faith alone without regard to works (2:24). Around AD 200, the *Kerygmata Petrou* (*Proclamations of Peter*) vilified Paul as the enemy, a helpmate of the evil one, and an impostor preaching a false gospel.[2] It attacked his legitimacy, calling him a liar for claiming an apostolic commission that came directly from Christ in a vision. If Paul were a true apostle, Peter continues, he would not contend with 'me', 'the foundation stone of the church' (*Clem. Hom.* 17.19.1–4).

While many suspected him of using dark, magical arts, others either were unacquainted with his letters or simply ignored them. In the second century, Ignatius, bishop of Antioch, was arrested and sent to Rome in chains to a martyr's death. In seven letters he wrote on the way to Rome he made only five or six references to the Pauline corpus, and even in those, Pauline influence was superficial. Although resemblances exist, Schneemelcher correctly notes, 'the theology of Ignatius is not Pauline, indeed has nothing to do [with Paul]'.[3]

Polycarp (AD 69–155), the simple, humble younger contemporary of Ignatius and a bishop in Asia, wrote a cover letter for a collection of Ignatius' letters in which he referred to Romans, 1 Corinthians, multiple Philippian letters, and possibly Galatians and Ephesians.[4] Yet he confessed that neither he nor anyone else could 'follow the wisdom of the blessed and glorious Paul' (*Letter of Polycarp* 3:2). That candour found expression in literary echoes of Paul's letters, yet there is no evidence that they were theologically important to Polycarp.[5]

While Ignatius did know who Paul was and what he did, Papias (ca AD 60–130), who knew about important leaders of the apostolic period, made no reference to Paul.[6] Given his millenarian beliefs, the absence of a single remark about Paul is astonishing.[7] Justin Martyr (AD 100–65), born of pagan parents in Samaria, and converted to Christianity in AD 130, became an important apologist for Christianity. Faint echoes of Paul's letters come from his writings, but they nowhere explicitly sound the name of the apostle. Theophilus, a second-century bishop of Antioch, drew on Romans 13 in his discussion of Christians and the state but made no reference to Paul.[8] This avoidance of Paul by these important personalities suggested to Schneemelcher that Paul was 'intentionally shoved aside'.[9] Whether it was intentional or unintentional, Marcion and Valentinus appear in mid century to rescue Paul from obscurity.

MARCION

Harnack's view that Catholicism was invented as a response to Marcion contains a grain of truth. To understand that dynamic we must trace the role Paul played in the fateful and protracted struggle between the proto-orthodox church and this 'heretic'.

Before discussing Marcion's legacy we must emphasize the diversity of second-century Christianity. In this period, no clean line divided orthodoxy and heresy and no single archimedian point could be summoned to verify the truth claims of any confession. Marcionites, Valentinian Gnostics, Ebionites, Montanists, the Roman church, and other groups made competing claims to be true Christians. It is anachronistic to begin a discussion of Marcionism as a 'heretical' movement, for in the second century 'orthodoxy and heresy do not stand in relation to one another as primary to secondary'.[10] That would change with Constantine's grant of imperial favour to Christianity in AD 312, and that endorsement gave the Roman church the power to rid itself of 'heretics' and to frighten away 'wild beasts from Christ's sheep' (Eusebius, *HE* 4.24).

Only the barest outlines of Marcion's biography are recoverable. Since not a single line from his own pen survives, we must rely on his critics for our reconstruction of his life and teachings. From their accounts we learn he was born near the end of the first century in Sinope, an important port on the southern coast of the Black Sea, and that he was acquainted with Jewish communities in the area. His knowledge of Jewish scriptures and religion hardly proves, however, that he and/or his parents were proselytes to Judaism before converting to Christianity.[11] Marcion's Christian background offers a sufficient explanation of his familiarity with Judaism. Hippolytus' report (AD 170–236) that Marcion's father, the bishop of Sinope, excommunicated him for seducing a virgin betrays a smear campaign to discredit him by portraying him as morally depraved.[12]

His origin in a family of wealth and influence explains his career as a ship owner (*nauclerus*), his reputation as a 'zealous student of Stoicism', and his lavish gift of 200,000 sesterces to the Roman church.[13] That past would also explain his significant educational achievement, his knowledge of texts, his critical assessment of their content and consistency, his keen text-critical eye, his rejection of exegetical conventions like allegory and typology, and his skilful redaction of troubling passages.

His theology was rooted in Paul's collected letters, which he encountered while he was still in Asia Minor. That corpus profoundly shaped his Christian outlook, moved him to correct 'mistaken' church doctrine, and led him to argue that the teaching of Paul and the theology of the church were irreconcilable.[14] That conviction led to a confrontation with Polycarp, who rebuked him as the 'first-born of Satan' for his rejection of the 'Old Testament' and his fabrication of a myth of two gods (Irenaeus, *AH* 3.3.4).

Speculation about why Marcion sailed to Rome, generously endowed the church there, and actively participated in its life varies wildly. Some believe that he was excommunicated by the church in Asia Minor; others argue that he chose Rome for the visibility the imperial capital would give his movement. His relocation could have been inspired by his hope to persuade the Roman church of the rightness of his understanding of Paul and his desire to enlist the church in his reforms.[15]

About the date of his sojourn there we are on firmer ground. Around AD 150 Justin Martyr moaned that Marcionite churches had spread throughout the Empire. His worry suggests that by the time he made the remark Marcion had already been spreading his gospel for a decade or two.[16] Such an early date for Marcion's mission would support scholars who see an anti-Marcionite polemic both in the Pastoral Epistles and in the Acts of the Apostles.[17]

In a hearing before the council of elders of the Roman church, Marcion presented his teachings, and perhaps his 'New Testament' and 'Antitheses'. Pointing to the foolishness of sewing new patches on old garments (Luke 5:36) or putting new wine in old skins (Luke 5:37–8) he vigorously defended his reform. The elders, however, remained unconvinced and condemned his teaching, returned his 200,000 sesterces, and banished him to 'a permanent excommunication'.[18]

This excommunication, however, energized Marcion, and his genius as an organizer, left over from his days as a shipmaster, paid handsome dividends. He promoted a reform that spread like a prairie-grass fire, and when he died around 160 he left a movement that threatened to eclipse the church that banished him. At the time of his death adherents to his reforms may have outnumbered other Christians.[19] By around 207 Tertullian fretted that Marcion's gospel might succeed 'in filling the whole world' (*AM* 5.19). While Irenaeus and Tertullian attest to Marcion's influence in the West, Bardesanes, Epiphanius, and Theodoret bear witness to a Marcionite success in the East that lasted well into the fifth century. To outsiders Marcionite and 'catholic' Christians were indistinguishable and martyrdom was visited on each indiscriminately. Their churches stood side by side with similar rites, clerical offices, and organization, and each had a collection of sacred scriptures. But an examination of Marcion's teachings will show sharp differences between them.

MARCION'S TEACHING

For Marcion, Paul was '*the* true apostle' (*AM* 3.13), whose *true* gospel conformed exactly to that of Christ. Claiming Paul's truth as *the* truth, Marcion submitted the preaching of the 'pillar apostles' to Paul for approval and found it wanting. Thus the way was clear to blame 'false apostles', Judaizing redactors, and clever users of allegorical and typological interpretation for corrupting Paul's gospel. Marcion sought to remove those defilements and to recover the 'true' gospel by reconstructing the primal texts of the apostle Paul and Luke's gospel. He rejected Matthew because of its endorsement of the law (Matt. 5:17). He probably did not know John. And he chose Luke over Mark because of its Gentile bias and ascetic emphasis. But even Luke had to be purged of Judaizing corruption. Through his deft use of the 'pruning knife', his brilliant text-critical and philological moves, and his reformist ideology Marcion produced a simple, graspable, defensible gospel based on Luke and the Pauline letters. His *New* Testament devalued the Old and provided an authoritative basis for a reform with such broad appeal that for a time it threatened to displace its 'catholic' rival entirely (*AM* 5.18). Hoffmann aptly summarizes the seriousness of this threat:

> by challenging the integrity of the first apostles he [Marcion] called into question the historical basis for christian teaching, and there could have been no more serious a threat to the backward-looking church of the second century.[20]

The core of Marcion's teaching was a stark contrast between the God of the New Testament and the God of the Old. He took Paul's reference to the 'God of this world' (2 Cor. 4:4) to refer to the lower, creator God of the Old Testament. This creator God exacted a harsh justice; the alien God offered mercy.[21] The creator God offered salvation to Jews only; the alien God gave salvation to all. The creator God gave the law; the alien God graciously offered the gospel. The creator God had Moses stretch out his hands to kill;

the alien God made Jesus Christ stretch out his hands to bless and to save. The creator God urged Joshua to violence; the alien God had Christ forbid violence. The creator God gave a law that requited an 'eye for an eye and a tooth for a tooth'. The alien God commanded his followers to 'turn the other cheek', and to 'repay no man evil for evil'. The creator God offered justification by works of the law; the alien God promised 'justification by faith' (Gal. 2:16). The creator God urged people to 'be fruitful and multiply and fill the earth'; the alien God commanded celibacy as a form of liberation from this world.

As Harnack showed, Marcion's view of the Old Testament was more complex than often assumed.[22] His citation with approval of Jesus' appeal to the law in Luke 10:26 to love God and the neighbour shows that even if Marcion thought that the Old Testament was inferior, he hardly saw it as valueless. The creator God and the alien God both hate evil and both regard the love of God and the neighbour as good.[23] Both testaments demand righteousness even if the creator's righteousness lacks mercy and unjustly excludes Gentiles. Both testaments speak of a Messiah even if the Messiahs are radically different. The creator God promised happiness to the rich; the alien God pronounced blessings on the poor (*AM* 4.38).[24] The contrast Marcion drew between the Old Testament and the New was sharp, but hardly total. He saw no contradiction between his rejection of the Old Testament and his acceptance of selected parts of that tradition to instruct the church.

Marcion's solution to the paradox of Jesus' association with the fallen world through his fleshly nature only later would be condemned as a docetic heresy. Jesus, he claimed, only *seemed* or *appeared* to be a fleshly creature; in reality he was the divine redeemer from the merciful, good, and loving alien God. He readily found in Phil. 2:6–8 support for these docetic views. To subordinate the Christ of the alien God to the created order of the inferior God would have been inconsistent and unthinkable. For how could the Messiah of the higher alien God be subject to the order of the lower, inferior creator God? Marcion did, however, affirm the suffering of Jesus as a human being even though his identity as a creature of this world was only apparent.[25]

At some points, however, Marcion's teaching exactly replicated the proclamation (kerygma) of the early church. Strongly influenced by his versions of Galatians and Romans, his soteriology sharply focused on a Christ who preached good news of God's love and mercy for 'Gentile sinners' (Gal. 2:15), and whose salvation was available to all who believe. His teaching that God sent his own Son as a sacrifice to save those in bondage to the creator God obviously differed radically from the teaching of 'catholic' Christianity. And, his rejection of the Old Testament and the history of Israel and his emphasis on Christ as totally new made it impossible for him to endorse a salvation history in which Jesus Christ appears as the fulfilment of Israel's hopes and expectations.

MARCIONITE PRAXIS

Marcion's teaching, simple and graspable as it was, was hardly the whole of Marcionism. Its success was due largely to Marcion's ability to weave theological conviction and institutional life into a seamless whole. The leadership, rituals, and ethos of the Marcionite church all bore a distinctive stamp. It was perhaps the first church to ordain women as priests commissioned to teach, to administer the sacraments, to practise the healing ministry, and to serve as bishops or presbyters (Tertullian, *On Prescriptions* 41).

Like the 'catholic' church, Marcionites practised baptism and celebrated the Eucharist. Although the outward form of the sacraments was quite traditional, their inner meaning was radically different. At baptism all believers embraced celibacy, renounced the lower world, and defied the command of the creator to 'be fruitful and multiply' (Gen. 1:28). Since Marcionism renounced sex as shameful, dirty, and death-producing, its future depended entirely on evangelistic efforts. This missionary strategy was driven by the belief that all non-Marcionites, whether 'catholic' Christians or pagans, were benighted souls in need of salvation.

The Marcionite practice of using water instead of wine in the Eucharist was entirely consistent with its stringent rule governing eating and drinking. The substitution of water for wine in the Eucharist expressed the Marcionite disdain for the enjoyment of food and drink; ironically, Marcionites saw no contradiction in the use of elements from the lower world to point to the higher.[26]

Because of the family resemblance of their ritual practices to those of the 'catholic' church, pagans and Christians alike found it difficult to distinguish Marcionite from other churches. Their generic appearance sometimes recoiled on Marcionites, making them vulnerable to bursts of persecution. But such episodes only further validated their status as citizens of a higher world and confirmed their rank as the redeemed living in a fallen world.

The surest sign of the terror that the Marcionite movement excited may be seen in the vicious attacks launched against it by other Christians. We have noted already the contempt of Polycarp, Irenaeus, Epiphanius, and Tertullian for the Marcionites. But, as Quinn and others have noted, the Pastoral Epistles may have offered an even earlier assault against Marcion and the Gnostics. The admonition to Timothy to avoid 'godless chatter and *antitheses*' (1 Tim. 6:20, my italics) which some 'falsely' call knowledge has the ring of an anti-Marcionite polemic. The condemnation of those who avoid certain foods and repudiate marriage (1 Tim. 4:3) and who allow for freedom of expression by men and women in the service of worship is also consistent with Marcionite practice. The *'gnosis'* of the adversaries was especially repugnant to the author of the Pastorals, and while Marcion was no Gnostic, second-century authors were unable to draw such a distinction.[27] The subordination of women, forbidding them to assume positions of authority over men or to teach, sounds like an attempt to impose on women restrictions that the Marcionite church had removed (1 Tim. 2:11–15).

Whatever one may say of Marcion, he was certainly a radical Paulinist who both understood and misunderstood Paul. He correctly saw Paul's emphasis on grace and newness, and elevated 'the loving will of Jesus' to the highest rank. He understood the radical nature of Paul's egalitarian tendencies. He saw the intimate connection Paul made between salvation and freedom. He obviously saw the import of Paul's gospel for the poor and for the disenfranchised. He understood the importance of the issues Paul addressed for the future of the church. And he correctly elevated Paul's occasional letters to scriptural status. But, at other points Marcion misunderstood, oversimplified, and even falsified Paul's message and was vulnerable to the barbs of his critics. To those we now turn.

IRENAEUS VERSUS MARCION

When Irenaeus was born around 140, Marcion and Valentinus had already set the agenda for his lifework. Although he recalled hearing Polycarp as a boy in his native Smyrna in Asia Minor, it is unclear whether he learned the gospel tradition from Polycarp or from his study in Rome (Eusebius, *EH* 5.5.8). After that study he served as a presbyter in the church at Lyons, and from there the resident bishop dispatched him on a diplomatic mission to carry letters to Pope Eleutherus pleading for tolerance of the Montanists. While he was away a spasm of persecution took the bishop's life, and he succeeded him around 178. His prolific polemics against the Gnostic, Marcionite, and Montanist 'heresies' offer our best source of information about Marcion and his successors.

As the first to take for granted the Marcionite association of Luke and Paul, Irenaeus charged that Marcion was truncating rather than creating the canon. Marcion's canon was in error, he maintained, not because it was truncated but because it contradicted apostolic teaching (*AH* 3.14.1, 7, 8, 9). By centring on God, Christ, and salvation-history Irenaeus aimed to discredit

Marcionite exegesis, to rescue Paul from the clutches of the 'heretics', and to domesticate him by affirming his 'orthodoxy'.[28]

Irenaeus based his theology on a small number of Pauline texts that contested Marcionite core convictions. In response to Marcion's teaching of the two gods, Irenaeus appealed to 1 Cor. 8:6, which refers to the 'one God, the Father, from whom are all things'. He added that the God of Jesus Christ and the God of the Hebrew scriptures are one and the same, and that 'by dividing God into two ... [Marcion] does in fact ... put an end to deity' (*AH* 3.25.3).[29] Against Marcion's docetic christology, which denied Jesus' full humanity, Irenaeus again invoked 1 Cor. 8:6 to make Paul's reference to the 'one Lord Jesus Christ' refer to a unity of the human Jesus and the lordly Christ. He met Marcion's aversion to salvation history by reading *telos* (end) in Rom. 10:4 to mean 'Christ is the *fulfilment* of the law' rather than Marcion's 'Christ is the *termination* of the law' (*AH* 4.12.3). And even while granting Marcion's point that the righteousness of God is manifested 'apart from law', Irenaeus, nevertheless, added from Paul that 'the law and the prophets bear' witness to that righteousness (Rom. 3:21). Because he found the Abrahamic theology intolerable, Marcion excised Rom. 3:31–4:25 and Gal. 3:6–9, 14a, 15–25 in their entirety. But, Irenaeus used Paul to forge a continuity between Abraham and Christ, and to argue that Abraham prefigured the church as 'children of Abraham' (Rom. 4:12f.; *AH* 4.5.3; 4.5.4). From this Irenaeus concluded contra Marcion that in Christ 'God's way of dealing with humanity has not changed in substance even if it has changed in the manner of its administration' (*AH* 4.21.1).[30]

While Irenaeus was eager to forge a strong continuity between the God of Jewish scriptures and God in Christ, he also recognized in Paul's gospel a radical discontinuity. Appealing to Rom. 5:12–21 he argued that the human legacy of sin and death initiated by Adam and recapitulated by all humanity was, in his view, being reversed. As the Lord of both 'the dead and the living' (Rom. 14:9), Christ links the past, present, and future. He viewed that future as no simple evolution of the past, but as a radical divine intervention in human history that resulted in the adoption of believers in Christ and their incorporation into Christ's body through the resurrection.

Congruities and incongruities between Irenaeus and Paul abound. His emphasis on the oneness of God, Christ, and salvation-history echo basic convictions of Paul. His belief that all humanity shared in Adam's legacy of sin and death was faithful to Paul. Like Paul, Irenaeus contrasted Christ and Adam, but his linkage of the incarnation to the existential fact of corporate sin and death sounds very alien to Paul. Also, Irenaeus' understanding of faith as assent to church doctrine and acceptance of the power of the sacraments differed entirely from that of Paul. Irenaeus was less interested in faithfully representing Paul's theology; he was more concerned to rescue him from powerful and popular rival interpreters, and to use Paul to legitimize a church doctrine that Irenaeus felt to be true.[31]

TERTULLIAN

Born to a Roman centurion and his wife (ca AD 160) in Carthage, North Africa, Tertullian enjoyed enormous privileges as a Roman citizen. He received a classical education in law and rhetoric and later practised law in Rome. After his conversion to Christianity in 195 he returned to Carthage, served as a catechist, was ordained as a priest, and wrote voluminously. Of his writings against heresies, those against Marcion (207) are the most voluminous and the most important. As the first theologian to write mostly in Latin, Tertullian drew a portrait of Paul which was nuanced and complex, deeply rooted in the Pauline letters and fully at home in the Graeco-Roman world. While Tertullian preferred Latin, his firm grasp of Greek, rhetoric and Hellenistic philosophy well equipped him for his war of words with the Marcionites and Valentinians.

Of Marcion's antagonists, Tertullian offered the most detailed exegetical challenge. Central to his position was Paul's reliance on the 'Old Testament' to secure the concept of salvation-history. He understood the arrival of the Messiah, the proclamation of the gospel, and the outpouring of the Holy Spirit as fulfilment of Old Testament prophecy. Isaiah's reference to the redeemer to come from the root of Jesse on whom the Spirit rests he understood as an allusion to Christ (11:1–3; *AM* 5.8). Metaphors like 'unleavened bread' and the 'passover' he read as 'Old Testament' references to the church and to Christ respectively (1 Cor. 5:7); and he wrote approvingly of the way Paul 'clothes us and Christ with symbols of the Creator's solemn rites' (*AM* 5.7). Rather than repudiating Old Testament law as Marcion had done, he called on Paul to reaffirm its importance (1 Cor. 9:9 *AM* 5.9). Fixing on Paul's rhetorical question in Rom. 7:7, 'Is the law sin? God forbid', Tertullian explodes in disgust, 'Fie on you, Marcion . . . (see how) the apostle recoils from all impeachment of the law' (*AM* 5.13).

Ironically, Tertullian's appeal to the 'Old Testament' was no endorsement of Judaism. God, he believed, took Paul away from Judaism 'for the erection of Christianity' (*AM* 5.6). He likened Paul to the 'wise master builder' (1 Cor. 3:10) whom 'the Lord of hosts' took away from Jerusalem in the prophecy of Isaiah (3:3; *AM* 5.6.10–11). Appealing to a beloved passage of Marcion in which Paul referred to his Hebrew lineage as 'dung' (Phil. 3:5–11), Tertullian countered that it was not the Hebrew background that Paul counted as 'refuse' but rather the 'stupid obduracy' of the Jews

(*AM* 5.20). Thus Tertullian oddly presented a Paul who was rooted in the religion of the Old Testament but who repudiated his native Judaism.

Tertullian took special umbrage at Marcion's *theo*logy and *christ*ology. At least superficially, certain Pauline texts did seem to support the distinction between the creator God of this world and the God in Christ, and Tertullian set out to reclaim them. For example, 2 Cor. 4:4 refers to the '*god of this world* [who] has blinded the minds of the unbelievers, to keep them from seeing the light of the gospel of the glory of Christ, who is the likeness of God' (RSV, my italics). In response, Tertullian stressed a traditional monotheism by moving the phrase 'of this world' to the end of the sentence to make it modify 'of the unbelievers'. This crude, astonishing displacement then made Paul say, 'God has blinded the minds of the *unbelievers of this world*' (my italics). Tertullian further understood 'unbelievers' to refer to 'Jewish unbelievers, from some of whom the gospel is still hidden under Moses' veil' (*AM* 5:11).

While the Council of Nicaea lay far over the future horizon, Marcion forced Tertullian to deal with the relationship of Jesus' divine and human nature. Paul's view that 'flesh and blood cannot inherit the kingdom of God' (1 Cor. 15:50) sounded consistent with Marcion's view of the creation as depraved and his denial of the resurrection of the flesh. This devaluation of the flesh, if sustained, would have brought the full humanity of Jesus into question. Against Marcion, Tertullian cited 1 Cor. 15:42–4 to support the resurrection of the body in form and substance (*AM* 5.10). Whereas Marcion took 1 Cor. 15:50 literally, Tertullian read 'flesh and blood cannot inherit the kingdom of God' to mean 'the *works* of the flesh and blood' deprive humanity of the kingdom of God (*AM* 5.10). Against Marcion's claim that in Jesus Christ 'there was nothing but a phantom of flesh' (Phil. 2:6–7), Tertullian argued that Paul 'could not have pronounced him [Jesus Christ]' to have 'become obedient unto death' (Phil. 2:8) if he 'had not been constituted of a mortal substance' (*AM* 5.20).

The linkage of Jesus to Christ was crucial to Tertullian's argument. In this formula was an implicit confession of the humanity of Jesus and the eschatological, divine significance of Christ. This articulation would play a key role in the later christological debates.

Throughout this debate Tertullian was working with a highly idealized portrait of Paul.[32] His imagined Paul appears as a saintly icon, as the teacher of the Gentiles (*AM* 5.7.10), as the 'most holy apostle' (*On Baptism* 17.2), and as the saint whose gaze is fixed on the world beyond. He is consumed by the desire to depart this world in order to be with Christ (Phil. 1:23). Almost as a concession to Marcion, Tertullian gives Paul's words scriptural status. His divine persona transforms his speech into a divine voice requiring obedience. This divine persona joins his Lord as a martyr painted in the garish colors of the Apocalypse.

Tertullian subscribed to the noble fiction that Paul's teachings were in strict harmony with those of the other apostles (*AM* 4.3.1). Even the shouting match between Peter and Paul at Antioch (Gal. 2:11–21) Tertullian cast in a favourable light. Paul did not, in his view, rebuke Peter because of erroneous teaching but rather because of an error in judgment. He withdrew from Gentile believers out of 'respect for persons' (*Prescriptions against Heretics* 23). Tertullian noted happily that Peter and Paul were co-equals in their status as martyrs (*Prescriptions* 24), and therefore co-equals in doctrinal purity. He concluded from this that Marcion's juxtaposition of the teaching of Paul with that of the apostles was flatly 'heretical' (*AM* 4.2.2–4). This smoothing of the jagged edges in apostolic discourse well reveals Tertullian's attempt to 'domesticate' Paul.[33]

While he depended on the works of Irenaeus, Tertullian's argument was fuller and more complex, and he was able more than any other to enlist Paul in the struggle against Marcion and Valentinus and to secure Paul's canonical status.

VALENTINUS

Excluding Marcion, the most influential Gnostic of the second century was surely Valentinus. Born in Egypt and educated in Alexandria (115–35), Valentinus spent most of his adult life in Rome promoting his Gnostic gospel, teaching his disciples, and writing letters, psalms, and homilies (135–65). For reasons unknown he left Rome for Cyprus, and his disciples later spread his teaching throughout Italy and the Orient. Their fertile imaginations prompted Irenaeus to moan: 'Every day one of them invents something new' (*AH* 1.18.5). Our composite sketch of the Valentinian myth is drawn from his antagonists' works and from the Gnostic codices found at Nag Hammadi, Egypt, in 1945.

This myth blamed a crisis within the godhead for the genesis of darkness, the creation of the lower world, and the partition of being into absolute opposites. The crisis erupted when Sophia's lust for the primal Father created a dark and evil presence in the Pleroma that required expulsion. This aborted element, or lower Sophia, gave birth to the Demiurge, the creator of the lower, evil world, and created a benighted humanity ignorant of its divine origin. Salvation from this ignorance was possible only for those retaining some spark of the divine fullness inadvertently brought from the Pleroma by the lower Sophia and arbitrarily lodged in some humans. Those with no divine spark were hopelessly and irretrievably trapped in stupefied ignorance. Redemption for the rest came from Christ, the redeemer, who descended from the Pleroma, merged with the earthly Jesus, and set out to awaken the spiritual elite (*pneumatikoi*) and unspiritual plodders (*psychikoi*) to their origin and destiny. This awakening to knowledge (*gnosis*) was synonymous with salvation itself.

For these Gnostics Paul was a source of inspiration and a fountainhead of secret, cosmic mysteries. When taken out of context many Pauline texts well lent themselves to legitimize what Irenaeus called 'the great blasphemy' (*AH* 2.3.2). Paul's desperate cry, 'nothing good . . . dwells in my flesh' (Rom. 7:18), his plea for rescue from 'this body of death' (Rom. 7:24), his flat assertion that 'flesh and blood cannot inherit the kingdom of God' (1 Cor. 15:50), and his unequivocal declaration that 'you are not in the flesh, you are in the Spirit' (Rom. 8:9; RSV) all appear to support Gnostic tenets.

Other texts also offered support. The reference in Eph. 3:21 to 'the aeon of the aeons' reinforced the Gnostic doctrine of the aeons. The neat distinction in 1 Cor. 2:6–3:3 between the spiritual (*pneumatikoi*), the unspiritual (*psuchikoi*), and the fleshly (*sarkikoi*) legitimized the Gnostic tripartite anthropology. The poem of the descent and ascent of the divine redeemer in Phil. 2:5–11 offered brilliant confirmation of the Valentinian myth of the descending and ascending redeemer. The statement in 1 Cor. 6:12 that 'all things are lawful' reinforced a libertarian ethic that released Gnostics from scruples about eating idol meat, emancipated them from the shackles of church rules and regulations, and rescued them from the 'stagnant' water of ecclesiastical teaching.[34]

Irenaeus heatedly responded that they totally misunderstood Paul and that their perceptions were sheer 'madness' (*AH* 4.41.3–4). He condemned their 'mad opinions' and their false utterances (*AH* 4.41.3–4). He bristled at their use of Paul to affirm the doctrine of the Pleroma (*AH* 1.3.4), and he huffed at their exploitation of Paul to validate their world rejection (*AH* 1.3.5). He snorted at their use of Paul to authorize their doctrine of Sophia (*AH* 1.8.2–3) and their tri-modal anthropology (*AH* 1.8.3). And finally, he challenged their use of Paul to authorize a libertarian lifestyle indifferent to law and church direction. Against them he linked Paul with Peter to certify the truth of the teaching of the Latin church, and he redefined faith in the Pauline letters to make it mean mental assent to the doctrines of the Roman church. Thus he transformed Paul, the apostle to the Gentiles, into the ecclesiastical Paul who defended the church from doctrinal error.

In spite of, or maybe because of, this vicious attack, Valentinian Gnosticism flourished. Irenaeus lamented the seduction of many bishops and deacons (*AH* 4.26.3). He complained that the Valentinian writings were a stumbling block (*Frag.* 51). He deplored their deceitful evangelization, their behaving like wolves in sheep's clothing (*AH* 4.41.3–4). Tertullian likewise bemoaned the defection of 'bishops, deacons, widows, and martyrs'. He asked rhetorically, 'How comes it to pass . . . that this woman or that man, who were the most faithful, the most prudent, and the most approved in the church, have gone over to the other side?' (*Prescriptions* 3). At this stage there was no way to know how the struggle would end, or how to anticipate their triumph over the Gnostics. They had no inkling that their interpretation of Paul would ultimately become normative, and consequently the struggle was bitter and protracted.[35]

THE ACTS OF PAUL AND THECLA

An important chapter in second-century Pauline reception history is found in the Acts of Paul and Thecla.[36] Out of reverence for the apostle, an anonymous presbyter collected, arranged, and interpreted legends about Paul in the late second century. The author, a native of Asia Minor, so successfully glorified Paul as the consummate celibate, the prodigious miracle worker, and the heroic martyr that his work eventually acquired canonical status in the Syrian and Armenian churches. He portrayed Paul less as the quintessential theologian than as an advocate for a very simple faith that could be summarized in a few short formulae and mediated in delightful stories. These legendary accounts lack the polemical harshness of the proto-orthodox Irenaeus and Tertullian and the internecine acrimony seen in Marcion and Valentinus. The issues facing their church both resembled and differed from those noted above – issues of sex, cultural tyranny, and desperate physical challenges. And, the stewards of these traditions found in Paul more than a model for a good death, more than a courageous, defiant witness, more than a fearless, composed, confident hero. They found in his model inspiration for times of repression and in him an instrument for the subversion of entrenched pyramids of power.

We see then how diverse the second-century Christian movement was, how animated or even vicious the polemics were between contending churches, and finally, how Paul was insinuated into these stormy exchanges. In the contest over the correct interpretation of Paul it is remarkable that the memory of the apostle survived to inform the discussion of the centuries ahead. Given Paul's privileged position with the highly popular Gnostics, it is amazing that he was not tarred with the same brush that was used to smear the 'heretics'. Schneemelcher suggests that the Roman church may have preferred to exclude Paul's letters from the canon altogether, but by the late second century it was too late. Paul enjoyed a status so legendary that exclusion was out of the question.[37]

Notes

1 E. Käsemann, 'Paul and Early Catholicism', *New Testament Questions of Today* (Philadelphia: Fortress, 1969) 249.
2 E. Hennecke, *New Testament Apocrypha*, ed. W. Schneemelcher, ET R. McL. Wilson (Philadelphia: Westminster, 1964), vol. 2, 111–27.
3 W. Schneemelcher, 'Paulus in der griechischen Kirche des zweiten Jahrhunderts', *ZKG* 75 (1964) 16.
4 *Letter of Polycarp* 3:2, in *Early Christian Fathers*, ed. C. C. Richardson (Philadelphia: Westminster, 1953).
5 H. von Campenhausen, *The Formation of the Christian Bible* (Philadelphia: Fortress, 1972) 7.
6 Schneemelcher, 'Paulus' 7–8.
7 Admittedly, our knowledge about Papias is scanty (Irenaeus, *Against Heresies* (hereafter *AH*) 5.33.3–4 and Eusebius, *Ecclesiastical History* (hereafter *EH*) 3.39.1; *AH* 5.33.4). Unless otherwise noted the citations are from *The Ante-Nicene Fathers*, ed. A. Roberts and J. Donaldson (Buffalo: Christian Literature Publishing Co., 1887).
8 Schneemelcher, 'Paulus' 8.
9 Ibid., 9.
10 W. Bauer, *Orthodoxy and Heresy in Earliest Christianity* (1934; ET Philadelphia: Fortress, 1971) 131.
11 A. von Harnack, *Marcion: The Gospel of the Alien God* (ET Durham, NC: Labyrinth Press, 1990) 15.
12 J. J. Clabeaux, 'Marcion', *ABD* 4.514.
13 Tertullian, *Against Marcion*, in Roberts and Donaldson, *The Ante-Nicene Fathers*, vol. 3, 5.30.1. Hereafter *AM*.
14 Clabeaux, 'Marcion' 4.514.
15 Harnack, *Marcion* 17, thought that Marcion migrated to the world capital to 'gain influence upon the whole of Christendom'.
16 Ibid., 44–7.
17 J. D. Quinn, *The Letter to Titus*, AB 35 (Garden City, NY: Doubleday 1990); J. Knox, *Marcion and the New Testament: An Essay in Early Christian History* (Chicago: University of Chicago Press, 1942).
18 Tertullian, *On Prescription against Heretics* xxx.
19 Clabeaux, 'Marcion' 4.515.
20 R. J. Hoffmann, *Marcion: On the Restitution of Christianity* (Chico, CA: Scholars, 1984) 153.
21 See Harnack's summary in *Marcion* 53–63.
22 Von Campenhausen's statement is too extreme that in 'Marcion's eyes the Old Testament was no longer valid in any sense whatever' (*Formation* 152). See Harnack, *Marcion* 65–92.
23 Harnack, *Marcion* 76.
24 Ibid., 97.
25 Ibid., 83. See Tertullian, *De carne Christi* 3.
26 Harnack, *Marcion* 96.
27 Knox, *Marcion* 74.
28 A. Harnack, *History of Dogma* (reprint: New York: Russell and Russell, 1961) vol. 2, 48 n. 2, 51.

29 R. A. Norris, 'Irenaeus' Use of Paul in his Polemic Against the Gnostics', in W. S. Babcock, ed., *Paul and the Legacies of Paul* (Dallas: Southern Methodist University Press, 1990) 85.

30 Ibid., 88.

31 Schneemelcher, 'Paulus' 19.

32 R. D. Sider, 'Literary Artifice and the Figure of Paul in the Writings of Tertullian', in Babcock, *Paul* 109–14.

33 Hoffmann, *Marcion* 237.

34 E. H. Pagels, *The Gnostic Paul: Gnostic Exegesis of the Pauline Letters* (Philadelphia: Fortress, 1975) 66.

35 Schneemelcher, 'Paulus' 11.

36 Hennecke, *New Testament Apocrypha*, vol. 2, 322–87.

37 Schneemelcher, 'Paulus' 11.

17 Paul's enduring legacy

ROBERT MORGAN

Victorian leaders in church and state are typically memorialized in rarely read volumes of *Life and Letters*. Paul too is known today from an account of his life and a collection of his letters, but the book in which both are preserved will continue to be read for as long as Christianity endures. Paul's impact on this religion and the cultures it has largely shaped began with his mission and the thought it stimulated but has been mediated by the records of both and magnified by their location in the New Testament. Elijah's cruse offers an image of scripture steadily nourishing faith communities without exhausting its deposit of oil; the financial metaphor of a legacy providing not only a regular income but varying dividends that sometimes exceed the original investment hints at Paul's revolutionary potential.

Religions depend on and live from their traditions, some especially from their scriptural traditions. Contemporary Christianity is heir to what Paul achieved historically and owes much to the example of his life, the teaching and inspiration of his letters, and their impact on other influential figures in Christian history. As a central part of Christian scripture his letters not only influence but partly *constitute* this religion by nourishing believers' response to God in different ways and at different levels. The history of doctrine shows how some of his ideas and myths have generated arguments that have left behind a doctrinal sediment; but that is secondary to the ways the epistles have informed and sustained different versions of Christian faith and life over centuries. The history of exegesis shows a church wrestling with its difficult and inspiring legacy, but it is in the interaction of that technical work with the practice of the religion that the power of Paul's legacy is to be seen.

The apostle's earliest influence on other believers' thinking is less visible than his contribution to the mission and expansion of Christianity, but probably no less fundamental. Wrede's description of Paul as 'the second founder of Christianity'[1] gives insufficient weight to pre-Pauline traditions and non-Pauline developments. The new religion taking shape in the theological conception of Luke–Acts combines traditions other than those which originate with Paul, and the growing influence of Gentile Christianity in the generation after Paul's martyrdom was accelerated by the fall of Jerusalem, but Wrede was right to insist that the faith proclaimed by Paul was new enough to justify calling it a different religion.

That was not Paul's intention, neither was he alone responsible. John's Jewish Christians were probably expelled from their synagogue on doctrinal grounds,[2] but when we ask what makes Christianity distinct from Judaism, it is to Paul that we turn first. The people from James at Gal. 2:11–14 were right. When Paul at Antioch defined the truth of the gospel in a way that made faith in Christ rather than observance of Torah the basis for association, the boundaries of what most Jews consider Judaism were overstepped and the messianic movement was losing its place as a sect within its parent religion.

Paul came to believe that his fellow-Jews would in the future be grafted back into what God was now doing, but that 'mystery' (Rom. 11:25) only underlines the present divide. On the other hand, Paul's strenuous efforts for acceptance of his Gentile mission by the Jerusalem church is also an inestimable part of his legacy. Gentile Christianity might otherwise have cut itself off from its Jewish roots long before Marcion. What is at stake here is nothing less than the identity of God according to the new religion. Paul thought that he remained a Jew, however 'radical'.[3] His retention of his Jewish scriptures was and is definitive of Christianity.

Paul's posthumous victory in the struggle for a law-free Gentile Christianity accelerated the split from the synagogue and the beginnings of a Christian literature. The New Testament contains in addition to his authentic epistles a narrative (Acts) and Pauline pseudepigrapha which throw some light on his contribution to the organization and belief-system which was already in his own apostolic activity becoming Catholicism. It also contains other writings probably (1 Peter) or possibly (Hebrews) influenced by his letters or (James) correcting them.

These first visible dividends on Paul's legacy of authentic epistles have in effect been added to the capital. For later readers of Christian scripture, 'Paul' means not only the seven almost certainly authentic epistles (Romans, 1 and 2 Corinthians, Galatians, Philippians, 1 Thessalonians, Philemon), but also six 'Pauline' letters which were probably written a generation (Colossians, Ephesians, 2 Thessalonians), or two (1 and 2 Timothy, Titus), later and also the anonymous epistle or homily (Hebrews) wrongly attributed to him for most of Christian history, as well as his story in Acts. They have all affected how the apostle has been heard, and this means that 'the canonical Paul' differs from Paul as he was, and even more from the 'historical' Paul constructed by modern scholars.

The canonical expansion of Paul helped secure him for emerging ortho-doxy at a time when his dualistic and antithetical formulations were com-mending him to gnostics and Marcion. It blunted one aspect of his legacy which was destined again to make history but otherwise caused no serious distortion because later writers have drawn mainly from the authentic epis-tles or from secondary material influenced by them, such as Col. 1:15–20. F. C. Baur thought Luke's portrait tendentious,[4] but few readers have noticed where it is suspect because their own Gentile interests have been closer to Luke's than to Paul's.

The main reason why subtracting Acts and Hebrews and the Pauline pseudepigrapha from theologians' perceptions of Paul has not made much difference is that these writings never prevented the authentic epistles from being heard more or less in the form that Paul wrote them. These were al-ready recognized by 2 Pet. 3:16 as dangerous as well as valuable. By including them in the canon the church bound itself to listen to a powerful witness that might have unpredictable effects, especially in situations thought anal-ogous to Paul's own. The early Pauline dividends did not conceal this Pauline legacy, but the canonical factor is relevant in other ways.

Firstly, when Paul's epistles were read as holy scripture their original contexts were lost and their content generalized. They were now heard in the echo-chamber created by the biblical canon. New connections were made with the Old Testament and Paul became part of a 'biblical world', an apostolic harmony, and a network of images. Being part of scripture affects not only the circulation of these letters but how they are read. Most Christians expect to learn from them something of God's engagement with the world in Jesus Christ, and perhaps to be themselves drawn further into that story. Students conditioned by the new historical and biographical interest in Paul can easily underestimate the religious spectacles through which he has been read, despite the combination of religious interests and historical methods in modern New Testament theology.

Secondly, Paul's canonical legacy has rarely been absorbed as a single en-tity. It is the scriptural *texts* which have been received, and particular words, phrases, and verses which have made most impact. Paul's contemporaries could contrast his personal presence with the letters (2 Cor. 10:10), but his heirs cannot. They have only the texts, and few remember them in a way that gives due weight to their literary, historical, and theological contexts. A mental image of Paul holds them together, but their powerful rhetoric im-presses most through words and phrases or favourite texts, some condensed in liturgy (e.g. the Prayer Book collects with their Augustinian background) and so embedded in minds shaped by Christian practice. Passages such as Phil. 4:4–9 are self-authenticating, but the impact of others is reinforced by the impression of Paul's personality and acceptance of his apostolic and canonical authority. The structure of his thought and the argument of an epistle are less accessible.

A third aspect of Paul's legacy may be called the snowball effect. The epistles pay immediate dividends in every generation, but their influence also grows and changes shape and density as it rolls through Christian history. The epistles have provided linguistic materials in the construction of doctrine and are appealed to in support of its scriptural basis, but building metaphors oversimplify the processes by which religious communities define their doctrine after long debate. Theology stems from actors and thinkers whose faith is nourished partly by scripture. It is the effect of Paul's epistles on such seminal figures as Origen, Augustine, and the Reformers which has proved decisive in the history of theology and so affected some later church doctrine. These theologians continue to influence parts of the church even when their writings (unlike Paul's) are no longer read except by students. Their Pauline-influenced theologies also affect how Paul is understood today, and there is enrichment as well as distortion here. Great literature, including religious literature, accumulates meanings unknown to the original author.[5] When modern theological interpreters of Paul bear the marks of the intervening tradition they may penetrate Paul's meaning more profoundly than some more strictly historical exegesis. One form of the snowball effect connects with the previous points. That is how much Paul has gained in translation. The Authorized Version of 1 Corinthians 13 and other purple passages of scripture is rhetorically more powerful than the original, giving added density to the text making its liturgical impact.

The effects of modern critical study on the reception and so the legacy of Paul constitute a fourth aspect of our topic. Like a blow-lamp turned on a snowball, historical exegesis melts away layers of interpretation, bad and good, superficial and profound, by reference to the author's intentions. This critical reduction is not new. The Reformers' rejection of allegorical interpretation devastated the delicate web of medieval exegesis. But the Reformers also intensified Paul's influence on theology and church life. That dividend remained powerful even when gospel criticism was subverting classical christology. Historical study has made little difference to the legacy of Paul because theologians such as Bultmann, Käsemann, and Martyn have integrated it in a series of Reformation theological interpretations of the epistles.

The sharper focus gained by discounting secondary pictures has not yet proved as significant as it might. Disputing the apostolic authorship of all the non-Pauline parts of the New Testament makes Paul the only first-century believer about whom much is known. He is now even more pivotal to the church's memory of its origins. If the character and credibility of this religion depend at all on that, Paul should become more central, as he has in modern New Testament theology. He will remain contested, even (perhaps especially) when most clearly understood. Recent historical and exegetical hypotheses have generated new and different interpretations of the epistles. Whether these strengthen or weaken his impact, they should remind us that what is 'enduring' in Paul's legacy is the epistles themselves. Interpretations are transient.

These preliminary considerations have directed the enquiry about Paul's legacy more to the religious lives of hearers and readers than to the history of doctrine or exegesis. This influence can be illustrated in the necessary brevity only by attending to the most influential writers, who are not surprisingly theologians and exegetes, but it is the way their religion is fired by Paul that is decisive, rather than those aspects of their theology that appeal to Pauline proof-texts.

The salvation-history framework by which Luke seems in retrospect to have preserved Paul for early Catholicism has much in common with how Irenaeus made him central for orthodoxy.[6] Language that might support Marcion or Gnosticism is made safe by the larger canonical context. Paul's Adam–Christ typology is developed to affirm the unity of creation and redemption. The idea of 'recapitulation' is taken up from Ephesians (1:10), and when Irenaeus' theology is called 'biblical' the canonical Paul provides much of the evidence.[7] It is surely more biblical than that of his opponents, and more true to the Jewish thinker Paul, but it lacks many of Paul's most characteristic emphases. The decisive question is whether his understanding of salvation in terms of divinization can claim any affinity with Paul's understanding of union with Christ.[8] If it can, this will be at the level of religion and experience rather than formal theology. The conceptuality is foreign to Paul, but the mystic who can claim to be co-crucified with Christ offers points of contact with the spirituality of the Greek Fathers.

Whereas Irenaeus secures Paul in the framework of Christian orthodoxy, Clement of Alexandria and above all Origen place him at the centre of Christian theology, exegesis, and spirituality. Origen's was the first systematic theology, and his biblical interpretation, including commentaries on Paul, has dominated Eastern and influenced Western (especially monastic) theology ever since. But his Christianity is a spirituality before it is speculation. What Wrede said about Paul can be said *mutatis mutandis* of Origen: his religion is theological through and through: his theology is his religion.[9] The soul's return to God by mystical ascent sounds remote from Paul, but Origen intends to live a biblical spirituality, and the most autobiographical biblical author by far is Paul, who says much about his own experience of life in the Spirit. His eschatological vision of rescue from this present evil age can be drawn on selectively to interpret a quite different account of the spiritual life.

What Paul wrote in 1 Corinthians encouraged Clement and Origen to identify with this true Gnostic, and their successors in the East and in Western monasticism followed him. The spiritual man teaches spiritual things to spiritual people (1 Cor. 2:13), revealing mysteries, explaining scripture allegorically (1 Cor. 9:9, 10:4 Gal. 4:24), and providing the beginnings of a hermeneutic to justify this: the letter kills, the Spirit gives life (2 Cor. 3:6). Paul was himself an ascetic (1 Corinthians 9), advocated celibacy (1 Corinthians 7), and constantly warned against the lusts of the flesh. The deutero-Pauline shadow was far more positive about marriage (Ephesians 5), and positively suspicious about celibacy (1 Tim. 3:2), but this was not allowed to obscure a more authentic Paul. The apostle gave instruction on prayer (1 Corinthians 14, Romans 8, and 1 Timothy 2) and suffering, was himself a charismatic whose experiences outshone everyone's, and was finally a martyr. He was above all a mystic who had been taken up into the third heaven (2 Cor. 12:2)[10] and looked forward to the vision of God (1 Cor. 13:12).

Paul taught the primacy of love. The way that Origen and his successors, above all Bernard of Clairvaux in the West, constantly quote Paul as they comment or preach on the Song of Songs[11] sounds strange to anyone unaccustomed to allegory. But scripture is read by believers to strengthen their relationship to God. Its moral exhortations and doctrinal content belong to that, but the constant echoes of the epistles in Origen's writings express and so sustain his ascetical religious practice.

When Paul fuels a particular spirituality so directly he is unlikely to challenge the religious frame of reference that determines how he is read. Allegorical interpretation further blunts his critical potential and makes him reinforce the dominant theology. Even where allegory was criticized, as by the Antiochenes, Paul was read in terms of the ruling paradigm. Grammatical exegesis alone is never powerful enough to shift this. Chrysostom's homilies on Paul boil with prophetic power, but within the Antiochene doctrinal framework. Those moral dividends on the Pauline legacy reach into the realms of political theory and Christian attitudes to homosexuality[12] without revising the basic understanding of Christianity. Paul can be omnipresent and yet some of his legacy lie dormant. Marcion's theological revolution had been defeated on rational exegetical grounds, but he had grasped an aspect of Paul which could overturn a dominant theology as the Christian Platonist reception of the epistles could not. The Greek

Fathers did not squeeze the Christian gospel into the procrustean bed of their philosophy. They revised their philosophy in the light of their understanding of scripture, and generally respected the textual authorial intention of the New Testament; but they missed the direction of Paul's polemic because their own problems and opponents were different. Origen did not evade the difficulties posed by the biblical text for his Greek thinking. He constantly returned to the most difficult Pauline text of all, Romans 9 on election and predestination. He knew from 2 Corinthians 3 and elsewhere that the gospel and the Spirit are about freedom, and to avoid denying free-will and so moral responsibility he took Romans 9 to mean that God foreknew what people would choose.

This shows Origen reading Paul against the grain. His opponents could appeal to passages in the epistles that supported Gnostic and later Manichaean determinism. Origen, like Irenaeus, neutralized that part of his ambiguous legacy. Other parts of it were unimportant to him or did not fit his frame of reference. Paul's arguments against circumcising Gentile converts were no longer of interest, though as an exegete Origen could see that Paul spoke of the law in different ways. The moral law was plainly important and the Old Testament was preserved for Christianity by the allegorical interpretation licensed by Paul. He tried to work the apostle's eschatology into his own systematic theology, but it was a poor fit. The apostle was valued above all as one who taught us to pray without ceasing (1 Thess. 5:17) and to peer beyond the created order with the mind's eyes that 'gaze at the glory of the Lord with unveiled face and that are being changed into his likeness from glory to glory'.[13] This 'sheer contemplation of God' is also what Origen's admirer, Gregory of Nyssa, finds in Paul. His *Life of Moses* draws more of its substance from 'Paul' than from the Old Testament. The words of 'the divine apostle' about 'straining forward to what lies ahead . . .' (Phil. 3:13–14) sum up this account of the Christian life.[14]

That sort of spiritual reading of Paul survives wherever Christian faith is understood as participation in the life of God through adoption and grace. It may be considered the most enduring dividend yielded by Paul's epistles, and yet it misses much of what Western Christianity has drawn from the apostle. The difference lies not only in Augustine's less sanguine assessment of the human condition after the fall and his psychological insight into the human will, but also in his appropriation of Paul's language of grace in an account of how the human will is being healed. Both the Origenist and the Augustinian traditions are drawn by the personal and autobiographical character of Paul's writings and what they imply about human nature and the search and need for God. But whereas the East and later humanists like Erasmus insisted on the free choice and moral responsibility required by God's justice, Augustine placed greater emphasis on what God in his love had done and was doing to save a lost world. His analysis of what was needed drew a theological anthropology out of Romans 7 and turned Western thought to the human subject. It is ironic that this concern for God's grace gave Western thought its pre-occupation with the human condition, whereas the more humanist East has better preserved Paul's sense of God's glory and transcendence.

Returning to the Catholic Church[15] by way of Platonism after a serious attraction to Manichaean determinism, Augustine insisted on human free-will in his early writings on Romans. It was only in 397, when he was answering Simplician's questions about Rom. 7:7–25, and especially Rom. 9:10–29, that further study of Paul led him to redefine the relation of grace and free-will and to see even faith as a gift of grace, accepting that God in his omnipotence and inscrutable will chooses some and not others.[16]

Pelagius thought that undermined morality and opposed Augustine.[17] The ensuing controversy over what the human will could achieve embraced disagreements about the origin of souls and the consequences of the fall. Following the condemnation of a disciple of Pelagius for rejecting the traducianist view that the soul is passed from parent to child and the sin of Adam inherited, and unbaptized children therefore damned, Augustine entered the controversy with a defence of his doctrine of grace, *On the Spirit and the Letter* (412).[18] This stunning interpretation of Romans and Christianity is exegetically sometimes mistaken. The immoral idea of original guilt found in the Latin mistranslation of Rom. 5:12d is not Paul's, even if those who held it could appeal to Rom. 5:19. Augustine's erroneous reading of Paul on sin and concupiscence has proved fateful, and yet also fruitful. He later referred the divided mind of Rom. 7:7–25 to Christian existence, in effect anticipating Luther's *simul iustus et peccator* and introducing 'the introspective conscience of the West'.[19] This made him the godfather of medieval mysticism, monastic penitential practice, and some more recent Western philosophy, literature, and psycho-analysis. But before and above all that, what Augustine learned from the epistles was that the religion of Jesus is essentially a matter of grace, not of reward for virtue.[20]

This was firstly a matter of experience and so of theological reflection. Augustine echoes the religious passion of the epistles (e.g. Gal. 2:19–20; Rom. 5:5), and like Paul's, his reflections flow into the doxological language that is characteristic of Christian talk of God. But he also saw the importance of criticizing distorted accounts of Christianity and enshrining the authentic experience and understanding of grace in church doctrine. Only then would God's gift to the world in Christ be communicated rather than obscured by a facade of moral and ascetic respectability. That instinct connected him with Paul's struggle for the truth of the gospel against those who insisted on their tradition.

Both sides in the Pelagian controversy wanted Paul's support for their answers to questions he never asked. Such extensions and extrapolations are inevitable when scripture is used as a doctrinal norm. The question is which ones best articulate Paul's gospel. It took a Welsh opponent devoted to the moral law to stimulate the first full dividend since Marcion on Paul's passionate language of grace. There was more to come.

The fertility of Paul's language as a resource for theology is nowhere clearer than in these Western arguments about 'the righteousness of God', the stated theme of the Epistle to the Romans (1:17), and one of the scriptural concepts (mainly drawn from the Psalter and Isaiah) by which he spoke of salvation. Augustine's recognition that Paul meant not only that God is righteous but also 'what he gives to man when he justifies the ungodly' (Rom. 4:5)[21] was so far lost by some of his successors[22] that Luther had to rediscover it for himself before finding confirmation in Augustine.[23] The phrase sounds more legal in Latin than in Greek, and when Anselm directed the discussion of salvation into moral and legal categories it sharpened the question of the relationship of God's justice to God's mercy. Anselm, unlike Paul, rooted God's saving action in philosophical reflection on God's nature, but he did not himself interpret God's justice as rendering to everyone their due.

That common misreading of Paul's phrase led much medieval and later Protestant atonement theology to find in Paul's obscure and ambiguous language at Rom. 3:25 the immoral idea that God's justice was satisfied by the sacrifice of an innocent victim. The verse speaks of God's gracious initiative in dealing with sin and evoking the response of faith. Augustine's insistence on the experiential and affective dimension of this saving faith was taken further in Abelard's subjective theory of the atonement based on his exposition of Romans. This does not grasp all that Paul says; Anselm's 'objective' theory also draws on the epistle. But Abelard is true to Paul in recognizing that God's grace evokes a loving response.

Scholastic exegesis made Paul as central to the new university theology[24] as he was to the monastic, and entrenched him in the medieval discussions of nature and grace. His echoes of Stoic natural theology found a place there, but it was still his doctrine of grace that was central. Augustine's Pauline doctrine of predestination was generally rejected, but his view of grace gradually healing the disabled will and making believers righteous provided the main rationale for the institutional church and its sacramental practice.

The polemical edge of Augustine's Pauline *sola gratia* was again dormant, but it revived and was sharpened in Luther's criticism of late medieval theology and practice. Origen had seen the *sola fide* implicit in Rom. 3:28, but it was only when 'the works of the law' were identified with a visible target that the medieval doctrine of justification rediscovered the polemical potential of Paul's antithetical language. *Faith* and faith alone became the Pauline banner under which the Reformers dismantled the medieval theology of grace, divided Western Christianity, and opened a door to modern Western individualism and the anthropocentrism[25] which has dominated Western thought since the Enlightenment. Neither Paul nor the Reformers can be credited with or blamed for this, and yet it owes much to their integration of talk of God with talk of humanity.

The Reformers did not see the sacramentalism which later historians of religion would find in Paul, but their new emphasis on the word of God was essentially Pauline and suited the new world that was dawning. The translation of the Bible into the vernacular and its availability in print and the growth of literacy were major factors in this new word-driven development of Christianity in Northern Europe. At its heart it was a rediscovery of Paul and the anti-Pelagian Augustine informed by massive exegetical scholarship also made widely available by printing. New emphases and new combinations of Pauline texts led to fresh developments in their understanding of his language of justification and sanctification, and (especially in Calvinism) predestination. Rom. 4:7 and medieval experience led to an un-Pauline emphasis on forgiveness and sins, and 1 Cor. 1:30 told Luther that justification involved Christ's righteousness becoming ours. Calvin pressed the logic of predestination further even than Augustine, whose reply to Simplician (see n. 17) had introduced the problem in the first place by systematizing Paul and connecting this dangerous idea with justification. Melanchthon introduced the idea of imputation (from Romans 4) into the new forensic account of justification in the Augsburg Confession (1530), and this became standard Lutheran doctrine. His *Loci Communes* of 1521, the first Protestant dogmatics, was modelled on Romans, and Calvin's *Institutes* owe more to Paul than to anyone. At the other end of the Reformation spectrum, antinomianism has always had Pauline roots, despite Rom. 3:8.

But it is in the religion of Protestants even more than in their theology that the legacy of Paul has continued to yield dividends. The title of John Bunyan's spiritual autobiography, *Grace Abounding to the Chief of Sinners* (1666), both echoes and personalizes Romans 5, and persecuted puritans were inspired by Paul's example. The perversion of Calvinist Paulinism is dramatized by James Hogg in *The Private Memoirs and Confessions of a*

Justified Sinner (1824). When the university theology of Germany became scholastic again, pietism recovered the experience of justification and in doing so was true to Luther as well as to Paul. John Wesley's experience of his heart being 'strangely warned' at Aldersgate in 1738 was stimulated by the reading of Luther's *Preface to Romans*. Experiences of conversion could always find a model in Paul.

Pauline ideas and phrases not only shaped the personal religion of Protestants, but also influenced the external organization of their churches and sects.[26] Any determination to recover the simplicity of the apostolic church in opposition to Catholic corruption would direct attention to the church-founder whose missionary work is well documented and whose teaching is authoritative. Catholicism can convincingly appeal to Ephesians, but Protestantism draws its ecclesiology and much of its practice from the real Paul reflected in his authentic epistles. Defining the church in terms of the word being preached and the (gospel) sacraments being celebrated, de-sacralizing the ministry, valuing the secular, and insisting that all believers have their vocation (*Beruf*) and ministry are all genuine Pauline emphases, even if national churches are not. The Protestant sects could appeal more directly to Paul in support of a more gathered church, and yet what the Reformers inherited from Augustine and Catholicism about God's concern for the whole of society has Pauline as well as Old Testament roots. God is Lord of all. Paul's claim that 'the powers that be are ordained by God', on the other hand, has had a massive and problematic influence, especially in Lutheranism.

Paul's throw-away remark about God justifying the ungodly (Rom. 4:5; cf. 5:6) gains its power from its reflecting Jesus' ministry. It has lent some support to modern secular Christianity by being glossed by an implied contrast to the salvation of the pious. The early Barthian critique of 'religion' ignored the religious contexts necessary for all Christian talk of God, but it reactivated aspects of both Jesus' and Paul's criticism of their religious opponents, and this is one of several points at which Paul can be said to be the truest interpreter of Jesus. Paul certainly and Jesus perhaps, like many prophets, spoke most incisively in polemical contexts, and Paul has been heard most clearly in new polemical contexts. His gospel of grace is 'the clearest gospel of all' (Luther) when pitted against something as 'holy, just, and good', indeed 'spiritual', as religion and morality. Paul himself was not opposing the idea of earning salvation, despite Rom. 4:4; 'without the works of the law' at Rom. 3:28 probably intended 'the works of circumcision or the sabbath, and others of this sort'.[27] Nevertheless, the Lutheran dialectic of law and gospel catches an abiding element of Paul's thinking which liberal interest in the 'religion' of the apostle understated. Its recovery by twentieth-century neo-Reformation theologies not only reasserted essential elements in the tradition against tendencies to minimize 'the scandal of the cross' (cf. 1 Cor. 1:18–25), but was also a distinctively Pauline theological response to the secularization of European culture. This renewal of Christian theological discourse was detonated by an interpretation of Paul's greatest epistle.

Luther had despised both scholasticism and the Erasmian humanism which preferred not to make assertions.[28] He appealed to Paul's 'Word of the cross' against all human wisdom (1 Cor. 1–4). Barth also repudiated the project of finding common ground with the contemporary culture. His insistence that the gospel judges all human achievement resonated after the First World War and strengthened Christian witness against totalitarian regimes. It remains an essential ingredient of biblical preaching. But even within the dialectical theology different theologians drew different kinds of inspiration from Paul. Bultmann admired Barth but reclaimed the neo-Reformation Paul for his revision of the nineteenth-century programme of speaking of God by speaking of the human condition. He speaks with Paul and Luther of humanity *coram Deo*, that is, from the perspective of faith. Presenting Paul's theology as a theological anthropology, and Paul himself as an existentialist theologian, requires some trimming of the textual data, but touches on his central concerns, which include how to speak appropriately and intelligibly of God.

The analyses of Bultmann's Pauline interpretation by such sympathetic critics as his pupil Käsemann[29] and the philosophical theologian Macquarrie[30] show that there is more to Paul's legacy than that penetrating reduction allowed. But these debates themselves lead back to the central question posed when Paul's epistles were read as Christian scripture by Origen, Augustine, and Luther: how does reading them inform and sustain another generation's Christian talk of God? Some of the answers can be found in the better textbooks of Christian doctrine. These reflect Paul's conviction and insistence (1) that God is identified as the God of Israel (see Rom. 9:4–5 and *passim*), which means the creator, and that the Jewish scriptures remain Christian scripture; (2) that talk of the crucified and risen Messiah, the Lord Jesus, is central to Christian discourse and that all talk of God and the Spirit is to be tested by reference to this man and his obedience unto death; (3) that the Spirit of God who is also the Spirit of Christ (Rom. 8:9) is the key to individual and corporate Christian existence, gifting individuals and building up communities, guiding the Christian life (Galatians 5) including its prayer (Romans 8; 1 Cor. 12–14), and spreading freedom (2 Corinthians 3), a life summed up in the dialectic of freedom and service (Galatians), or in faith, hope, and above all love (1 Corinthians

13); (4) that talk of God always involves talking of that authentic human existence but also points beyond this world to a future that can be spoken of only imaginatively (1 Thessalonians 4 1 Corinthians 15).

These basic convictions are found in the epistles which constitute Paul's enduring legacy. When the epistles are read with due receptivity by Christians they sometimes reactivate and rejuvenate similar convictions of the readers or hearers. Their potential for breaking down barriers within the Christian community (Gal. 3:28) has been only slowly and imperfectly realized, and their possibilities for motivating a new respect for the environment have scarcely yet been assessed. These wider perspectives invite some evaluation of Paul's legacy to Western culture outside the Christian churches. The epistles are public property. But their broader impact has usually been mediated through Christian faith, and is unlikely to endure outside that proper context. It can be explored by cultural historians interested in what remains of a body of religious thought when it is no longer heard to speak of the living God. Paul himself would not be interested, unless he thought that by becoming a post-theist to the post-theists he might by all means save some.

Notes

1 *Paul* (1904; ET London, 1907) 179.

2 See the debate stimulated by J. L. Martyn, *History and Theology in the Fourth Gospel* (New York, 1968; 2nd edn, Nashville, 1979), especially D. Rensberger, *Johannine Faith and Liberating Community* (Philadelphia, 1988) = *Overcoming the World* (London, 1989).

3 See D. Boyarin, *A Radical Jew: Paul and the Politics of Identity* (Berkeley, 1994), K.-W. Niebuhr, *Heidenapostel aus Israel*, WUNT 62 (Tübingen, 1992).

4 F. C. Baur, *Paul: The Apostle of Jesus Christ* (1845; ET 2 vols., London, 1873, 1875).

5 See M. Bakhtin, *Speech Genres and Other Essays* (ET Austin, 1986) 4.

6 See H. von Campenhausen, *The Formation of the Christian Bible* (ET London, 1972.

7 E.g. J. Lawson, *The Biblical Theology of Saint Irenaeus* (London, 1948); R. Noormann, *Irenäus als Paulusinterpret* (Tübingen, 1994).

8 F. Normann, *Teilhabe – ein Schlüsselwort der Vätertheologie* (Münster, 1978), hints at this.

9 *Paul* 76.

10 This account of Paul's rapture was discussed at length by Augustine (*De Gen. ad Litt.* XII.27–37, *PL* 34 cols. 453–86) and Aquinas (*ST* II.2, 175.3–6) and provided a model for Dante's *Paradiso.*

11 Origen's Prologue to the *Commentary on the Song of Songs* is translated by R. Greer in the *Origen* volume of The Classics of Western Spirituality (New York and London, 1979); and Bernard's eighty-six sermons on the same book in the Cistercian Fathers Series (3 vols., Michigan, 1979–83). On Origen's understanding of Paul, see T. Heither, *Translatio Religionis* (Cologne, 1990).

12 See his Homily 23 on Romans 13, and Homily 4, which attacks homosexual practices (not homoerotic love) as unnatural in an echo of Rom. 1.26–7 which stretches from Clement (*Paidagogos* 2.10) to the present day. The later discussion of Romans 13 may be illustrated by Aquinas (*ST* ii.2, 42 art. 2) following John of Salisbury, *Policraticus* 8) in denying that it forbids tyrannicide, and the Council of Constance (1415) deciding otherwise. German theologians under Hitler were also restrained by the weight accorded to this passage in Lutheran tradition. See E. Käsemann, 'Römer 13.1–7 in unserer Generation', *ZTK* 56 (1959) 316–76.

13 Origen, *On Prayer* ix.2. ET in Greer, *Origen*, 99.

14 Ed. A. J. Malherbe and E. Ferguson (New York/London, 1978).

15 The contribution of Rom. 13.13–14 to his conversion is told at *Confessions* 8.

16 The relevant parts of this are available in ET in *Augustine's Earlier Writings*, ed. J. H. S. Burleigh, LCC 6 (Philadelphia/London, 1953) 372–406. His crucial 'reconsideration' (*Retractiones* ii.1) of Romans 7 is also included (370).

17 In his *Commentary on Romans*, ed. T. de Bruyn (Oxford, 1993), which was indebted to Rufinus' translation of Origen's commentary.

18 ET J. Burnaby, *Augustine: Later Works*, LCC 8 (Philadelphia/London, 1955).

19 Krister Stendahl's phrase in his 1961 lecture which signals a reaction against the classical Reformation interpretation of Paul, in *HTR* 25 (1963) 62–77; reprinted in his *Paul among Jews and Gentiles* (Philadelphia, 1976; London, 1977).

20 A. McGrath, *Justification by Faith* (Basingstoke, 1988) 43, emphasizes Augustine's appeal to the parable of the labourers in the vineyard (Matt. 20:1–10).

21 See also *De Trin.* xiv.15; ET Burnaby 114.

22 Not all. H. Denifle, *Die abendländischen Schriftausleger bei Luther über Iustitia Dei (Rom. 1.17) und Iustificatio* (Mainz, 1905), showed how far it was preserved.

23 See his autobiographical Preface to his Latin writings (1545).

24 See Aquinas' admirable *Expositio in Ep. Omnes Divi Pauli Apostoli* (1593, reprinted 1948–50).

25 Parodied by Feuerbach in *The Essence of Faith according to Luther* (1846; ET New York, 1967).

26 Menno Simons' organization of Anabaptist congregations in mid-sixteenth-century Holland was analogous to and modelled on Paul's mission. See also R. Allen, *Missionary Methods: St Paul's or Ours?* (1912; 2nd edn,1927) for indications of the missiological importance of Paul's example.

27 So Pelagius, *Commentary on Romans* 83.

28 *De Servo Arbitrio* 1 (*WA* 18.603-5), ET *Luther and Erasmus*, ed. G. Rupp with A. N. Marlow, LCC 17 (Philadelphia/London, 1969) 105–9.

29 See D. Way, *The Lordship of Christ* (Oxford, 1990) for a penetrating account.

30 J. Macquarrie, *An Existentialist Theology* (London, 1968).

18 Contemporary perspectives on Paul

BEN WITHERINGTON, III

Fresh winds are blowing through the corridors of Pauline studies, and in many ways it is an exciting time to be studying the apostle to the Gentiles' correspondence. In this chapter we will be exploring four areas where new perspectives and methodologies have led to further light being shed on the Pauline corpus. The areas of our discussion will include: (1) Jewish perspectives on Paul; (2) feminist and liberationist perspectives on Paul; (3) rhetorical studies of Paul's letters; and (4) the examination of Paul's letters as scripture.

SAUL THE PHARISEE/PAUL THE CHRISTIAN IN JEWISH PERSPECTIVE

The study of Saul of Tarsus' life and works by Jewish scholars is certainly not an entirely new phenomenon. A generation ago, H. J. Schoeps wrote a lively account of the apostle's life and work, and there were always a few treatments, like that of S. Sandmel, which suggested that the subject deserved closer scrutiny by Jewish scholars. But in recent years some of the most influential studies on Paul have been offered by Jewish scholars such as A. Segal, D. Boyarin, or M. Nanos. We will briefly consider the promise and problems with each of these studies, but before doing so it is worth making a few preliminary observations.

Firstly, the new wave of Jewish studies of Paul is part of the wider re-examination of Jesus and his first followers by Jewish scholars. This renewed interest in the origins of Christianity has to some extent been fostered by scholarly discussions in major universities, but also by inter-faith dialogue between Jews and Christians, and by interaction between Jews and Christians since Jews began returning to the Holy Land in 1948 and Christians increasingly have gone on pilgrimage to Israel in the last fifty or more years. In other words, recent Jewish scholarship on Paul is part of a wider social phenomenon sparked in part by the ever-growing social networks between Jews and Christians, and between the West and the Middle East.

Secondly, it is precisely because of the enormous ongoing contemporary debate about what makes a Jew a Jew that earlier discussions by Paul and others on this very matter (e.g. Romans 9–11) have been given close scrutiny by Jewish scholars. The study has then in part been generated by the fact that Paul appears to address issues of contemporary relevance and urgency for people of Jewish faith and others interested in early and/or modern Judaism.

Thirdly, the study of Paul has been undertaken by Jews also because since the Jewish Holocaust in the 1940s, there has been enormous concern about texts that were and indeed continue to be used in anti-Semitic ways. It is not accidental that S. Sandmel wrote not only a study of Paul and his life, but also a scholarly monograph entitled *Anti-Semitism in the New Testament*.[1] Paul, or at least later Paulinists, have been seen as some of the real instigators of anti-Semitism in the church and in Western culture in general.[2] Even though most scholars would make a distinction between a radical critique of early Judaism and anti-Semitism (for it seems odd to accuse an early Jew such as Paul, who drew on and affirmed a great deal of his heritage, of being anti-Jewish), one still finds some scholars, for example H. Maccoby, who largely blame Paul for corrupting the Jesus movement, and indeed inventing a form of early Christianity hostile to Judaism.[3]

(1) Segal and the apostasy of the apostle

One of the issues which have always been pressing when the Jewishness of Paul has been under discussion is whether or not one should speak of Paul's conversion to Christianity, and thus of his apostasy from early Judaism. It is interesting that Jewish scholars such as A. Segal *are* prepared to talk about Paul's conversion, while various scholars of Christian extraction such as Krister Stendahl wish to insist that Galatians 1 and other such texts only speak of the call, not the conversion of the apostle.[4] Both sides of this discussion are agreed that Paul was indeed a Jew, the issue being whether he was a good or a bad Jew, a judgment which depends, of course, on one's view of what makes for a good Jew.

Segal's study of Paul in part builds on his earlier work on early Jewish mysticism. It is Segal's view that Paul himself was a mystic and part of a social phenomenon later associated with *merkabah* mysticism. While this view rightly points to the visionary nature of some of Paul's experiences (2 Cor. 12:1–7), it fails to place them in the right context, for they are experiences which reflect the influence and impact of early Jewish apocalyptic, not later Jewish manifestations of throne-chariot mysticism.

More helpful is Segal's study of conversion and early Judaism, and he demonstrates at some length that by any normal definition of conversion,

Paul seems to have experienced one. 'Mystical experience started or aided Paul's conversion. Whether the conversion took place gradually or suddenly the effect was an about-face. Whether or not Paul also tried to missionize Jews, the change is most easily described as a decision to change commitments from one religious community to another.'[5] It is very ironic that a Jewish scholar insists not only on this conclusion, but also on the conclusion that Paul the convert did not believe that faith in Mosaic legislation was the equal (and equally valid) to faith in Christ, while scholars in the Christian tradition such as K. Stendahl, J. Gager, and L. Gaston think that Paul operated with a two people of God and a two-track salvation model (one for those in Christ, another for Jews outside of Christ).[6] Indeed Segal concludes from texts like Rom. 10:12–13 that for Paul, the name of God is Jesus the Christ, a truth discovered in his ecstatic or mystical conversion experience, and he hopes for the day when 'all Israel will be saved' in and by Christ (11:26). Paul then is not to be seen as an early advocate of religious pluralism. What distinguishes Segal and various traditional Christian interpreters of Paul is that the latter would see Paul as helping to bring Judaism to its proper climax or completion in Christ, while the former would speak of Paul's defection or apostasy from true Judaism.

(2) Boyarin and the difficulties of difference

Equally intriguing is the study by D. Boyarin, who sees Paul as an advocate of a universal religion which transcends both differences and hierarchy. He takes Gal. 3.28 as the essence of Paul's view of things and believes that Paul raises for all the question, 'Are the specificities of human identity, the differences, of value, or are they only an obstacle in the striving for justice and liberation?'[7] Boyarin thinks that Paul's universalism manifests itself in a particular sort of hermeneutics in dealing with Torah and Jewish traditions – namely, the letter kills, but the Spirit gives life. In an odd twist, Boyarin sees his own reading of Paul as closest to that of F. C. Baur. The end result is an attempt to read Paul as very much like Philo in the way he interprets sacred texts often in an allegorical and symbolic sense, including the allegorizing of what the term or sign 'Israel' means.[8] Paul then is a dualist in his anthropology and in his interpretation of scripture, like unto Philo. Boyarin concludes about Paul: 'If there has been no rejection of Israel, there has indeed been a supersession of the historical Israel's hermeneutic of self-understanding as a community constituted by physical genealogy and observances and the covenantal exclusiveness that such an understanding entails.' This approach, 'while not anti-Semitic (or even anti-Judaic) in intent . . . nevertheless has had the effect of depriving continued Jewish existence of any reality or significance in the Christian economies of history'.[9]

The problem with this conclusion is that it does not grapple sufficiently with what Paul envisions in Romans 11 when he speaks of 'all Israel' being saved in the future. Paul does not deny a future for Israel, or even the present of Israel, much less its past. He simply insists that its future is in Christ. Boyarin's conclusion quoted above also entails his view that by 'works of the law' Paul means the boundary-defining rituals such as circumcision and sabbath laws, so that Paul's critique of the law turns out to be less radical than is often thought.[10] But this conclusion does not sufficiently grapple with what Paul says about the law in Galatians 3–4 and in Romans 10. If the law as a whole is the slave guardian of God's people until Christ comes, then a new situation exists since that time, and 'we' (by which Paul means even a Jew like himself) are no longer under the law.

(3) Nanos and the nature of Paul's gospel

Yet another stimulating reading of Paul can be found in the recent and award-winning book by M. Nanos on Romans. Like Boyarin, Nanos finds a less radical Paul in the Pauline corpus than has often been thought. Thus, for instance, Paul is seen as not arguing for a law-free gospel, but rather a law-observant one for Jews and a law-respectful one for Gentiles. Paul is encouraging Jews in Rome to continue to observe the Torah. Further, Paul taught Gentiles in Rome not only to respect Jewish Christians who observe the law and be tolerant of them but to welcome such people, and in fact to accommodate and even to adopt such practices. 'They were to observe the halakhic behavioural requirements of "righteous gentiles" in their relationship with Jews, whether Christian or not.'[11]

Surprisingly, then, Paul sounds remarkably like James and/or the author of the apostolic decree found in Acts 15, at least if that decree is interpreted as imposing a modicum of Jewish Laws on Gentiles.[12] Furthermore, Paul's ministry to the Gentiles had as its ultimate goal having 'stumbling' Israel reconsider the gospel for themselves. Paul did not seek to disassociate the new Christian movement from the synagogue. To the contrary he encouraged subordination to the leaders of synagogue and their interpretation of what was appropriate behaviour by righteous Gentiles (Rom. 13:1–6). They were to pay temple taxes and obey applicable halakhah (Rom. 13:7). The 'early Roman Christian communities were functioning as subgroups within the larger synagogue communities at the time of Paul's letter.' If his audience heeded the exhortations in Romans, then Gentiles would be heard extolling the one true God of Israel in the midst of the synagogue. Thus 'the Paul of Romans believed that faith in Christ "established" Torah; it certainly didn't make it obsolete'.[13]

To a very real extent, what one concludes about Paul's views on Israel and the Law will be determined by where one thinks the starting point of the discussion ought to be. Do we begin with Romans and then try to explain Galatians and other texts in light of Romans, or do we begin with the chronologically earlier Galatians and work our way towards Romans? In my view, if one starts with Galatians and believes that Paul did not radically alter his views between the time he wrote Galatians and when he wrote Romans,[14] the reading of Romans by Nanos becomes quite improbable. It is true enough that Paul is no supersessionist, but he does indeed believe that Jew and Gentile united in Christ is the ultimate or final form of the people God, otherwise known as Israel. The centrality and indispensability of Christ is no less evident in Romans than it is in Galatians, and the locus of God's people as being 'in Christ' is equally clear. But one must applaud the attempt to offer a sympathetic and fresh reading of Paul the Jew and his most famous letter, even if at the end of the day it appears to be a reading which does not do full justice to the data either in Romans or elsewhere in the Pauline corpus. One can only be thankful that scholars of both Jewish and Christian heritage are once again vigorously debating the significance of Paul and his letters.

FEMINIST AND LIBERATIONIST APPROACHES TO THE PAULINE CORPUS

Since 'Feminist biblical interpretation is a species of liberationist hermeneutics',[15] it is certainly justifiable to treat the two approaches to Paul's letters as two variations on one theme. What is assumed in both these approaches is that a hermeneutics of suspicion should be applied to the Pauline corpus, so that the apparent meaning of the text should not be taken at face value. It is assumed that the text is not neutral, nor is any reader of the text 'objective'. In other words, the suspicion applies to both the text and the various interpreters of Paul's letters.[16] Yet it must be said that equal suspicion is not applied to all Pauline texts by all feminist interpreters of Paul. In the brief space allotted to this part of our discussion we will concentrate on three examples of feminist interpretation of Paul and one example of a wider liberationist perspective.

(1) Fiorenza and the apostle of equality

Certainly the most influential of feminist Pauline interpreters is Elizabeth Schüssler Fiorenza. Fiorenza's treatment of what Paul says about women is always carefully researched and stresses that Paul and his churches were simply one part of a larger Christian missionary movement, which she believes was essentially egalitarian because of the nature of the movement Jesus himself founded. In other words, Paul inherited an egalitarian movement already in progress, and his churches owe the prominence of women not to Pauline innovations or policy but to the already existing situation when Paul began his missionary work. Thus, for example, while Gal. 3:28 is not a Pauline but a pre-Pauline formulation, it is one Paul is prepared to use.

Fiorenza adds that Paul does not simply conclude that the formula in Gal. 3:28 has a spiritual significance (all are one in Christ) but also a social one, for one could argue that much of Paul's ministry was geared to the breaking down of the barriers between Jew and Gentile in Christ. She rightly urges that the clause 'no male and female' likely means that patriarchal marriage and sexual relationships are not what constitute the new Christian community. 'Paul's interpretation and adaptation of the baptismal declaration of Gal. 3:28 in his letters to the community of Corinth unequivocally affirm the equality and charismatic giftedness of women and men in the Christian community.'[17] Yet Fiorenza in the end sees Paul as something of an ascetic who because of his preference for the single state restricts the participation of wives in worship, and his characterization of his apostleship as a form of fatherhood leaves the door open for the reintroduction of patriarchal values in the church. She also thinks that what Paul says about hair and headcoverings (offered originally to help outsiders distinguish Christian practice from that of the orgiastic cults) was subject to misreading when the Pauline churches were re-patriarchized.

In the end, Fiorenza feels that the impact of Paul's dictates on women was a mixed blessing, helping to free single women for ministry but further restricting Christian married women. It was, in her view, the latter restrictions which were to be emphasized and amplified in the post-Pauline and pseudo-Pauline tradition. It is somewhat ironic that in most respects Fiorenza, of all the feminist interpreters of Paul's letters, least manifests the hermeneutics of suspicion as applied to Paul, and yet she was in part the impetus for such a move by later feminist interpreters.

(2) Wire and the hermeneutics of suspicion

Less influential, but more controversial, is the feminist interpretation of 1 Corinthians offered by A. C. Wire. She suggests that there was a group of radical Christian prophetesses in Corinth whom Paul felt compelled to correct at various points in 1 Corinthians. They were at odds with Paul in regard to matters ranging from sexual morality to the wearing of headcoverings. Wire suggests that these women may have been urging singleness and asceticism. But if this was the case, then Paul's own advice in 1 Corinthians 7 on the surface would not seem to be a corrective to this problem. Indeed it would seem that his original teaching in Corinth may have fostered such an approach. It is interesting that the feminist hermeneutics of suspicion about Paul leads Wire to argue for the inclusion of 1 Cor. 14:33b–36 as part of the original Pauline content of the letter.[18] It also leads her to assume that Paul is trying to curtail Corinthian women's acts of prophecy and tongue-speaking, when in fact Paul rather seems to encourage such behaviour on the part of women and men in 1 Corinthians 11 and 14 so long as it is carried out decently and in good order. In fact, the evidence of 1 Corinthians taken as a whole suggests that the real targets of Paul's criticism in 1 Corinthians are relatively high-status Gentile Christian males who did not want to disengage from certain practices, like sexual promiscuity and attending idol feasts, which had been a regular part of their pagan past.

(3) Castelli and Pauline power plays

E. Castelli provides an interesting reading of Paul's use of power and apostolic authority.[19] She suspects Paul of using mimetic language ('be imitators of me') in a coercive fashion in order to establish himself at the top of the ecclesiastical hierarchy. Paul may sound as if he is a caring individual advocating the growth and eventual independence of his converts, but much of this sort of language is in fact to be seen as an emotional ploy used to secure Paul's position of power and authority.

This interpretation is not viable, however, when one understands the function of mimetic language in a deliberative discourse, and when one further understands that Paul goes on to say that he is imitating the servant leadership of Christ. Paul pointedly distinguishes himself from the sort of figure the Emperor or the Sophists might be, especially by inserting the hardship catalogue in 1 Cor. 4:9–13. Imitating Paul who is imitating Christ means being conformed to the pattern of Christ's suffering and death. This is not the stuff of self-aggrandizement.

(4) Elliott and the problem of the later Paulinists

N. Elliott has applied the liberationist hermeneutics of suspicion in a different manner in order to try and rescue Paul from his later canonical handlers. Elliott's fundamental approach is to suggest that the later Paulines, especially the Pastorals, not merely domesticated Paul but in fact gutted his letters of the radical social critique one finds in text like Gal. 3:28 or Philemon. Unlike most feminist approaches to Paul, Elliott sees not Paul himself but his later handlers as the real problem for liberationists. Paul is seen as a social crusader who focuses on the cross as an example of historical and political oppression rather than as an atoning sacrifice (unlike the later document Hebrews). But such a reading, while right that there is a social reforming edge to Paul's message,[20] ignores the rather clear thrust of crucial texts such as Rom. 3:21–6. It also may be doubted that the later Paulines, especially if written by Paul's own disciples, really so badly misrepresent the apostle to the Gentiles.

THE RHETORICAL INTERPRETATION OF PAUL'S LETTERS

(1) The rhetorical background

The decline of the requirement of classical studies in the twentieth century in Western schools and universities has without question taken its toll on NT studies in the twentieth century. In the middle of that century a whole generation of NT scholars arose who either had not studied the Latin and Greek classics and ancient Graeco-Roman rhetoric, or had never been shown the relevance of such studies for understanding Paul's letters. Yet it was not always so. In the nineteenth and at the beginning of the twentieth century major commentaries were written by scholars as diverse as J. B. Lightfoot and J. Weiss which were cognizant of the importance of rhetorical studies for understanding Paul. The revival of such an approach to Paul's letters came in the late 1970s and early 1980s as first H. D. Betz published a landmark rhetorical study on Galatians and then G. A. Kennedy showed the relevance of Graeco-Roman rhetoric for studying various parts of the New Testament.[21] The discussion was carried forward by the students of these two scholars and has blossomed in the 1980s and 1990s into a major area of interest in Pauline studies.

To date, while rhetorical analysis has been applied to all of Paul's letters, those which have been most illumined by such an approach are 1 Corinthians (a deliberative argument for concord in a factious congregation), Galatians (a deliberative argument meant to produce reconciliation between Paul and his converts), 2 Cor. 10–13 (a forensic *tour de force* attacking Paul's opponents and shaming his converts), Philippians (a deliberative argument meant to nurture Paul's relationship with the Philippians while persuading them not to send any more gifts), and Philemon (a personal deliberative arm twisting meant to persuade Philemon to free and return Philemon's slave Onesimus to Paul).

The analysis of Paul's letters as rhetoric is predicated on a series of deductions: (a) the evidence seems strong that these letters were surrogates for oral communication; (b) these letters reveal the apostle Paul trying to convince or persuade his converts of various things, and the ancient art of persuasion was rhetoric; (c) Paul lived in a rhetoric-saturated environment, an environment in which rhetoric was a staple item in the curriculum for both primary and secondary education.

(2) Pauline rhetorical practice

Rhetorical devices within Paul's letters have always been noticed by commentators (e.g. rhetorical questions), but the analysis of the structure of entire letters, minus the epistolary opening and closing elements, as examples of rhetorical speeches is a new emphasis in Pauline studies, though well grounded in the manner in which many ancient commentators on Paul (e.g. John Chrysostom) analysed his letters during early church history. Such an analysis sheds fresh light on: (a) the importance of Paul's opening remarks (e.g. the thanksgiving prayer, or lack thereof, in Galatians); (b) the function of the emotional final exhortations (*peroratio*) found in Paul's various letters; (c) Paul's satirical and caustic remarks in 2 Cor. 10–13 which reflect conventions of inoffensive self-praise, mock-boasting, and *tour de force* shaming of one's opponents by such rhetorical ploys; (d) and finally the purpose or function of such Pauline letters (are they mainly a defend or attack forensic sort of letter, mainly an advise and consent deliberative sort of letter, mainly a praise or blame epideictic sort of letter?).

It is important to emphasize that Paul was a master of rhetoric, so much so that various modern commentators' failure to recognize the rhetorical signals in the letters has led to false conclusions (e.g. that Paul is defending his apostolic office in 1 Corinthians, particularly 1 Corinthians 9; or that 2 Cor. 10–13 shows that Paul was a arrogant and boastful person). Perhaps most importantly, Paul's use of rhetoric shows that he would rather persuade than command, rather treat his converts as free and intelligent persons who must make up their own minds about the issues he is addressing. Paul preferred the church to function like the ancient Greek *ekklesia*, in democratic fashion, especially when it came to debated or disputed matters.

PAUL'S LETTERS AS HOLY WRIT

There is evidence that Paul's letters were some of the earliest Christian documents to be collected and studied as sacred texts. It is suggested in 2 Pet. 3:15–16 that this process was already underway during the New Testament era. Not only is there reference here to Paul's letters as comparable to 'the other scriptures' (or writings), but it is implied that they require and repay the kind of careful study that the learned can afford to give them. On the other hand, ignorant and unstable persons are likely to distort Paul's meaning, especially the more difficult portions of his letters. In recent years various scholars have attempted to make suggestions about how to approach

Paul's letters as scripture. We will focus on the efforts of two scholars – B. Childs' canonical approach, and D. Trobisch's historical investigations of the collection of Paul's letters and the final redaction of the New Testament.

(1) Childs and the canonical approach

It must be admitted at the outset that more historically oriented NT scholars have been suspicious of canonical approaches to Paul's letters. This concern has been manifested in part because of the way specialists in Pauline theology have long used the whole or most of the corpus of Paul's letters as a quarry for constructing a synthetic presentation of his thought.[22] The recent SBL Seminar on Pauline Theology manifested these tensions in a rather obvious way as it tried to present the theology of or in particular discrete letters and then in combination with other letters. But it could be argued that letters do not have theologies: people do.

In theory a canonical approach to Paul's letters would entail not only interpreting a particular Pauline letter or passage in light of the rest of the Pauline corpus, but also looking at the impact of the earlier Paulines on the later ones, and of the Pauline corpus on other parts of the canon (e.g. Hebrews). Further, a canonical approach would involve examining Paul's letters in light of the rest of the NT and of the Hebrew scriptures.

There is perhaps already within one of Paul's earliest letters justification provided for a more canonical approach to the Pauline corpus. In 1 Thess. 5:27 the Thessalonians are exhorted to have the letter written to them read 'to all the brothers'. This might mean that the Thessalonians are to make copies of the letter and send it on the church in Beroea or Philippi (or even further afield) perhaps; or it may mean, as seems more likely to me, that there were several house churches in Thessalonike and Paul is concerned that the letter be read out in all the house churches in that particular locale. But more clearly Col. 4:16 shows that already during the NT era and probably during Paul's own time it was believed that there was sufficient 'universal' content in various of Paul's letters to be useful and applicable in a variety of Pauline congregational settings. The 'canonical' approach no doubt grew out of such texts as Col. 4:16 and out of a widespread belief that Paul's letters were of enduring value even in widely diverse cultural situations.

It is perhaps right to notice that those who take a canonical approach to Paul's letters do indeed see them as sacred texts, and therefore it is assumed that we should expect a certain coherency of thought throughout these documents. In addition, B. Childs avers that the major 'function of the church's canonical literature i[s] providing its own normative interpretive context which is not necessarily to be identified with the original author's intention'.[23] Herein, we see the inherent tension between a historical approach to Paul's letters and a canonical approach. The canon, or some sort of *analogia fidei* within the canon, is used as a hermeneutical tool to determine how certain Pauline texts, perhaps especially the more prolix ones, should be understood. N. Dahl rightly saw, however, that the fundamental obstacle to both the canonizing of Paul's letters and the canonical approach to Paul's letters is their particularity. 'How can occasional letters written to specific churches and concerned with particular situational conflicts function canonically as an authoritative norm?'[24] It is a fair question, and the question is not adequately answered by simply referring to eternal principles expressed in particular practices, for some of the ideas are used in an *ad hoc* fashion as well.

Childs also thinks that the canonical approach to Paul's letters may overcome some of the historical problems raised in regard to the authorship of Paul's letters. For instance, Childs suggests that while the Pastorals were not likely written by Paul, they present us with an interpretation of Paul which makes serviceable various of Paul's letters for a later church situation. But if the canonical Paul is at odds with the historical Paul, which is to be taken as normative for the church today? Can, as Childs suggests, a non-historical theological construct be given normative status at the expense of the historical Paul and his actual views and teachings? Should we take a 'school' approach to Paul's letters with the (possibly) Deutero-Pauline letters seen as faithful extensions by disciples of essential Pauline insights to new situations? If this is the case historically speaking, then a canonical approach could be seen as a hermeneutical approach which does not do violence to historical enquiry. Historical criticism and canonical criticism could be seen as basically congruent. Yet the greater the apparent or perceived differences between Paul and later canonical Paulinists, the more likely that a canonical approach represents the triumph of hermeneutics over history.

At the end of the day, Childs finds justification for a canonical approach on the basis of a certain reading of the development of the Pauline corpus, namely, that the canonical letters include both Pauline and post-Pauline elements, all seen as in some sense normative for the church. Yet this disputable historical judgment seems an odd foundation on which to base a canonical approach. Surely a canonical approach must be concerned not just with theological or ethical truth but also historical truth, which in the case of the Christian faith is the foundation for theological reflection. It is questionable what sort of normative force a text can have for the church if it is not from the putative inspired author whose authority lies behind the text.

(2) Trobisch and the Hauptbriefe

Of a different ilk is D. Trobisch's approach to these matters. Trobisch argues that not only do Paul's own letters already show a unifying tendency (cf. above on 1 Thess. 5:27 and Col. 4:16), but in fact Paul himself collected and edited some of his own letters, providing the authorized recension of these documents. Trobisch suggests that Paul composed 1 and 2 Corinthians, then Romans and Galatians, and sent them all with a cover note (Romans 16) to Ephesus. These four letters were intended to be read as a unit in the form in which we now find them. Paul 'published' this canon of letters because of the conflict with the Jerusalem authorities as an attempt to show what distinguishes Christian views from purely Jewish ones. At the same time, the reason Paul grouped these letters together is that they all share the concern of the collection for Jerusalem. Thus Paul himself gave birth to the Christian canon at least *in nuce.*[25]

Interesting as this theory is, it seems to have little basis in historical fact. For one thing, the detailed work of R. Jewett has shown that Romans 16 is probably addressed to the church in Rome, not in Ephesus, and indeed that Romans 16 seems likely to have been connected originally with Romans as a letter of commendation for Phoebe.[26] It is thus not a later addition to Romans meant to serve as a cover letter for the four-letter corpus. It is also questionable whether the mentioning of the theme of the collection is sufficient reason to group these four letters together. Why shouldn't Philippians also be included since it also addresses the delicate issue of money and support for Christian leaders such as Paul or the Jerusalem church leaders?[27] One suspects that the real reason for picking the four letters Trobisch chooses is that they have long been seen as a sort of canon within the Pauline canon, especially by German scholars who have dubbed them the *Hauptbriefe.* Yet there is perhaps a way to salvage Trobisch's thesis by recognizing that Paul may have written his letters not just for the specific audiences to which they are addressed, but also with one eye on the larger group of Pauline churches, as Col. 4:16 intimates.[28] This might provide justification for treating Paul's letters as a fundamentally coherent corpus of thought, which the apostle put together bearing in mind what he had said and positions he had taken previously, and not merely as reactions to *ad hoc* situations.

What is basically missing in the discussions of both Childs and Trobisch is any sort of theory of inspiration and its relationship to the authority of the apostle and his letters. If indeed the Pastoral Epistles raise the issue of the inspiration and authority of sacred texts, and they do (see 2 Tim. 3:16), and there is evidence that Paul's own letters were seen as scripture during the NT era (so 2 Pet. 3:16), then it follows that the issues of inspiration, authority, canon, and scripture ought to be addressed together. Some of the earliest Christians seem to have attempted to do so, as the canonizing process itself shows.[29] Perhaps the next phase of the discussion of Paul's letters as scripture will seek to deal with some of these inter-related matters.

As R. W. Wall says, while the differences between the Pauline letters are well known, as are the tensions between various Pauline letters and other NT documents (e.g. James or Hebrews), not enough consideration has been given to what it means to recognize these tensions and at the same time treat these books as scripture.[30] In a sense this conversation has just begun in the field of Pauline studies. It remains to be seen whether it will produce more heat or more light, whether the historical issues will be sublimated in favour of a theological construct, or whether they will be squarely faced, as the attempt is made to integrate historical and theological concerns and insights.

CONCLUSIONS

This chapter has sought to expose the reader to various recent or new perspectives on Paul and his letters. Of course none of these avenues of approach are entirely new, and some, like rhetorical criticism, have very ancient precedents indeed. It may also be said that the jury is still out on the usefulness of most of these ways of evaluating the Pauline corpus. It remains to be seen whether the legacy of any or all of these approaches is enduring or ephemeral.

Notes

1 (Philadelphia: Fortress, 1978).
2 See most recently N. Elliott, *Liberating Paul: The Justice of God and the Politics of the Apostle* (Maryknoll: Orbis, 1994).
3 H. Maccoby, *Paul and the Invention of Christianity* (New York: Harper & Row, 1986).
4 K. Stendahl, *Paul among Jews and Gentiles* (Philadelphia: Fortress, 1976/London: SCM, 1977).
5 A. F. Segal, *Paul the Convert: The Apostolate and Apostasy of Saul the Pharisee* (New Haven: Yale University Press, 1990) 117.
6 See Segal's critique of such a view (ibid., 279–80).
7 D. Boyarin, *A Radical Jew: Paul and the Politics of Identity* (Berkeley: University of California Press, 1994) 3.
8 But the allegory of Sarah and Hagar in Galatians 4 is the exception rather than the rule if we are asking how Paul normally handles the Hebrew scriptures.
9 Boyarin, *A Radical Jew* 32.
10 Ibid., 53. Here he is following J. D. G. Dunn, *Jesus, Paul and the Law: Studies in Mark and Galatians* (London: SPCK/ Louisville: Westminster John Knox, 1990).

See my critique of this view in *Grace in Galatia* (Edinburgh: T. & T. Clark, 1998) 341–56.

11 M. Nanos, *The Mystery of Romans: The Jewish Context of Paul's Letter* (Minneapolis: Fortress, 1996) 336.

12 Against which view see my treatment of this issue in my 'Not so Idle Thoughts about *Eidolothuton*', *Tyndale Bulletin* 44/2 (1993) 237–54.

13 Nanos, *Mystery* 338.

14 A view only rarely advocated by Pauline scholars.

15 S. M. Schneiders, 'Feminist Hermeneutics', in J. B. Green, ed., *Hearing the New Testament* (Grand Rapids: Eerdmans, 1995) 349–69 (here 349).

16 Ultimately this approach is grounded in a postmodern epistemology which assumes that objectivity is not really possible for anyone, because everyone, unavoidably, has a point of view and an axe to grind. Furthermore it is questioned whether objective reality is really knowable in any case. In other words, though historically critical biblical scholarship has traditionally been grounded in the Enlightenment faith in the abilities of human reason to learn and know objective reality, modern feminist hermeneutics builds on a very different foundation and epistemology. The same could be said about the epistemic presuppositions for reader-response criticism.

17 E. Schüssler Fiorenza, *In Memory of Her* (New York: Crossroad, 1994) 235.

18 A. C. Wire, *The Corinthian Women Prophets: A Reconstruction through Paul's Rhetoric* (Minneapolis: Fortress, 1990) 151–2.

19 E. Castelli, *Imitating Paul: A Discourse of Power* (Louisville: Westminster John Knox, 1991).

20 See my *The Paul Quest: The Renewed Search for the Jew of Tassus* (Downers Grove, IL: IVP, 1998) 218–29.

21 H. D. Betz, *Galatians* (Philadelphia: Fortress, 1979); G. A. Kennedy, *New Testament Interpretation through Rhetorical Criticism* (Chapel Hill: UNC Press, 1984).

22 On which see my *Paul's Narrative Thought World* (Louisville: Westminster John Knox, 1994).

23 B. Childs, *The New Testament as Canon: An Introduction* (Philadelphia: Fortress, 1984) 251.

24 Ibid., 424.

25 D. Trobisch, *Paul's Letter Collection: Tracing the Origins* (Minneapolis: Fortress, 1994) 55–96 sums up his argument neatly.

26 See especially his forthcoming commentary on Romans (Philadelphia: Fortress).

27 See my *Friendship and Finances in Philippi* (Valley Forge: Trinity, 1995).

28 This suggestion is similar to that made by R. Bauckham and his fellow essayists about the gospels in *The Gospel for all Christians* (Grand Rapids: Eerdmans, 1998).

29 I am thinking also of some of the criteria applied in the second and following centuries to determine what ought and ought not to be in the canon, and especially the concern about the authorship and apostolicity of the included documents.

30 R. Wall and E. E. Lemcio, *The New Testament as Canon* (Sheffield: Sheffield Academic Press, 1992) 164.

Select bibliography

General

Babcock, W. S., ed., *Paul and the Legacies of Paul* (Dallas: Southern Methodist University Press, 1990)

Balch, D., 'Household Codes', in D. E. Aune, ed., *Greco-Roman Literature and the New Testament* (Atlanta: Scholars, 1988) 28–50

Banks, R. J., *Paul's Idea of Community: The Early House Churches in their Historical Setting* (Grand Rapids: Eerdmans, 1980)

Barrett, C. K., *Paul: An Introduction to his Thought* (London: Chapman, 1994)

Baur, F. C., *Paul: The Apostle of Jesus Christ* (1845; ET 2 vols., London: Williams & Norgate, 1873, 1875)

Becker, J., *Paul: Apostle to the Gentiles* (Louisville: Westminster/John Knox, 1993)

Beker, J. C., *Paul the Apostle: The Triumph of God in Life and Thought* (Philadelphia: Fortress, 1980)

 Heirs of Paul: Paul's Legacy in the New Testament and in the Church Today (Minneapolis: Fortress, 1991)

Best, E., *Paul and his Converts* (Edinburgh: T. & T. Clark, 1988)

Bornkamm, G., *Paul* (London: Hodder & Stoughton, 1971)

Boyarin, D., *A Radical Jew: Paul and the Politics of Identity* (Berkeley: University of California Press, 1994)

Bremer, J. N., ed., *The Apocryphal Acts of Paul* (Kampen: Kok Pharos, 1996)

Bruce, F. F., *Paul: Apostle of the Free Spirit* (Exeter: Paternoster, 1977)

Bultmann, R., *Theology of the New Testament* (London: SCM, vol.1, 1952)

Campenhausen, H. von, *Ecclesiastical Authority and Spiritual Power in the Church of the First Three Centuries* (1953; ET London: A. & C. Black, 1969)

 The Formation of the Christian Bible (Philadelphia: Fortress, 1968)

Capes, D. B., *Old Testament Yahweh Texts in Paul's Christology*, WUNT 2.47 (Tübingen: Mohr Siebeck, 1992)

Casey, P. M., 'Monotheism, Worship and Christological Developments in the Pauline Churches', in C. C. Newman, J. R. Davila, and G. S. Lewis, eds., *The Jewish Roots of Christological Monotheism*, JSJS 63 (Leiden: Brill, 1999) 214–33

Cerfaux, L., *The Church in the Theology of Saint Paul* (New York: Herder & Herder, 1959)

Clabeaux, J. J., 'Marcion', *ABD* 4.514–16

Dahl, N. A., *Studies in Paul* (Minneapolis: Augsburg, 1977)

Davies, W. D., *Paul and Rabbinic Judaism: Some Rabbinic Elements in Pauline Theology* (London: SPCK, 1948; 4th edn, 1981)

Dibelius, M., and Kümmel, W. G., *Paul* (London: Longmans, 1953)

Donaldson, T. L., *Paul and the Gentiles: Remapping the Apostle's Convictional World* (Minneapolis: Fortress, 1997)

Dunn, J. D. G., *Jesus, Paul and the Law: Studies in Mark and Galatians* (London: SPCK Louisville: Westminster/John Knox, 1990)

　The Theology of Paul the Apostle (Grand Rapids: Eerdmans/Edinburgh: T. & T. Clark, 1998)

　'Who did Paul Think he was? A Study of Jewish Christian Identity', *NTS* 45 (1999) 174–93

Elliott, N. *Liberating Paul: The Justice of God and the Politics of the Apostle* (Maryknoll: Orbis, 1994)

Fee, G. D., *God's Empowering Presence: The Holy Spirit in the Letters of Paul* (Peabody, MA: Hendrickson, 1994)

Fitzmyer, J. A., *Paul and his Theology: A Brief Sketch*, 2nd edn (Englewood Cliffs, NJ: Prentice Hall, 1989)

Furnish, V. P., *Theology and Ethics in Paul* (Nashville: Abingdon, 1968)

Grant, R. M., 'Gospel of Marcion', *ABD* 4.516–20

Hawthorne, G. F., et al., eds., *Dictionary of Paul and his Letters* (Downers Grove, IL/Leicester: IVP, 1993)

Hays, R. B., *The Faith of Jesus Christ: An Investigation of the Narrative Substructure of Galatians 3:1–4:11* (Chico: Scholars, 1983; 2nd edn, Grand Rapids: Eerdmans, 2002)

　Echoes of Scripture in the Letters of Paul (New Haven: Yale University Press, 1989)

　The Moral Vision of the New Testament: A Contemporary Introduction to New Testament Ethics (San Francisco: HarperCollins, 1996/Edinburgh: T. & T. Clark, 1997)

Hengel, M., *The Pre-Christian Paul* (London: SCM/ Philadelphia: TPI, 1991)

Hengel, M., and Schwemer, A. M., *Paul between Damascus and Antioch: The Unknown Years* (London: SCM, 1997)

Hock, R. F., *The Social Context of Paul's Ministry: Tentmaking and Apostleship* (Philadelphia: Fortress, 1980)

Hoffmann, R. J., *Marcion: On the Restitution of Christianity* (Chico: Scholars, 1984)

Horsley, R. A., ed., *Paul and Empire: Religion and Power in Roman Imperial Society* (Harrisburg, PA: TPI, 1997)

Howard, G., *Paul: Crisis in Galatia: A Study in Early Christian Theology*, SNTSMS 35: (Cambridge: Cambridge University Press, 1979; 2nd edn, 1990)

Hultgren, A. J., *Paul's Gospel and Mission: The Outlook from his Letter to the Romans* (Philadelphia: Fortress, 1985)

Hurtado, L. W., *One God, One Lord: Early Christian Devotion and Ancient Jewish Monotheism* (Philadelphia, Fortress/London: SCM, 1988; 2nd edn, Edinburgh: T. & T. Clark, 1998)

　'Convert, Apostate or Apostle to the Nations: The "Conversion" of Paul in Recent Scholarship', *Studies in Religion/Sciences religieuses* 22 (1993) 273–84

　'Pre-70 CE Jewish Opposition to Christ-Devotion', *JTS* 50 (1999) 35–58

Jewett, R., *Paul the Apostle to America: Cultural Trends and Pauline Scholarship* (Louisville: Westminster/John Knox, 1994)

Keck, L. E., *Paul and his Letters* (Philadelphia: Fortress, 1982)

Kim, S., *The Origin of Paul's Gospel* (Tübingen: Mohr Siebeck, 1981; 2nd edn, 2002)

Knox, J., *Marcion and the New Testament: An Essay in Early Christian History* (Chicago: University of Chicago Press, 1942)
  Chapters in a Life of Paul (1950; revised edn, Macon, GA: Mercer University Press, 1987)
Kreitzer, L. J., *Jesus and God in Paul's Eschatology*, JSNTS 19 (Sheffield: JSOT, 1987)
Longenecker, R. N., ed., *The Road from Damascus: The Impact of Paul's Conversion on his Life, Thought, and Ministry* (Grand Rapids: Eerdmans, 1997)
Maccoby, H., *The Mythmaker: Paul and the Invention of Christianity* (New York: Harper & Row, 1986)
MacDonald, M. Y., *The Pauline Churches: A Socio-Historical Study of Institutionalization in the Pauline and Deutero-Pauline Writings*, SNTSMS 60 (Cambridge: Cambridge University Press, 1988)
Martin, R. P., *Reconciliation: A Study of Paul's Theology* (London: Marshall, Morgan & Scott, 1981)
Martyn, J. L., *Theological Issues in the Letters of Paul* (Edinburgh: T. & T. Clark, 1997)
Meeks, W. A., *The Writings of St Paul* (New York: Norton, 1972)
  The First Urban Christians: The Social World of the Apostle Paul (New Haven: Yale University Press, 1983)
Meggitt, J. J., *Paul, Poverty and Survival* (Edinburgh: T. & T. Clark, 1998)
Minear, P. S., *Images of the Church in the New Testament* (Philadelphia: Westminster, 1960)
Munck, J., *Paul and the Salvation of Mankind* (London: SCM, 1959)
Murphy-O'Connor, J., *Paul: A Critical Life* (Oxford: Clarendon Press, 1996)
Murphy-O'Connor, J. and Charlesworth, J., eds., *Paul and the Dead Sea Scrolls* (New York: Crossroad, 1990)
Newman, C. C., *Paul's Glory-Christology: Tradition and Rhetoric*, NovTSup 69 (Leiden: Brill, 1992)
Nock, A. D., *St. Paul* (London: Oxford University Press, 1938)
O'Brien, P. T., *Gospel and Mission in the Writings of Paul* (Grand Rapids: Baker, 1995)
Pagels, E. H., *The Gnostic Paul: Gnostic Exegesis of the Pauline Letters* (Philadelphia: Fortress, 1975)
Rapske, B., *The Book of Acts and Paul in Roman Custody* (Grand Rapids: Eerdmans/Carlisle: Paternoster, 1994)
Reumann, J., *Righteousness in the New Testament* (Philadelphia: Fortress, 1982)
Richardson, N., *Paul's Language about God*, JSNTS 99 (Sheffield: Sheffield Academic Press, 1994)
Roetzel, C. J., *The Letters of Paul: Conversations in Context* (Atlanta: John Knox, 1975; 2nd edn, 1982)
  Paul: The Man and the Myth (University of South Carolina Press, 1997)
Rosner, B., ed., *Understanding Paul's Ethics: Twentieth-Century Approaches* (Grand Rapids: Eerdmans, 1995)
Sampley, J. P., *Walking Between the Times: Paul's Moral Reasoning* (Minneapolis: Fortress, 1991)
Sanders, E. P., *Paul and Palestinian Judaism* (London: SCM, 1977)
  Paul (Oxford: Oxford University Press, 1991)
Sandmel, S., *The Genius of Paul* (1958; Philadelphia: Fortress, 1979)
Schoeps, H. J., *Paul* (London: SCM, 1961)
Schrage, W., *The Ethics of the New Testament* (Edinburgh: T. & T. Clark, 1988)

Schweitzer, A., *Paul and his Interpreters* (London: A. & C. Black, 1912)

Segal, A. F., *Paul the Convert: The Apostolate and Apostasy of Saul the Pharisee* (New Haven: Yale University Press, 1990)

Stendahl, K., *Paul among Jews and Gentiles* (Philadelphia: Fortress, 1976/London: SCM, 1977)

Stuhlmacher, P., 'The Pauline Gospel', in P. Stuhlmacher, ed., *The Gospel and the Gospels* (Grand Rapids: Eerdmans, 1991) 149–72

Theissen, G., *The Social Setting of Pauline Christianity* (Philadelphia: Fortress/ Edinburgh: T. & T. Clark, 1982)

Trobisch, D., *Paul's Letter Collection: Tracing the Origins* (Minneapolis: Fortress, 1994)

Whiteley, D. E. H., *The Theology of St Paul* (Oxford: Blackwell, 1964)

Wiles, M. F., *The Divine Apostle: The Interpretation of St Paul's Epistles in the Early Church* (Cambridge: Cambridge University Press, 1967)

Witherington, B., *Paul's Narrative Thought World* (Louisville: Westminster/John Knox, 1994)

  The Paul Quest: The Renewed Search for the Jew of Tarsus (Downers Grove, IL: IVP, 1998)

Wrede, W., *Paul* (London: Philip Green, 1907)

Wright, N. T., *The Climax of the Covenant: Christ and the Law in Pauline Theology* (Edinburgh: T. & T. Clark, 1991)

Ziesler, J. A., *Pauline Christianity*, 2nd edn (Oxford: Oxford University Press, 1990)

On particular letters
Romans

Cranfield, C. E. B., *Romans*, ICC (Edinburgh: T. & T. Clark, vol. 1, 1975, vol. 2, 1979)

Donfried, K. P., ed., *The Romans Debate* (Peabody: Hendrickson, 1991)

Dunn, J. D. G., *Romans*, WBC 38 (Dallas: Word, 1988)

Fitzmyer, J. A., *Romans*, AB 33 (New York: Doubleday, 1993)

Haacker, K., *The Theology of Romans* (Cambridge: Cambridge University Press, 2003)

Jewett, R., 'Honor and Shame in the Argument of Romans', in A. Brown et al., eds., *Putting Body and Soul Together*, R. Scroggs Festschrift (Valley Forge: TPI, 1997) 257–72

  'The Basic Human Dilemma: Weakness or Zealous Violence (Romans 7:7–25 and 10:1–18)', *Ex Auditu* 13 (1997) 96–109

Käsemann, E., *Romans* (Grand Rapids: Eerdmans, 1980)

Lampe, P., *From Paul to Valentinus: The Christians in the City of Rome of the First Three Centuries* (Minneapolis: Fortress, 2000)

Moo, D. J., *Romans* (Grand Rapids: Eerdmans, 1996)

Nanos, M., *The Mystery of Romans: The Jewish Context of Paul's Letter* (Minneapolis: Fortress, 1996)

Reasoner, M., *The Strong and the Weak: Romans 14.1–15.13 in Context*, SNTSMS 103 (Cambridge: Cambridge University Press, 1999)

Stuhlmacher, P., *Paul's Letter to the Romans* (Louisville: Westminster/John Knox, 1994)

Corinthians

Barrett, C. K., *1 Corinthians*, BNTC (London: A. & C. Black, 1968)

  2 Corinthians, BNTC (London: A. & C. Black, 1973)

Best, E., *Second Corinthians*, Interpretation (Louisville: Westminster/John Knox, 1987)

Conzelmann, H., *1 Corinthians*, Hermeneia (Philadelphia: Fortress, 1975)

Fee, G. D., *1 Corinthians*, NICNT (Grand Rapids: Eerdmans, 1987)

Furnish, V. P., *2 Corinthians*, AB (New York: Doubleday, 1984)

    The Theology of the First Letter to the Corinthians (Cambridge: Cambridge University Press, 1999)

Hays, R. B., *First Corinthians*, Interpretation (Louisville: Westminster/John Knox, 1997)

Mitchell, M. M., *Paul and the Rhetoric of Reconciliation: An Exegetical Investigation of Language and Composition of 1 Corinthians* (Louisville: Westminster/John Knox, 1991)

Murphy-O'Connor, J., '1 & 2 Corinthians', *NJBC* (London: Geoffrey Chapman) 798–829

    The Theology of the Second Letter to the Corinthians (Cambridge: Cambridge University Press, 1991)

    St. Paul's Corinth: Texts and Archaeology (Collegeville: Liturgical Press, 1992)

Sampley, J. P., '2 Corinthians', *NIB* 11 (Nashville: Abingdon, 2000) 1–180

Thiselton, A. C., *1 Corinthians*, NIGTC (Grand Rapids: Eerdmans, 2000)

Thrall, M., *2 Corinthians*, ICC (Edinburgh: T. &. T. Clark, 1994, 2000)

Witherington, B., *Conflict and Community in Corinth* (Grand Rapids: Eerdmans, 1995)

Galatians

Barclay, J. M. G., *Obeying the Truth: A Study of Paul's Ethics in Galatians* (Edinburgh: T. & T. Clark, 1988)

Barrett, C. K., *Freedom and Obligation: A Study in the Epistle to the Galatians* (London: SPCK, 1985)

Betz, H. D., *Galatians*, Hermeneia (Philadelphia: Fortress, 1979)

Bruce, F. F., *Galatians*, NIGTC (Grand Rapids: Eerdmans, 1982)

Dunn, J. D. G., *Galatians*, BNTC (London: A. & C. Black, 1993)

    The Theology of Paul's Letter to the Galatians (Cambridge: Cambridge University Press, 1993)

Hays, R. B., 'Galatians', *NIB* 11 (Nashville: Abingdon, 2000) 181–348

Longenecker, B. W., *The Triumph of Abraham's God: The Transformation of Identity in Galatians* (Edinburgh: T. & T. Clark, 1998)

Longenecker, R. N., *Galatians*, WBC 41 (Dallas: Word, 1990)

Martyn, J. L., *Galatians*, AB 33A (New York: Doubleday, 1997)

Witherington, B., *Grace in Galatia* (Edinburgh: T. & T. Clark, 1998)

Ephesians

Arnold, C. E., *Ephesians: Power and Magic*, SNTSMS 63 (Cambridge: Cambridge University Press, 1989)

Best, E., *Essays on Ephesians* (Edinburgh: T. & T. Clark, 1997)

    Ephesians, ICC (Edinburgh: T. & T. Clark, 1998)

Lincoln, A. T., *Ephesians*, WBC (Dallas: Word, 1990)

Lincoln, A. T., and Wedderburn, A. J. M., *The Theology of the Later Pauline Letters* (Cambridge: Cambridge University Press, 1993)

Muddiman, J., *Ephesians* (London: Continuum, 2001)
O'Brien, P. T., *The Letter to the Ephesians* (Grand Rapids: Eerdmans, 1999)
Perkins, P., 'Ephesians', *NIB* 11 (Nashville: Abingdon, 2000) 349–466
Schnackenburg, R., *Ephesians* (Edinburgh: T. & T. Clark, 1991)

Philippians
Bockmuehl, M. N. A., *Philippians*, BNTC (London: A. & C. Black, 1997)
Fee, G. D., *Philippians*, NICNT (Grand Rapids: Eerdmans, 1995)
Hooker, M. D., 'Philippians', *NIB* 11 (Nashville: Abingdon, 2000) 469–549
Lightfoot, J. B., *Philippians* (London: Macmillan, 1883)
Marshall, I. H., and Donfried, K. P., *The Theology of the Shorter Pauline Letters* (Cambridge: Cambridge University Press, 1993)
Martin, R. P., *Carmen Christi*, SNTSMS 4 (Cambridge: Cambridge University Press, 1983)
O'Brien, P. T., *Philippians*, NIGTC (Grand Rapids: Eerdmans, 1991)
Witherington, B., *Friendship and Finances in Philippi* (Valley Forge: Trinity, 1995)

Colossians and Philemon
Arnold, C. E., *The Colossian Syncretism* (Grand Rapids: Baker, 1996)
Bartchy, S. S., 'Philemon, Epistle', *ABD* 5.305–10
   'Slavery', *ABD* 6.65–73
Crouch, J., *The Origin and Intention of the Colossian Haustafel*, FRLANT 109 (Göttingen: Vandenhoeck & Ruprecht, 1972)
Dunn, J. D. G., *The Epistles to the Colossians and to Philemon*, NIGTC (Grand Rapids/Carlisle: Eerdmans/Paternoster, 1996)
Fitzmyer, J. A., *Philemon*, AB 34c (New York: Doubleday, 2000)
Francis, F. O., and Meeks, W., eds., *Conflict at Colossae* (Missoula: Scholars, 1973)
Furnish, V. P., 'Colossians, Epistle', *ABD* 1.1090–6
Lincoln, A. T., 'Colossians', *NIB* 11 (Nashville: Abingdon, 2000) 551–669
Lohse, E., *Colossians and Philemon*, Hermeneia (Philadelphia: Fortress, 1971)
O'Brien, P. T., *Colossians, Philemon*, WBC 44 (Waco: Word, 1982)
Wedderburn, A. J. M., and Lincoln, A. T., *The Theology of the Later Pauline Letters* (Cambridge: Cambridge University Press, 1993)

Thessalonians
Donfried, K. P., and Marshall, I. H., *The Theology of the Shorter Pauline Letters* (Cambridge: Cambridge University Press, 1993)
Donfried, K. P., and Beutler, J., *The Thessalonians Debate: Methodological Discord or Methodological Synthesis?* (Grand Rapids: Eerdmans, 2000)
Hendrix, H. L., 'Thessalonica', *ABD* 6.523–7
Krentz, E. M., 'Thessalonians, First and Second Epistles', *ABD* 6.515–23
Malherbe, A. J., *Paul and the Thessalonians: The Philosophic Tradition of Pastoral Care* (Philadelphia: Fortress, 1987)
   The Letters to the Thessalonians, AB 32b (New York: Doubleday, 2000)
Marshall, I. H., *1 & 2 Thessalonians*, NCB (Grand Rapids: Eerdmans, 1983)
Milligan, G., *St. Paul's Epistles to the Thessalonians* (London: Macmillan, 1908)

Mitchell, M. M., 'New Testament Envoys in the Context of Greco-Roman Diplomatic and Epistolary Conventions: The Example of Timothy and Titus', *JBL* 111 (1992) 641–62

Smith, A., 'Thessalonians', *NIB* 11 (Nashville: Abingdon, 2000) 671–772

Wanamaker, C. A., *The Epistles to the Thessalonians*, NIGTC (Grand Rapids: Eerdmans/Exeter: Paternoster, 1990)

Pastorals

Barrett, C. K., *The Pastoral Epistles* (Oxford: Oxford University Press, 1963)

Bassler, J., *1 Timothy, 2 Timothy, Titus*, ANTC (Nashville: Abingdon, 1996)

Davies, M., *The Pastoral Epistles*, NTG (Sheffield: Sheffield Academic Press, 1996)

Dibelius, M., and Conzelmann, H., *The Pastoral Epistles*, Hermeneia (Philadelphia: Fortress, 1972)

Donelson, L. R., *Pseudepigraphy and Ethical Argument in the Pastoral Epistles* (Tübingen: Mohr Siebeck, 1986)

Dunn, J. D. G., '1 & 2 Timothy, Titus', *NIB* 11 (Nashville: Abingdon, 2000) 773–880

Harrison, P. N., *The Problem of the Pastoral Epistles* (London: Oxford University Press, 1921)

Hultgren, A. J., *1–2 Timothy, Titus* (Minneapolis: Augsburg, 1984)

Johnson, L. T., *1 and 2 Timothy*, AB 35A (New York: Doubleday, 2001)

Marshall, I. H., *The Pastoral Epistles*, ICC (Edinburgh: T. & T. Clark, 1999)

Mounce, W. D., *Pastoral Epistles*, WBC 46 (Nashville: Thomas Nelson, 2000)

Oden, T. C., *First and Second Timothy and Titus*, Interpretation (Louisville: Westminster/John Knox, 1989)

Quinn, J. D., *The Letter to Titus*, AB 35 (New York: Doubleday, 1990)

Young, F. M., *The Theology of the Pastoral Epistles* (Cambridge: Cambridge University Press, 1994)

Index of references

General index